The Fear of French Negroes

r literature beyond strictly national and disciplin-
by their historical grounding and their theoretical
udies that engage theory without losing touch with
out falling into uncritical positivism. FlashPoints aims
humanities and the social sciences concerned with mo-
and transformation. In a Benjaminian mode, FlashPoints
ature contributes to forming new constellations of culture and
now such formations function critically and politically in the present.
online at http://repositories.cdlib.org/ucpress.

Series Editors: Ali Behdad (Comparative Literature and English, UCLA); Judith Butler (Rhetoric and Comparative Literature, UC Berkeley), Founding Editor; Edward Dimendberg (Film & Media Studies, UC Irvine), Coordinator; Catherine Gallagher (English, UC Berkeley), Founding Editor; Jody Greene (Literature, UC Santa Cruz); Susan Gillman (Literature, UC Santa Cruz); Richard Terdiman (Literature, UC Santa Cruz)

The Fear of French Negroes

Transcolonial Collaboration
in the Revolutionary Americas

Sara E. Johnson

UNIVERSITY OF CALIFORNIA PRESS
Berkeley · Los Angeles · London

THIS BOOK IS MADE POSSIBLE BY A COLLABORATIVE GRANT
FROM THE ANDREW W. MELLON FOUNDATION.

iOO̶OISi62

University of California Press, one of the most distinguished university presses in the United States, enriches
lives around the world by advancing scholarship in the
humanities, social sciences, and natural sciences. Its
activities are supported by the UC Press Foundation
and by philanthropic contributions from individuals
and institutions. For more information, visit
www.ucpress.edu.

University of California Press
Berkeley and Los Angeles, California

University of California Press, Ltd.
London, England

Library of Congress Cataloging-in-Publication Data

Johnson, Sara E. (Sara Elizabeth)
   The fear of French negroes : transcolonial
collaboration in the revolutionary Americas / Sara E.
Johnson.
     p. cm. — (Flashpoints ; 12)
   Includes bibliographical references and index.
   ISBN 978-0-520-27112-8 (pbk. : alk. paper)
   1. Blacks—Caribbean Area—History—19th century.
2. Blacks—Gulf Coast (U.S.)—History—19th century.
3. Blacks—Race identity—Caribbean Area—History—
19th century. 4. Blacks—Race identity—Gulf Coast
(U.S.)—History—19th century. 5. Blacks—
Migrations—History—19th century. 6. Haiti—
History—Revolution, 1791–1804—Influence. I. Title.
F2191.B55J65 2012
305.896'969729—dc23

                              2012005111

Manufactured in the United States of America
20 19 18 17 16 15 14 13 12
10 9 8 7 6 5 4 3 2 1

In keeping with a commitment to support environmen-
tally responsible and sustainable printing practices, UC
Press has printed this book on 50–pound Enterprise, a
30% post-consumer-waste, recycled, deinked fiber that is
processed chlorine-free. It is acid-free and meets all ANSI/
NISO (Z 39.48) requirements.

For my Egun
For Kenneth and Carolyn
For Julián and Amaya

Contents

Illustrations

Acknowledgments

This book was researched and written over many years, and the debts that I have incurred are numerous. Many thanks to the Library Company of Philadelphia, especially Jim Green, Philip Lapansky, and Linda Wisniewski. It was a true pleasure to work there, where I first studied many of the primary sources, both textual and visual, that I used in this and other projects. Thanks are also due to the New York Public Library, the Archives Nationales d'Outre Mer, Tulane University's Special Collections, the Yale Center for British Art, and the Outer Banks History Center. Barbara Rust at the National Archives, Southwest Regional Office, Fort Worth, Leslie Tobias-Olsen at the John Carter Brown Library, Siva Blake at the Historical New Orleans Collection, Richard Phillips at the University of Florida's Latin American Collection, Tony Lewis at the Louisiana State Museum, and Howard Margot at the New Orleans Notarial Archives were all especially kind about answering questions and locating sources.

This project has been graciously funded by the Ford Foundation Postdoctoral Program, the University of California President's Postdoctoral Fellowship, the University of California San Diego Academic Senate, the Hellman Fund, and the Modern Language Initiative. Early versions of chapters 1, 2, and 4 were published as "'You Should Give Them Blacks to Eat': Cuban Bloodhounds and the Waging of an Inter-American War of Torture and Terror," *American Quarterly* 61.1 (2009):

65–92; "*Cinquillo* Consciousness: The Formation of a Pan-Caribbean Musical Aesthetic," in *Music, Writing and Caribbean Unity*, edited by Timothy Reiss (Trenton, NJ: Africa World Press (2005), 35–58; and "The Integration of Hispaniola: A Reappraisal of Haitian-Dominican Relations in the Nineteenth and Twentieth Centuries," *Journal of Haitian Studies* 8.2 (2002): 4–29. Thank you for permission to reprint.

I'd also like to express my deep gratitude to the many teachers that I have had over the years. The Baltimore city public school system created and fostered my love of languages and literatures. Thanks to Ms. Celestine Carr, Mrs. Sally Daneker, and Ms. Rocca. My professors in African diaspora studies at Yale nurtured my passion for the field: Hazel Carby, Cathy Cohen, Vera Kutzinski, Chris Miller, and Robert Stepto. At Stanford, Mary Louise Pratt, Elisabeth Boyi, and Richard Rosa were the first readers and helpful critics for the early iterations of this project. I'd also like to thank Al Camarillo, Claire Fox, John Rickford, Yvonne Yarbro-Bejarano, and all of the folks at Stanford's Center for Comparative Studies in Race and Ethnicity for providing such a supportive, intellectually stimulating environment. Vèvè A. Clark deserves special mention for teaching me what a mentor can and should be. For almost fifteen years her guidance through myriad "epistemic" models, backward-facing check marks in the margins of my work, and endless wisecracks provided both serious and humor-filled continuity to my work. You are deeply missed.

My intellectual debt to the scholars whose work has made this book possible are enormous. I'd like to thank Judith Bettelheim, Robin Blackburn, Jean Casimir, J. Michael Dash, Joan (Colin) Dayan, Laurent Dubois, Katherine Dunham, Raul Fernández, Sybille Fischer, Barry David Gaspar, David Geggus, Edouard Glissant, Sandra Gunning, Saidiya Hartman, C. L. R. James, Robin D. G. Kelley, Franklin Knight, Jane Landers, J. Lorand Matory, Sidney Mintz, Julius S. Scott, Rebecca J. Scott, and Michel-Rolph Trouillot for inspiring me with their engaging work on the revolutionary period in the extended Americas and the interconnections among black folk in general.

Special thanks are also due to the four anonymous readers from the University of California Press and Duke University Press. Your suggestions are sincerely appreciated and have been integrated throughout. Many thanks to Ken Wissoker for his unflagging support for the manuscript, and a big shout-out goes to Susan Gillman, who has been an enthusiastic reader and tireless advocate for the Flashpoints series from the very beginning. My editors at UC Press and the Modern Language Initiative have been a pleasure to work with as this project came to a close: Mari Coates, Mary Francis, Kim Hogeland, Elisabeth Magnus, Tim Roberts, and Eric Schmidt. Finally, thanks to Dixa Ramírez for her help editing the bibliography, and to Marilyn Bliss for compiling the index.

My eternal thanks to the crew for the many hours spent working together, exchanging ideas, and just generally hanging out. You warm friendships have been invaluable over the years: Leslie Alexander, Ingrid Banks, Rob and Mialisa Bonta, Evelyn Cruz, Robin Derby, Zaire Dinzey, Fatima El-Tayeb, Ada Ferrer, Heather Fowler, Sharon Holland, Nancy Ho-Wu, Stephanie Ivy, Tara Javidi, Ede Jermin, Tracy Johnson, Meta DuEwa Jones, Nicole King, Kimberly Lindsay, Lisa Lowe, Gina Marie Pitti, Cherise Smith, Lynnea Stephan, Ula Taylor, Kay and Gabriela Torres, Reshima Wilkinson, Erin Lee Gurney, Helen Yoon, and last, but certainly not least, Lisa Ze Winters. And thanks to my wonderful colleagues and friends at the University of California who have provided insightful feedback about this project over many gourmet meals: Luis Alvarez, Jody Blanco, Ross Frank, Tak Fujitani, Rosemary George, Jin Lee, Yen Lespiritu, Curtis Marez, Nayan Shah, Stephanie Smallwood, Shelley Streeby, and Lisa Yoneyama.

Writing this book literally would not have been possible without the dedicated care of Saige Walding and Mitch Lehman. Thank you for the many hours spent keeping me healthy. Likewise, many thanks to Fa'irawo Amos Dyson for everything.

And of course, my acknowledgments would not be complete without thanking my family. Much love to my amazing parents, Ken and Carolyn Johnson, who have always been my greatest source of unconditional affection, guidance, and support in all things. Thanks to my three wonderful aunts, Barbara Azeltine, Ava Johnson, and Lorraine Washington, all of whom treated me as a daughter and a friend. We lost you too soon. The entire Johnson-Dischert clan has been an inspiration, especially Geylon and Minnie Johnson, who toiled tirelessly in rural Mississippi so that subsequent generations could have an easier life. Likewise, the extended Widener family—Carolyn, Edra, Mike, and Renee—your warmth and sustenance are sincerely appreciated. Thank you, Jennifer, you're still my best friend after all these years. Mahalik, Mia, Elias and Benjamin, I'm always hopeful that you and Jennifer will all move to California one of these years. And Danny, words are inadequate to express my appreciation for the love, generous idea exchanges, and boundless goodwill you've shown as you have read the many drafts of this project. This book would not be the same without you. Finally, my undying thanks to Julián and Amaya for being a daily source of inspiration and laughter. Aburu aboye abosise.

Preface

The Fear of "French Negroes"

Billowing smoke and fire pour from an elegant plantation in ruins. Black figures armed with swords and bayonets battle uniformed soldiers. Women, children, and an infirm elder flee empty-handed as they reluctantly leave their fallen menfolk behind. In the center, a male and female white couple looks back as a black insurgent pursues them; the man's elegant attire and the woman's décolletage stand out amid the chaos. Meanwhile, a ship is anchored in the harbor as its passengers engage in battle, and those fleeing for their lives desperately seek passage on the ships that will eventually land them in neighboring Jamaica, Cuba, or one of the port cities of the eastern United States. The image (figure 1) depicts the 1793 conflagration of Cap Français (Le Cap). Known as the "Paris of the Antilles," Le Cap was the economic and cultural capital of the wealthiest Caribbean colony of the eighteenth century. The racialized class war that pitted French, British, and Spanish imperial armies against hundreds of thousands of slaves and free people of color was in full swing, and the conflagration of the city marked a point of no return. Graphically capturing what the painting's title notes as the "troubles, ravages, murders, fires, devastations and massacres" of the Haitian Revolution from a blatantly sensationalized perspective of the white elite, the image encapsulates what contemporary audiences came to recognize as the "horrors" of Saint-Domingue as they were perpetrated against white victims. It is a classic example of

FIGURE 1. *Incendie du Cap; Révolte générale des nègres. Massacre des Blancs.* Watercolor. Cover plate of *Saint-Domingue, ou Histoire des ses révolutions, contenant le récit effroyable des divisions, des troubles, des ravages, des meurtres, des incendies, des dévastations et des massacres qui eurent lieu dans cette île, depuis 1789 jusqu'à la perte de la colonie* (Paris: Chez Tiger, Imprimeur-librairie, 1815). Courtesy of the Library Company of Philadelphia.

the "white fright" images that circulated in the Atlantic world during the first decades of the nineteenth century.

Another image lends a different perspective to the one captured above. At the entrance to a public inn, three white men gesticulate as they watch a fourth figure falling backwards. This collapsing figure is black and is depicted in the act of slitting his throat. A carriage waits in the foreground, and to the far left a black woman and child look back upon the scene (figure 2). Published by the anonymous Humanitas in an 1803 pamphlet, the image comments on events from the previous year, when an inquest was conducted in New York to investigate the sudden death of Romain, a black man from Saint-Domingue. The inquest ruled that it was a case of "Suicide, Occasioned by the Dread of Slavery, to Which the Deceased Knew Himself Devoted." While Romain's decision to take his life rather than continue in the custody of his owner falls within the long tradition of slave suicide, the macabre spectacle on a northern urban thoroughfare provoked horrified reaction, and a volley of articles appeared documenting the case. Of the events immediately preceding the suicide, Humanitas writes:

> And here it may not be unnecessary to reflect on the situation of the unfortunate man's mind at this moment. He well knew the cruelties inflicted on slaves in the West Indies. . . . He was, therefore, not only unwilling, he was determined not to return. . . . Maddened with the thought, and rendered desperate by the complicated misery of his situation, from which he had now no prospect of release, but still determined to be free, he adopted his dernier resort, took a pruning-knife from his pocket, and dreading a spark of life should remain, whereby he might be restored, he three times cut his throat across, and fell dead on the pavement, thereby emancipating himself from the grasp of avarice and inhumanity. (13–15)[1]

Inquest records determined that Romain, twenty-seven years of age, had arrived at the hotel under guard, in the company of his wife, Marie, and their young child. They had resided in the environs of Trenton, New Jersey, with their owner Anthony Salaignac since 1795, when the latter had relocated there after leaving Saint-Domingue. Periodicals from the time reveal that Romain had a previous record of resistance and that many of Salaignac's slaves had escaped during their residence in the United States.[2] By 1802, Salaignac felt confident enough to return to Saint-Domingue in order to reclaim his property, most likely because Napoleon Bonaparte's massive expeditionary force had recently arrived in the island to restore slavery. Although we can only

FIGURE 2. Frontispiece of Humanitas, *Reflections on Slavery; with Recent Evidence of Inhumanity, Occasioned by the Melancholy Death of Romain, A French Negro* (Philadelphia: R. Cochran, 1803). Courtesy of the Library Company of Philadelphia.

speculate about the particulars, evidence suggests that the apprehension occasioned by returning to Saint-Domingue and its ancien régime was profound enough for Romain's family to resist relocation. Marie and her child escaped; Romain slew himself. Romain probably did not know that by the time of his proposed departure Napoleon's brother-in-law, General-in-Chief Charles Leclerc, was dying of yellow fever and the black revolutionary army had control of all but a small part of the island. Within less than two years, most of the remaining white inhabitants of the island would be dead or in exile, and their former slaves free. Had they returned, Romain and his family would have been included in this final emancipation, one that was won by the force of arms, not decreed by words emanating from the distant, vacillating French metropolitan capital.[3]

I open this story with both images, as they vividly capture the circumstances that occasioned the hemispheric movement of thousands of people from diverse racial and socioeconomic backgrounds as a result of the Haitian Revolution (1791–1804). Exact figures recording the total number of refugees who left Saint-Domingue are not available. We do know, however, that the largest relocation sites in the Americas were Cuba, Louisiana, and Jamaica. Nowhere did this relocation matter more than in eastern Cuba and New Orleans, where the influx of refugees doubled the size of local populations and permanently altered the character of local life.[4] Norfolk, Charleston, Philadelphia, New York, and Baltimore also proved popular resettlement sites. Secondary migrations often led to Trinidad, Puerto Rico, and the islands of the Lesser Antilles such as Martinique and Guadeloupe. Most resettlement thus occurred in slave-holding territories, effectively guaranteeing either continued servitude or a precarious freedom for migrants of African descent.

The images also embody very different ideas of what Saint-Domingue and its revolution meant to diverse populations of the colonial Americas. For some, the prerevolutionary days were ones of privilege and leisure; for others, a time of bondage and forced labor. I am interested in how the dread felt by Romain and his family and the gruesome nature of his suicide convert the oft-touted horrors of Saint-Domingue away from those chronicled by white refugees, to the horrors of slavery itself as practiced both on the island and during the subsequent diaspora occasioned by the revolution. It is important to remember that slavery in Saint-Domingue was "a genocidal state of affairs maintained by an astounding rate of slave consumption; in the last decades of the eighteenth century, the single colony became the largest buyer of slaves in the Northern Hemisphere, importing more than twice as many persons as the rest of North America. . . . [It] extracted on average ten to fifteen years of labor from captive men and women before they were driven to death" (Garraway, *Libertine Colony* 240).

The "fear of French negroes," an oft-mentioned phrase in contemporary accounts of the revolution, should thus draw our attention to the fears felt by blacks themselves, not simply the implied anxiety of their oppressors. When told from the perspective of the displaced elite, narratives of revolution tend to revolve around two axes. The first is one of pillage, fire, and the massacre of innocent victims at the hands of a ferocious mob. Conversely, many of these same refugee families cherished fond memories of their slaves, and their stories contain depictions of their servants' selfless devotion to their owners.[5] Romain's suicide and the stories surrounding it, however, provide an alternative to planter accounts that attempt to manage the paradox between frenzied and indiscriminate black rage and the idealization of content, loyal slaves. While Humanitas's abolitionist rendition of the story is couched in the sentimental language of melancholy and dread as opposed to that of black self-determination, there is little doubt that Romain understood there could be no middle ground accommodating the irreconcilable nature of a slave economy and his humanity. His highly visible resistance to his fate provides its own commentary on two of the choices he felt were available to him—life in freedom or death.

Romain's actions hence afford a dramatic window into how historical players of his hue and circumstances created and reacted to the radical transformations of the era. The stories that follow trace black people's responses to the breakdown and restructuring of colonial life in the aftermath of the Haitian Revolution. I examine the migration of people, ideas, and practices across colonial boundaries from the 1790s to the 1840s. In each case, the migrations were informed by the upheaval on the island. I focus on the experiences of people who had little expectation that their stories would be preserved. For the most part their stories were not written down, and their traces have to be reassembled from fragmentary sources. Such reassembly is still an important task, as many studies of Saint-Domingue exile communities privilege white refugee experiences.[6] While this is in part because the printed archival record is skewed in their favor, even influential historians in the field who have proven sensitive to the silences in their sources blithely make statements such as "The luckiest [planters] were able to save a few slaves" (Debien and le Gardeur 199). While the colonists would no doubt consider themselves fortunate, the extreme "unluckiness" of Romain's plight serves as a reminder of the contrasting choices available to those compelled to relocate.

The Fear of French Negroes thus prioritizes the stories of a wide variety of black voices. The title is meant to be deliberately thought-provoking, depending on whether one understands "French negroes" as subjects experiencing fear or as the objects of others' fears The more common interpretation highlights the alarm invoked by the very idea of black revolt, especially the sensationalist specter of black violence and revenge. However, contained within this modality of fright is also the possibility of seeing "negroes" as subjects rather than objects, as the agents of radical change in hemispheric economic and social relations. Once they become subjects, the full range of their emotional and physical reactions to life during the time period is open to study. I wish to provide a nuanced discussion of what could easily be seen as two poles of abjection—the extremities of either white or black brutalization and misery. I highlight the creativity and resolve of people during uncertain times, their fight to achieve some measure of influence, even control, over their lives.

To date, much excellent work has been done about the consequences of the revolution and its demographic, legal, economic, and cultural impact on neighboring parts of the Americas.[7] For example, painstaking archival work has filled in the gaps in people's lives as they migrated—whom they married, their occupations, how they socialized; has documented legislation designed to restrict the arrival of French immigrants; and has traced the impact of coffee and sugar-growing technologies as these traveled from Saint-Domingue to places such as Cuba and Louisiana. *The Fear of French Negroes* uses these behaviors to further speculate upon the nature of expressive consciousness—how was the revolution's import captured in a variety of popular late eighteenth- and early nineteenth-century artistic genres? At both the practical and more imaginative levels, how did free people of color and slaves each articulate what they considered to be the most desirable postrevolutionary political subjectivity? How does culture help us understand this moment?

Revolutionary Haiti hence occupies a central space in the book, but one that emanates out in multiple cultural, political, and socioeconomic directions. The result of a thirteen-year war with the most technologically advanced armies of imperial France, England, and Spain, the 1804 Declaration of Independence that marked the passage of power from Saint-Domingue to Haiti made the new nation the first independent Caribbean and Latin American country, and the only nation born out of a successful slave revolt. As is the case with all true social revolutions, events in colonial Saint-Domingue resulted in a pocket of newfound liberty surrounded by both intense reactionary antipathy and curious onlookers seeking inspiration. Whether they viewed the revolution as anathema to be contained at all costs so as not to "contaminate" neighboring slave-holding regimes or, conversely, as a source of hope and new opportunities, the populations under examination all grappled with the revolution as a factor in their quests for profit, freedom, and sanctuary. This book shows how cultural forms—textual, visual, musical, and movement based—illuminate the engagements of people of African descent in physical and ideological collaborations across imperial frontiers as one path toward political ends that would convert fear to possibility. Transcolonial collaborations offered black actors unique opportunities to negotiate mobility, liberty, and self-expression from within a hemispheric system of chattel slavery.

Introduction

Mobile Culture, Mobilized Politics

Communication networks between subjects of different European empires in the Americas have always thrived, despite being closely regulated and habitually proscribed. Given the climate of competitive mercantilist politics in the region, imperial officialdom militated against unmediated interactions between their colonies and other metropoles. However, contact, most importantly in the form of trade, was essential to the survival of early Caribbean and North American societies that imported basic foodstuffs, luxury items, and enslaved men and women from neighboring territories. Black markets existed alongside sanctioned ones, and colonial officials were known to turn a blind eye to activities that offered a financial incentive.[1] Voluminous primary sources document these interactions: ship manifests from archival customs records, travel chronicles of itinerant wanderers, and records of sale for both the official and contraband market in African slaves "seasoned" and traded from one island to another. Contemporary sources make it clear that a merchant living in Saint-Domingue might have had contact with family in Philadelphia or New Orleans, and a slave who had run off to Cuba or Spanish Florida in search of freedom under a writ of Catholic sanctuary might try to share news with fellow slaves back home in South Carolina or Jamaica. There are abundant examples of communication networks that flourished in the interstices of empires, calling into question strict colonial loyalties or imperialist isolation.[2]

Whereas contact and exchange between colonial empires have always occurred, the Age of Revolution as it unfolded in the Americas marked interactions on an even larger scale than had hitherto been the case.[3] As David P. Geggus points out, "The decades flanking the turn of the nineteenth century . . . were quite exceptional. Most colonies suffered either foreign invasion or internal revolt when, from 1793 to 1802, and with lesser intensity to 1815, war between the European powers sent tens of thousands of soldiers into the region, displaced thousands of refugees, and disrupted local shipping on a massive scale" ("Slavery, War" 2). *The Fear of French Negroes* attempts to capture the essence of a unique moment, one of chaos, upheaval, and the possibility of fundamental disruptions to the status quo. Virulent debates about the birth of new nations through revolutionary struggle, the future of slavery, and the nature of declining European power and growing U.S. expansionism in the region were just a few of the signs that flux, not stability, was the reigning order of the day. The repercussions of the "big bang" created by the Haitian Revolution are at the heart of this narrative, but the protagonists in the pages that follow participated in other seminal armed conflicts of the age, including the Second Maroon War in Jamaica, the War of 1812 as it unfolded in Louisiana, Latin American independence movements, and the Seminole Wars.

One result of this "turbulent time" was increased awareness of life in other colonial spheres of influence and a corresponding insight into the potential advantages to be gained by collaborating on projects of mutual interest (Geggus and Gaspar). The search for opportunities that involved movement across colonial frontiers was constant, and the transcolonial became a meaningful terrain for vastly different people. This was especially the case for those of African descent. I examine the lives of figures as diverse as Romain and his family, armed black soldiers and privateers, female performers, and newspaper editors in an effort to uncover how and why they brokered alliances.

I use the idea of transcoloniality as both a geopolitical and a methodological concept. First, *transcolonial* describes the conflicts and collaborations that occurred between the residents of American territories governed by separate political entities—in this study France, Spain, and England. All three nations had extensive, extremely lucrative empires in the Caribbean Basin, and the region became the theater of their struggles for global dominance. A map produced in the 1730s (figure 3) provides an excellent visual depiction of the rival European empires in the immediate area; New France, New Spain, and the British Americas all coexisted within relatively close proximity around the Gulf of Mexico and the Caribbean Sea (noted as the North Sea). Hispaniola is just right of center, and one can imagine waves of people leaving the island for neighboring territories such as Cuba, Jamaica, Louisiana, or Maryland. I adopt the modifier *transcolonial* as opposed to *transnational* both because the latter would be anachronistic in most of the examples under study and because the concept of empire carries connotations of global connectedness that are often lost in the national frame. Even as imperial borders in the Americas were in the process of becoming national ones, the world examined here was conceived and regulated to bring the maximum benefit to the colonial state.

As a methodological approach, transcoloniality takes as its starting point the inventiveness and viability of intercolonial contact zones. The creation and dissemination of the artifacts under study provide a counternarrative to the linguistically and disciplinarily isolated fields of American and Caribbean studies that still tend to compartmentalize the region according to categories such as francophone, hispanophone, anglophone, and Dutch-speaking territories. This book seeks to mitigate this balkanization, both to more accurately grasp how actors in the past negotiated their own realities and to provide a holistic approach to studying the region in the present. For example, it is commonplace to acknowledge the web of connections linking Saint-Domingue and neighboring Louisiana. This is due to the generations of people and their cultural practices that moved between the two formerly francophone colonies. Much may be gained, however, by placing Spanish Santo Domingo in juxtaposition with Louisiana. Both territories were "traded" back and forth between the Spanish and French, and their populations evinced remarkably similar sentiments about having their lives uprooted by treaties that challenged their local customs. Or reconsider the aforementioned ties between Cap Français and Philadelphia. What for many contemporaries was a headlong flight on the first ship available represents in retrospect an evocative meeting between the most determined remnants of a profitable plantocracy and the citizens of one of the hemisphere's most antislavery cities. In each case we are reminded that the meaning of this historic moment for people of African descent must be asked across as well as within assumed geographies.

While we are more familiar with transcolonial conflict, this book is about collaboration; it was often uneasy, and it always occurred

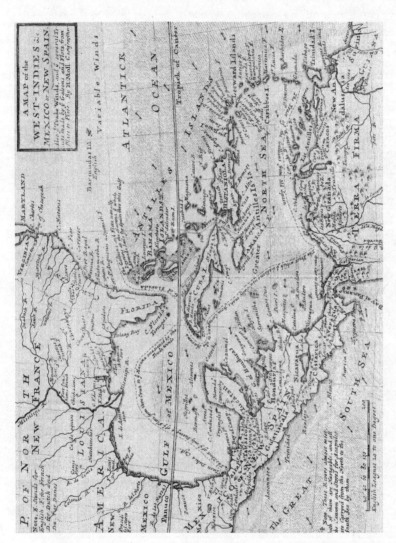

FIGURE 3. Herman Moll, *A Map of the West Indies etc. or New Spain; Also ye several tracts made by ye galeons and flota from place to place.* In *Atlas Minor or a Set of Sixty Two New and Correct Maps of All Parts of the World* (London: Thomas and John Bowles, ca. 1730). Courtesy of the Outer Banks History Center, Manteo, North Carolina.

within a larger context of tension between and among states and local residents. Cooperation between subjects of different empires was regarded with deep suspicion, as it could potentially result in autonomy (economic and political) from the metropole. The colonial state was even more threatened by virtually all cooperation on the part of the black enslaved majority and their collaborations occurred amid a climate of fear and repression. I use the term *collaboration* in its original sense of working together, of commingled labor for a common cause. By definition, partaking in most collaborative processes involves sharing complementary, mutually beneficial information. In the following chapters we see people developing experiential practices— torture techniques, religious ritual, smuggling knowledge, performance expertise, reading and writing habits—into knowledge bases with regional influence.

In contrast to the sense of optimism that often accompanies invocations of the transnational, I argue that transcolonial collaborations were not intrinsically emancipatory or progressive. Quite the opposite was often the case. This book was born out of a desire to document alternative community formations that contested the racialized violence endemic to European imperialism and creole nation-building projects. The evidence I have accumulated, however, suggests that extreme racial violence remained a constant reality for the majority of inhabitants of the region during this era, whether perpetrated by the imperial state, creole nationalists, or groups such as slave-trading pirates that functioned in the interstices of state domination. As a point of clarity, I use the term *creole* here to refer to people born in the Americas. The racial, class, and gender fault lines that defined colonial and national life also existed in the transcolonial sphere. This social stratification played a direct role in restricting the circumstances under which people could interact with one another. That said, for black residents of the region and economically marginalized whites, the appeal of transcoloniality often contained an idealistic impulse to imagine another world that could result in improved material circumstances. Their struggle to connect was where a hopeful politics existed, sometimes even thrived.

This book uses a series of case studies from the 1790s to the 1840s to demonstrate that there were disparate visions of transcolonial exchange, what I deem competing inter-Americanisms. Much as competing inter-American analytical frameworks are the hallmarks of the current moment, they likewise marked the turn of the eighteenth century two hundred years ago. The renewed interest in inter-American collaboration on the scholarly level that flourished in the mid-1990s is undoubtedly linked to events such as the creation of the North American Free Trade Agreement (NAFTA) and the more contemporary existence of networks such as the Alianza Bolivariana para los Pueblos de Nuestra América (ALBA). These projects have obvious roots in inter-American cooperation and antagonism, informing ongoing debates about governance in the age of neoliberal globalization. Just as such concepts might be imagined from divergent points of view—for example, ones that favor wealthy corporations and others that are imagined by the working poor, ones that privilege those north of the U.S.-Mexican border and ones that prioritize indigenous development strategies to the south—so too we must examine how there were competing visions of early nineteenth-century inter-Americanness.

Not surprisingly, two key axes upon which these earlier visions revolved were race and class. Transcolonial American collaborations were racialized and differed in substance and means of expression between people of color and white populations, just as they differed according to the economic circumstances of the actors involved. For example, the white planter elite discussed in chapter 1 participated in proslavery, inter-American collaborations whose objectives were diametrically opposed to those fostered by people engaged in the hemispheric Underground Railroad network that stretched from Canada to Mexico. Once we understand opposing agendas such as these, it is essential to recognize that within the black community differences of status linked to skin color and economic station were also of critical importance. The cultural forms under examination here highlight the contrasting worldviews held by black populations throughout the region, providing a more nuanced picture of the communities that they inhabited and imagined. Some of the more familiar divisions emerge—slave/free, black/mulatto, African/creole. Other, more surprising ones do as well. Take, for example, how the performers in chapter 4 articulated simultaneously overlapping and antagonistic identities such as Congolese-French-Jamaicanness in a strategic attempt to assert their creative autonomy.

The stories I have assembled lead me to claim that there is no way of neatly theorizing black transcoloniality as an absolute. It is too contradictory and internally diverse, faced with the challenge of encompassing the worldviews of people as distinct as "saltwater" slaves and black slaveholders. The black transcolonial world of the late eighteenth and early nineteenth centuries resists reduction into a single framework capable of encompassing such divergent priorities and aspirations. Rather, the story worth telling is about the unruliness of its persistent iterations. The critical constant I wish to emphasize is that in the cases under examination there was a conscious choice about a way of being in the world, a perspective that had its grounding outside what are commonly considered the twin specters of colonial versus national subjectivity. That said, the three dominant ideological frameworks that I consider throughout—colonialist, transcolonial, and nationalist—were not mutually exclusive but often able to cohabit the same space. For example, when an aesthetic developed out of transcolonial contact, whether in a musical rhythm or a religious ritual, it did not necessarily lose a sense of its component parts. Home, often Saint-Domingue, migrated and became something new; it was rooted and routed, although the roots may have been more grounded in a particular community identity as opposed to a territorial state as such.

The revolutionary period in the extended Americas has much to teach us, and the cultural artifacts I examine tell a story different from one that might emerge from more settled historical moments. One of the great political lessons of the Haitian Revolution is that the possibility of radical change hinges upon an ability to form strategic bonds, whether across racial and class lines, across imperial boundaries, or across gendered and ethnic affiliations. The enemies of yesterday become temporary allies, and coalitions, often fragile ones, are born. This struggle to form alliances, to find common cause with people whose agendas might intersect at particular historical moments, is at the heart of the narrative that follows. The conflicts that defined the tripartite racial and class structure of colonial Saint-Domingue and played a direct role in the unfolding of the revolution are well documented by scholars in the field—they occurred not only between white owners and black slaves but between whites and *gens de couleur libres* / free people of color and, equally importantly, between *gens de couleur* and slaves. C. L. R. James's astute exposé of these rifts and their successful, if short-term, sublimation is the classic example. Yet studies of the cultural and political legacies of the revolution in a larger context have paid less attention to the intrablack dimensions of these conflicts. The ever-shifting loyalties and opportunistic collaborations that emerged in colonial Saint-Domingue were likewise evident in the Saint-Domingue diaspora, and certainly in the larger hemispheric black world of the time. Hence for some, fostering alliances with slave-trading pirates seemed a more expedient choice than becoming antislavery activists. By documenting these struggles for unity within a context of strife and division, I hope to show the richly varied manifestations of collectivist activities of the time.

Despite the diversity found within the communities under study, some constitutive elements of black transcolonial politics emerge. The framework shaping this type of politics was that state institutions were not going to function as a primary mechanism of protection or advancement; they were likely to be antagonistic. Haiti was an exception to this rule, and its promise of racial equality explains why people were drawn to its example, both in the immediate aftermath of the revolution and decades later. The evidence I gather demonstrates how knowledge circulated among a population for whom the governing structures of colonial and national society were either inaccessible or intentionally being circumvented. These regulating structures included political assemblies, policing mechanisms, educational institutions, publishing houses, and so forth. Control over knowledge production and dissemination occasioned great anxiety for people of African descent in a context of arbitrary and extreme violence, lack of citizenship status, censorship, and exclusion from the right to attain skills such as reading and writing. As a result, expressive cultural forms had great significance and potential. They provided a location to process, create, contest, and disseminate meaning. These forms placed a high value on accurate information sharing; contained the roots of both anticolonial and antinational critique; and were often performance oriented, expressed in movement and orality.

From the vantage point of the present, this focus on the migration of people and culture across colonial boundaries requires recapturing the process by which inter-American sensibilities were subsumed by the eventual concretization of national boundaries. What follows are not "what ifs," precisely, but traces of forgotten possibilities, the "world that we have lost," to use Peter Laslett's terminology. I invoke the concept of crossroads to show the value of the paths that were not memorialized, the importance of a world of ideas and behaviors subsumed not only by the passage of time but by campaigns to silence nonconformist perspectives on how the rigidly hierarchical societies (both colonial and creole nationalist) of the era might be reordered to better suit the needs of people of African descent. Why has the memory of transcolonial American collaborations faded? Historiography from the late nineteenth century until the recent past has tended to downplay the importance attributed to these encounters. What is the explanatory value of cultural productions to recover these stories? I believe that the cultural artifacts studied here are where the results of collaboration retain their life and alternative histories are embedded and transmitted across generations.

METHODOLOGICAL CONSIDERATIONS

In the late eighteenth and early nineteenth centuries, the majority of people of African descent in the Americas were slaves. A smaller percentage were born free men and women or acquired their liberty by purchasing themselves or being manumitted by their owners. Their lives, while strictly circumscribed on a daily basis in terms of labor demands, were also mobile ones. As slaves, they were sold or forced to travel with their owners; when free, they were always in search of a place where they could live with dignity and equality. While they may have moved across colonial frontiers with less frequency than they moved within them, blacks were frequently compelled to relocate under duress or, conversely, tempted to escape or migrate across colonial frontiers in search of better life opportunities.

A long history of scholarship has explored the various ways that black populations moved beyond and between colonial/national boundaries. Referred to in varied contexts as "the common wind," "hydrarchy from below," the "Black Atlantic," "poetics of relation," "translocalism," "transnational black studies," "black cosmopolitanism," or the "black international," these theories posit nuanced explanations of interactions between people of African descent who proactively used movement and their common experiences of subjugation to advance their interests.[4] Migration is a defining characteristic of New World blacks, from the Atlantic crossing, to the Great Migration, to the more contemporary return of urban blacks to the U.S. South. The genesis of African diaspora studies as a site of inquiry is attributable to a perceived need for relations with a world beyond one's immediate boundaries—understood as imperial, religious, linguistic, economic—a world that potentially held ideological convictions that called slavery and discrimination into question. These ruminations were frequently transcolonial/transnational in nature precisely because many people of African descent recognized that their struggles for self and community would be betrayed by both colonial and national power centers that depended on their continued oppression for profit. My research is grounded in diaspora studies (both African and Haitian), using mobility as a framework to study the transfer of people, knowledge, and meaning.

A quick set of examples suffices to illustrate why people were wary of state control. In the context of imperial subjugation, colonial officials were deeply tied to the slave trade. For example, royal governments initially oversaw the West African trading companies, and colonial representatives in the colonies frequently owned plantations, allowed illegal importations of slaves, and acted as executive and judicial controls to back slave owners' absolute dominion over their property. With regard to nationalist movements, Gordon K. Lewis reminds us that "the argument of political liberalism, with its traditional support for colonial liberties, became identified with the proslavery ideology, while the political ideas of the abolitionists became identified with continuing supervision from the metropolis. . . . The upshot of all this was that, ironically, the defense of anything approximating a doctrine of Caribbean nationalism passed, for the time being, into the hands of the proslavery apologists themselves" (*Main Currents* 245). This was especially the case in the French and British colonies, where there was a powerful abolitionist momentum in their corresponding European metropoles between 1790 and 1810. Creole nationalisms in the modern era were thus often ambivalent about, when not in direct opposition to, black equality. An August 5, 1837, edition of the African American newspaper the *Colored American* succinctly confirms the limits of white creole nationalism in the North American context. The editors note that "a thought, as humiliating to America, as it was glorious to England, threw itself across our minds. It was this—Had Republican America remained a colony of Great Britain, the first of August 1834 would have emancipated every slave, and made us a nation of FREEMEN." Hence the American Revolution's most glaring failure for these writers was that it almost doubled the time that North American blacks were denied their freedom compared to their West Indian contemporaries.[5]

The texts most commonly associated with any study of black mobility and transcoloniality/transnationality in the era of slavery often include the now canonical autobiographies and essays of former slaves and free people of color who wrote their own stories or told them to others for the express goal of publication. Usually members of the antislavery movement, these authors include Olaudah Equiano, Nancy Prince, Frederick Douglass, Ramón Betances, and Martin Delany. I do not examine autobiography, essays, or fiction by these authors in detail, in large part because Afro-diasporic texts of these genres have received a great deal of critical attention, especially in the anglophone world.[6] They have withstood extensive exegesis because of their rich complexity.

My transcolonial approach demands and reveals an alternative, complementary archive. This book focuses on the stories of people who did not have an expectation of having their voices recorded for posterity. With the exception of the black newspapers examined in chapter 5, they left few, if any, written records documenting their own lives. Yet they created idioms that formulated and disseminated various expressions of black collectivity in an age during which literacy was proscribed. As a result, I have assembled an archive of fragmentary sources to tease out their experiences. My evidentiary base is capacious and includes visual images; newspaper articles and advertisements; orally transmitted songs, poetry, and speeches; and rhythms, instruments, and costumes. I also sift through memoirs, court depositions, and other state records for traces of how people of African descent negotiated the upheavals occasioned by the various conflicts of the Age of Revolution. The materials examined exemplify the corpus of early inter-American cultural studies.

As a literary historian, the "historian" part of my job is more prevalent in the study that follows. My material came to determine my method. I read, view, and listen closely to my sources. For example, I am attentive to the ways in which visual records are useful, as they remain an underexplored resource for studies of this era.[7] This is not because iconography is somehow objective, or that it provides an unmediated "window" into the past. These images are subject to all of the ideological agendas that texts are. Yet contemporary observers frequently caught glimpses of black creativity and resourcefulness, sometimes in spite of their own biases. As we shall see, images are likewise extremely helpful in comparative work across geographic and temporal boundaries. With regard to close listening, performative music and dance repertoires also tell fascinating stories of transcolonial collaborations. Rhythms, and the instruments on which they were played, migrated and became a living tapestry of conversations that helped to "institutionalize" black experiences.

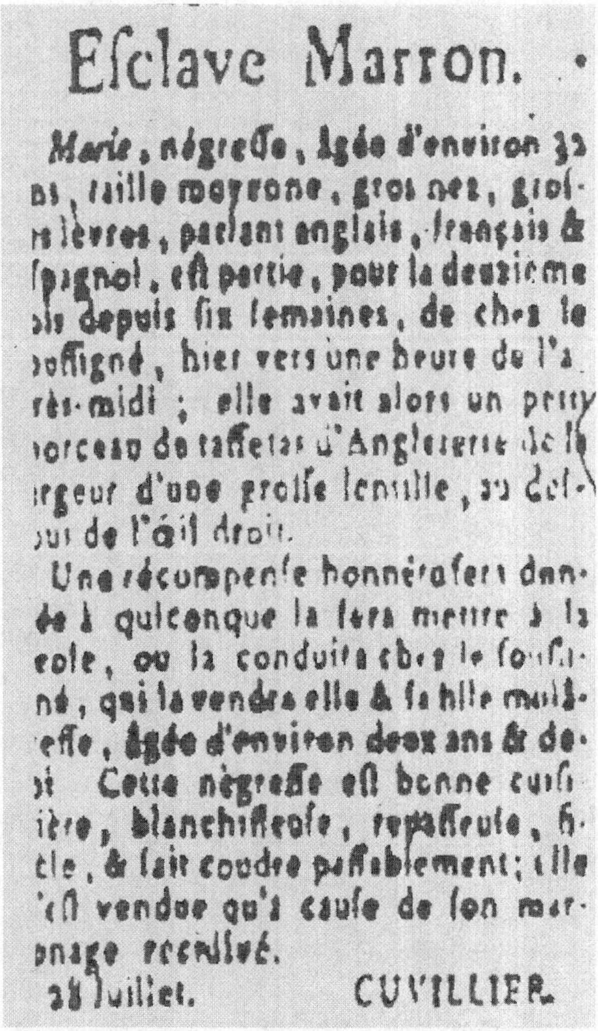

Efclave Marron.

Marie, négrefle, âgée d'environ 33 ans, taille moyenne, gros nez, grof-es lèvres, parlant anglais, français & fpagnol, eft partie, pour la deuxième fois depuis fix femaines, de chez le fouffigné, hier vers une heure de l'après-midi ; elle avait alors un petit morceau de taffetas d'Angleterre de la largeur d'une groffe lentille, au def-fus de l'œil droit.

Une récompenfe honnérafera donnée à quiconque la fera mettre à la geôle, ou la conduira chez le fouffi-né, qui la vendra elle & fa fille mulâ-effe, âgée d'environ deux ans & de-mi. Cette négrefle eft bonne cuifi-ière, blanchiffeufe, repaffeufe, fi-cle, & fait coudre paffablement; elle 'eft vendue qu'à caufe de fon marronnage recidivé.

28 Juillet.   CUVILLIER.

FIGURE 4. Advertisement for Marie, a runaway slave. *Moniteur de la Louisiane* (July 28, 1809).

It bears noting that a multilingual approach is critically important throughout, given that the people who cross these pages did not live in a monolingual world: language acquisition and mastery were necessary tools for both survival and subterfuge. I have chosen to reprint many of the original-language citations in the body of the book as a reminder of this reality. A series of advertisements from contemporary newspapers provides a case in point. Consider

Ranaway,

On the 23d instant, a French Negro MAN, named JOSEPH, about 22 years of age, tall and strong made, of a dark complexion, full face, with small eyes, has a slow pronunciation, speaks English, beside his native language ; is well known on the wharves of this city, where he used to work. He had on when he went away, a pair of blue trowsers and jacket.

All masters of vessels are cautioned against taking him on board, as he may probably attempt to make his escape in that way.

Ten Dollars reward will be given for apprehending the said Negro, and lodging him in the Work-House, or for any correct information, such as may tend to his being apprehended and effectually secured by the owner. For particulars, enquire of the Printers.

April 26   eod 3

FIGURE 5. Advertisement for Joseph, a runaway "French negro." *City Gazette and Daily Advertiser* (April 27, 1808)

Louisiana's first newspaper, *Moniteur de la Louisiane*. The periodical was founded in 1794 by the printer Louis Duclot, himself a refugee from Saint-Domingue. During the 1809 influx of more than ten thousand multiracial Saint-Domingue refugees to Louisiana following their expulsion from Cuba, he published many notices for runaway slaves / *esclaves marrons* and slaves for sale / *nègres à vendre*. For every advertisement seeking to sell or apprehend escaped "French negroes" in *Moniteur*, there are others in newspapers all over the region where French-owned slaves, including those from Saint-Domingue, resettled with their masters. In one advertisement (figure 4), readers were told of Marie, a "black woman about thirty-two years old, medium build, big nose, big lips, speaking English, French, and Spanish" ("une négresse âgée d'environ 32 ans, taille moyenne, gros nez, grosses lèvres, parlant anglais, français & espagnol"; July 28, 1809). The owner did not wish to part with her since she was a "good cook, laundress, and ironer" ("bonne cuisinière, blanchisseuse, repasseuse"). However, her "marronage recidivée," or recidivist escapism, made it necessary to sell her and her two-and-a-half-year-old "fille mulâtresse."[8] Another advertisement solicited the return of two slaves who had fled from the Habitation Jacques Fortier. It asked for information and/or the capture and return of "the black man Devis, of the Ibo nation, of good stature, speaking

French and English" ("le nègre Devis de nation Ibo, d'une belle taille, parlant Français & Anglais") and "the black woman Nancy, a creole of Charleston, speaking English and French" ("la négresse Nancy, créole de Charleston, parlant Anglais & Français"; May 6, 1809). Information presented in an advertisement from Charleston, South Carolina's *City Gazette and Daily Advertiser* (figure 5) likewise speaks of a runaway, multilingual "French negro" named Joseph. Both of the latter ads warned that the runaways were likely to flee by sea, and one specifically prohibited any ship captains from furnishing aid. One can imagine that being sold between islands or to owners from different territories resulted in the acquisition of French, English, and Spanish. If these men and women managed to avoid recapture, living as free persons in neighboring territories would certainly have been easier given the great linguistic dexterity each seems to have possessed. Of course, one cannot romanticize these skills or the history of cultural contact that was required to give them birth. Regardless of the language employed to issue a command, regardless of what king or what republic was ultimately receiving the revenue generated from this forced labor, slavery was remarkably brutal throughout the region. The struggle to assert one's humanity was arduous and often doomed to fail. That said, for people willing, or forced, to take risks, windows of possibility promised improved life conditions, if not complete freedom.

A generation later, at the close of my study, we have the case of Joseph Michael, a free man of color. In an advertisement from an 1834 edition of the aforementioned newspaper the *Colored American*, he solicits employment as follows: "The Subscriber, student of the African Seminary, located at Parsippany New Jersey . . . has subsequently visited England and France, and resided for some time in the West Indies and several parts of South America; and having acquired a tolerable knowledge of the French and Spanish languages; and having made the moral improvement of his colored brethren one of his principal objects, he offers his services to them, to teach the following Branches—Reading, Writing, Arithmetic, Geography, English and French Grammar; mathematics, Rhetorick *[sic]*, Natural Philosophy, the Use of the maps and Globes, &c, &c." Michael was evidently educated, well traveled, multilingual, and like many northern U.S. blacks, eager to share his Protestant religious beliefs with communities where he traveled.[9] His worldview was expansive, and he sought to make a living providing specific skill sets to those whom he consciously identified as his "colored brethren" living throughout the Americas.

These brief glimpses into five lives provide an entrée into the quotidian details of black inter-American consciousness. In each chapter, we see people fighting to establish personal and communal spaces that afforded some measure of control, however fleeting, over their own lives. This may have been through reform, rebellion, or revolution. How did they imagine communities where they might belong? What tangible attempts did they make to settle in or create these communities? While desirous of making connections with those with whom they imagined common interests, could they successfully negotiate the challenges attendant to living in vastly different geographic locales with diverse cultures?

At this juncture, I would like to provide some further context and parameters for this study. My focus on black transcolonial life in the revolutionary Americas situates my work at the intersection of inter-American studies and Haitian revolutionary studies. The last ten years have witnessed a groundswell of research dedicated to the methodological, political, and cultural parameters of both fields, as evidenced by the publication of many monographs, several collective volumes, and special issues of prominent literary journals.[10] The fields speak to one another in productive ways, and the former has particular parameters and possibilities when seen from a Caribbeanist perspective. For example, slavery was a principal pillar of eighteenth- and nineteenth-century political economies, and abolition of the transatlantic slave trade and the potential abolition of slavery itself were arguably the most hotly debated issues of the day.[11] As a result, research on inter-American topics from this era, both intra- and transcolonial, needs to be grounded in slavery and slave resistance studies, as a great deal of regional activity was occasioned by this socioeconomic system.[12] Indeed, given that colonial Saint-Domingue and its revolution can easily sit at the center of scholarship dealing with topics such as the viability of large-scale plantation models, anti-slavery movements, independence struggles, intraregional migration, and the birth of local artistic idioms, it provides a thought-provoking model for understanding key debates on a hemispheric scale.

The interplay between slavery, abolition, and independence struggles adds another unique challenge to inter-American studies from the vantage point of the Caribbean. Whereas in the colonial United States or Latin America battles were waged against one metropole

(England and Spain), and abolition occurred in stages through the 1860s, in the Caribbean five major European powers fought to dominate the region, and historical time lines fluctuate tremendously both between and within empires. Hence, one former French Caribbean colony (Haiti) achieved independence and abolition in 1804, while others (Martinique, Guadeloupe, and Guyana) ended slavery (for the second time) in 1848 but remain part of France in the present. Cuba did not officially abolish slavery until 1886 and defeated the Spanish in 1898; neighboring Jamaica freed its slaves in 1838 but achieved its independence from England almost 125 years later, in 1962. The complex series of events behind each of these dates is indicative of the rich terrain that must be contextualized in any study of the circumstances that both facilitated and hindered collaborations between subjects of different empires. This trajectory of what Eric Williams has theorized as "staggered development" in the region is particularly poignant when one considers the motivations behind and potential success of transcolonial freedom-seeking efforts among populations of color.[13] In the case of Saint-Domingue refugee movement, for example, slaves who arrived in the United States or Cuba during the 1790s would probably have had their offspring consigned to one or two generations longer of bondage than if they had arrived in Jamaica. Movement between empires was perilous and had long-term consequences.

With regard to terminology and geographic scope, I use the terms *inter-American, regional,* and *circum-Caribbean* interchangeably to delineate a space comparable to the one outlined by Peter Hulme in his work on Europe and the indigenous populations of the Caribbean.[14] My book focuses on specific coordinates in this geopolitical space, with an emphasis on the islands of the Greater Antilles and what became the U.S. state of Louisiana. Precisely because I do not privilege either the colony or the nation as my primary focus of analysis, I weave in and out of localized activities and larger questions of how these same activities had specific value to black actors because of their regional, transcolonial nature. To a great extent, such microscopic and macroscopic views are made possible by focusing on people's lives. I have opted to narrate much of what follows around individual figures—those whose compelling experiences served as examples as they traversed colonial boundaries and created ties with family and associates.[15]

I have divided the book into five chapters. All demonstrate that beyond functioning as an intellectual and cultural framework, transcoloniality involved material linkages that bound together ostensibly different colonial entities. Proslavery and antislavery agendas vie for dominance in the pages that follow, and each chapter demonstrates how inter-Americanist, transcolonial interests were pursued alongside imperialist and nationalist ones.

Chapter 1 sets the stage by establishing a vivid contrast. The material presents an anomaly in that I focus on black people as objects rather than subjects. Although scholarly work with an inter-American approach tends to study collaborations that highlight unity among the oppressed, I open with a discussion of a torture technique made possible by sophisticated mercantile networks between the "axes" of slave-holding powers in the region. I explore the exportation of Cuban bloodhounds and their handlers to Saint-Domingue, Jamaica, and territorial Florida, sites of the three largest-scale conflicts pitting the white colonial state against African and indigenous combatants during the time period under consideration. Uniting against the threat of nonwhite enemies, local colonists collaborated across colonial frontiers to ensure their continued hegemony.

Chapter 2 focuses on the eastern part of the island of Hispaniola, what is now known as the Dominican Republic. I examine how antislavery politics were institutionalized through a succession of Haitian efforts to unite the island under one aegis. To demonstrate how Dominican slaves deliberately adopted a transcolonial politics that allowed them to endorse Haitian objectives as their own, I use iconographic sources and orally transmitted ones such as speeches and poetry. Cross-border armed insurgency, religion, and popular revolt offer an alternative narrative to conventional Dominican historiography that posits an antagonistic view of relations between the two countries.

Chapter 3 examines the privateer communities of the Gulf of Mexico, particularly those established just south of New Orleans in Barataria, and subsequently on Galveston Island. Primarily associated with the infamous pirate Jean Laffite, these smugglers have a legendary stature that persists to this day in Louisiana and Texas lore. I examine how free black refugee soldiers from Saint-Domingue became involved with these privateers, creating opportunities for themselves as mercenaries and slave smugglers. Plundering under the "official" sanction of letters of marque from the newly declared republics of Mexico and Colombia, these men established their own highly profitable outlaw communities that provided a spirited challenge to North American, Spanish, British, and French attempts to control the fate of the region. This chapter uses court depositions, historical chronicles, and nineteenth-century novels and poetry to showcase how "desperate," armed black men fought for their advancement by enslaving others.

In chapter 4 I study the costumes, instrumentation, and rhythms of the *tumba francesa*, *bomba*, and *bèlè* as evidence of how performance exemplifies the cultural life that linked the enslaved across colonial frontiers. I am interested in how the "fear of French negroes" became ritualized in performance. My methodology seeks to negotiate between a conventional approach that focuses on the role of male "public intellectuals" as a guiding dynamic to the study of regional philosophy (think Eugenio Maria de Hostos, Eric Williams, Aimé Césaire) and a model that also acknowledges the "intellectual public." Women were especially important carriers in the performance repertoires under examination, fiercely competitive, innovative practitioners of what became vibrant communal traditions. This intellectual public of musicians and dancers created highly sophisticated, learned compositions that would eventually be co-opted by various national traditions, and their collaborations provide an important model for the transmission of oral and movement-based knowledge with its own logic of pleasure and resistance.

Chapter 5 closes the book, showcasing debates from the perspective of prominent middle-class black journalists. I focus on three periodicals of the black press—*L'Union* (Haiti), the *Colored American* (the United States), and the *Revue des Colonies* (Paris/Martinique). Three decades after the Haitian Revolution, periodicals mobilized their readerships by capitalizing on intricate networks of reporting and editorializing that voiced the continued importance of the revolution in the inter-American public sphere. These journalists placed domestic struggles for black liberty and equality in an internationalist framework, connecting a network of black activists that was regional in scope. The papers encouraged people of African descent to learn about one another by promoting particular reading material, encouraging migrant labor, and speculating about the advantages of a regional political federation. Their comprehensive perspective on the Americas, their polyglot character, and their insistence that regional strength depended on black equality make them a critical precursor to the more well-known movements of the 1860s and 1890s, when the notion of Caribbean federation was further pursued among intellectuals of the Spanish Caribbean as a strategic means of protecting the region's autonomy in the face of European imperialism and U.S. expansion.

Hence I place revolutionary Saint-Domingue at the center of a web of artistic practices, political projects, and human migration. The narrative that follows begins with the outbreak of the Haitian Revolution in 1791 and concludes with the establishment of Dominican independence in 1844. These decades mark a distinct revolutionary historical moment, one that witnessed the flowering of multiple political and cultural imaginings about the interdependence of the extended Americas and how people of African descent could best struggle to become both the architects and the builders of their own future.

As servitude is nothing less than a veritable state of war, the slaves are and should be the enemies of their masters, and the sound of their chains ceaselessly warns the latter that vengeance is awake and stirring around them.

Ainsi la servitude n'étant qu'un véritable état de guerre, les esclaves sont et doivent être les ennemis de leurs maîtres et le bruit de leurs chaînes avertit sans cesse cet dernier que la vengeance veille et s'agite autour d'eux.

—Médéric Louis Élie Moreau de Saint-Méry, 1785

Have they not hung up men with heads downward, drowned them in sacks, crucified them on planks, buried them alive, crushed them in mortars? Have they not forced them to eat shit? And, having flayed them with the lash, have they not cast them alive to be devoured by worms, or onto anthills, or lashed them to stakes in the swamp to be devoured by mosquitoes? Have they not thrown them into boiling cauldrons of cane syrup? Have they not put men and women inside barrels studded with spikes and rolled them down mountainsides into the abyss? Have they not consigned these miserable blacks to man-eating dogs until the latter, sated by human flesh, left the mangled victims to be finished off with bayonet and poniard?

Ont-ils pendus des hommes la tête en bas, noyés, renfermés dans des sacs, crucifiés sur des planches, enterrés vivans [sic], pillés dans des mortiers? Les ont-ils contrains de manger des excrémens humains ? Et après avoir mis leurs corps en lambeaux sous le fouet, les ont-ils livrés vivans à être dévorés par les vers, ou jetés dans des ruches de fourmis, ou être attachés à des poteaux près des lagons pour être dévorés par les maringouins ? Les ont-ils précipités vivans dans les chaudières à sucre bouillantes ? Ont-ils fait mettre des hommes et femmes dans des boucant hérissés de clous, foncés par les deux bouts, roulés sur le sommet des montagnes pour être ensuite précipités dans l'abime avec les malheureuses victimes ? Ont-ils faits dévorer les malheureux noirs par des chiens antropophages [sic], jusqu'à ce que ces dogues, repus de chair humaine . . . se refusassent à ne plus servir d'instrument à la vengeance de ces bourreaux, qui achevaient les victimes, à moitié dévorées, à coup de poignard et de bayonnette?

—Pompée Valentin Vastey, 1814

CHAPTER I

Canine Warfare in the Circum-Caribbean

As captured in the epigraphs, slavery in the plantation Americas was a "veritable state of war" between opposing factions: masters, whose rights were upheld by a legal, social, and cultural fabric of institutions that guaranteed their dominion over human beings designated as property, and the women and men compelled to work as slaves. Despite the apparent distance suggested by these third-person assessments, Moreau de Saint-Méry and Baron de Vastey were creole intellectuals who were intimately familiar with the system. The first was proslavery, albeit unusual in that he left copious and nuanced ethnographic descriptions of black life.[1] The latter was a former slave who eventually served as a statesman under King Henri Christophe of Haiti, authoring well-known "defenses" of the black race and its possibilities. Both of their statements conjure up graphic images of abuse and excess. Moreau writes of rattling chains and a simmering, omnipresent desire for vengeance on the part of the enslaved. Vastey provides a litany of cruel bodily tortures inflicted upon slaves, tortures reminiscent of the worst excesses of the Spanish Inquisition. In doing so, he rhetorically questions who were the true barbarians of the age. Their remarks capture the perennial violence that was a constitutive element of slave societies, violence that was common to territories across the region regardless of which European metropolis was in charge.

I open the book with an examination of the proslavery dimensions of transcolonial encounters. I do so to provide a context in which to understand one critical dimension of competing inter-Americanisms—the master/slave divide. If we understand that slavery was a state of war, how and when did opposing factions mobilize across colonial frontiers to meet their needs? By focusing on proslavery initially, I demonstrate the international resources (military, diplomatic, intellectual, material) that were mobilized to perpetuate the viability of slave-holding systems. I wish to emphasize that transcolonial, inter-American collaborations were used for decidedly brutal and oppressive purposes. What follows is a story linking colonial Cuba with revolutionary events in Saint-Domingue, colonial Jamaica, and territorial Florida during three of the largest-scale conflicts pitting the white colonial state against African and indigenous combatants from the 1790s to the 1840s. This chapter is about one modality of transcolonial contact that occurred over a fifty-year period in moments of crisis: the use of canine torture.

Uniting across frontiers, French, British, Spanish, and North American slave-holding powers collaborated in subduing nonwhite enemies to ensure their continued hegemony, using warfare techniques that dated back to the Spanish Conquest. Dogs were regularly used as a slave-catching device throughout the region. However, my examples highlight the inter-American networks of trade and terror that employed specially bred dogs to track down and feed upon black flesh. These dogs were raised in Cuba by professional trainers, the *chasseurs*, and they acquired a reputation for cruelty and efficacy that sent neighboring colonists and their imperial representatives on expeditions to the island to procure their services. While canine warfare has garnered a certain notoriety within the context of specialized national historiographies, a transcolonial methodology brings to light how interimperial cooperation facilitated such atrocities as part of a regional proslavery agenda.

This chapter thus sets the scene by highlighting the violence that black hemispheric populations were up against. It signals the stakes for the engagement of populations of color with modes of struggle and community identification that challenged colonial hierarchies determined to keep them at the bottom of the social order. The content here differs significantly from that of subsequent chapters in that people of color are not subjects. They are acted upon, objectified in arguably the most profound physical and psychological ways possible. Yet the very need for such a dire torture technique circulating among the slave-holding powers demonstrates that black populations across the hemisphere were very much prime movers, formidable combatants that could not easily be subdued. Their subject-hood, what amounted to an affirmation of their humanity within a system that legally counted them as objects, was affirmed by their actions. As insurgent slaves, maroons in revolt, and steadfast native populations resisting relocation, they are driving the narrative that follows, however much the particulars emphasized spotlight different protagonists.

I also wish to foreground the role of culture. This study relies heavily on visual iconography, and I corroborate visual narratives with eyewitness historiographies and to a lesser extent with fiction. I highlight conflicts and continuities across multiple colonial frontiers—political, linguistic, and conceptual. By the latter I refer to frequently invoked categorizations that rely on dichotomies such as enlightened/savage, metropolitan/creole, imperial isolation / transcolonial collaboration. These texts offer a nuanced interpretation of the meanings of such pairings.

CUBAN BLOODHOUNDS AND TRANSCOLONIAL TERROR NETWORKS

A black woman looks on in terror as two large dogs maul her, attacking from both sides. A babe in arms clings to her neck. To her immediate left, a black man is being killed by a third dog, whose jaws are locked around his skull in the final act of execution. His left hand is already missing, and with his remaining hand he clings to the arm of an unconscious male figure barely visible under the skirts of the woman. This victim is likewise being bitten and licked on the head by a vicious hound. In the right background, a bare-chested black man unsuccessfully fends off an assault by a fifth dog who attacks his throat. The idyllic rural setting of the Haitian *mornes* at sunset belies the expressions of agony and terror depicted on the faces of the well-dressed victims, members of a family surprised by the vicious assault. The image, *Blood Hounds Attacking a Black Family in the Woods* (figure 6), provides a valuable counterpoint to the scenes of carnage and destruction in the *Incendie du Cap* painting presented in the preface (figure 1); while women and children remain front and center, in this instance the helpless victims are black.

This disturbing engraving forms part of a series of plates included in Marcus Rainsford's 1805 *An Historical Account of the Black Empire of Hayti*. Rainsford, a British captain in the Third West-India Regiment, was stationed in Saint-Domingue during the Haitian Revolution

FIGURE 6. *Blood Hounds Attacking a Black Family in the Woods.* Engraving. Marcus Rainsford, *An Historical Account of the Black Empire of Hayti* (London: James Cundee, 1805). Courtesy of the Library Company of Philadelphia.

and later wrote one of the few sympathetic analyses of the Haitian people's bid for independence to appear during the nineteenth century. He made the initial drawings for his text, believing that "mere description conveys not with so much force as when accompanied by graphic illustration those horrors which are wished to be impressed upon the public mind" (xix). The author was concerned with bringing one particular horror to the attention of the public: the use of bloodhounds to hunt and kill enemies of war.[2]

Rainsford's stated purpose was to "excite the detestation he urges against the very idea of ever again introducing these animals under any pretexts to the assistance of an army" (428). In a remarkable reversal of the "horrors of Saint-Domingue" away from tales of hatchet-wielding slaves, Rainsford indicts the French, "a great and polished nation," for "not merely returning to the barbarism of the earliest periods, but descending to the characters of assassins and executioners; and removing the boundaries which civilization had prescribed even to war, rendering it a wild conflict of brutes and a midnight massacre" (xi). His outraged indictment of the French nation for effectively being nothing short of uncivilized brutes is curious, however, given that Rainsford was aware that his own government had also employed dogs against black rebels. Less than a decade earlier, the British used this same canine torture technique in its own conflict on the neighboring island of Jamaica during the Second Maroon War (1795–96).[3]

The viciousness of this strategy was a topic of strident debate for contemporary observers both in the metropole and at home in the plantation zone. Although local colonists tended to support the measure, public opinion in Europe and the northern United States was very much divided. Hence, in addition to elucidating the material conditions of the commercial inter-American trade, a study of regional canine warfare showcases the intellectual debates that became central to creole self-fashioning. Although white creoles across the Americas developed discourses of pleasure and self-sufficiency to define themselves vis-à-vis Europe, violence and forced labor were central, even foundational, to the creole way of life. Support for the circulation of attack dogs bound the white creole slave-holding world together when confronting opposition from both black and native insurgents, as well as from their metropolitan detractors. In all cases, the use of dogs as a means of torture showcased the legal nonpersonhood and subhuman status of the colonized as a way of asserting planter control.

The means that the colonial state was prepared to resort to in order to retain this control are exemplified in an 1803 letter written by Donatien-Marie-Joseph de Vimeur, the Vicomte de Rochambeau. General Rochambeau assumed command of the Napoleonic expedition sent to restore slavery in the French Caribbean after the death of his predecessor, General Charles Leclerc. Legendary for his cruelty, he allegedly massacred hundreds of people by drowning, burned others alive, and generally orchestrated a campaign of terror to salvage the last hopes of preserving Saint-Domingue under French control. He frames the strategy employed by the French army as follows: "I send you my dear commandant . . . twenty-eight 'bouledogues.' These reinforcements will allow you to entirely finish your operations. I don't need to tell you that no rations or expenditures are authorized for the nourishment of the dogs; you should give them blacks to eat" ("Je vous envoie, mon cher commandant . . . 28 chiens bouledogues. Ces renforts vous mettront à même de terminer entièrement vos opérations. Je ne dois pas vous laisser ignorer qu'il ne vous sera pas passé en compte ni ration, ni dépense pour la nourriture de ces chiens; vous devez leur donner à manger des nègres"; Madiou 2: 555).[4] Thomas Madiou and Beaubrun Ardouin, the influential historians of nineteenth-century Haiti, incorporated detailed accounts of Rochambeau's torture methods into their analyses of how the initial slave revolts evolved into an outright war of independence. These accounts circulated widely, becoming the basis for the lore surrounding the dogs' use as a gruesome weapon in the French arsenal.

The Vicomte de Noailles, a French aristocrat best known for his service in the American Revolution, traveled to Cuba at Rochambeau's request to purchase these dogs. Ardouin states that they were acquired at an enormous cost to the colonial treasury, and demonstrations of the dogs' ferocity were made center stage.[5] Upon their initial arrival, they were paraded around town. Next, a black man, the domestic servant of a French general, was sacrificed to the starving dogs on a special platform erected in the town square for that purpose. Amid initial applause that soon turned to "consternation," the dogs "devoured his entrails and didn't abandon their prey until they had gorged themselves on the palpitating flesh. Nothing was left on the post but bloody bones" ("dévorent ses entrailles et n'abandonnent leur proie qu'après s'être assouvis de chair palpitante. Il ne resta plus contre le poteau que des ossements ensanglantés"; Madiou 506–07). These executions were a frequent spectacle, and the horror they occasioned motivated many residents of the city, both white and black, to relocate to neighborhoods far from these "accents of death" (507).

The psychological intent of this civic spectacle was crucial. Not only were the dogs employed to hunt down black rebels; they were used to publicly consume them in a staged performance of white supremacy and domination. Much like the goal of a public lynching, these performances were designed as a stark warning, and the presence of community observers provided an air of legitimacy to the terror. The slave's torture served as the ultimate example of his and, by extension, all slaves' expendability. His literal conversion into an edible object was a more extreme mode of persecution and execution than other forms of torture, for example, whipping or time in the stocks. Being consumed alive by dogs pitted an animal against a human being. Inasmuch as one can suppose that the human species' most primal fear is that of being killed and eaten by wild animals, the deliberate use of semi-domesticated dogs as weapons made it clear that the state was a fearsome predator ready to cannibalize human flesh by proxy. Of course, such a method of marking black prey as legitimate entailed a simultaneous paradox: designating them as nonhumans while showcasing their human vulnerability to promote an ambience of anxiety and fear.

A second plate included in Rainsford's account, *The Mode of Training Blood Hounds in St. Domingo and of Exercising Them by Chasseurs* (figure 7), also attempted to provoke reader outrage at the treatment meted out to fellow human beings by European armies and the colonial militia. Just as the image of an innocent family being dismembered was meant to shock and disgust, so too was the depiction of a defenseless, bound victim being fed to snarling dogs.[6] The victim depicted is actually a mannequin designed to resemble a black person, a training practice that confirms the premeditated brutality of slave abuse. As commentary to the figure, I cite Rainsford's appendix at length below:

> With respect to the dogs, their general mode of rearing was latterly in the following manner. . . . They were confined in a sort of kennel, or cage, where they were but sparingly fed upon small quantities of the blood of different animals. As they approached maturity, their keepers procured a figure roughly formed as a negro in wicker work, in the body of which were contained the blood and entrails of beasts. This was exhibited before an upper part of the cage, and the food occasionally exposed as a temptation, which attracted the attention of the dogs to it as a source of the food they wanted. This was repeated often, so that the animals with redoubled ferocity struggled against their confinement . . . till, at the last extremity of desperation, the keeper resigned the figure, well charged with the nauseous food before described, to their wishes. While they gorged themselves with the dreadful meat, he and his colleagues caressed and encouraged them. By these means the whites ingratiated themselves so much with the animals, as to produce an effect directly opposite to that perceivable in them towards the black figure . . . The common use of them in the Spanish islands was in chase of runaway negroes in the mountains. When once they got the scent of the object, they immediately hunted him down . . . and instantly devoured him. . . . With horrid delight the chasseurs sometimes preserved

FIGURE 7. *The Mode of Training Blood Hounds in St. Domingo and of Exercising Them by Chasseurs.* Engraving. Marcus Rainsford, *An Historical Account of the Black Empire of Hayti* (London: James Cundee, 1805). Courtesy of the Library Company of Philadelphia.

the head to expose at their homes, as monuments of their barbarous prowess. (427–29)

Severe physical torture, heads of gored victims kept as trophies—these methods of control were results of the well-documented regime of terror employed on the plantations in colonial Saint-Domingue as well as throughout the Americas. This terror was an ambient one in that extreme violence could strike at any time and was routine, rather than employed solely during "officially" declared wars and revolutions. Moreau and Vastey allude to this constant state of war in the epigraphs above. Confirming this idea, C. L. R. James poignantly states that the fundamental dynamic in slave societies was that "though one could trap them like animals, transport them in pens, work them alongside an ass or a horse and beat both with the same stick, stable them and starve them, they remained, despite their black skins and curly hair, quite invincibly human beings; with the intelligence and resentment of human beings. To cow them in the necessary docility and acceptance necessitated a regime of calculated brutality and terrorism, and it is this that explains the unusual spectacle of property-owners apparently careless of preserving their property: they had first to ensure their own safety" (12).[7] A roughly hewn black figure made out of wicker and designed as a target for ravenous animals is a harrowing reminder of this institutionalized violence. In an era that witnessed an active, regional counterplantation resistance that ranged from small-scale, quotidian opposition to the formation of semi-independent maroon communities, there was always evidence of nonconformity to the system that demanded planter reprisals.

On the neighboring island of Jamaica, another war to the death had just taken place. The Trelawney Town Maroons renewed hostilities against the British Jamaican colonial regime in 1795 in what came to be known as the Second Maroon War.[8] Combat between maroon guerrilla forces and approximately five thousand British soldiers and militia led to a stalemate, and it was this inability to get the upper hand that purportedly motivated the Jamaican Assembly to resort to canine warfare and import dogs from Cuba. R. C. Dallas, author of the earliest account chronicling this conflict, *The History of the Maroons from Their Origin to the Establishment of Their Chief Tribe at Sierra Leone, Including the Expedition to Cuba, for the Purpose of Procuring Spanish Chasseurs* (1803), credited the dogs with putting an "end to a war, in which force and military skill alone might have been foiled for years" (2: 3). The frontispiece of volume 2, an engraving entitled *A Spanish Chasseur of the Island of Cuba*, features the hunter with his three large, muzzled dogs, intimating that their story was at the center of the ensuing action (figure 8).

The nature of the hostilities with the maroons was such that elite contemporary observers feared that the 1795–96 conflict had "all the appearance of being an endless evil, or rather one that threatened the entire destruction of the island." Witnesses of all the wars discussed

FIGURE 8. *A Spanish Chasseur of the Island of Cuba.* Engraving. Frontispiece to vol. 2 of Robert C. Dallas, *The History of the Maroons* (London: Longman and Rees, 1803). Courtesy of the Library Company of Philadelphia.

here focused on the epic nature of events, the outright contest to the death between those that fought for their privileged lifestyles and those that were determined to attain their liberty. The latter were portrayed consistently as insurgent, bloodthirsty barbarians, rather than acknowledged as human beings fighting for freedom and self-determination. In Jamaica, this anxiety about the total collapse of British colonial society was in part due to the fact that several maroon communities (for instance, those in the Blue Mountains and those in the Cockpit country) had the potential to destabilize neighboring plantations. In the worst-case scenario for white landowners, they would join forces with the slaves in "a permanent and successful opposition to the government" (Dallas 2). This did not prove the case, and as a result of this conflict the surviving maroons from Trelawney Town were deported and exiled to Nova Scotia and Sierra Leone.[9]

Dallas's two-volume history begins with the settlement of Jamaica and concludes in the early nineteenth century. In a lengthy side story, Dallas interrupts his tale to include the adventures of Colonel William D. Quarrell, a local planter and member of the legislature who traveled to Cuba at the behest of the Jamaican Assembly to contract the *chasseurs* and their dogs.[10] I note the information Dallas provides concerning Quarrell's trip for several reasons. First, it provides a glimpse into the activities of the multiracial, economically precarious inhabitants who existed on the margins of plantation societies throughout the region. Quarrell laments that because of the haste with which he departed, his crew was composed of four British seamen, twelve Curacao negroes [from the Dutch colony], and eighteen Spanish "renegadoes." Once in Cuba, this "vagabond" crew mutinied, and the Cuban coast guard was reluctant to interfere because they "were afraid of a banditti that neither acknowledged, nor was acknowledged, by any government; rascals that cared not against what country they fought so they could but plunder" (8, 46). Men and women similar to those depicted in a sensationalist manner here tended to be at the forefront of transcolonial collaborations, often illegal ones. Seminal historical scholarship by Franklin Knight (*Caribbean*) has classified them as "transfrontiersmen," and the language used to describe them has much in common with the "masterless men" and "many-headed hydra" examples explored by Julius Scott ("Common Wind") and Linebaugh and Rediker.[11] Figures such as these make appearances, however fleeting, in a remarkable cross section of texts from the time period, providing a reminder that much as the plantation has come to center discussions of development in the circum-Caribbean, those who operated on its peripheries have equally compelling tales to tell.

Quarrell's narrative is also critical to Dallas's work because it situates white planter anxiety in a regional context. Once he arrived in Cuba, he proceeded inland to the small town of Bejucal on the outskirts of Havana. There he met with the Marquesa de San Felipe, a woman who exercised "supreme authority" in her district and had many of the desired dogs and their trainers in her employ. Quarrell lost no time informing her of "the horrid war waged by the Maroons of Jamaica against the white inhabitants; and the barbarities of it were strongly represented to her, in order that the impression made upon her mind might interest her the more in favor of the mission to Cuba" (Dallas 35). After receiving her blessing, he visited the captain general of the island, who, while receiving him pleasantly, "expressed surprise at the commissioner's supposing that he would sanction the recruiting of men in the dominions of his Catholic Majesty, and particularly in favour of a Power at war with another with which a treaty of peace was just concluded. For the purpose, however, of taking care of the dogs that had been purchased, he consented" (75). The complicated geopolitics involved with procuring state sanction illustrate that despite official policies that often discouraged population movements and other collaborations between the warring French, Spanish, and British nations and their colonies, each acknowledged that this particular endeavor was temporarily in their common interests.

Insofar as contracting the dogs and their masters was the reason for his trip, Quarrell comments extensively on the *chasseurs,* the breeding of their animals, and their particular aptitude for the hunt.[12] The descriptions are graphic about the training required to turn the dogs into killers and the resultant punishment meted out to their victims. For instance, Quarrell says that "these people live with their dogs, from which they are inseparable. At home the dogs are kept chained, and when walking with their masters, are never unmuzzled, or let out of ropes, but for attack" (qtd. in Dallas 57). "The chasseurs beat their dogs most unmercifully, using the flat sides of their heavy muschets [*sic;* i.e., machetes]" (64); "[their] coat, or skin, is much harder than that of most dogs, and so must be the whole structure of the body, as the severe beatings he undergoes in training would kill any other species of dog" (57–58). The dogs "are perfectly broken in, that is to say, they will not kill the object they pursue unless resisted. On coming up with a fugitive, they bark at him till he stops, then they crouch near him, terrifying him with a ferocious growl if he stirs. In this position they continue barking to give notice to the chasseurs, who come up and secure their prisoner" (56). He goes on to report that the chasseurs "receive good pay from the Government, besides private rewards for particular and extraordinary services. They are a very hardy, brave, and desperate set of people, scrupulously honest, and remarkably faithful. . . . The activity of the chasseurs no negro on earth can elude" (59–61). The picture painted is one of acute violence: the dogs are raised so savagely that they cannot go unmuzzled and unleashed even in the company of their owners. Lauded for their dependability, fidelity, and skill, the *chasseurs* police the slave population to keep them under constant control. They are the classic middlemen necessary to the smooth functioning of all colonial regimes.

When Quarrell finally arrived back in Jamaica, he was accompanied by forty *chasseurs* and 104 dogs, only 36 of which had been completely trained (Dallas 109). This question of partial training was important, as without the requisite preparation the dogs "fly at the throat, or other part of a man, and never quit their hold, till they are cut in two" (67). As was the case in Saint-Domingue, the dogs provoked terror upon their arrival with their "wild and formidable appearance," attacking everything in sight, including animals and people. As Dallas documents events, "The streets were cleared [and] the doors of the houses shut" (119–20). Even General Walpole, leader of the British expeditionary force sent against the maroons, "found it necessary to go into the chaise from which he had alighted" when dogs attacked him and his horses (129). Additional descriptions testify to the constant aggression and virtual uncontrollability of these animals.[13]

Thus both Rainsford's and Dallas's engravings and commentaries provide a vivid glimpse of three key facets of canine warfare in plantation America, even as they arrive at different conclusions as to its justification. First, they detail the use of torture (starvation techniques, beatings) to train the animals to be dependable executioners. Second, they provide a sense of the effect that this warfare had upon its victims. The evidence makes it clear that slaves and free blacks (the maroons) were ultimately treated worse than the dogs themselves. They were routinely brutalized and in some cases literally forced to watch their own flesh being consumed as a reminder of their legal nonpersonhood. Occasions that "justified" the use of dogs, from running away to outright revolt, were assertions of the slaves'/maroons' humanity

FIGURE 9. *Hunting Indians in Florida with Bloodhounds.* Lithograph. Published by James Baillie (New York: 1848). Courtesy of the Library of Congress Prints and Photographs Division.

that necessitated an extreme response: negating that same humanity by treating them as prey for wild animals. Third, and most importantly for the present study, these chronicles show how the dogs and their trainers were a multi-state-sponsored mercenary force of repression. The actual process of mobilizing this Cuban labor force abroad necessitated coordinated tactical planning and corresponding commodities: correspondence between officials, recruitment of the *chasseurs,* cages to restrain the dogs, ships to transport them, and so forth. While creole planters were at the forefront of these collaborations, such an involved project also mandated the participation and sanction of the governing European authorities.

This regional market for Cuban hounds and their handlers persisted into the 1840s. For example, the Florida territorial government procured thirty-three dogs to fight Native American and African populations in the Second Seminole War.[14] A conflict that raged between 1835 and 1842, the war pitted federal U.S. troops against the native population and their African American allies, the latter comprising both free and fugitive blacks from the neighboring regions of Georgia, Florida, and the Carolinas. General Zachary Taylor, himself a slave-holder and the head of U.S. Army forces in Florida at the time, favored using the dogs in his campaigns, though with little success. Eventually elected the twelfth president of the United States in 1848, he found that his decision to employ dogs against the Seminoles would follow him throughout his political career, becoming the focus of many anti-Whig party caricatures disseminated by his opponents.[15]

An 1848 print entitled *Hunting Indians in Florida with Bloodhounds* is one such campaign attack (figure 9). The image depicts a chaotic scene of canine warfare in which uniformed U.S. military figures are advancing upon the Seminoles. Native bodies litter the ground as dogs charge them, and one Seminole warrior attempts to shield a woman and young baby as a dog seizes him by the throat. This section of the print is strikingly similar to Rainsford's *Blood Hounds Attacking a Family in the Woods.* In the caption Taylor proclaims, "Hurra Captain, we've got them at last, the dogs are at them. . . . Let not a red nigger escape, show no mercy, exterminate them, this day we'll close the Florida War; but remember Captn, as I have written to our Government to say that the dogs are intended to ferret out the Indians . . . for the sake of consistency and the appearance of Humanity, you will appear not to notice the devastation they commit." The cartoon suggests that concern about using dogs as executioners during combat supposedly motivated Taylor and his colleagues to shield their intended homicidal use from scrutiny. Again, "ferreting" out victims appeared to be a much milder strategy than consuming them. Managing public relations during times of war made it especially necessary to control the discursive terms of the debate.

While the use of combat animals, including dogs, dates back centuries in Europe, the novelty of these cases in modern times in the extended Americas was employing dogs to kill as part of a strategy designed to maintain racial slavery. They were engaged to function as lethal "weapons" as opposed to doing police investigative work.[16] That is, conventionally dogs were used to sniff out hiding places, detect ambushes, and so forth. This was the initial justification offered in the Saint-Domingue, Jamaica, and Florida cases. Dogs were more efficient than men in conducting a chase, especially in difficult terrain such as the mountains or the swamps. The specificity of their use was thus their tracking ability. In the evidence presented here, however, it was abundantly clear to contemporary observers that the animals were likely to maim and/or kill their prey, not simply to capture them in the course of pursuit. They were used as part of a strategy of total annihilation, what Lord Balcarres, the aggressive new governor of Jamaica at the onset of the Second Maroon War, referred to as the key to permanently "reducing the Enemy" (Campbell 229).

My focus on Cuban dogs raises the question, Why were dogs from Cuba in such demand in the circum-Caribbean? Didn't other colonial powers have their own slave-catching dogs? To be certain, the answer to the latter question is affirmative. However, knowledge concerning the skills of the Cuban *chasseurs* and their dogs must have circulated widely.[17] This fact suggests the viciousness of Cuban slavery in the late eighteenth century and first years of the nineteenth century, complicating a truism associating the collapse of Saint-Domingue with the escalation and corresponding brutalization of Cuba's system.[18] The system was already ruthless. This observation aside, it is striking that the turn of the eighteenth century would see the most powerful imperial slaveholders almost simultaneously use these dogs against those that presented the biggest threats to the system. The method of brutalizing them in preparation for their tasks made them sought-after commodities to the extent that Cuban torture methods came to signify effectiveness in the regional imaginary. More specifically, both the dogs and their *chasseurs* were commodities, as the dogs alone were no good without their masters. The former could not simply be purchased, since the technology required trainers to "rein in" the terror so that it was not indiscriminately used against whites. Ironically, despite their training to the contrary, the dogs sometimes proved "ignorant of color prejudice." For example, in one March 1803 battle between the French and the former slaves in Saint-Domingue, the imported dogs "attacked those who were fleeing, who, in this circumstance happened to be white" (Dubois, *Avengers* 292–93).[19]

Thus, although the ferocity of canine warfare as enacted in the Haitian, Jamaican, and Florida conflicts is well documented and forms part of the legends that have grown up around these pitched confrontations, it is crucial to remember that the colonists' commissioning of dogs was not an isolated occurrence. Rather, the decision resulted from a common network of trade (in torture techniques and the necessary supplies) across empires. Spain, an ally sought by both the French and British during the height of their imperial wars in the 1790s, took advantage of its position as a purveyor of goods to make a profit and simultaneously repress insurgents in neighboring American colonies. Dog-purchasing trips provide evidence of transcolonial cooperation, albeit with an unusual cargo. While these arrangements were carried out with the sanction of the metropolitan states involved, local creoles also had an interest in building relationships with their counterparts in other colonies. This was especially the case during times of crisis and self-preservation. Creole elites throughout the extended Americas could presumably identify with the travails of their neighbors. For example, we have seen that a prime objective of Quarrell's aforementioned trip was to elicit sympathy and material aid from prominent Cuban slaveholders. Likewise, representatives from the Saint-Domingue Colonial Assembly later pled for aid from Jamaicans who might be expected to understand the threat of living at the mercy of revolting blacks.

Both British and French colonial governments in favor of using canine warfare were well aware that they were contending against Spain's reputation for cruelty when conquering the indigenous populations. Elsewhere I have commented on how the Spanish set the historical precedent for this mode of torture during the Conquest.[20] Dallas writes that "the Assembly of Jamaica were not unapprised that the measure of calling in such auxiliaries, and using the canine species against human beings, would give rise to much animadversion in England and that the horrible enormities of the Spaniards in the conquest of the new world would be brought again to remembrance" (9–10). Ardouin, writing a generation later, reminds us that Rochambeau, le

Vicomte de Noailles, and their conspirators risked the reputation of renewing "in the nineteenth century the spectacle of the cruelties committed by the Spanish conquistadors of the sixteenth century against the unfortunate indigenous population on the island of Haiti" ("au 19ème siècle le spectacle des cruautés commises dans le 16ème par les conquérans espagnols, sur les infortunés aborigènes de l'île d'Haiti"; 5: 74). In spite of this avowed fear of being thought to behave as brutally as the Spanish, the British, French, and Floridians opted to turn to Spain's tried-and-true techniques in an hour of need. Cuban *chasseurs* had acquired the former reputation of the conquistadores, serving as a local, creole base, for the dissemination of canine soldiers. Thus, although concerned about angering public opinion and acquiring the stigma of Spain's abuses, British, French, and North American forces simultaneously sought to renew this centuries-old military strategy for their own ends. I now turn to a further discussion of the active debates in both the transatlantic and inter-American public spheres surrounding this torture method.

A DISCURSIVE BATTLE OF WILLS

Writing at the dawn of the nineteenth century, Rainsford suggested that "with the persons who breed and have the care of these animals in Spanish America, the public are already sufficiently acquainted" (424). This statement implies that the prowess of Cuban dogs was a matter of common knowledge. That said, contemporary public opinion was quite varied about the ethical merits of canine warfare. Debates did not fall along a simple pro- and antislavery spectrum, as even those with no abolitionist leanings had qualms about such a mode of combat. Below I examine one axis upon which public opinion tended to be established: a creole-versus-metropolitan division. This "center/periphery" distinction was also the case in territorial Florida, where land acquired from Spain had yet to become a state in the union and the governing metropole was Washington, D.C. Creole public opinion expressed itself in language that defensively asserted better knowledge of realities in the war zone, a knowledge they believed made local residents more qualified to make decisions about their welfare and the future of the nonwhite enemies they fought. This attitude is in evidence across the colonial spectrum and provides a sense of how creoles imagined solutions to their "problems" by looking at the experiences of their closest neighbors. Transcolonial collaboration became a strategy for preserving their way of life.

At the time of Quarrell's 1795 trip to Cuba, evidence shows that this military strategy was the subject of spirited discussion in both England and Jamaica. Lord Balcarres did not wish to bargain with the maroons; much like his contemporary Rochambeau, he was in favor of employing any and all means to subdue them. An 1803 issue of the London *Anti-Jacobin Review* confirms that certain members of the British public balked at his decision to use canine warriors. In an extensive commentary of Dallas's book the reviewer states, "When the circumstance was first heard of in this country, we may remember what a clamour it raised. The humane bosom of an Englishman revolted at the seeming barbarity of the expedient, and Lord Balcarres was not only stigmatized by the public prints and pamphlets of that time, but attacked in the House of Commons, where even his friends were at a loss to defend him" (247).[21] King George III also weighed in, demanding that the dogs be removed from the island because of his "abhorrence of the mode of warfare" (Campbell 230).[22]

To justify this strategy, the desperate planters and their allies in government who were "solicitous of their welfare" took pains to shift the terms of the debate (Dallas 17). In Jamaica, the strategy was presented as a "preventive measure of sparing the effusion of human blood, by tracing with hounds the haunts of murderers, and rousing from ambush, savages more ferocious and blood thirsty than the animals which track them" (12). The initial victims of the slave trade were portrayed as the aggressors, their attempts to defend themselves couched in terms of savagery that denied the possibility that they even shared "human" blood with their enemies. They were characterized as more vicious than the dogs themselves, and their right to share the island was questioned even though they had been recognized as legitimate co-owners of the land since the original Maroon Treaty of 1739. Those propagating the measure prevailed, and it was determined that use of the dogs against the maroons posed no ethical violations. While arguing that some aggression *was* beyond the pale, specifically the "slaughter of captives, subjecting them to indignities or torture, and the violation of women," none of these violations obtained because "these very enormities were practiced, not by the colonists against the Maroons, but by the Maroons against the colonists" (14). Hence, in language of removing a contagion that threatened the safety of the body politic, canine combat was discursively figured as a preemptive attack undertaken as an act of self-preservation rather than as an act of aggression.[23]

In the context of the Florida conflict with the Seminoles, popular opinion was likewise divided about the use of bloodhounds. Opinion was divided about the nature of the Second Seminole War in general on grounds as varied as concern over its exorbitant costs, to concern regarding how the potential incorporation of additional slave states would upset the delicate balance established in the 1820 Missouri Compromise. One letter from J. R. Poinsett, a South Carolina planter and secretary of war in the Van Buren administration, warned that "the cold-blooded and inhuman murders lately perpetrated upon helpless women and children by these ruthless savages render it expedient that every possible means should be resorted to, in order to protect the people of Florida" (Giddings 268). Orwellian sophistry allowed local Florida residents to blithely refer to the dogs hired to pursue and destroy rebel Seminoles as "hounds of peace" (Covington 117). A litany of hate-inducing portraits of "red" men bearing tomahawks or throat-slitting, duplicitous Africans was employed in the rhetorical and actual battles waged to acquire new slave-holding territories.

However, as the mocking tone of the 1848 print examined above indicates, not all shared this perspective. Most famously, a congressman from Ohio named Joshua R. Giddings used the war as a way of avoiding the gag rule prohibiting discussions of slavery on the House floor. As one historian writes, "The gist of his constitutional argument was simple: If what the slaveholders were always saying was true—that the federal government had no business making laws about slavery—then the same logic should hold in Florida, where the federal army should therefore have no business hunting fugitive slaves. If the southern doctrine of states' rights meant no federal interference with slavery, then surely it also meant no federal protection for the institution."[24] In an 1841 speech that provoked the ire of his southern colleagues, Giddings cited voluminous documentary evidence linking the federal government with slave-holding interests. He quotes a letter from General Jessop, leader of the forces before the arrival of Zachary Taylor, that stated, "If you see Osceola [a principal Seminole chief], tell him I shall . . . take all the negroes who belong to the white people [the fugitives or those claimed as such]. . . . Tell him I am sending to Cuba for bloodhounds to trail them; and I intend to hang everyone of them who does not come in." Outraged by both the justification for fighting the war and the means used to do so, Giddings concludes that the national flag "seems to have been prostituted in Florida to the base purpose of leading on an organized company of negro catchers. . . ."[25]

He documents the tension between soldiers on the ground and local planters with regard to this policy, noting that the former were "duly conscious of the dishonorable employment in which they were engaged; that they were daily subjected to dangers and death for the purpose of enabling the people of Florida to seize men and women and sell them into interminable bondage; nor can we wonder that the consciousness of these facts should have created a feeling of hostility between our regular troops and the slaveholders of Florida, who were constantly charging them with inefficiency and want of energy in the capture of negroes" (Giddings 279). The tension alluded to in this context is similar to Rainsford's disaffection with the imperial government's complicity with creole slaveholders' extremist tactics.

With reference to Saint-Domingue, both Ardouin and Madiou noted that some residents chose to relocate further away from the scene of public dog maulings, and they mention several French generals who refused to participate in the spectacles. However, some planters offered justifications for the use of contested torture techniques to "save" the island and its white inhabitants. Leonora Sansay, a contemporary observer of the last days of the French occupation of Saint-Domingue, confirms the disjuncture between metropolitan and local attitudes. She writes, "The Creoles shake their heads and predict much ill. Accustomed to the climate, and acquainted with the manner of fighting the Negroes, they offer advice, which is not listened to" (*Secret History* 9). Later in the same work she comments that the Creoles "had supposed that the appearance of an army of thirty thousand men would have reduced the negroes to order; but these conquerors of Italy, unnerved by the climate, or from some other cause, lose all their energy, and fly before the undisciplined slaves" (34). The anonymous author of another first-person eyewitness account of the Haitian Revolution also weighs in on these issues. He writes, "For those who question the discipline under which they [the slaves] live, it is certainly not more rigorous than that which is observed for soldiers and sailors; and when one realizes that thirty thousand whites are in the center of six hundred thousand semi-barbaric Africans, one should not hesitate to say that discipline is necessary" (de Puech Parham 25, 40). Convinced that the slaves rebelled only because of outside agitation, he refers to abolitionists as "egoistic pedants who, from the depths of their libraries, judge everything by hearsay, and make a pretence of feeling compassion for some unfortunates whom they have never seen or known" (40). In a letter to Napoleon, a group of planters further exemplifies the typical remonstrances leveled against "armchair philosophers." They praised Rochambeau as "the leader they needed" ("le chef qu'il faut") because he was "distanced by his principles and his morality from those vain abstractions of false philosophy, inapplicable in a country where only Africans could cultivate the soil under the force of harsh discipline" ("éloigné par ces principes et sa moralité, de ces vaines abstractions d'une fausse philosophie, inapplicables dans un pays dont le sol ne peut être fécondé que par des Africains, qu'une discipline sévère doit comprimer"; Ardouin 5: 75).

Thus, in all three locales, local colonists portrayed opponents of canine warfare as out of touch with reality. They publicly countered objections to their political and military strategies by claiming that the "safety of the island and the lives of the inhabitants were not to be sacrificed to the apprehension of perverse misconstruction or willful misrepresentation in the mother country" (Dallas 11). The so-called "friends of the blacks," and other purported negrophile advocates were blamed for inciting controversy and bloodshed because of their abstract principles and "sickly sentimentality" (Giddings 264). Different measures were argued to obtain in certain types of societies, in this case plantation America vis-à-vis metropolitan Europe or the northern United States. A state of exception was invoked for combat against nonwhite others. Indeed, to the extent that the fundamental paradox of the Age of Revolution was the subtext in these debates, whether liberty, fraternity, and equality were universal rights that pertained to native populations and Africans and their descendants in the Americas, the colonial Caribbean states and the new U.S. republic responded with a decisive negative. Black and native insurgents had to be viewed as expendable nonhumans for the rhetoric of self-preservation to have weight. This ideology facilitated the inhuman violence routinely perpetrated upon other human beings.

The planter positions presented here are ultimately predictable as they aligned with their class and racial interests. Violence was the modus operandi for sustaining elite creole lifestyles. Participants in an inter-American slave-holding economy, the interested parties established mobile repressive technologies. What bears closer examination is the outrage expressed by Rainsford and other contemporary witnesses about the use of dogs as weapons of war. Was their chief objection grounded in the knowledge that these animals were used to kill rebellious opponents rather than to capture them? Was a more stringent code of honor to be enacted between opponents on the battlefield than those in place during times of peace? I contend that any use of dogs specifically bred to track and destroy human beings is evidence of a state of war. Can one ever speak of a peaceful cohabitation of the enslaved and free in the context of slavery such that the use of dogs in the quotidian context is much different than during a declared state of full rebellion? While words such as *warfare* and *torture* may conventionally describe supposedly discrete, bounded activities (a military encounter between multiple states, a particular moment of cruelty) that have utilitarian purposes (the achievement of military goals, the extraction of information), plantation America poses a challenge to conventional understandings of these terms.

Although the ethical dimensions of using dogs may have been more publicly discussed during these massive late eighteenth- and mid-nineteenth-century wars, their visibility there does not essentially change the nature of their presumptive function. Unlike the case for white civilian populations during times of peace, for those of African and native descent living as slaves or runaways throughout the early Americas, the threat of being killed by white owners/settlers was constant and not relegated to moments of politically declared wars. Hence what does one make of a sadistic technique considered beyond the pale in communities that by their very nature effectually existed in a state of permanent warfare between masters and slaves, societies that routinely resorted to physical and psychological torture to maintain the status quo?[26] Rainsford et al.'s conviction that the use of dogs in war was against "human nature," a crime against humanity that should be universally deplored (xviii), effectively relegated the extreme repressive use of violence to the animal world. There was a displacement of human atrocities onto dogs, and the *means* of subduing black victims became the focus of the critique rather than the *system* that necessitated those means. As a result, a discussion of slavery itself as an institution based upon terror got sidelined. Few dared to critique the explicit links between war policy and metropolitan economic dependence on slave-holding industries.

When the employer of the dogs was no longer an anonymous planter but the state, which used them in a state-sanctioned battle, the stakes were higher for those who might otherwise have turned a blind eye to the systemic functioning of plantation life. For a trained military man such as Rainsford, using bloodthirsty dogs to fight one's enemies was distasteful: it had none of the organized, mechanistic efficiency of professional warfare. At a historical moment when people sought to

define modernity partially through evocations of enlightened rational-
ism, the guillotine was the era's contemporaneous weapon par excellence. It was most famously put to use in Europe during the Terror
phase of the French Revolution (1793–94) precisely because of its perceived humanity: it was controlled and effective and didn't make its
victims suffer needlessly. Having living human beings ripped to pieces
by dogs was quite the opposite. Rather than distant and scientific, the
method was raw and unpredictable. The very attributes that made
dogs a preferred weapon in the colonial arsenal, their sense of smell
and superhuman strength, also made them a danger. Once they were
unleashed, they were still wild beasts and no appeal to their "reason"
was possible.

In an era when a nascent creole sensibility began to claim opposition to Old World tyranny as a formative patriotic ideal, the debate
over the military use of dogs allowed European observers to revive
long-held associations regarding the inherent depravity of creole life.
In the context of revolutionary struggles on both sides of the Atlantic,
the debate complicated the articulation of clear boundaries between
the civilized and the barbaric, the rational and the irrational, the discrete campaign and the total reign of terror. This was a meaningful division, for as C. L. R. James reminds us, the growing fissure
between Old and New World whites would contribute decisively to
the fortunes of black rebels in Saint-Domingue. Ultimately, however,
these objections to canine warfare did not keep Cuban dogs away
from their prey.

CULTURE AND PUBLIC MEMORY

I conclude by affirming the critical role that cultural production plays in
documenting, disseminating, and bringing the memory of these events
to life. Rainsford's above-mentioned conviction that images wield the
power to influence public opinion is one pertinent example. The prints
under examination invited sympathy, outrage, curiosity, and a host of
other emotions at the time of their production much as they do in the
present moment. Using iconographical narrative techniques, they present a truth that is stranger and more disturbing than fiction. The striking correspondence between warfare strategies across the Americas is
immediately discernible. The images establish temporal continuities
across four decades, as well as evidence of transcolonial alliances that,
however temporarily, overcame the official imperial balkanization of

the region. This is not to say that fiction has not lent its considerable descriptive and analytical weight to the subject. Caribbean and African American artists in both the nineteenth and twentieth centuries have documented the collaborations that brought Cuba to the forefront of regional consciousness as a source of canine terror.

Before turning to fiction, however, I cite one of the few extant testimonies written by a victim who survived such an assault. One of the most memorable descriptions in Juan Francisco Manzano's *Autobiografía* (1840), Latin America's only known slave narrative, concerns his capture and mauling by dogs. The scene is rural Cuba, and Manzano writes:

> He [the slave catcher] took out a rope of flimsy hemp, tied me up like a criminal, mounted his horse, and pushing me ahead, ordered me to run. . . . We had gone about a fourth of a league when tired of running in front of the horse, I tripped and fell. No sooner had I hit the ground than two dogs or two beasts, which were following him, attacked me. One of them, holding my entire left cheek in his mouth, sank his fang all the way through to my molar. The other one perforated my thigh and my left calf, with the utmost voracity and speed. These scars persist in spite of the twenty-four years that have transpired since then. The overseer leaped from the horse onto the dogs and separated them. I was bleeding profusely, especially from my left leg, which fell numb. He grabbed me with one hand by the rope that bound me, hurling a stream of obscenities at me. This yank dislocated my right arm, which has not yet healed. (95–97)

> Sacó una cuerda de cáñamo delgada, me ató como a un facineroso, se montó a caballo y, echándome por delante, me mandó correr. . . . Fatigado de correr delante del caballo, di un traspié y caí. No bien había dado en tierra cuando dos perros o dos fieras que le seguían se me tiraron encima. El uno metiéndose casi toda mi quijada izquierda en su boca, me atravesó el colmillo hasta encontrarse con mi muela. El otro me agujereó un muslo y la pantorrilla izquierda, todo con la mayor voracidad y prontitud. Estas cicatrices están perpetuas, a pesar de los 24 años que han pasado. El mayoral se tiró del caballo sobre los perros y los separó. Mi sangre corriá en abundancia, principalmente en la pierna izquierda, que se me adormeció. Me agarró por la atadura con una mano, echando una retahíla de obscenidades. Este tirón me descoyntó el brazo derecho, del que aún no he sanado. (94–96)

The description presented here provides some of the most explicit details of how physical punishment was experienced personally as bodily violation. This account is all the more striking given that first-person hemispheric slave narratives as a genre tend to provide ample evidence of slave torture without lingering over the more unsettling, bloody details. If one extrapolates this scene time and again—orders shouted in different languages depending on the local setting, victims of different sexes and ages—Manzano's palpable terror is magnified. The ubiquitous documentation of dog torture is in part explained by the violence of such assaults. Common in occurrence yet uncommonly extreme in their viciousness, such tactics have left their mark on collective memory.[27]

Given that scenes such as these were unfortunately frequent, it is not surprising that Cuba's most famous nineteenth-century novel, Cirilo Villaverde's *Cecilia Valdés* (1882), mentions dogs as a slave-hunting mechanism in a domestic scene set in the 1830s. One of the protagonists is horrified that a runaway slave has been bitten and conjectures, "What if they've torn him to pieces! It's more than likely. Those dogs are like wild beasts. Good heavens, how horrible!" (331) ("¡Si le habrán despedazado! Es probable. Esos perros son como fieras. ¡Qué horror, Dios mío!"; 202–03). Moving outward from the island to Saint-Domingue, the aforementioned Leonora Sansay, in *Zelica, the Creole* (1820), captures the pall cast by the dogs' presence there. At one point the protagonist entreats Rochambeau to "remove, I pray you, these frightful dogs from the city, whose dismal howlings fill me with terror, and torment me day and night." Rochambeau replies, "These dogs are our means of defence, . . . but they shall be removed as far from the possibility of annoying you as the limits of our town will allow" (251). At first glance, the protagonist's comments seem like a superficial response to "bothersome" noise, especially given her critique of how the French army is losing the war. However, her comments imply a deep unease with the extreme tactics used by her "defenders" to protect her way of life. Unnerved by the dogs' presence, she cautiously critiques those who deem it appropriate to employ them, even if the military authorities seek to justify their use by invoking colonial security.

The dogs' continued international reputation in an everyday context in 1850s North America is also evident in the first African American novel. In William Wells Brown's *Clotel* (1853), a visitor to the South remarks upon an astonishing sight at a neighboring plantation. It was "a kennel of bloodhounds . . . ferocious, gaunt, and savage-looking animals. They were part of a stock imported from Cuba" (114). Wells must have been acquainted with their use, as he portrays these dogs hunting down a runaway slave belonging to one of the main characters. Twentieth-century texts continued to keep this memory alive. During the anxiety-producing days following abolition in the British Caribbean in the mid-1830s, the white creole child protagonist of Jean

Rhys's *Wide Sargasso Sea* (1966) waits in fear that her former slaves will harm her. She fervently wishes that she "had a big Cuban dog to lie by my bed and protect me" (22). Evidently the memory of these dogs' brutality when employed in Jamaica was still vivid more than one hundred years later when Rhys composed her prequel to *Jane Eyre*.

In perhaps the most famous example of historical fiction memorializing the particular aptitude of Cuban dogs for slave repression, Alejo Carpentier opens a chapter of *El reino de este mundo (The Kingdom of This World;* 1945) with a discussion of "The Ship of Dogs." The chapter's title is a double entendre, as the following pages first introduce the Leclerc expedition, literally a convoy of French ships coming to wreak terror on the island. Foreshadowing life in Saint-Domingue under Leclerc and Rochambeau, the narrator states "this was the road leading straight to horror" (102). Carpentier was well aware of Rochambeau's penchant for torture, and his protagonist, Ti Noel, witnesses a French official provisioning a ship bound for Cap Français with Cuban dogs.[28] He writes: "One morning the harbor of Santiago was filled with barking. Chained to each other, growling and slavering behind their muzzles, trying to bite their keepers and one another, hurling themselves at the people watching behind the grilled windows, hundreds of dogs were being driven with whips into the hold of a sailing ship. . . . Where are they taking them? Ti Noel shouted above the din to a mulatto sailor. . . . 'To eat niggers!' the other answered with a guffaw" (89) ("Una mañana el puerto de Sanitago de Cuba se llenó de ladridos. Encadenados unos a otros, lanzándose hacia las gentes asomadas a las rejas, mordiendo y volviendo a morder sin poder morder, centenarios de perros eran metidos a latigazos, en las bodegas de un velero. . . . ¿Adónde los llevan? Gritó Ti Noel a un marinero mulato. . . . ¡A Comer negros! Carcajeó el otro"; 69). The characters' glee at the thought of dogs consuming and regurgitating human beings illustrates just how macabre such events were; the spectacle has excited public interest, both disgust and acclaim, for well over a century.

I cite these literary examples from North America and the anglophone, francophone, and hispanophone Caribbean for two reasons. First, they are evidence that artists have ruminated upon and creatively engaged the late eighteenth- and early nineteenth-century transcolonial networks of repression under study here. Given the long cultural life of these canine villains it is reasonable to suppose that they occasioned deep trauma. Can a human being ever be inured to the sight of another person deliberately consumed by a dog? With very few exceptions, we have little direct evidence documenting the sentiments of the victims and their families; like the man sacrificed by Rochambeau and his lieutenants on stage, they are the nameless maimed and dead. We do know that those who witnessed these horrors passed the stories down, however, and that they have been reworked time and again as evidence of the contested extremities employed by the colonial state in a bid to maintain power.

Finally, these narratives point to the continued importance of a transcolonial approach in the production of academic scholarship about these same events. Unfortunately, these accounts often get critiqued within nationalist contexts (e.g., Haitian or Jamaican or U.S. history), despite the circuits of travel that brought Cuban dogs to foreign shores to begin with. The novels cited above highlight inter-American connections, and their authors demonstrate that the plantation zone depended upon both transatlantic and equally importantly, intraregional supplies of labor and goods to survive.

In the following chapters, the image of these dogs can serve as a constant reminder of the stakes involved for those who employed transcolonial collaborations as a way of fighting for their survival, improving their quality of life, or gaining their freedom. Much as "Remember the Alamo!" and "Remember the Maine!" became rallying cries for white settler nationalism or U.S. imperialist goals within the context of regional, intercolonial warfare, attack dogs symbolized what was most feared by a hemispheric stratum of black men and women who continued to be tracked down, maimed, and killed by these representatives of the state and the creole plantocracy.[29] In one critical context, however, a forceful inversion would produce equally poignant and contested counterimages of armed power and state authority. As the Haitians emerged victorious from their decade-long struggle, many of their neighbors to the immediate east in the Spanish colony of Santo Domingo found the nascent ideology of black power both fearsome and compelling. I now turn to the postrevolutionary landscape of Hispaniola.

CHAPTER 2

"Une et indivisible?"

The Struggle for Freedom in Hispaniola

In 1845, a local Dominican artist published one of the first engravings in the Dominican Republic (figure 10).[1] *General haitiano en marcha (Haitian General on the March)* is striking for several reasons. First, the image is a visual representation of what both the creole plantocracy and metropolitan authorities most dreaded during the age of the Haitian Revolution—armed, organized slaves and free people of color ready and able to protect their interests. These are the "French negroes" so feared and vilified throughout the Americas. Significantly, the general is forcibly dragging a dog behind him, dominating the animal in a way that denotes a stark reversal of the power relations in evidence in my discussion of regional canine torture. Competing transcolonial American formulations could not be more starkly drawn between these two chapters, as the project of radical antislavery embodied in Haiti was vying directly with regional proslavery efforts designed to crush it. Rather than tormented victim, the man depicted here is confident and at ease, dressed in military regalia that combine a traditional European-styled uniform with local adaptations—casual rolled-up pants and rustic sandals. He is "on the march," proactively fighting for his well-being in a world that, until very recently, considered him chattel and accorded him no rights whatsoever.

That the earliest published example of Dominican iconography is an image of a Haitian general is also telling. This speaks volumes for the centrality of the Haitian presence in nineteenth-century Dominican

FIGURE 10. Domingo Echavarría, *General haitiano en marcha*
(1845). Engraving. Reproduced in *La caricatura y dibujo en
Santo Domingo*, ed. Emilio Rodríguez Demorizi (Santo Domingo: Editora Taller, 1977).

life. Rich and contradictory, the image can be read in myriad ways that
provide insight into relations between the former neighboring colonies
of French Saint-Domingue and Spanish Santo Domingo, territories with
a complex, antagonistic history.[2] This chapter highlights the figure of
the Haitian military general, seen as historical personage, iconographic
representation, and fictional character. I explore the ideological stakes
involved in depictions of the Haitian presence in Santo Domingo—from
elite anxieties about black rule to a counterculture where the general
symbolized pride, strength, and hope in a new regime. Beyond being
associated with military prowess, the figure was coupled with popular
religiosity, specifically Vodou. Successive nineteenth-century Haitian
constitutions promised the free exercise of religion, and I examine how
depictions of spiritual practices have been manipulated in Hispaniola

to signify difference—of national origin, of presumed civilization—as well as to mark belonging and resistance.

As the only land militarily incorporated into the postrevolutionary Haitian state, the eastern territory allows me to show how transcolonial collaborations transformed themselves into intraisland nationalism. This was an anomalous postcolonial project in the region, both because Haiti was only the second independent country in the hemisphere at the time and because it was a black independent state in the midst of slave holding territories. Promoting a philosophy of an island that was, in the words of Toussaint Louverture, intended to be "one and indivisible," successive Haitian leaders redefined what had hitherto been foreign into the domestic. This institutionalized integration involved collusion between black populations on both sides of the border separating the French and Spanish colonies. Former slaves and free people of color on the French side employed transcolonial policies in order to protect their tenuous, newly proclaimed personal freedoms and national sovereignty. To the east, many people of African descent likewise embraced the Haitian cause, as the new state was their best chance to gain their freedom and be integrated into a system that recognized and protected them as equal citizens. Abolition predated the formation of the Dominican nation and served as a rallying cry for those who envisioned a new social order predicated on freedom from chattel slavery and its corresponding regulation of labor arrangements, kinship networks, and all aspects of everyday life.

Moving in rough chronological order from the 1790s through the 1840s, this chapter thus examines three moments of active mobilization to unite the island and the debates about the meaning of freedom that occurred during each. The first was in 1801, when Saint-Domingue was still a "special" French colony controlled by Toussaint Louverture; the second occurred in 1805 under the leadership of Jean-Jacques Dessalines; and the next lasted from 1822 to 1844 during the presidency of Jean-Pierre Boyer. I demonstrate how a variety of classes come to understand Toussaint's language of "indivisibility" in these tumultuous times. Those who favored an islandwide alliance were forced to compete with the desire of foreign empires (and their local sympathizers) to reincorporate the island as a colonial territory and protonationalist sentiments seeking Dominican independence.

Again, I privilege popular cultural production when telling these stories, focusing on visual images, orally transmitted speeches, and poetry that bring a variety of black voices to the discussion. I also mine memoirs, official records, and prose fiction looking for fragmentary traces of how people of color both represented themselves and were represented during the era. It is worth remarking that nontextual sources served an especially important expressive and communicative function for the majority of the island's population at the time, a population for whom literacy was largely inaccessible.

Knowledge production concerning these events continues to shape political life in the Dominican Republic. As a whole, dominant discourse posits an inherent antagonism between the two countries and views the aforementioned series of military campaigns waged by Haitian leaders during the first five decades of the nineteenth century as savage wars of conquest.[3] The very semantics of the discussion focuses on "occupation" as opposed to unification and integration. Indivisibility is blithely reconstituted as predatory and rapacious. In the discussion that follows I deliberately eschew the language of occupation, as it taints any attempts to imagine an alternative interpretation of events. Dominican nationalism is deeply mired in anti-Haitianism, and during the colonial period the specter of a black republic was anathema to the ruling class. Over a century later, Emilio Rodríguez Demorizi, one of the nation's most prolific historians, could still refer to the Haitian presence as "the blackest days of Ethiopian domination ("los más negros días de la dominación etíope"; *Pintura y escultura* 31).[4] Dominicans who favored political and cultural alliances between the island's populations have been marginalized by successive governments, both past and present, that had a stake in fostering antagonism among the majority black populations on both sides of the border so that a small governing elite could maintain its power.[5] Ultimately, I am interested in the different stories that emerge when we catch glimpses into the lives of those for whom, to cite the Haitian national motto, *l'union faisait la force:* unity rendered them strong.

"L'ÎLE D'HAITI FORME LE TERRITOIRE DE LA RÉPUBLIQUE": THE EARLY YEARS OF ANTISLAVERY BORDER POLITICS

I begin this story of black transcolonial collaboration by exploring the history of José Campos Taváres. This general and his remarkable career provide a window into the complicated historical struggles that culminated in a series of Haitian maneuvers to unify the island. A mulatto slave of the Dominican priest Don Pedro Taváres, he went on to serve as a distinguished general in the Haitian army during the first decades of the nineteenth century. Campos Taváres's official titles indicate his commitment to a united Dominican-Haitian cause in the face of imperial attacks from Europe and the local elite. He served as "Colonel of the Haitian Army, Commander of the Yaque Battalion integrated by blacks and mulattos in Santiago, Governor of the Department of the Cibao under Dessalines, signer of Christophe's 1806 Constitution with the rank of Assistant General of the Haitian Army, Haitian Ambassador before the Spanish Governor Carlos Urritia in 1811, occupying the rank of Baron of Taváres, Brigadier General of the Haitian Army and Aide-de-Camp of His Majesty King Christophe" (Cordero Michel 106). A resident of Santiago de los Caballeros in the north-central region of the Dominican Republic, Campos Taváres consciously decided that his interests lay with the neighboring "sable Republic," which he served under a number of its most distinguished leaders. His representation of the Cibao region is especially interesting given that many Dominican scholars have traditionally considered this central plain the cradle of a Hispanicized campesino culture, understood as white and Catholic, a "region where the national soul conserves its autochthonous characteristics" and a place that "served as a defense of the nation against invasion from the west" (Ryan 24, 29).

Although Campos Taváres was a much decorated general, his name is not frequently cited in Dominican history books. He is in fact rather obscure.[6] Given his exceptional military career under some of the most distinguished leaders of the antislavery and anticolonial struggles in the Americas, the omission is noteworthy. A Dominican leader with Haitian sympathies was, and continues to be, extremely threatening to many Dominicans. As was the case with Joseph Savary, a black military figure examined in the following chapter, Campos Taváres became an "impossible" patriot, a figure whose blackness and politics rendered him inassimilable in the nationalist narrative that emerged in the latter part of the nineteenth century and blossomed during the Trujillo era.

Campos Taváres's life is largely chronicled in a manuscript edited in 1814 by a Dominican planter, Gaspar de Arredondo y Pichardo. A description of events from the late 1790s to 1805, the fifteen-chapter manuscript serves as a lens for viewing how the white Dominican elite coped with the Haitian presence. The son of "rich, virtuous, and well-born parents" ("unos padres ricos, virtuosos, de esclarecido nacimiento"), Arredondo served as an emissary from Santiago de los Caballeros to the Haitian government before going into exile in Cuba in 1805. He maintains that he wrote the memoir so that posterity would understand how those "born in opulence" ("nacido en la opulencia") had experienced the abrupt reversal of their fortunes, noting that "I wouldn't dare to write it if in every corner of Cuba there were not many émigrés, witnesses who participated with me in those disasters" ("No me atrevería a escribirla, si no hubiera en cada rincón de esta isla [Cuba] . . . muchos emigrados testigos presenciales de aquellos desastres de que participaron junto conmigo"; Arredondo 122–23).[7] Migrations from Hispaniola gave rise to an international production of "reversal-of-fortune" memoirs in France, the United States, and the Caribbean, continued evidence of the centrality of the Haitian Revolution to Caribbean creole letters.[8]

Arredondo's narrative mentions Campos Taváres on several occasions. The first time he appears as Arredondo's travel companion during an 1804 trip to Guarico (Cap Haitien, formerly Cap Français) when the two served together on a delegation of Cibaeños meeting with Emperor Jean-Jacques Dessalines. The stated purpose of the mission was to protest what the Dominicans considered the overly expensive tribute demanded by the Haitians following the integration of the island.[9] When the city of Santiago could not present the required sum, the Haitians put Campos Taváres in command of "200 *negros*" to exact payment. Informed that Taváres has been promoted to "chief of the brigade and interim commander of the plaza" ("gefe *[sic]* de brigada y comandante interino de la plaza"), Arredondo expresses relief at this appointment, noting that "Campos Taváres, although mulatto, was Spanish and maintained his regard and respect for us from the time he lived under another system" ("Campos Taváres, aunque mulato, era español y nos conservaba aquel prestigio de miramiento y de respeto del tiempo en que vivió bajo otro sistema"; 143). On the basis of old regime customs that mandated black slave subservience, Arredondo thus expects Campos Taváres to continue showing deference for his social "betters." Interestingly, Arredondo identifies him as "español," even as Campos Taváres himself has adjusted his mode of self-identification to reflect multiple new possibilities. He is Spanish, a native Dominican, and a de facto Haitian as well.

Arredondo's relief at Campos Taváres's appointment proves to be short-lived. During a narrative description of the 1805 defeat of a small group of landowners living in Santiago, Arredondo transcribes the entire speech given by Campos Taváres under the heading "Words of Campos Taváres from the Banks of the Yaque River" ("Palabras de Campos Taváres desde las orillas del Yaque"). The speech is worth quoting at length, both in the original Spanish and in translation, as it is one of the few extant eyewitness testimonies from a black soldier who participated in the island's struggles for racial equality. Although mediated by Arredondo's own perspective, this address provides a glimpse into the mind-set of a remarkable individual. Notable for his passion, directness, and aggressively pronativist stance, Campos Taváres addresses his audience of fellow Dominicans as follows:

Citizens: I am from the country where you were born. I have been your comrade, and I could never forget the affection I have always held for you. . . . I still have family in this land that is about to be destroyed. I honor those persons, who when I was their slave, always treated me like a free man, dispensing their attention and affection. . . . I know the situation in which you find yourselves. *I see the forces of the army with which I have come united.* I have penetrated its intentions. The orders we have are terrible and very rigorous in the event that we encounter any opposition to our passing; they are also rigorous [in their discipline] against our troops if they misbehave or if any of you are offended in the least by one of us, provided that you cede us passage to the capital where we go to battle the French who occupy it. That is the only thing that the *indigenous government* desires. Open your eyes, reflect . . . I speak to you as a friend, as a Spaniard, as a countryman. Our chief comes in good faith. . . . *My heart would infinitely regret having to come to my native land only to bathe it in blood,* leaving my friends strewn in the middle of its streets and plazas. . . . As God is my witness, in giving you this advice I have no other intention, nor any other interest than saving you and saving all of the innocent. . . . Do not attempt resistance. If you do not comply, count on your extermination. . . . *I say goodbye to you, my dear friends, as I go to incorporate myself into the army that you see ahead.* (italics mine)

Ciudadanos: Yo soy del país en que vosotros nacisteis. Yo he sido compañero vuestro, yo no podré jamás prescindir del afecto que les he merecido siempre. . . . Tengo todavía parientes en ese suelo que va a destrozarse. Venero aquellas personas que siendo su esclavo, me tenían siempre sobre el rango de la clase libre, dispensándome sus cuidados y atenciones. . . . Conozco la situación en que se hallan. *Veo las fuerzas del ejército a que vengo unido.* He penetrado sus intenciones. Son temibles las órdenes que tenemos y muy rigurosas para en caso de encontrar oposición a nuestro tránsito, así como son también fuertes contra la tropa cuando se desmande, o sea cualquiera de ustedes ofendido en lo más leve por uno de nosotros, dejando libre el paso que queremos para la capital, a batirnos con los franceses que la ocupan. Esto nada más quiere *el gobierno indígena.* Abran los ojos, reflexionen. . . . Yo les hablo como amigo, como español, como paisano. El gefe nuestro está de buena fé. . . . *Sentiré el lo infinito de mi corazón llegar a mi patria a inundarla de sangre, y dejar a mis amigos yertos en medio de sus calles y plazas.* . . . Pongo a Dios por testigo de que en darles este aviso no tengo otra intención, ni me lleva otro interés que el de salvarlos y salvar tantos inocentes. . . . No traten de resistencia. . . . Si así no lo hacen cuenten con su exterminio. . . . *Yo me despido de vosotros queridos amigos, y voy a incorporarme al ejército que tenéis a la vista.* (Arredondo 155–56)

Campos Taváres placates the egos of his paternalistic former owners, only to threaten them with "extermination" ("exterminio"), their bodies "strewn in the middle of the streets and plazas" ("yertos en medio de sus calles y plazas") if they do not surrender to the Haitian army. The friendship and respect he claims for his "compañeros" do not make him waver. By deliberate choice, he comes "united" ("unido") with this army, insisting on his commander's "good faith" ("buena fe"). In six different phrases he affirms his patriotic love of his *native* land, while unequivocally stating that it is in his land's best interest to fight alongside the Haitian forces. Citing the strict orders and discipline by which his fellow soldiers are bound, he refutes accounts of barbarous hordes and indiscriminate violence that eventually came to dominate accounts of the Haitian military presence in the eastern territory. In a remarkable statement of belonging, Campos Taváres speaks in the name of an "indigenous government" ("gobierno indígena") that has rightful claim to the entire island. Those who resist are traitors. Significantly, he invokes the language of *indigènes*, a terminology used to identify the rebel black army vis-à-vis the French in the latter years of the Haitian Revolution.[10]

Campos Taváres's speech has verbatim passages from a May 1804 proclamation by Emperor Dessalines.[11] In it, he accuses Spanish inhabitants of the east, especially the priests, of being in league with French forces and demands that they remain neutral in Haitian attempts to definitively expel the French from the island. The French occupying the capital of Santo Domingo were the remnants of the 1802 Napoleonic army sent to crush the government of Toussaint Louverture and to reestablish slavery. As we have seen, this was the same army that imported Cuban dogs to fight against their enemies. As a political expedient, the Haitian state regarded possession of the east as a necessary safeguard against continued attacks that could be launched against the new nation from adjacent land. Campos Taváres serves as a cipher for Dessalines's / the Haitian state's will, but he inserts a local context into the demands that indicates how his own personal experiences must have resonated with the causes espoused by Haiti.

The Haitian presence thus provides a mechanism of social and political ascension for Campos Taváres and others. He fights for his freedom, and once he gains ownership over his own body, he chooses to serve a state that acknowledges his worth and declares him a citizen. As was the case with creole nationalism throughout the Americas, one needed force to transform sentiment into a viable political project. This is one of the earliest hemispheric examples of how black claims to indigeneity, understood as entitlement to the land and its fruits, were prioritized as a key element in violent revolutionary struggle.

Campos Taváres's example demonstrates the existence of divergent viewpoints between the slave-holding oligarchy and the oppressed about the future of the colony, specifically with regard to abolition and the creation of a unified and independent island republic. Members of various social classes were aware of the potential ramifications of unity, some fearing it and others lending the mandate their support. If we consider integration attempts as a historical arc that stretches from 1801 through the 1840s, several chronicles and travelogues further elucidate the trajectories of belonging and displacement that characterized transcolonial interactions in Hispaniola at each of the three aforementioned junctures: 1801, 1805, and 1822–44.[12]

Any examination of the independence struggles of both Haiti and the Dominican Republic must necessarily evaluate relationships between France and Spain, as efforts to unite the island originated as a result of imperialist politics. The 1795 Treaty of Basle ceded Spain's two-thirds of Hispaniola to the French as part of Spain's capitulation to France during the continental wars sparked by the French Revolution. Figure 11 is a map from the 1790s depicting the French and Spanish parts of the island, as well as major borders and cities. Note the mountainous Cibao region in the center of the map, the scene of many of the stories I document here. In 1801, Haitian troops, under the command of Toussaint Louverture, marched into the east to take possession of the colony in France's name. This inter-European "exchange" of American colonies was not uncommon in and of itself; take the Spanish, then U.S. acquisition of the formerly French Louisiana Territory, or the exchange of islands such as Saint Lucia and Dominica between the French and the British. However, this was the first and only time that stipulations of a European treaty were implemented by a black-led army. The six years between the signing of the treaty and Louverture's takeover marked an exodus of the Spanish Dominican population as well as of the French colonial exiles who had taken refuge in the east

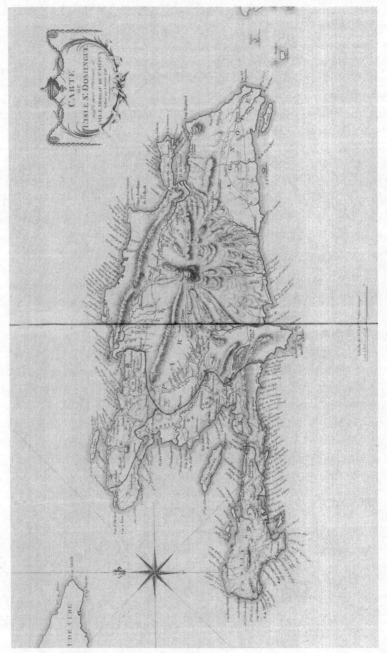

FIGURE 11. *Carte de l'île de Saint-Domingue.* Nicolas Ponce, *Recueil de vues des lieux principaux de la colonie françoise de Saint-Domingue* (Paris: Chez Moreau de Saint-Méry and M. Phelipeau, ca. 1791). Courtesy of the John Carter Brown Library.

when fleeing their homes in Saint-Domingue.[13] Frank Moya Pons estimates that between January and February 1801 alone, more than two thousand people fled to Venezuela, Cuba, and Puerto Rico (*Dominican Republic* 106).

Of essential interest is a December 1795 decree issued by the French republican governor general of Saint-Domingue, Etienne Laveaux, shortly after the peace accord was signed. This legislation goes to the heart of the issue of "exporting" the Haitian and French revolutions in the Caribbean region. One of the treaty's conditions was that the Spanish inhabitants were granted one year to leave the island with their possessions. Many of them wished to leave with their most valuable belongings—their slaves. We see this highly charged economic and ethical issue surrounding forced migration and continued enslavement of people who had been emancipated by the 1794 French abolition decree recurring in many of the stories under examination—in the case of Romain and his family in New Jersey, or the case of "French" slave performers in Jamaica. In the Dominican context, Laveaux categorically denies their owners' right to do so. In no uncertain terms he tells the Spanish governor general Joaquín García and other petitioners:

> The inhabitants of this part of Santo Domingo who for whatever motive prefer to transport their belongings to the Possessions of her Catholic Majesty will be able to do so within the space of a year. Whoever says "inhabitants" is speaking of all men, whatever color they may be. The French nation doesn't recognize slaves but men; hence your so-called slaves, being here in the land conceded to the French Republic, have acquired their liberty. . . . The body of a man is not looked at as property, as a good belonging to another man. . . . The inhabitants can move their belongings, but the Republic has decreed that a man cannot be the property of another.

> Los habitantes de la parte de Santo Domingo que por motivos de intereses u otro prefiriesen transportarse con sus bienes a las Posesiones de S.M.C. podrán hacerlo en el espacio de un año. Quien dice "habitantes" dice todo hombre cualquiera, de cualquiera color que sea. La nación francesa no conoce Esclavos ni conoce sino hombres, luego vuestros pretendidos esclavos hallándose sobre el suelo concedido a la República Francesa, han adquirido la libertad. . . . El cuerpo del hombre no es mirado como propiedad, como un bien perteneciente a otro hombre . . . . Los habitantes podrán trasladarse con sus bienes, la República ha decretado que el hombre no puede ser propiedad de otro. (F. Franco, *Negros* 81, 83)

Such French republican zeal and commitment to racial equality are remarkable given the subsequent reversal in French politics under Napoleon I, when the French state reinstated slavery in its colonial

FIGURE 12. *Moi Egal à toi.* Engraving by François Bonneville
(Paris: Rue du Théâtre Français, No. 4, undated). Courtesy of
the Art & Architecture Collection, Miriam and Ira D. Wallach
Division of Art, Prints and Photographs, The New York Public
Library, Astor, Lenox and Tilden Foundations.

possessions. If the slave population were informed that they were under no obligation to emigrate with their former masters as "property"
at this historical moment, however, one can reasonably suppose that
many local inhabitants would see Toussaint's army as a liberating one
fighting in their interests.[14]

   Consider an image from the heady, hopeful days following France's
abolition of slavery (figure 12). Created by the French engraver François Bonneville, the print plays on the well-known "Am I not your

FIGURE 13. *Ne suis-je pas ton frère?*
Engraving. Cover plate of *Adresse à
l'Assemblée nationale, pour l'abolition
de la traite des noirs. Par la Société des
amis des noirs de Paris* (Paris: De l'Imp.
de L. Potier de Lille, 1790). Courtesy of
the John Carter Brown Library.

brother?" ("Ne suis-je pas ton frère?") language common in much British, French, and American abolitionist literature (figure 13). The rhetorical questioning is gone, replaced by an assertive "I am your equal"
("Moi egal à toi"). Rather than depicting the generic profile of a suppli-
cative slave in chains, the newly liberated black woman is shown facing
forward. Her features are sharply drawn; her face is expressive and her
short afro is exposed. French republican iconography made extensive
use of women as liberatory muses; in this context, Bonneville's idealized figure is not only racialized but Caribbeanized as well.[15] Instead of
the Phrygian liberty cap, she wears a plaid madras headwrap. I examine the communicative power of such headwraps in chapter 4. The
point I wish to emphasize is that for a few short years in France and its
colonies this image was a comprehensible one. A black woman boldly
proclaiming her equality in public propaganda was an idea supported
by official state policy. A political space was opened in which a black
subject could be a citizen clothed in republican regalia. This ideal had
no counterpart anywhere else. The promise of such freedom, a message delivered by Laveaux's decree or iconographically via broadside,
provoked widely divergent reactions among slaves, free people of color,
and their masters.

Abolition would have been a critical motivating factor in the decisions of all segments of the population to stay or flee. In 1794, the total
population of the eastern part of the island was 103,000 inhabitants.
Of this number, approximately 35,000 were white, 38,000 freedmen,
and 30,000 slaves (F. Franco, *Negros* 72). Contrary to the assertions

of many Dominican writers, an insurgent Haitian army propagating the ideal of *liberté* may not have invoked feelings of widespread terror for the majority. To be clear, I am not asserting that people of African descent in Santo Domingo would have automatically sided with their western neighbors. For example, the east housed a large rural population of free blacks, in addition to a substantial maroon population, both of which lived beyond the easy reach of the Spanish state. If events in Saint-Domingue and postcolonial Haiti are any indication, groups similar to these had an uneasy relationship with the Haitian military, sometimes working with them for a common goal, other times existing in conflict.[16] That said, it is unrealistic to discount the motivation many people of color would have had for forming alliances.

It is also important to remember that there was a history of popular revolt in Santo Domingo at this time. In addition to the surprisingly understudied uprising on the Boca Nigua plantation in 1796, there were other signs of unrest. Raymundo González's excellent article on the "people eater" *(comegente)* or "unknown black" *(negro incógnito)* presents a wealth of primary-source documents to this effect. He outlines how in the last decades of the eighteenth century Crown officials, the church, and landowners decided to escalate the export economy. Once this decision was made, the dispersed rural population, many of them free blacks living independently in isolated areas of the mountains, became a threat precisely because they did not have "ties to an estate, cattle farm, or officially recognized person. A lack of affiliation became synonymous with vagrancy" ("lazos a una estancia, hato o persona de oficio reconocido. La falta de afiliación se convierte en sinónimo de vagancia"; R. González 209). A series of laws passed between 1792 and 1793 mandated the capture of "all of those persons, especially blacks, about whom you have the least suspicion" ("todas aquellas personas especialmente negros contra quienes alcanzasen la más leve sobspecha" *[sic]*).[17] This was quickly expanded to specifically include "foreign blacks" ("negros extranjeros"), most from the French part of the island. Through vagrancy, autonomy thus became criminalized in an attempt to root out suspicious elements and provide a ready and dependent labor pool to local hacendados.[18]According to González's sources, when rural violence moved close to the capital city of Santo Domingo, local slave owners formed a Junta of Proprietors / *Junta de Hacendados* to initiate roving patrols (194–98). In 1793, the Crown also appointed an official regulator, Pedro Catani, to investigate. Many of his reports to the state outlining his suspicions and frustrations have survived; they paint a rich picture of the Dominican underclass, and equally telling, the colonial government's anxiety about them. In one letter from April 1793, Catani vows to "clean this land of the lazy, vagabonds, drunks, and thieves . . . this class of men [that] doesn't have small plots, or any other honest calling with which to maintain themselves. . . . These are the ones who destroy haciendas, who kill cows, horses and other animals, causing big problems for the landowners . . . This state of affairs must be seen in order to be believed: it's a haunt of pícaros, without law, without religion. . . . And tell me sir, of what good are these kind of people in a republic?" (198–200).[19] By May of that same year, Catani claims that this aforementioned class of men is in part "animated by the example of the French" ("animados por el exemplo de los franceses") and that they are "infesting all of the roads and part of the mountains of the island, committing horrible murders ("han infestado todos los caminos y parte de los montes de la ysla [sic], cometiendo horribles asasinatos"; 202–03).

We thus have evidence of resistance and rebellion among residents of the east, however inconclusive the evidence may be about the alleged role of black "French" insurrectionists in events. Notably, the Crown viewed not only slaves but also free blacks as a threat. Perhaps the unfolding of events in the French side, where free people of color led the initial revolt against the white landowners, served as a cautionary tale. The lengths that these sectors of society were willing to go to in order to apprehend any "indolent" black shows just how tenuous freedom was in a slave-holding society. This makes the appeal of Haitian integration all the more understandable both for former slaves like Campos Taváres and for free people of color.

Arredondo's narrative provides anecdotal evidence that popular unrest continued throughout the 1790s and early years of the next century. He states that in 1799 "some anonymous papers called 'ensaladillas'" circulated throughout the city that were insulting to families of "virtuous" reputation and "full of insults and invective against the altar ministers" ("llenos de insultos y de invectivas contra los ministros del altar"; 126–27). He speculates that these attacks against the elite and the church, combined with the general "disorders that were beginning to be felt," were instigated by "lost people" ("gente perdida"). Just who constituted these forsaken people? With hindsight, considering this written propaganda indicative of the "calamities" to come, Arredondo notes that some of these same subversive materials began to be circulated in verse, "with worse and more indecent words" ("con peores y más indecentes palabras") and "malignant ideas" ("malignas ideas"; 127).[20]

Outlaws and assassins versus model citizens, "lost people" with dangerous ideas as opposed to families of good reputation: such are the dichotomies established in many accounts written about the Haitian Revolution by the white ruling class throughout the Caribbean. Old established Dominican families, many of whom could trace their antecedents back to the Conquest, fled, and many reestablished themselves in other parts of the Spanish Empire. One such refugee, Don José Francisco de Heredia y Mieses, documents the aftermath of the Treaty of Basle in his 1812 address to the Ayuntamiento. Heredia laments that

> this part of Hispaniola has suffered a series of calamities capable of ruining the best organized state, and even more so for a colony which had just started to enjoy . . . prosperity. . . . Her very rights to enjoy the respect of the government for having been the cradle of the Spanish Empire in the New World . . . did not save her from the sad fate of seeing herself ceded, as the cost of peace, to the new French Republic, which with its very name is an insult. . . . . All of the Spanish population resolved to emigrate to another soil and only those who absolutely could not stayed. . . . This island lost the biggest and best part of its civilized and hard-working population, and almost all of the circulating capital that gave it life.

> ha sufrido esta parte de la Española una serie de calamidades capaces de arruinar al estado mejor constituido, cuanto más a una colonia que apenas comenzaba a divisar aquella especie de prosperidad.... Sus justos derechos a la consideración del Gobierno por haber sido la cuna del imperio Español en este nuevo Mundo . . . no la salvaron de la triste suerte de verse cedida, en precio de la paz, a la nueva Republica Francesa, que solo con su nombre nos insultaba. . . . Toda la población española resolvió emigrar a otro suelo, y no lo hizo el que absolutamente no pudo. . . . Perdió la isla la mayor y mejor parte de su población civilizada y laboriosa, y casi todos los capitales que circulaban en ella y animaban su industria. (162)

I quote this firsthand account of the takeover to establish the shock felt by members of the upper-class "civilized" and "hardworking" oligarchy as they saw themselves changed into "miserable wretches" ("pobres miserables"). Heredia continues with the conclusion that the eastern part of Hispaniola "finds itself in a worse state today than at the time of our grandfathers because everything, or almost everything, must be built again and we don't have the million indigenous [workers] on which they could count on then" ("se halla hoy en peor estado que al tiempo de su ocupación por nuestros abuelos, porque todo o casi todo debe levantarse de nuevo, y no tiene el millón de indíjenas con que . . . se contaba entonces"; 165–66).[21] This candor regarding the frustration of the hacendados when confronted with the lack of a workforce, in this case both Native Americans and the newly emancipated people of African descent, is revealing. Class and race ideologies mandated a strict hierarchy that governed who was supposed to do what work. The idea of slave emancipation was one that Heredia and many of his station found disastrous.[22]

Arredondo provides one final example of the disturbing position in which the white elite found itself. He writes:

> We remained in this state tolerating an equality that we saw accompanied in all directions by ignominy and cruel threats, since the black officials now came forward to pursue relations with the principal señoritas of the country, with every step compromising family honor. . . . Some were able to leave the island for other parts of the Spanish monarchy at the cost of personal and financial sacrifices, humiliating themselves in front of the concubines of that monster [Dessalines] with copious flattery, so that they would mediate in the attainment of a passport, which is the only thing one needed to get away from a government sustained only by tyranny and where the worst of crimes was to be white and to have owned slaves.

> En este estado permanecimos tolerando una igualdad que veíamos acompañada por todas partes de la ignominia y de la cruel amenaza, pues ya se adelantaban los oficiales negros a pretender relaciones con las principals señoritas del país, comprometiendo a cada paso el honor de las familias . . . algunos pudieron lograr la salida de la isla para otros puntos de la monarquía española a fuerza de sacrificios personales y pecunarios, humillándose a las concubinas de aquel monstruo con gratificaciones cuantiosas, para que mediasen en la consecusión de un pasaporte, que era todo lo que se pretendía, para alejarse de un gobierno sostenido solo por la tiranía, y donde el primero de los delitos era ser blanco y haber tenido esclavos. (134)

Arredondo's distaste at being subject to "a government that was an enemy to our color" ("un gobierno enemigo de nuestro color"; 135) is palpable, as are his feelings of humiliation, rage, and helplessness. His diction is fascinating, especially the phrase "tolerating an equality." Rather than interpret equality as a concrete, hard-won political agenda in keeping with international debates about the nature of modernity, he experiences it as outrage on an individual level. Former slaves are disrespectful, and his very manhood is threatened, as he cannot protect the "maidens" ("señoritas") of his country from black suitors. He and many slave owners proved incapable of adjusting to the new order, where, according to articles 4 and 5 of the 1801 Haitian Constitution, "all men, regardless of color, are eligible to all employment [and] there shall exist no distinction other than those based on virtue and talent."

The Santo Domingo exiles cited above were thus against integration into one unified island state largely because it marked an end to the class and race advantages enjoyed by a relatively small percentage of the population. As they produced memoirs and essays about their experiences from abroad, they were greatly invested in how these events were presented, eager to write themselves as victims and/or valiant protectors of the homeland's way of life. When evaluating the larger import of the Haitian Revolution, Sybille Fischer elegantly asks, "What might have happened if the struggle against racial subordination had carried the same prestige and received the same attention from posterity as did the struggle against colonialism and other forms of political subordination? What might have happened if the prestige associated with racial equality equaled that of political independence?" (2–3). She concludes that "the suppression and disavowal of revolutionary antislavery and attendant cultures in the Caribbean was also a struggle over what would count as progress, what was meant by liberty, and how the two should relate" (24). These questions go to the heart of understanding how the Haitian Revolution was experienced as an actual event and how it was later wielded as an epistemological tool within Caribbean letters. The chasm of interpretation evident in the histories of Arredondo and Campos Taváres is clear, and it is the former's exegesis that has triumphed. Even in the present day, Arredondo's narrative has been reissued with the provocative promise of telling "the terrifying story of the genocides in Moca and Santiago, written by a survivor."[23] No studies have given Campos Taváres the in-depth attention his life merits.

Louverture's 1801 arrival and its accompanying social changes ended abruptly with the aforementioned landing of Napoleonic troops under the command of General Leclerc in 1802. As noted in Campos Taváres's speech, although the French eventually conceded defeat in the newly independent Haiti and abandoned the western coast, a small force refused to withdraw, staying in Santo Domingo and the Cibao under the leadership of generals Louis Ferrand and François Kerveseau. In total opposition to the ideals elaborated in General Laveaux's letter cited above, Ferrand encouraged residents of the former Spanish side to capture "insurgents" ("sublevados") of color, and an 1805 decree "authorized armed incursions into Haiti for the purpose of hunting black children less than fourteen years old to be sold as slaves in the colony and abroad" (Moya Pons, *Dominican Republic* 111).[24]

FIGURE 14. *Cristobal comandante del Ejercito, recorre la Isla de Santo Domingo incendiendo y matando a los infelices colonos de ella [Christophe, commander of the army, moves throughout the island of Santo Domingo burning and killing its unfortunate colonists].* Engraving. Louis Dubroca, *Vida de J.J. Dessalines, gefe de los negros de Santo Domingo con notas muy circunstanciadas sobre el origen, caracter y atrocidades de los principales gefes de aquellos rebeldes desde el principio de la insurrección en 1791* (Mexico: Mariano de Zúñiga y Ontiveros, 1806). Courtesy of the John Carter Brown Library.

Given the aggressive encroachments of their former masters, the Haitians once again entered the east under the command of Jean-Jacques Dessalines in 1805. Convinced that Haiti would never be free as long as a foreign power, especially their French ex-owners, still had a foothold on the island, Dessalines attempted to drive them out once and for all. It was at this moment that Campos Taváres definitively joined forces with the Haitians. Although it is appropriate to view these events as prompted by questions of national security, I believe that for the *indigène* army they were interpreted more personally. Destroying the French was a matter of physical security, personal and collective self-defense of the right to exist as free men and women. When they were forced to concede defeat and end the siege of the capital Santo Domingo prematurely, the Haitians destroyed the path of their retreat using the same guerrilla annihilate-and-burn strategy that had won them the war against France. This military maneuver is perhaps the most oft-cited justification of anti-Haitian sentiment to this day.[25]

Louis Dubroca, a French propagandist for Napoleon's regime, wrote a history of Dessalines that was translated and published in Spain (1804) and Mexico (1806). The volume includes an image of the former slave and future king of Haiti, Henri Christophe, burning the island during the course of the revolution (figure 14). I introduce this depiction of the merciless Haitian general because it accords well with Dominican descriptions of the 1805 encounters and provides a visual precedent for the "horrors of Saint-Domingue" genre of images produced later in the century, both in the Dominican Republic and elsewhere. The engraving foregrounds Henri Christophe holding a sword aloft in one hand and a torch in the other. Despite the elaborateness of his uniform, which includes embroidered cuffs and a plumed hat, his feet are bare and he wears a large hoop earring. His sword's scabbard hangs between his legs like an enormous phallus. Behind him several white male colonists plead for mercy as their children and womenfolk look on in fear. Juxtaposed to the strong black general, they appear weak and emasculated. Smoke pours from the buildings that have been set on fire, and crowds of people are running about in the background. The image leaves little to the imagination as the worst fears of white colonists are realized. In Dubroca's image, the colonists are iconographically caught "entre la espada y la pared" ("between the sword and the wall"), in this case a burning wall that marks the point of no retreat.

In his eyewitness testimony, Arredondo describes the "horrendous butchery" ("carnicería horrorosa") that marked the second siege of

Santiago de las Vegas, the largest city in the Cibao. Although he affirms that he and his colleagues were fighting alongside General Ferrand, Dessalines's/Haiti's fiercest enemy, the Haitians are depicted as unprovoked aggressors. The author loads his narrative with invective against "the brutes for whom the voice of pardon and pity was blasphemy" ("feroces para quienes la voz del perdón y de la misericordia era una blasfemia"). Verbs such as "sacking" ("saqueando"), "devouring" ("devorando"), and "throat-slitting" ("degollando") appear with frequency. His diatribes against the "tropa negra" ("black hordes") focus on the massacre of infants, young (virgin) women, and the elderly, much as was the case in the image above and in *Incendie du Cap; Révolte générale des nègres. Massacre des Blancs* (figure 1). He also repeatedly mentions that "the ground and the altars" ("el suelo y los altares") were stained with blood. Arredondo's likely exaggeration aside, the organized Catholic Church may have been singled out for vengeance given that the altars and priests emerged as targets for the Haitians, as demonstrated in Dessalines's speech, as well as the "lost people" native to the eastern territory.[26] I return to the importance of this possibility below.

When relating how a small group of landowners fought against the Haitian troops, he writes that "the native whites and all people of color, free or enslaved, were forced to take up arms against those that came from the outside" ("a los naturales blancos y a toda la gente de color, libres o esclavos, los obligaron a que tomaran las armas contra los que venían de afuera"; Arredondo 146). Once this mandate was enforced, eventually "the blacks were afraid and the following attack caused them to abandon their posts and disperse in disorder" ("los negros temieron y el suceso siguiente los redujo a dejar el puesto y a la disperción en desorden"; 146). If we read between the lines, a different possibility emerges. For those "obligated" to fight, desertion may have been motivated by a sense of common cause with the enemy as opposed to fear of them. General Campos Taváres is the perfect example, one provided by Arredondo's narrative itself.

The language of indigeneity served as a contested code for marking ideological positions and is thus key to understanding the stakes involved. Campos Taváres's above-cited assertions of belonging and the right to govern the land as one of its natives are noteworthy given that throughout Arredondo's narrative he deliberately designates his own white allies as the "naturales." Many white criollos identified with their native land and saw themselves as distinct from the metropolitan Spanish. As the white population felt more

threatened, however, even those with strong Dominican, nativist loyalties reverted to pretensions of Spanishness, understood as Catholic,
white, and "civilized." These pretensions on the cultural level had
political ramifications as well, as many residents solicited Spain to
occupy the country again, ushering in a twelve-year Spanish presence
colloquially referred to as the period of "la España boba" (1809–21).
The Dominican elite fought the logic inherent in claims of island indivisibility, preferring continued colonization to an independence affili-
ated with the Haitians.

The Haitians kept their sights on the east, however. Under the leadership of the newly elected president Jean-Pierre Boyer, himself a military veteran of the Haitian Revolution, they again succeeded in inte-
grating the island. Before Boyer's arrival, José Núñez de Cáceres, one
of the leaders of the Trinitario movement, had declared the eastern
part of the island independent in November of 1821. He named it the
Free State of Spanish Haiti and offered to place it under the control
of Bolívar's newly formed union of Gran Colombia.[27] This short-lived
independence was terminated in January of 1822, when Cáceres gave
up the keys to the capital to Boyer's army. The new integration would
last for twenty-two years.

THE MEANING OF FREEDOM

How did the Haitians come to integrate the entire island for twenty-
two years? While some Dominican historiography insists on the far
superior size of the Haitian forces, most often depicted as barbarous "hordas salvajes," historical reality was certainly more nuanced
(Balaguer, *Centinela* 9). I have shown that many inhabitants of the
east had vested interests in welcoming the arrival of their Western conquerors, as Boyer definitively abolished slavery throughout the island
in 1822. This act made Santo Domingo the first island in the Spanish
Caribbean to abolish slavery, predating Cuban and Puerto Rican abolition by more than fifty years.

Scholars rightfully observe that Dominican slavery was always
small in scale compared to the system in neighboring Saint-Domingue
and that most slaves were domestic ones. By inference the argument
follows that slavery was hence very "mild" and "familial." Such decep-
tive labels imply that the motivation for freedom would somehow be
less pressing. Similar assumptions about slaves' desires and motivations

appear in other American contexts. Consider the example of slaves in revolutionary-era North America. When presented with Lord Dunmore's 1775 promise of freedom if they fought for the British army, many slaves decided to adopt the loyalist cause as theirs. Their owners, heretofore convinced of their loyalty and contentment, were shocked by how quickly they decided to flee (Nash 26–35). A few years later, Mum Bett, subsequently known as Elizabeth Freeman, successfully sued the Massachusetts Legislature for her freedom. Though a domestic slave in New England, a place where slavery was reputedly milder than in the North American South, she was one of countless slaves who bore physical and psychological scars from years of forced servitude.[28] She eloquently stated, "Any time while I was a slave, if one minute's freedom had been offered to me, and I had been told I must die at the end of that minute, I would have taken it just to stand one minute on God's airth a free woman, I would" (Nash 22). We must take seriously this claim that freedom mattered, no matter the reputed "mildness" of slavery or the eventual contingencies that circumscribed its expression.

Dominican verses from the period corroborate this point succinctly. Similar to Campos Taváres's speech, the verses are an orally transmitted snapshot of black popular culture and were transcribed by a listening public.[29] They feature a Dominican slave woman asserting the value of her newly granted liberty.

So mercé no dice	Doesn't my mistress say
Que yo soy fea?	That I am ugly?
Pué yo me bá	Then I'm going
Y buque otra negra	And you can look for another
Pa trabajá	black woman to work
Dice mi señora	My mistress says
Que me va a bendé	That she's going to sell me
A Doña Ana Ponce	To Doña Ana Ponce
Que pringa con mié	Who will work me mercilessly
Levántate negra	Get up black woman
A hacé café,	Make some coffee
Levántese uté,	Get up yourself
Que estos no son los tiempos	These are no longer the times
De su mercé.	Of my mistress
Dios se lo pague	May God bless
A papá Boyé,	Papá Boyer
Que nos dió gratis	Who gave us freely
La liberté	Our liberty

Mocking her abusive mistress, the speaker tells her to "get up and make her own coffee," since her time as a member of the slave-holding elite has come to an end. In just a few lines she speaks of psychological abuse, a demanding owner, and living under the threat of being sold off if recalcitrant. The speaker affirms her worth as a racially oppressed subject on two levels. First, she acknowledges her value as a laborer who can no longer be forcefully compelled to work under degrading conditions. Second, she asserts her self-esteem as a woman who is unwilling to tolerate the abuse of others, notably two female mistresses, who use her skin color and vulnerable social status as an excuse for persecution.

The poem contains only one French word: *liberté*. It is arguably the most important, as it refers to the freedom granted to the community of slaves in the eastern part of the island by their French and French Creole-speaking neighbors to the west. The slave's grateful invocation of "Papá Boyé" refers to the aforementioned Haitian president Jean-Pierre Boyer. The French Revolution's ideals of "liberty, fraternity, and equality" were thus brought to bear as a reality for residents of the east via the Haitians. Given that the speaker's freedom resulted from Boyer's policies, it is clear that slavery continued during the seventeen intervening years between Dessalines's 1805 retreat and the Haitians' return. This time line makes Campos Taváres's military career especially telling. By the second decade of the 1800s he was serving as brigadier general and aide-de-camp under King Henri Christophe. He was the Haitian representative *to* his homeland in 1811 as opposed to *from* it. Most likely, he would have risked being re-enslaved had he returned to live in the east.

This slave woman's story is hence one of alliances between populations on both sides of the border. Her testimony substantiates the observations of a British observer of the time. T. S. Heneken reported that residents of Santiago actively "invited" Boyer's 1822 invasion. According to his testimony, "While Nuñez and the Francophiles conspired, Boyer watched them very closely and with the word of his spies he found out, to his great satisfaction, that among the black populations and the mulattos of the Spanish part of the island, there were individuals who desired annexation to Haiti, preferring Haiti to a badly organized Republic or a French protectorate" (390).

Given the decidedly masculinist, militarist nature of postrevolutionary life, it is all the more important to uncover how women on both sides of the border fit into the new body politic. Despite their struggles for the revolutionary cause, women in France and postrevolutionary

Haiti were not granted equal rights to men; gender inequality remained the norm.[30] For example, Mimi Sheller has convincingly argued that the postrevolutionary Haitian state routinely excluded women from public life and subjected them to second-class citizenship. She writes, "Article Nine of the first constitution states, 'No one is worthy of being a Haitian if he is not a good father, a good son, a good husband, and above all a good soldier,' foreshadowing the militarization of the state, the marginalization of women, and the depiction of citizens as male protectors of family and nation" ("Sword-Bearing Citizens" 244). As with emancipation enterprises throughout the hemisphere, freedom was contingent and partial, different from, yet too often chillingly familiar to life under slavery and patriarchy more generally.[31] It was a compromised freedom, and the Haitian case is no different, however much we hold Haiti to a higher standard because of its revolutionary struggle and official claims of black equality.

In the east, it still remains to be seen what role women may have played during the fierce battles against Ferrand's French occupying forces or in struggles against Spanish slave owners. Arredondo describes those of his class as having to "humiliate" themselves before Dessalines's lovers (whether Dominican or Haitian women it is unclear) in order to obtain passports and describes the shame of being forced to dance with one of his former female slaves while a black audience watched (132). One can tease out the quotidian ways that women exercised the shift in power relations. If we understand that the fundamental reality of freedom (to do what one wanted, when one wanted, in the company of one's choice) was always being negotiated, there are signs that these new Spanish-speaking Haitian *citoyennes* did see an improvement in their quality of life. Certainly for the female speaker in the poem this was the case. Her poetic praise-song is frozen in time, however, and her future experiences under an integrated island regime are unknown.

Unfortunately, narrative accounts of this twenty-two-year period from the point of view of both women and the nonruling elite more generally are rare.[32] Franklyn Franco is one of a small group of Dominican historians who have declined to take the complaints of planters such as Arredondo at face value. He argues that on a fundamental level Haitian rule marked "a reversal in the mode of production and the material structure of colonial society that inevitably brought about a new order on the level of social, political and economic relations" ("el viraje en el orden de las relaciones de producción, en la estructura material de la sociedad colonial, que iba a traer, irremisiblemente, todo un nuevo ordenamiento en el plano de las relaciones sociales, políticas y económicas"; *Negros* 79). Substantiating Heneken's firsthand account, he cites other texts that support this thesis. Even by the 1840s, when the Haitian presence was overwhelmingly unpopular, there were still those who preferred to reform the union rather than disintegrate it in the name of independence or recolonization under Spain or the United States.[33]

I conclude this discussion of the three attempts to unify the island during the first half of the nineteenth century by returning to the concept of Hispaniola as "one and indivisible." For the elite, a unified island signified the spread of both French revolutionary republicanism and intimate contact with the "disaster" next door as personified by former slaves-turned-Haitian generals. Consciously or unconsciously, they masked the political stakes of events by obsessing about the indignities they suffered in everyday life; they invoked the contrast between "pícaros" and their own "civilized" lifestyles as a barrier to integration. Language, in this case Spanish (as opposed to French or Creole), and religion (Catholicism as opposed to Vodou) stood as markers of difference from the "brutes" to the west. For slaves and free people of color, a unified island promised protection, liberty, and social advancement, the contours of which remained to be seen. As an individual, Campos Taváres can be seen as a symbol of both fear and potential. Shifting from historical personage to cultural icon, a discussion of *Haitian General on the March* also illustrates that where some saw the figure that most represented the destruction of the old regime, others saw armed justice and new possibilities.

HAITIAN GENERALS: OGOU ICONOGRAPHY ON BOTH SIDES OF THE BORDER

At this juncture, a closer examination of *General haitiano en marcha (Haitian General on the March)* is appropriate. Loaded with what I argue is unmistakably Vodou iconography, the image demonstrates how representations afford critical insight into how intraisland consciousness was articulated during the first half of the nineteenth century. The cultural artifacts and practices considered throughout this chapter extend our analytic scope beyond the language and symbols we've come to expect of revolutionary republicanism in the French style (liberty caps, secularism, and so forth) toward a set of native cultural texts. I continue my examination of iconography that employs some variation of the Haitian military uniform. While this uniform is portrayed derisively by foreign artists, it has been used in art produced in Hispaniola in a more nuanced way.[34] A comparative reading of the 1845 image with the work of renowned Haitian artist and religious leader André Pierre demonstrates how subversive the military uniform can be when read according to an alternative epistemological framework.

General haitiano en marcha has been classified as the earliest example of published caricature art in the Dominican Republic, and the image was published in the newspaper *El Dominicano* (Rodríguez Demorizi, *Pintura y escultura* 138). It was anthologized by the aforementioned historian Rodríguez Demorizi, who explained that the figure "represents a Haitian general on the march, overloaded with military braids, in contrast to his rustic sandals, which corresponds to reality, because the Haitian soldier of that epic was more preoccupied with his military decorations than with his shoes" (138). Rodríguez Demorizi's derisive commentary presents as fact rather than conjecture the idea that the image is a caricature, a statement that assumes that its intended purpose was to exaggerate, mock, and/or distort the figure it represented.[35] He further implies that the general is representative of all Haitian soldiers because of his presumed preference for military decorations over shoes. Clearly insignia that symbolize victory over an oppressive slave-holding system should not be cavalierly dismissed, however, and a lack of shoes is indicative of economic necessity, not an indicator of racial intelligence. By undermining the pride that Haitian soldiers may have placed in their uniforms, Rodríguez Demorizi subtly undermines their military prowess and questions their common sense. They become unshod savages dressed up for play.

The image depicts a man in an elaborate, long-sleeved military uniform that includes a waistcoat, knee britches, epaulettes, and a French-style tricorn hat (figure 10). A very long sword hangs from his waist; the angle at which it falls is suggestive of a tail. He smokes tobacco, and he has a large ring in his ear. His physical traits, while not portrayed as overtly grotesque, are slightly enlarged around the head and nose. Finally, as mentioned above, he drags an emaciated dog forcibly by the collar behind him. Perhaps Echavarría drew the dog as a symbol of the Dominican nation, literally strangled and oppressed while under Haitian rule. Of course, a black general dragging a dog, an animal that people of color the world over associated with slave-catching violence, also epitomized rebellion and power.

The image closely resembles the Dubroca engraving, as it incorporates the elaborate military uniform, exposed calves, large hoop earring, and prominent sword. Although Echavarría may have seen the earlier image, since it was available in the Spanish-speaking world, his work depicts some distinct differences. An observer versed in Afro-Caribbean religious systems could read certain symbols in very precise ways. The image is loaded with Vodou iconography, from the military uniform itself to the foods depicted.[36] Specifically, the general is shown carrying a pole with fish, corn, and plantains. All of these foods are used in ceremonies as offerings, or *manje lwa*, to the spirit deities. The presence of the cigar, the dog, and the sword are especially noteworthy, as they are associated with a specific *lwa*, the warrior Ogou.

What seems so obviously a representation of Ogou is telling. After all, who is this *lwa*, and what does he represent? In her introduction to a collection devoted to Ogun worship in Africa and throughout the Americas, Sandra Barnes writes: "Ogun is popularly known as the god of hunting, iron, and warfare. . . . In the minds of followers, Ogun conventionally presents two images. The one is a terrifying specter: a violent warrior, fully armed and laden with frightening charms and medicines to kill his foes. The other is society's ideal male: a leader known for his sexual prowess, who nurtures, protects, and relentlessly pursues truth, equity and justice" (2). Karen MacCarthy Brown, in her discussion of the *lwa*'s attributes in Haiti, explains that "the Ogou are soldiers or politicians. . . . [They] operate in extreme social situations—in difficult, trying, perilous times—and so the strength they exhibit in themselves and call forth in their devotees is the strength of someone pushed to the limit. . . . Ogou is a protective weapon for those who serve him . . . [tapping] the deepest source of human energy; anger, the final defiant refusal to admit defeat" (71–74). Finally, in her landmark study of Haitian Vodou, Maya Deren adds that "Ogoun is deity of fire and red is the color sacred to him. . . . Power too resides in the saber or machete which is sacred to [him]" (132–33).

Ogou's dress is frequently portrayed as military in keeping with his warrior status. Many scholars conjecture that in the years between the revolution and the reestablishment of the Catholic Church in Haiti in 1847, the Vodou religion solidified its base. Worshippers consequently incorporated much of the military regalia to be found in the country into ritual practices. Given that the uniform is a source of pride and symbol of independence, it is fitting that powerful *lwa* such as Ogou are depicted wearing it.[37] The Haitian Ogou is the military general par excellence, guarantor of justice in the face of overwhelming odds. It is thus no coincidence that major Haitian leaders such as Toussaint Louverture, Jean-Jacques Dessalines, and Jean-Bertrand Aristide have all been iconographically shown as Ogou.[38] This *lwa* makes a strong statement about the political ambience of any given time—he sends a message of might, not of compromise; of power, not submission. Patrick Polk suggests that "depictions of Ogou as St. James Major are emblematic of military and spiritual triumph in much the same way as photo-reproductions of embattled U.S. marines. They represent a shining moment in victory: a defining point not just for a nation's military power, but for its citizens' conceptions of self" (347).[39]

The equation of an image with a community's conception of self is helpful when evaluating *General haitiano en marcha*. Many of Ogou's attributes correspond to Echavarría's image: the show of military might, the presence of fire, certain ritual foods, and a saber, representing the *lwa*'s dominion over iron. Why would an 1845 image read so readily as a representation of Ogou? This very ambiguity makes the image engaging. If it were meant to poke fun at Haitians, why use the iconography associated with one of the most powerful, militaristic *lwa*? It is not far-fetched to conjecture that Echavarría was familiar with the outward symbols of Vodou practitioners given the long history of population movements between the two sides of the island. Hence he may have known that corn, tobacco, and dogs were among the ritual foods served to various *lwa*, even if he did not specifically associate them with Ogou. While he perhaps signified on this knowledge for satirical ends, it is debatable whether much of the Dominican-Haitian population of the time period would necessarily have read the image as insulting. Rather, it could have been self-affirming for practitioners of Vodou, residents of the east and west. Cultural interchanges, including religious practices, were likely some of the strongest manifestations of free, runaway and enslaved populations' engagements with each other for generations.

Further discussion concerning spiritual practices on the island is apropos. As evidence that religious interchanges were occurring, several historians of Dominican religion have cited the 1862 edict from the Bando de Policía y Buen Gobierno. The edict states that because "disorders and scandals are being very frequently committed in the so-called dances *holandés, danois, tango, bambulá,* and *judú,* they are prohibited and can occur only if one obtains a license from the authorities. . . . The dance called *judú* is prohibited" ("siendo muy frecuentes los desórdenes y escándolos que se cometen en los denominados bailes holandés, danois, tango, bambulá y judú, quedan prohibidos y solo podrán verificarse obteniendo una licencia de la autoridad. . . . Queda prohibido el baile llamado judú"; Deive, *Vodú* 163). Carlos Esteban Deive and Martha Ellen Davis read the very existence of such edicts as proof that Dominicans were practicing the religious dances associated with Vodou in the 1860s, if not earlier. Popular poetry from the 1860s on confirms the participation of Dominicans in Vodou ceremonies. Juan Antonio Alix (1833–1918), arguably the most famous *décima* poet of the Dominican Republic, authored several selections that refer to the practice of Vodou in the Dominican Republic at the turn of the century.[40] In his oft-cited poem "Las bailarinas del judú en la calle Santa Ana," he sings of how the police entered one of these "fandangos africanos," where they "surprised four women, who danced *judú* with great pleasure along with a Haitian" ("sorprendió cuatro mujeres, que bailaban con placeres, el judú con un haitiano"). Describing the altar in front of which they danced, he states that "on that altar, there was a roasted plaintain, corn and toasted peanuts" ("en aquel altar, había un plátano asado, maíz y maní tostado"). The food items cited are in large part the ones in the Echavarría image, and interestingly the participants in the ceremony are women: three are Dominican and one is from "la tierra borinqueña [Puerto Rico]" (Alix, *Décimas* 44–45). The fact that women surround the Haitian, and that one of the women in the poem enters into a trance, suggests that they were *ounsis*, the female dancing *serviteurs* of the *lwa*. Alix closes by warning that "al fin comeremos gente, si Dios no mete su mano" (45). This popular reference to the act of "comer-gente" equates Haitians with cannibalism and satanic religion. Of course Dominicans, like the *comegente / negro incognito* discussed below, are also implicated. Whatever else might be said about the anti-Haitian sentiments revealed in Alix's poetry, there is no denying his intimate knowledge of Haitian culture. His characters speak Creole, regularly cross the border for trade, and are knowledgeable about many aspects of everyday life, including cuisine and festivities.

Many Dominican historians downplay these expressions of transborder culture, however, asserting that only Haitians resident in the country, and not Dominicans themselves, participated in these rites. These are the eternal questions that underlie any discussion of Dominican religion—Was there a native Afro-Dominican practice that evolved alongside Haitian Vodou in the Dominican Republic? If so, how was it similar to or different from the ritual practices of its neighboring religion? If Alix is to be believed, Dominicans did indeed have their own version of this religion. In the *décima* "Los Brujos y Adivinos Expendedores de Guangua," he warns that "now there is no choice but to emigrate to faraway lands because there are Dominicans with such powerful *guangua*, we have them here now, worse than the Haitians" ("Ya no hay más sino emigrar / para paises lejanos / Porque hay dominicanos / tan Fuertes con el guanguá / Que aquí los tenemos ya / Peores que los Haitianos"; 98). *Guangua* or *ouanga* in this case derives from the Central African / Bantu *nganga*, a term for an object that serves as a weapon against one's enemies. An 1802 dictionary assembled by a Saint-Domingue exile describes it as a "charm or sorcery" ("charme ou sorcilège"; Baudry de Lozieres). It is a term usually associated with witchcraft or black magic. In contrast to Santo Domingo, where Catholicism was the only tolerated religion, Haiti, in successive constitutions, beginning with Dessalines's Constitution of 1805, guaranteed freedom of religious worship. Despite this guarantee, the Haitian state has had a long and vexed relationship with Vodou, and campaigns to attack its practitioners date back to the revolutionary era and the founding years of the nation.[41]

A debate from the last years of the integration period demonstrates how religion became a point of contention between inhabitants of the island. The Haitian historian Madiou notes that during deliberations surrounding the proposed 1843 Constitution, delegates from the eastern provinces raised objections to this guarantee and used it as one justification for wishing to separate from Haiti. Madiou writes, "They demanded, without success, that the Catholic, Apostolic and Roman religion be declared the state religion; their Spanish education had led them to consider that all religions freely practiced, recognized, and protected were an instrument of decadence and degeneracy" ("Ils avaient demandé sans succès, que la religion catholique, apostolique et romaine fût déclarée celle de l'Etat; leur éducation espagnole les portait à considérer tous les cultes librement exercés, reconnus et protégés, comme un instrument de décadence et de dégénérescence"). We have seen that decades earlier elite residents of Santo Domingo were already decrying the assault on their altars and proclaiming that a presumed black religiosity embodied all that was a threat to their civilization.[42] Madiou concludes that "despite the efforts of the eastern deputies," the assembly approved article 28, stating that "all religions are equally free. Everyone has the right to profess and freely exercise his religion provided that it does not disturb the public order" ("Tous les cultes sont également libres. Chacun a le droit de professer sa religion et d'exercer librement son culte pourvu qu'il ne trouble pas l'ordre public"; Madiou 8: 81).

Thus the revolutionary new order that pervaded the east spoke not simply in the language of antislavery appeals or republicanism but through an official policy of religious tolerance that may have opened up a space to worship previously proscribed deities. The people engaged in the struggle to unite the island politically also brought their spiritual beliefs and intermingled them with those that they found locally. For example, the soldiers and bureaucrats who made integration a reality used a set of religious cultural texts that had crossed the ocean from Africa and were creolized in Hispaniola as manifestations of Ogou. This mobilization of the *lwa* for political ends has been demonstrated in Sheller's aforementioned work on postrevolutionary society on the island. She writes of how "the national [Haitian] symbol, appearing on the flag and on coins, was a palm tree, symbol of liberty throughout the Caribbean, topped with the republican liberty cap, and surrounded with a bristling array of spear-tipped banners, cannon, bayonets, and military drums. . . . The vèvè for Ogou Feray is an abstraction of the Haitian coat of arms" ("Sword-Bearing Citizens" 244–45). A vèvè is a ritual image drawn on the ground and used in Vodou ceremonies to invoke the deities; its integration into official objects demonstrates how popular spirituality undergirded state practices. Importantly, a philosophy of integration into a strong black state, symbolized visually, was available to the illiterate as well. This latter fact is especially important, given that even editors of the aforementioned *El Dominicano* acknowledged that the paper faced the challenge that "here no one writes because no one reads, and no one reads because no one writes" ("Aquí no se escribe porque nadie lee, y no se lee porque nadie escribe"; F. Franco, *Cultura* 114).

Many scholars have examined how Haitian rule was implemented and how it worked its way into Dominican national consciousness. We have seen how even the "name of the French republic was an insult" to many. Antimonarchical beliefs, atheism, and abolition became the imported bogeymen from the west. It goes without saying that the Haitian period was about the perceived threat not only of French culture but of African culture as well. Fischer describes the process of disavowal that occurred, a deliberate attempt to suppress the tenets of radical antislavery and the modernization associated with the Haitians. While for much Dominican historiography and literary production this means gross generalizations about dangerous black men who lived to do no more than rape and massacre innocent Dominican women, we must question what Africanist influences actually meant ideologically.[43] Religion is a case in point. The assumption that the Haitian state imported a French republican secularism is only part of the picture. Evidently there were communities that found African-derived, creolized religions a potent force of common community markers.

Returning to the image at hand, one can speculate about its reception among audiences of the 1840s. The ambiguity remains. Echavarría may have expressly depicted the Haitian military general as a *lwa* to symbolize power and adaptation to the local environment (hence the sandals). Rather than an example of disdainful political caricature, the image can be read as a multifaceted, iconographic confirmation of the centrality of Haitian political and cultural presence in Dominican life. Conversely, Vodou's reputation as witchcraft in the minds of an extended American public was damning in and of itself. As tales of bloodthirsty slaves killing their former masters circulated, the Haitian Revolution was linked to tales of black magic and sorcery. Hence associating the Haitian military general and his uniform with any Afro-Caribbean religion could have been Echavarría's way of perpetuating negative stereotypes of the "African savages" and their struggling nation. Threatened by the interconnectedness of populations on both sides of the border, Echavarría and commentators of his work may have needed to ridicule the very attribute that led to the formation of the unified Haitian-Dominican state—a military struggle that successfully defeated the combined forces of metropolitan France, Spain, England, and native French and Spanish creoles. Regardless of the intentions of the artist, the image was undeniably capable of evoking mixed reactions among its public.

A brief discussion of the sacred art of Vodou provides a relevant point of comparison. The work of Haitian painter and *oungan* André Pierre illustrates how the Haitian uniform has been employed toward an end that is anything but satirical and mocking.[44] Although painted over a century later, Pierre's calabash *Ogoun Badagry* (figure 15) is strikingly similar to the aforementioned Dominican image *General haitiano en marcha* (figure 10). While the Echavarría representation is facing east (toward the Dominican Republic) and Pierre's to the west

FIGURE 10. Domingo Echavarría, *General haitiano en marcha* (1845). From page 50.

FIGURE 15. André Pierre, *Ogoun Badagry* (ca. 1950s). Painted calabash. Collection of Halvor and Astrid Jaeger. Reproduced in *Sacred Arts of Haitian Vodou*, ed. Donald Cosentino (Los Angeles: UCLA Fowler Museum of Cultural History, 1995).

(toward Haiti), both figures are depicted smoking tobacco that emits a great deal of smoke, both have swords at their waists suspended from a sash crisscrossed around the chest, and both wear heavily decorated, long-sleeved shirts. Pierre's Ogou wears a sombrero rather than French-style headgear. Because the calabash is painted in color, the red scarves and red-sheathed sword of Ogou are immediately recognizable. The upturned bottle in his right hand connotes this *lwa*'s love of rum, and the sword/machete's placement to the front of the hip eliminates the potential tail-like monkey effect that comes across in the Dominican print. These differences in detail subtly shift the overall impact of the works so that Pierre's calabash lacks the negative connotations that can be read into Echavarría's.

Despite these dissimilarities, however, the resemblance between the two pieces is undeniable. The symbolism present in both can be deconstructed toward different ends depending on an observer's epistemological framework. Pierre, a Vodou practitioner, uses the ritual trappings of his religion, including the Haitian military uniform, to express veneration. In the case of Echavarría's image, the uniform is an emblem of either respect or ridicule.

GUANGUA PANGNOL PI FORT PASÉ OUANGA HAITIEN

I close with a discussion of the *comegente*, or the *negro incógnito*, a figure of Dominican legend that relates to the story at hand. The story has been preserved in historical documents, orally transmitted tales, and popular literature. The *comegente* provides a vivid example of how intraisland politics, revolutionary generals, and popular religion merge in Dominican cultural production. In its various versions, the story centers on a black serial killer who terrorized the Dominican countryside, probably between 1790 and 1793.[45] Interestingly, the environs of La Vega and Santiago seem to have been the location for most of his crimes. The Cibao thus emerges once again as the heart of rebellion and unrest, despite the efforts of later historians to claim it as the country's idealized white heartland.

The earliest records of the *comegente* date from the time of his alleged activities. A 1792 manuscript attributed to Padre Pablo Francisco de Amézquita y de Lara, a native Dominican, provides a summary of his activities and a list of his victims, their locations, and the nature of their deaths and injuries. Francisco Mariano de la Mota made a copy of Amézquita's manuscript in 1867, and this copy was reprinted several times in the nineteenth century, and then again in the 1930s and 1940s during the Trujillo dictatorship. In his analysis of the *comegente* story, Raymundo González includes excerpts from the memos of many official Crown and municipal authorities that corroborate much of the information found within Amézquita's version. The tale was also incorporated into *Episodios dominicanos,* an unpublished, undated story by Casimiro N. de Moya. After an examination of the 1790s material, I concentrate on Moya's reinterpretation. It is of special interest because the tale's narrator presents the *comegente* as a character reviled for his sadism, his cannibalism, and his ties to Haiti; however, he is simultaneously converted into a hero capable of foiling the plans of two of the most powerful Haitian generals, Henri Christophe and Jean-Jacques Dessalines. He accomplishes this feat by using a Dominican *guangua* that is "much more potent" ("pi fort pasé") than anything produced in the western part of the island. Like Alix, then, he confirms not only the practice but the perceived power and efficacy of African-derived religion among the Dominican campesino population.

The 1792 manuscript claims that the *comegente* was of African birth, though of what "nación" the chronicler is unsure. Whether African or creole, the unknown *negro* is said to have burned homes, destroyed fields, and killed both people and animals, the latter always described as "defenseless people" ("gentes indefensas") such as the elderly, women, children, and the infirm (Rodríguez Demorizi, *Tradiciones* 269). Over the course of a few years twenty-five people were killed and another twenty-nine wounded. The *comegente*, while presented in the manuscript as extremely cowardly, was also incredibly difficult to apprehend, although he was pursued relentlessly over the course of a few years. According to Amézquita, he was finally captured by rural residents and their dogs and was executed in Santo Domingo. Another contemporary source notes that before his execution he was instructed in "the sacred dogmas of Our Sainted Religion because he was an idolater" ("los sagrados Dogmas de Nuestra Santa Religion, a causa de ser idólatra"; Catani, letter dated December 18, 1793, qtd. in R. González 206). I mention this historical reference to his perceived idolatry given the persistent mention of non-Catholic spirituality. As we shall see in Moya's text, the *comegente* was assumed to be a practitioner of an African-derived religion and was rumored to have "much wisdom" "mucha sabiduria"; 187). Accounts from the 1790s confirm that the local population attributed supernatural powers to him and that the Crown did its best to downplay such subversive ideas (R. González 180–81, 185–86).

I wish to properly emphasize the nature of the crimes attributed to this unknown black man. Many victims were slaves ("una mulatica de D. Agustín de Moya, un negrito de Victoriano Sanchez . . ."), all remaining nameless and noted only as someone's property. Other victims were named and identified as both free people of color and whites. Moya works these victims into his narrative as well, citing them by name. The gory details of the murders and mutilations are astonishing; the crimes perpetrated against women are particularly horrific. A characteristically detailed list of his victims notes how some were "cut up, others split open, from the sternum to the pubis, a pole driven through their private parts, some hands cut off, the heart cut out and [some] faces covered with their own entrails; from another he ripped out all of the pubic area and clitoris. . . . He made off with all of the parts that he cut off" ("unos cortados, otros abiertos, desde el hueso esternón hasta el pubis inclusive, clavado un palo por sus pudendas, cortada alguna mano, sacado el corazón y cubierto todo el rostro con sus mismas entrañas; otro le arrancaba todo el pubis y clitoris. . . . Se llevaba todos los miembros que cortaba"; Rodríguez Demorizi, *Tradiciones* 271).

It is critical to contextualize the *comegente*'s violence, as it was part and parcel of a sadistic society that mutilated its victims as a matter of control. As we have seen, torture in its various guises was an integral part of slave-holding societies. One Spanish *cédula*, for instance, remarked "that it was convenient to apply severe laws that ranged from whipping to the brutal castration of genital organs" ("Era conveniente . . . aplicar leyes severas que fueran desde la pena del látigo hasta la extirpación brutal de los órganos genitales").[46] Considering the lurid nature of the claims, it is also important to study Amézquita's text more particularly as a product of the 1790s. As always, when discussing the question of violence in the era of the Haitian Revolution, it is easy to fixate on well-publicized examples (the alleged white baby immolated on a stake is the most well known) and forget the quotidian violence of slave-holding societies that might provoke extreme violence in turn. That said, the text stands out among other eighteenth-century Caribbean texts that document extreme torture because of its graphic depiction of the sexualized mutilation of the body. Like the witnesses for whom there were no words to describe "the compassion we felt at the sight of the cadavers, so impiously destroyed" ("la compasión que nos causa la vista de los cadávares, tan impiamente destrozados"), a reader cannot remain unaffected by the image painted of the victims' bodily remains (271).

It is thus difficult to ascertain what may have been either extremely psychopathic, misogynistic behavior or revolutionary intent on the *comegente*'s part; the two things probably were not mutually exclusive. As we saw in the previous chapter, it is a well-documented strategy of the dominant classes to criminalize the insurgency and to understand revolutionary warfare as pathological and/or criminal insanity. Burning homes and fields does not at face value make the unknown negro a "monster." Many of the victims listed in Amézquita's appendix were killed in August 1791, which is suggestive given that the initial revolts in Saint-Domingue occurred that month and year. In this environment, an anonymous black man killing in what appeared to be an indiscriminate manner was extremely alarming to the authorities, as it could have indicated rebellion against the dominant economic and social system in the eastern part of the island. Significantly, Catani, the aforementioned head of the search party sent to investigate criminal activity in the environs of Santo Domingo, concluded that there was not one *comegente*, but many. A free black was eventually convicted for the crimes and executed, but authorities believed that he had accomplices throughout the island, even others who might have used his example as inspiration for their own activities. Catani firmly believed that "esta clase" of people whom he so reviled were in league with one another, posing a danger to the whole island.

I'd like to linger on the implications of this story for Caribbean historiography. Whereas in other parts of the Caribbean and North America there are well-studied conspiracies and revolts, such as José Aponte's activities in Cuba or Denmark Vessey's in South Carolina, there is no corresponding set of well-known examples in colonial Santo Domingo. The rebellions on the Columbus estates in the early sixteenth century and the revolts on the Boca Nigua plantation are the exceptions to the rule. Black revolt and revolutionary events are usually associated, not with Dominicans themselves, but with blacks from "afuera," the Haitians and the revolution they brought with them. Is it coincidence that in a colonial society that prided itself on having practiced a paternalistic, family-oriented form of slavery, vengeful violence of the *comegente*'s nature is inexplicable? As work such as Raymundo González's demonstrates, evidence of popular black revolt is available. If the fight against slavery had come to occupy the same importance in the Dominican Republic as struggles for independence from Spain or Haiti, then perhaps the Dominican "unknown black" would be memorialized, or at the very least studied, in the same way that Haiti's anonymous *nègre marron* has come to symbolize Haitian freedom. At the very least, we would see interesting parallels between the *comegente* and other black freedom fighters of the era. For example, accounts of the *comegente* have fascinating parallels with that of Macandal, the former slave who led a poisoning campaign in 1750s Saint-Dominguc. In popular accounts of both, they were masters of guerrilla warfare aided by a network of accomplices, and their magical abilities gave them shape-shifting powers and made them virtually impossible to track.

These speculations aside, I now return to Moya's short story. His text borrows generously from earlier sources, especially the 1792 account, while making some interesting adaptations. To begin with, the *comegente* is named Luis Beltrán. Moya describes him as a free black from Santiago de los Caballeros who begins to commit his crimes in the early 1790s. He is physically attractive, able to read and write, and Moya writes that he decides to "go and learn something in the French part of the island" ("irse a aprender algo en El Frances"; 177). Settling in Limbé, he works as an overseer on a French plantation, where he comes into contact with Carabali slaves. These slaves teach him their "witchcraft" ("brujerias"). Once he exceeds them in power, they put a spell on him in an effort to be rid of his presence. Losing his mind, Beltrán returns to his homeland, where he starts "setting fire to houses in the countryside and tobacco farms" ("pegando fuego a algunas casas de campo y ranchos de tabaco"; 178), attacking those in power and making off with their slaves.

Moya's text thus puts Beltrán at the center of popular revolt in Saint-Domingue during the 1790s. What do we make of his settlement in Limbé, a region of revolutionary activity in the Northern Plains associated with Bois Caïman, the site of the Vodou ceremony that is credited with unleashing the floodgates of revolution? As in Catani's official report to the Crown, there was a presumed relationship between free blacks and the "brigands" from the western part of the island. Presumably a contemporary Dominican reader was supposed to draw the conclusion that connections with colonial Saint-Domingue, specifically with African-born *bosales*, were the source of "contamination" for Beltran.[47] The revolutionary, bloodthirsty fervor of the neighboring colony infected his reason and somehow explains his belligerence upon returning; "El Frances" stands in for sorcery and aggression. Even at this early stage, though, the author suggests that Beltrán's capabilities exceeded those of his evil mentors and could not be contained.

Like so many nineteenth-century Dominican tales, certain historical events are reworked into new forms, usually to sensationalist effect. This is the case for Haiti-identified offenses in particular, for example the oft-decried massacres at Santiago and Moca and the murders of the Virgins of Galindo, events that occurred around the 1805 Haitian military campaign. The *comegente*'s serial appearances over the course of several centuries are in keeping with this tradition, and Moya's invention of Beltrán's supposed ties to Haiti could be interpreted as part of the Dominican nationalist discourse of Haitian aggression, in this case perpetrated through a dangerous Dominican black.

While following the formulaic plot of the dangerous Haitians/Africans and their "brujeria," however, the story takes an unusual direction. *El comegente* becomes a hero of sorts, his miraculous abilities capable of defeating the powerful Haitian generals most often associated with violent depredations against the Dominican people. A local Dominican wins the day and by inference saves his *patria*. To convert the *comegente* into an unlikely nationalist savior, Moya employs a literary framing technique that begins and ends with scenes of storytelling. The year is 1842, and in a small Dominican village a group of multigenerational Dominicans listens eagerly to the story as presented by a community elder, Señó Domingo. The storyteller claims acquaintance with the killer's family and details many of his attributes, including Beltrán's mystical ability to disappear and travel long distances in an instant, his overpowering odor, and his uncanny knack of eluding the authorities by disappearing whenever his feet touch water. After regaling (disgusting) his young audience with vivid descriptions of the *comegente*'s vicious crimes, he explains that a local *montero*, or rural peasant, finally managed to capture the *comegente* by hunting him with dogs and tying him up with a magical *bejuco*.

Señó Domingo adds a coda to the tale, and this coda bears closer attention. Titled "The *Comegente*'s Will" ("El Testamento del Comegente"), the conclusion gives the history of the unknown *negro* relevance in the present moment of the narrative. Supposedly the trunk of a certain tree bears inscriptions that none of the locals has ever been able to read. Years after his death, in 1805 to be exact, Generals Henri Christophe and Dessalines enter a secluded woods where they stumble upon these inscriptions. Summoning their most powerful *Papa bocó*, a Vodou authority who accompanied the Haitian army on its travels, they ask him to interpret the meaning of the words.[48] The *bocó* immediately begins to cry and shake, removing his hat (and requiring Henri Christophe to do the same) as a mark of respect toward the being that once inscribed the words before him. The *comegente*'s will warns that "they haven't caught me and they never will" ("ni me han cogido ni me cogerán"; 190).

The will proceeds to claim that in fifty years' time the *comegente*'s granddaughter will emerge from a spring and have mystical powers of her own. He warns, "Health and science for those who respect me, pain and death for those who reject me" ("Salud y ciencia para los que me respetan; dolor y muerte para los que renieguen de mi"; 191). The *bocó* then remarks in Haitian Creole, "Oh tragedy, oh tragedy my son, Spanish *guangua* is much stronger than Haitian *ouanga*" ("Ah malher, malher, mon fils a mouin! Guangua pangnol pi fort pasé ouanga haitien"). In case his audience of Haitian soldiers is slow to catch on, the *bocó* informs them that "the land that produced such a wizard was a land superior to their own and that as a consequence, he considered it temerity to try to conquer it, as while they might have a surprise victory at the beginning, they would pay for it dearly in the long run" ("la tierra que produjo lo necesario para domar al boude era tierra superior a la de ellos, y por consiguiente consideraba una temeridad el tratar de conquistarla, pues si por la sorpresa se podía conseguir un triunfo al principio, a la larga lo pagarían muy caro"; 193). His final advice: leave the Dominicans alone and never dare to cross the Massacre River that divides the territories again. In a surprised rage, Henri Christophe relates this news to his superior, General Dessalines, and the two decide to retreat from the east, destroying everything in their wake and "never daring to return."

The story ends with the wide-eyed listeners hopeful that "our *guangua* was stronger than theirs. . . . It could be that the *Papa bocó* was right and who knows, perhaps the day approaches of proving it fully" ("nuestro guangua era más fuerte que el de ellos. . . . Senores puede ser que ese Papa boco tuviera razon y quien sabe si esta ya cercano el dia de probarlo plenamente"; 194–95). The frame narrative is set during the last years of Haitian integration, and it allows the listeners and the readers to hope that independence from Haiti is on the horizon. Beltrán's mystical daughter is predicted to reappear in fifty years, and not surprisingly, the end of the story marks the passage of that time exactly. Her birth presages the birth of a new nation. The figure of Luis Beltrán, he who "will never be truly caught," thus serves as a contradictory source of inspiration. A perverted outlaw, he also serves as a symbol for a homeland that can never be dominated by Haitian military invaders.

In a classic case of having one's cake and eating it too, Dominicans assert that they don't practice magic but that if they did it would be more powerful than that practiced by the Haitians. There is thus a simultaneous disavowal and embrace of this figure and the power he represents. Only something supernatural in strength could vanquish the Haitians; a black man who terrorizes the country and is associated with everything dark and violent is also the weapon against blacks from the other side of the border. Black counterculture is narrowly construed as having nationalist potential. The usual equation of "good, Catholic" religion versus "dangerous, satanic" ritual is disrupted somewhat, and mystical practices, such as they are portrayed in the text, are a viable location for dissent and resistance. However, the reader is left in no doubt that *guangua* is still witchcraft, and there is never an acknowledgment of the value of alternative religious cosmologies that flourished on both sides of the border.

It is tempting to see irony in the Dominican recourse to black spiritual warfare. Rather than irony, however, I see a glimpse of something more important. Moya's *comegente* demonstrates that at the moment when the Dominicans are using black spirituality as a weapon, at the moment he becomes their hope of redemption, one cannot tell the two sides apart. That is, for a brief interlude it is impossible to tell what distinguishes the opposing factions. Transcolonial collaborations on the island create this moment of possibility. They enable Campos Taváres's life story as well. Although conflicts on both sides of the border make this moment unsustainable, the fragments themselves are illuminating. They point to how the attempted consolidation and expansion of the Haitian state provided a multifaceted language for asserting new forms of black subjectivity.

CHAPTER 3

"Negroes of the Most Desperate Character"

Privateering and Slavery in the Gulf of Mexico

In August 1817, a customs officer in New Orleans named Beverly Chew voiced grave concerns about the smuggling activity occurring in the Gulf of Mexico. In a letter to William Crawford, the U.S. secretary of the Treasury, he wrote: "I deem it my duty to state that the most shameful violations of the slave acts, as well as our revenue laws, continue to be practiced with impunity, by a motley mixture of freebooters and smugglers at Galveston, under the Mexican flag, being in reality little less than the re-establishment of Lafitte's [sic] Barataria bands, somewhat more out of reach of justice. . . . The establishment was recently made there by a Commodore Aury, with a few small schooners from Aux Cayes, manned in a great measure, with refugees from Barataria, and mulattos. . . . On the part of these pirates we have to contend with, we behold an extended and organized system of enterprise, of ingenuity, of indefatigability, of audacity" (Bollaert 439–40). The details included in the letter are incredibly rich. Chew's warning encompasses many of the most high-profile actors and events concerning the privateering world in the Gulf of Mexico during the first decades of the nineteenth century.[1] While the geographic points named here may now be less well known, Chew's combination of Spanish, soon to be Mexican Texas (Galveston), the newly admitted state of Louisiana (Barataria), and postrevolutionary Haiti (Aux Cayes) in one breathless litany demonstrates how a transcolonial black market economy thrived between various Gulf Coast communities. The U.S. government had long been aware of the activities of these smugglers. For example, in a letter from March 1813, former governor of Louisiana W. C. C. Claiborne cautioned that "an organized plan, for introducing Slaves & Merchandize into this State illegally, was formed on Lake Barataria, & with such combinations as to render Military and Naval aid essential . . ." (Claiborne to Wilkinson, Rowland 6: 216). Claiborne elsewhere expressed great concern about how visitors in New Orleans associated with the Barataria community included "some St. Domingo negroes of the most desperate character, and no worse than most of their white associates" (Claiborne to Andrew Jackson, September 20, 1814, Bassett 2: 56). Due east of these smuggling settlements in Barataria and Galveston Island, the same French commodore Aury was also setting up business in Florida. A contemporary eyewitness of his operations fearfully announced that "his great dependence . . . is upon about one hundred and thirty brigand negroes—a set of desperate bloody dogs. . . . Aury's blacks make their neighborhood extremely dangerous to a population like ours." Another observer saw "African rowers ferrying slaves from ship to shore almost continuously," believing that "Aury sold more than one thousand Africans in less than two months . . ." (Landers, *Black Society* 245–46).

This chapter explores the complex histories that occasioned the "desperate" character of these "brigand negroes." In them we glimpse the circumscribed choices free people of color made at a moment when revolutionary activity both abetted and hindered their advancement. A hemispheric fear of French negroes simmers in these comments. The idea of desperation likewise provides a glimpse into the needs and fears of black people themselves. Yet what should also draw our attention in the above commentaries is that these black privateers were actively engaged in the most lucrative business of the time: slave trafficking. Hence, as opposed to the usual association of Saint-Domingue with slave revolution, this "motley" group of smugglers was collaborating with infamous privateers such as the Laffite brothers and Louis-Michel Aury to illicitly sell African men and women into bondage.

While the changeover from Saint-Domingue to Haiti inevitably invokes a trajectory of slavery to freedom, most studies of the Haitian Revolution show time and again that free people of color and slaves belonged to distinct social castes and that they were often in conflict. The shifting alliances, constant negotiations, and strident violence between black revolutionaries are as critical to our understanding of the revolution as the major conflict between French slaveholders and black insurgents. I believe that these struggles are equally important for an examination of the Saint-Domingue diaspora. In many hemispheric American societies, free people of color functioned as a buffer group in a tripartite hierarchy, living in what one observer called "a useful intermediary state between slavery and freedom" ("un état mitoyen entre l'esclavage et la liberté"; Moreau, "Discours sur les affranchis" 3). In addition to occupying the role of skilled artisans, they provided stability to the system by serving in the colonial militia and acting as policing agents, especially in their role as fugitive slave catchers. Hence they served to "keep the outside enemy at bay and contain the enemy within" ("repousser l'ennemi du dehors, à contenir ceux du dedans"; 3). The notion that "blackness" was in and of itself enough to unify people and trump critical differences in socioeconomic circumstances is an anachronistic idealization.

My discussion of transcoloniality brings intrablack class conflict into focus. These intrablack tensions in turn provide more evidence that transcolonial endeavors were often no more emancipatory than the imperial and national powers that gave birth to and succeeded them. Universal black liberty and equality was rarely a priority for the actors I study here. Black figures in privateering communities in Louisiana, Texas, and Florida serve as a reminder that I am not drawing a simple equation that equates transcoloniality with emancipatory and progressive aims, and nationalism with retrograde racisms. What follows is a story of collusion that depended on regional movement, a narrative about competing visions of inter-American collaboration that ran the gamut from slave smuggling, to protonational anticolonial struggles, to experiments in communalism. As in every chapter, I examine the strategic alliances and coalitions built by people of color, in this case ones that led free blacks to join armed groups of mercenaries who fought under a variety of flags, probably including the Jolly Roger.

I use a combination of cultural sources—court depositions, poems, memoirs, and maps—to bring the masterless world of the Gulf South in the 1810s into focus. These stories foreground the peak moment of transcolonial privateering alliances just as they began to give way to the early national era in the extended Americas. Ultimately the activities I trace demonstrate the blind spots of methodologies that privilege national liberation and expansionist struggles as a paradigm for historical progress. The people who embraced this lifestyle saw the world in ways that did not always prioritize allegiance to either colonial or emerging American nation-states. Their stories are challenging to write precisely because some of the most historically in-depth analyses about them has been produced using either a nationalist framework or one of state history, in this case of Louisiana and Texas. However, such a focus on territorial affiliation, often through the lens of patriotism, loses sight of alternative, well-organized, and entrepreneurial community formations that flourished at the time. I highlight how black people collaborated with those who exploited the conflict between European imperial forces and creole nationalists of a variety of races for their own profit-driven objectives. Many of the key players in these moments overlapped, and I reveal these stories primarily through the lives of two figures. The first is Joseph Savary, a free man of color from Saint-Domingue who had ties to the Baratarians and was a leader in the black refugee community. The other is the notorious privateer Jean Laffite.

While Laffite has become a cultural icon, the darker members of his enterprise remain in the shadows of academic discourse and popular culture. I contend that the lack of public attention devoted to these figures has varied motivations. In social and political spaces dominated by slaveholders, the exploits of groups of black itinerant soldiers/mariners/mercenaries were not bandied about. This was especially true during the late antebellum period, and in the post-Reconstruction climate of Jim Crow oppression in the United States, when stories of Laffite's exploits were very popular.[2] Both in the past and in the present, it has also been rather inconvenient to dwell on the fact that black leaders during the Haitian Revolution were in fact slave traders, slave owners, and allies of the mechanisms of power (planters and merchants) that kept the system running. For example, historians with revisionist desires to include forgotten black actors into nationalist histories, whether of Haiti, Latin America, or the United States, are circumspect about these people who were, like many during the Age of Revolution, walking contradictions.[3] In my discussion, I use the idea of contradiction as an analytical tool that places seemingly incongruous elements side by side to create something new. My engagement with these paradoxes allows us to better understand the importance of slave trading to freedom-seeking movements, both nation-based and non-nation-based ones.

These black privateers and their allies thus provide another perspective on the idea of "hydrarchy from below" documented in Linebaugh and Rediker's influential work on maritime life during an earlier era of mercantile expansion. Using words such as *proletarian* and *oppositional* to describe the nature of this hydrarchy, they focus on the antislavery, emancipatory nature of the relationships that developed aboard ships and in maritime centers (taverns, docks, etc.) that contributed to revolutionary activism in the early Atlantic world. This interpretation privileges the adversarial, noncooperative and nonconformist characteristics of people who built lives that humanized them in the midst of oppressive state regimes on land and at sea.[4] The activities of the seagoing black military men that I examine here did not conform to the more progressive elements of this ideology in key ways. Nonconformist, economically marginal, and determined to create their own possibilities, they were "masterless" men who achieved some degree of independence through the profitable business of depriving others of their freedom.[5]

RACE, PRIVATEERING, AND THE GULF SOUTH IN THE 1810S

In the bayou region of Barataria, eighty miles south of New Orleans at a strategic opening to the Gulf of Mexico, the brothers Jean and Pierre Laffite ran a privateering/pirating base. Despite inconclusive evidence about their early lives, it is generally agreed that they were residents of Saint-Domingue and that they left the island during the Haitian Revolution.[6] They built a powerful smuggling enclave between 1809 and 1814, which was broken up by an armed U.S. raid just prior to the Battle of New Orleans. As alluded to in Chew's comments, the smugglers regrouped on Galveston Island, Texas, for several years under the auspices of the new Mexican revolutionary government. The conventional narrative has the Laffites and their band of men working closely with Andrew Jackson to save the city and preserve the independence of the United States during the final skirmish in the War of 1812 against Great Britain. These figures are thus preserved in historical memory as part of a patriotic story of triumph for the young North American republic. Jean Laffite in particular has become larger than life, a cultural icon inscribed and reinscribed over the years as a roguish (anti) hero, the "pirate-patriot, gentleman rover."[7] Celebrated as flashy corsairs, these men and their deeds are immortalized in novels, several feature-length films, a state park, souvenir shops throughout the French Quarter, a Disneyland ride, and an annual festival called Contraband Days in Lake Charles, Louisiana, that commemorates the many legends surrounding the Laffites' buried treasure.[8]

Their roguish outlaw images to the contrary, the Laffite brothers were closely tied to the elite. From their base in Barataria, the Laffite crew maintained contacts with the most important merchant houses in New Orleans, in addition to developing strong ties to local political leaders. Many of these merchants, Saint-Domingue refugees themselves, had elaborate holdings in privateering ventures and owned shares of the Laffite enterprise.[9] The Laffites' reported flair for the dramatic—audacious thefts, putting a ransom on the governor's head—made their activities something of a deliciously scandalous *on dit* among the local population. Business boomed, and the Barataria islands became known for their auctions of plundered material acquired during privateering raids throughout the Gulf. Arsène Lacarrière Latour, an acquaintance of the brothers and author of one of the earliest and most-cited histories of Louisiana (1816), writes:

> Social order has indeed to regret that those men, mostly aliens, and cruising under a foreign flag, so audaciously infringed our laws as openly to make sale of their goods on our soil. . . . From all parts of Lower Louisiana people resorted to Barataria, without being at all solicitous to conceal the object of their journey. In the streets of New Orleans it was usual for traders to give and receive orders for purchasing goods at Barataria, with as little secrecy as similar orders are given for Philadelphia or New York. The most respectable inhabitants of the state, especially those living in the country, were in the habit of purchasing smuggled goods coming from Barataria. (14–15)

In addition to furniture, jewels, liquor, and other items, the most lucrative merchandise they marketed was slaves. The latter was of special importance, as the U.S. government had officially banned the importation of foreign slaves in 1808 at a moment when a large-scale plantation economy was escalating in the Louisiana Territory. Planters were hungry for labor, especially when acquired at relatively bargain prices. In his work on the post-1808 slave trade, Ernest Obadele-Starks is one of the few scholars who foregrounds the primacy of slave smuggling to the Laffite enterprise, identifying them as "the most ruthless of all Gulf Coast slave smugglers" who "spearheaded a slave-smuggling operation that for a good part of the nineteenth century served as a chief supply source for slaves in the region" (34, 4).[10] Believing that slavery was absolutely necessary to the future development of the territory, authorities at all levels of government often collaborated with these smugglers. Conversely, they were sometimes motivated to enforce the law prohibiting the importation of foreign slaves when they could financially benefit by reselling the slaves they confiscated.

Contemporaries described the business, a source of great profit to many, in ways that echo Chew's and Claiborne's concern about the national and racial composition of the "association." Portrayals of the supposed nature of this community routinely indicate a veritable Babel of nations, languages, and ethnic groups; its inhabitants came from everywhere. One extant crew list of a Laffite schooner lists members from Italy, Saint-Domingue, and France.[11] Jose Rodríguez, a victim of the Laffites' privateering ventures, spent one month in Barataria after his ship was captured and reported that "the crew of the armed vessel was composed of Spaniards, French, English, Americans, Italians and others—that their cargo was sold there by Jean Laffite."[12] The threat that they represented to the legal system was due as much to their foreignness as to their disregard of revenue laws. As a consequence, their loyalties to the United States, which had just acquired the land as a result of the 1802 Louisiana Purchase, were suspect. The political climate was volatile, and the fledgling United States was at a critical stage in its national consolidation because of an ongoing struggle over ownership of the Mississippi Valley and the Gulf. The question of borders—where U.S. rights ended vis-à-vis the Spanish, the best way to police continued French interest in the region, and how to keep the British from reestablishing the dominance that they had lost in the American Revolutionary War—was extremely salient.[13]

When any generalizations were made as to the privateers' nationality, the preoccupation seems to have been about their Frenchness, hence rumors circulated of the dangers of the "lair of New France" (W. Davis 109–10). This "French lair" was more specifically dangerous for two associations often made with it. The first was the Saint-Domingue origins of many; the second, the presumed French republican sympathies attributed to them. With regard to the first, it is crucial to remember that in 1809–10, the years immediately preceding the heyday of the Barataria establishment, ten thousand Saint-Domingue refugees, approximately six thousand of them slaves and free people of color, had arrived in Louisiana from their exile in Cuba. Expelled by the Spanish colonial authorities in response to Napoleon's 1809 deposing of the Spanish monarch Ferdinand VII, these refugees doubled the size of New Orleans. They became the bulwark of the French and French Creole–speaking population during the territorial American period and continued to exist as a recognized subgroup with a vibrant cultural life well into the late nineteenth century.[14]

With regard to the latter, many former French generals had taken up residence in New Orleans. Apprehensions about the potentially "radical" nature of their revolutionary politics combined with concern about their high-profile recruitment of men for filibustering expeditions into the American Southwest, Central and South America, and the Caribbean.[15] Figure 16, a map of the Gulf of Mexico region, is a visual reminder of the relative proximity of the area. What Kirsten Silva Gruesz calls the "supersaturated site for nineteenth-century visions of the Spanish imperial past, as well as the commerce-driven US empire of the future," the Gulf was a sea that connected the continental United States not only with its Caribbean neighbors but also with the lucrative ports of Central and South America ("Gulf of Mexico System" 470). Hence privateers such as those based in Barataria moved between locales such as Santiago de Cuba, Tampico, Campeche, the Floridas, Haiti, and Louisiana regularly; adventurers commonly met in a New Orleans café or gathered in Aux Cayes to plan the future of places such as New Granada or New Spain.[16] Below, I return to the importance of two French republican generals, Louis-Michel Aury and Jean-Joseph Humbert, as they were both associated with Joseph Savary and other free men of color from Saint-Domingue and postrevolutionary Haiti.[17]

In sum, these privateering enclaves thus made use of the profits from the prize cargo they seized during raids, cargo consisting heavily of men and women captured as slaves, to challenge the governing pretensions of both burgeoning nation-states and Old World monarchies. Setting themselves up in geographic locales with good harbors and enough proximity to potential markets to be viable, they intentionally gathered on the margins of society so as to be out of the easy reach of armed attack and suppression. For a brief window of time, these communes, like the pirate/buccaneering haunts that thrived in sixteenth-century Tortuga, enjoyed some degree of self-rule and served as a temporary refuge from the juridical control of multiple states, namely the U.S., Spain, and the fledgling Mexican revolutionary junta.[18] I use the word *commune* here as a way of denoting an organized group of people who intentionally decide to live and work together for mutual benefit. In a controversial journal that may or may not have been written by Laffite himself, *commune* is his word of choice when describing these settlements.[19] The author claims that he formed an "egalitarian empire" that desired to "confiscate the goods of rich exploiters" and redistribute "those riches to those in need in the majority class"[20] Capitalizing on generations of inter-American trade and social networks that both preceded and resulted from the Haitian Revolution, the privateers worked as mobile parasites that made the everyday maritime trade routes in the Gulf region highly dangerous and unpredictable.[21]

National struggles, however, Old World and New, were absolutely necessary to the success of such enterprises. These men were dependent on both and played them against one another, effectively having some degree of mobile sovereignty themselves. A novel by J. H. Ingraham captures the possibilities inherent in such risk taking. He writes, "From privateers-men, sailing under the flag of a South American state, emboldened by success and power, they became rovers of the wide blue sea, independent of every flag but their own bright-red banner, and acknowledging no commission but that written upon the edge of their gleaming sabres . . ." (52). This observation suggests that they were "independent of any flag," but it bears remarking that they were also disconcerting because they could simultaneously claim to be European, Texan, Mexican, Haitian, or whatever nationality was convenient.[22] To be clear, I do not want to dismiss what in some cases was likely a strong anticolonial, burgeoning nationalist sentiment among some of the privateers. Mercenaries, defenders of the rights of emergent nations, savvy smugglers—these labels were not mutually exclusive.

Returning to the issue of interracial alliances, how did free people of color and slaves fit into this privateering world? What were their networks of work, information sharing, and socialization in a profession that entailed both maritime trade and soldiering?[23] We have seen that their presence in these communities stoked fears among white inhabitants and government authorities in the region. Yet the outlaws evidently welcomed them as allies. Below I present a sampling of primary-source evidence coupled with fictional accounts to establish that people of African descent undeniably participated in the Laffites' privateering enterprise. I believe that it is critical to clearly spell out this involvement because little of the voluminous secondary work on the Laffites discusses the men of color, free or slave, who associated with their "marine banditti." As slave traders, the Laffite communities had regular contact with people of African descent, but the men and women who actually lived and worked with them remain shrouded in mystery.

Mention of the people of color associated with both the Barataria and Galveston communes comes in tantalizing bits; the sources invite speculation. One reason that it is hard to pin down these darker members of the community is precisely that they needed to stay below the radar. After 1808, it was illegal for free men of color over fifteen years

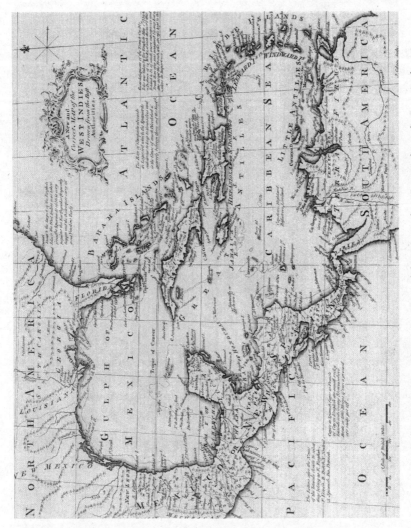

FIGURE 16. J. Gibson, *A New and Correct Map of the West Indies, Drawn from the Best Authorities.* (London: A. Millar, and J. & R. Tonson, 1762). Courtesy of the John Carter Brown Library.

of age to remain in the Louisiana Territory (Bell 39). On top of their very presence being illegal, if they were involved in contraband activities they were not likely to advertise it. As a result, they rarely appear in census records, lists of crews and passengers belonging to ships in port, and so forth. Fortunately, court depositions, letters, and novels contemporaneous to the period provide evidence of their ubiquity.

I begin with a July 18, 1813, deposition by Andrew Whiteman, a privateer who served with Laffite and later testified against him. When describing a raid against U.S. Customs officials, Whiteman stated that he and "one other white man named Scott and a mulatto rowed in their boat after the Lafourche boat. . . . They then boarded the boat . . . when Scott said something to him in French upon which a musket was fired from the cabin." Then "Lafite [sic] and two . . . mulattos boarded the boat much about the same time deponent's party did."[24] John Foley, a customs agent who was wounded in the course of the above skirmish, offers further documentation of the multiracial nature of the Laffite enterprise. In a letter dated May 1, 1813, he writes, "About four weeks ago the brother of the celebrated M. Lafite [sic] passed through the Canal heading from the Attapakas with a number of persons say 20 consisting of Whites, Blacks, Mulattos, Spaniards. . . . Yesterday the celebrated one, he who is so well known in New Orleans, arrived here with about ten persons chiefly mulattoes, and immediately the two brothers departed for the Sea and I have no doubts but their intention is to introduce cargo into N. O. via Barataria."[25] Yet another court statement made by Pierre Laffite himself describes recruiting "mulattos" for an upcoming mission (W. Davis 103).

In all of these juridical records, the mixed-race and black actors are integral participants in the action, yet they remain unnamed. For instance, in Whiteman's play-by-play account above, mulattoes, probably free since they were not identified as slaves, boarded the targeted boat directly alongside Laffite. Everyone racialized as white has a name—Scott, Whiteman, and Laffite himself, while the other three Laffite associates are simply anonymous people of color. Is this oversight indicative of the witnesses' own biases, or does it reflect a scale of worth and power among collaborators in the Laffite enterprise? Elsewhere Toni Morrison has brilliantly observed what she calls the "Africanist presence" in anglophone literary culture, even as canonical American authors have denied black characters names and voice. These historical documents demonstrate a similar narrative construction: black figures form a backdrop to the action; their labor is necessary, yet their individual lives are unremarked. They are simultaneously present and invisible.

Undoubtedly some of these black and mulatto laborers who worked in Barataria and Galveston were from Saint-Domingue. For example, Claiborne's and Chew's aforementioned letters both directly associate people of color from Saint-Domingue with these privateering communities. The activities of certain key privateering/soldier figures such as the Laffites, Joseph Savary, Louis-Michel Aury, and Jean-Joseph Humbert help to solidify the claims of the North American authorities. The latter three were soldiers who ended their careers with the French military after fighting in the Haitian Revolution; all of them became entangled in the Gulf of Mexico's privateering and filibustering communities. While only Savary was of African/ Saint-Domingan descent, primary sources indicate that all of them worked closely with a larger network of black associates. Below I provide three additional examples to corroborate these connections. The Spanish revolutionary Juan Picornell noted Pierre Laffite's influence over "the Santo Domingan free colored people of New Orleans" (Faye, "Great Stroke" 739). Pierre Laffite notes in an 1817 letter to his brother Jean that Commodore Aury and Colonel Savary were close and that Savary was "a man in whom Mr. Aury has much confidence." He was happy to report that despite this close relationship, he had "succeeded in separating from Aury's service fifteen sailors to whom I have given passage in the brig. Fourteen young colored men are with me from among those of Colonel Savary" (Faye, "Great Stroke" 774). Finally, court and ecclesiastical records also reveal that Pierre Laffite's long-term mistress and mother of some of his children was a free woman of color named Marie Villard who lived in the Faubourg Marigny, a neighborhood inhabited by many *gens de couleur* from Saint-Domingue (W. Davis 23, 478). It was a world Pierre Laffite circulated in easily, and one can conjecture that he had social interactions with potential accomplices.

The noteworthy presence of these actors in the historical record of the time is echoed in the fictional one. I do not wish to simply gesture to moments of representation: that is, my point is not to find every instance when a black figure appears in literature immortalizing Barataria. Rather, I find it fascinating that in the tens of thousands of pages produced about Laffite over the last 150 years, so little attention has been paid to either his black accomplices or his slave victims. This is especially remarkable given that in the popular imagination of the early nineteenth century inhabitants of these communities decidedly lived in a multiracial ambience, both during raids and at their bases.

Two novels that helped proliferate the romanticized Laffite legend prior to 1840, *Laffite, or the Baratarian Chief: A Tale Founded in Facts* (1828) and J. H. Ingraham's aforementioned *Laffite: The Pirate of the Gulf* (1836), provide useful cultural context. Anonymously published in New York, the former was the earliest to document Jean Laffite's supposed exploits, and it went through several editions. Of note are descriptions of Laffite's band of marauders. This "fact-based" work portrays black actors wielding the boarding pikes and fighting to the death alongside their chief. The anonymous writer describes one assault scene as follows: "His decks exhibited a motley assemblage of ferocious looking villains, black, white and yellow, whose horrid imprecations and oaths were enough to appal [sic] the bravest heart. . . . 'Have at the rascals then,' shouted Anson, as he thrust his sword to the hilt through the body of a huge negro. 'The sharks may have him in welcome if they can stomach the black dog'" (22, 24). In the above scene, it is taken as a matter of course that the multiracial "villains" worked together.

Just a few years later, Ingraham's novel, which one critic called "one of the most popular fictions ever issued from the American Press," features a deformed black protagonist, an "orangutan"-like slave named Cudjoe, who works closely with Laffite as his minion.[26] More interestingly, Ingraham provides a glimpse of life on shore at Barataria between raids. He imagines that "half a dozen boys, white, black and yellow, whose heads displayed all the varieties of carroty, wooly, and strait black hair, were gathered about him, their coal black eyes sparkling with glee. Each of these neophytes to the trade of buccaneering, was naked to the waist. . . . One of these youths, whose robes would have required much enlargement to rival the primitive fig leaf—was occupied in pricking, by way of practicing his profession, the hams of the suspended monkey; and delighting himself, and his parti-coloured companions, in the contortions and yells of the animal" (153). Ingraham makes his characters partake equally in cruel activities, existing in a state of seminudity and wanton abasement. Phenotypical traits—skin color and hair texture—again point to the multiethnic nature of these pirates in training. In both novels, the term *yellow* refers to a person of mixed-race African descent. This descriptor was common at the time, indicative of larger hemispheric systems of classifying people by gradations of skin color. In addition to phenotypical markers, both racial

admixture and Africanity were designated through terminology borrowed from the animal kingdom; the above scene with the monkey is
a less-than-subtle way of suggesting the commonalities between these
children and their victim.

As the century progressed, however, black characters virtually disappear altogether in most fictional accounts. Over time, what was an
acknowledged black presence in the first three decades of the nineteenth century was whitewashed, so to speak, so that the Laffites' associations with people of African descent, perhaps dependence on their
labor, was left unremarked.

TO FIGHT ABLY AND VALIANTLY AGAINST ONE'S OWN RACE

I now return to the figure of Joseph Savary. Though he was one of the
better-known Saint-Domingue free men of color who sought refuge in
Louisiana, few details are certain about his life. A hero of the Battle of
New Orleans, he fought bravely beside Andrew Jackson and received
a veteran's pension.[27] In the weeks leading up to the battle, the North
Americans desperately needed soldiers and Jackson and then-governor
Claiborne commissioned two regiments of color. The first was composed of black Americans who had formerly fought under the Spanish colonial government. The second was mobilized by Savary, who
"virtually single handedly raised a second battalion from among the
free Negro émigrés from Santo Domingo, most of whom had fought
as loyalists under the French flag in their native land. It was a Her-
culean task, but Savary procured sufficient personnel." In December
1814, 256 of them were mustered into the service of the United States
(McConnell 70–72). Of note, a few years earlier, in November 1813,
Savary had offered the service of five hundred free men of color to
the aforementioned French General Humbert, then commander of a
Mexican revolutionary filibustering force recruiting participants in
New Orleans. Between 1813 and 1815, then, half of his fellow free men
of color were no longer available. What happened to them? Over two
hundred free men of color, presumably well versed in the art of warfare, could not have passed unnoticed in the slave-holding city of New
Orleans. This intriguing fact aside, Savary was obviously an influential
figure in the local Saint-Domingue diaspora, able to mobilize forces of
free men of color quickly and efficiently.

Following the Battle of New Orleans, Savary enters the historical record in the environs of Galveston. Historian H. Gaylord Warren cites the May 1817 deposition of a Captain Juan Domingo Lozano, who notes that Savary and others arrived in Galveston with "150 men, of whom 110 were Americans commanded by [Colonel Henry] Perry and 40 were colored persons under Savary" ("Documents" 1092). William C. Davis, author of one of the most recent and exhaustive biographical studies on the Laffites, cites a deposition by Manuel Gonzáles, a mariner who lived in the Galveston commune in 1818, in which Gonzáles mentions that Colonel Savary had a woman slave who was "attending upon Lafitte" (353).[28] Savary thus frequented the Galveston establishment and owned at least one slave, a woman who perhaps provided sexual services to both her owner and his famous associate. Given the scarcity of information about women in this privateering world, her presence is significant. This female slave was intimately connected with events in these communities, yet she remains nameless. As is the case for Pierre Laffite's partner Marie Villard, details about her life would undoubtedly shed much light on the role of women in these enclaves.

Charles Gayarré, in his canonical *History of Louisiana* (1866), offers more clues. Describing Savary's role in the Battle of New Orleans, he writes:

> A colored man named Savary, *who had distinguished himself in the wars of St. Domingo, by fighting ably and valiantly against those of his own race, undertook to form a battalion of refugees from that island, who had cast their lot with the whites when they had fled to Louisiana* on being overpowered by their enemies. They had thus given a remarkable proof of attachment to the superior race for which it might have been supposed that they entertained feelings of hatred and envy. Savary obtained the grade of Captain, and was remarkably successful in his efforts to raise a company. . . . The new battalion was soon formed, and its command was entrusted to Major Daquin, of the Second Regiment of Militia, who was one of the white refugees from St. Domingo. . . . The whole corps of colored men . . . , it must be understood, were all free. None had been taken from the slaves. *Many had a certain degree of education, and some possessed considerable property.* (4: 406; italics mine)

Any black of so distinguished a reputation in slave-holding circles must certainly have fought against his fellow blacks. It remains crucial to piece together more information concerning Savary's activities in Saint-Domingue in order to get a better sense of the details concerning his exile. Did he arrive with the Saint-Domingue exodus from Cuba? Was he one of André Rigaud's men who fled Saint-Domingue during the civil war with Toussaint Louverture and returned as a soldier with the 1802 Leclerc expedition? How did he become associated with slave smugglers during the first decade of the nineteenth century, a time when Haiti had already proclaimed universal abolition of both the trade and slavery itself?

In a hemispheric context, we must remember that "the holding of African slave property by free people of colour was customary throughout the Americas and most colonial governments guaranteed the property rights of their free black citizens" (Hanger, "Free Blacks," 49). With regard to Saint-Domingue and Savary in particular, Gayarré's testimony is corroborated by scholarship on the island's affluent class of propertied *gens de couleur*. At the time of the revolution, free people of color owned a significant percentage of plantations and slaves on the island.[29] After local white planters refused to obey the 1792 French Assembly decree granting them equal rights, many of them joined the rebelling slaves. It is precisely when the oppressed make common cause that radical change is possible, and this coalition proved decisive for the outcome of the revolution. However, tension between free people of color and slaves had long been an everyday characteristic of colonial life, a conflict often related to one's racial heritage and skin color, namely being black or of mixed race, one's economic resources, or one's status as a creole or an African (figure 17).[30] Free people of color were likewise an internally diverse group of people with potentially conflicting interests.

Given that Savary was not only free but probably a landowner and slaveholder himself in Saint-Domingue, it is not surprising that he did not cast his lot with enslaved Africans. One can only speculate whether he and his fellow black privateers felt any sympathy with those they held in fetters. For every Olaudah Equiano who decried the depredations of the maritime slave trade as they were forced to labor for its benefit, there were doubtless men such as Savary or the "Curacao negroes" from chapter 1, those who made up the crew on the dog-procuring mission from Jamaica to Cuba. Slaves and free blacks belonged to different legal and social categories at the same time that they held fundamental things in common. There is no doubt that racial solidarity grew out of common experiences of subjugation. The black maritime underclass was not a monolithic community, however, and one cannot expect that people of African descent would have had common agendas. For the actors involved, this would have seemed obvious.

FIGURE 17. *Négresse, et femme mulâtre de St. Domingue.*
Engraving. Jacques Grasset de Saint-Sauveur, *Encyclopédie
des voyages* (Paris: 1795–96). Courtesy of the Collections of
the Louisiana State Museum.

This side of Savary's rather unsavory past is not the focus of revisionist scholarship. In books such as Roland McConnell's *Negro Troops of
Antebellum Louisiana*, or in Caryn Cossé Bell's popular *Revolution and
Romanticism*, no direct analysis of this proslavery side is mentioned.
McConnell, for example, is interested in demonstrating that black troops
were true patriots who contributed immeasurably to both Louisiana's history and that of the country. Bell locates him as a pivotal figure in what
she terms the "Afro-creole protest tradition," stating, "In New Orleans,
the entry of Colonel Savary and other Saint Domingue free black soldiers
in the 1809 refugee movement strengthened the city's community of free
people of color. Above all, they introduced the city's Afro-Creole leaders
to a strain of radical republicanism that had triumphed over slavery and
racial oppression in Saint Domingue/Haiti" (64). What do certain terms

such as *republican* or *radical* mean within this context of slave owning and slave trading? How was it possible for Savary to be a beacon of the successful triumph over slavery if he was known to be closely associated with slave traders? His class loyalties to others like him who "had some education and property" in colonial Saint-Domingue make him a fascinating figure that brings into focus the variety of black subjectivities and political coalitions formed at this precise historical moment.

Contrary to the case of white Saint-Domingue refugees who chronicled their sudden impoverishment and exile in personal memoirs and early nineteenth-century periodicals, direct testimony from people of color themselves describing their experiences is more difficult to find. Savary's biography suggests that we need to look elsewhere for evidence documenting how some people of color also experienced the reversals of fortune that so obsessed their white counterparts. This change in status was likely to be even more permanent for blacks, as the main locales of refugee resettlement, Cuba and Louisiana, gradually tightened control over free populations of color as their plantation economies boomed.[31] Laws barring them from myriad activities—from what professions they could hold to how they could congregate in public and private—were upheld by the constant threat of physical violence. The prerevolutionary black elite of Saint-Domingue would never regain their economic power in the region.

Instead, these formerly prosperous elite free men of color from Saint-Domingue now found themselves in the same second-class legal and social position they were relegated to at home, but with fewer financial resources. I turn briefly to the bitter words of a free person of color in the neighboring United States to provide a comparative perspective concerning the precariousness of this group's existence on a regional level. An editorial from an African American newspaper published in New York City poignantly demonstrates the challenges faced by free blacks of all classes. The author writes, "Free Man of Colour. What an empty name! what a mockery! Free man, indeed! when so unrighteously deprived of every civil and political privilege . . . when prejudice binds the most galling chains around him! drives him from every mechanical employment, and situations of trust, or emolument. . . . No man of colour, be his talents, be his respectability, be his worth, or be his wealth what they may, enjoys, in any sense, the *rights of a free-man*."[32] This strident statement deems the very term *free man of color* a rhetorical oxymoron. I return to a discussion of the limits of freedom within a slave-holding society in chapter 5. What I wish to emphasize is how race and class status were mutually constitutive. That is, for the few free men and women who did manage to attain financial stability, even some degree of affluence, this security could crumble in a moment because free people of color were seldom afforded the full protection of the law. In addition to bearing the burden of economic and social inequality, these men and women lived in an insecure state of bodily freedom, given that they could be captured and sold despite their free status. As Jeffrey Bolster notes in his work on black maritime culture during this same time period, seafaring "became an occupation of opportunity for slaves and recent freedmen." Despite the dangers involved, they were well aware that "discrimination and kidnapping . . . were also hazards of shore life" (4–5).

With regard to the appeal of transcolonial intrigue to Savary and others, it is evident that for most people involved smuggling provided desperately needed employment. For whites and blacks, those who were always poor, and those who were once wealthy, privateering was potentially a very lucrative undertaking; the attraction of a large payout made the risks involved worth taking. A state of flux and disorder caused by interimperial rivalries and creole nationalist struggles presented opportunities for entrepreneurial, desperate, and visionary individuals. Blacks with military expertise had opportunities to carve out a niche for themselves that was not available at other historical junctures when the threat inherent in their firsthand knowledge of warfare would have overridden its usefulness. In the context of a "masterless" Caribbean, racial status was less important than competency in sailing, smuggling, or combat. For creole militants seeking state power, men as different as Simon Bolívar and Andrew Jackson, reliance on the arms and laborers recruited in Haiti and its diaspora, or the incorporation of black troops, was a deeply uncomfortable, yet necessary choice in a time of crisis. As Bolívar remarked in an 1815 letter to a Jamaican newspaper, "When men are desperate, they are not fastidious in choosing the means to extricate themselves from danger" (Maingot 58). This logic cut both ways, for a president-to-be and for his unlikely auxiliaries. The demonstrated economic need of the recruits helps to explain their motivations.[33] McConnell reports that many of those who fought with Savary were destitute, reportedly having "no shoes or blankets" (72). In a letter from April 1815, Governor Claiborne begged federal authorities to use public funds to aid Humbert's men, who were "without rations, lodgings or the means of procuring them." He entertained "serious apprehensions that if the men, late of

Humbert's Legion, Composed as I learn of all Colours and description of Character, should longer remain in this City, and in a State of Suffering, they may and will depredate upon the properties of the Citizens" (Rowland 6: 357–58). Again, the poverty of these privateers for hire appears to have been extreme.[34]

By the 1850s, William Bollaert, a man largely credited for disseminating the story of Laffite that would be taken up by future generations, could summarize the attributes of the Baratarians as follows. "A majority of the outlaws were those who fled from the island of Santo Domingo during the troubles there. . . . Doubtless volumes might be written by the novelist upon the occurrences at Barataria, and those connected with that haunt. It was indeed a refuge for the destitute, and for such classes of men who for their crimes had been driven from society" (436). The disapprobation Bollaert and others evince toward "such classes of men" connected their uncontrollability to their international origins, and arguably more importantly their lower-class and racialized status. Their poverty and disquieting mobility earned them the reputation of riffraff with ties to revolutionary, when not criminal, pasts.

Such paranoid and melodramatic language was not limited to descriptions of the masterless, interracial group operating in Louisiana and Texas: events in the mid-1810s find intriguing parallels in other territories. Like New Orleans and Galveston, parts of Florida, as well as Aux Cayes and Port au Prince, were coastal communities that hosted a variety of smugglers and became recruiting spots for various missions—Latin American independence expeditions, privateering ventures, and other legitimate and illicit business negotiations. For example, Louis Aury was also active in the Floridas, establishing himself along with "more than one hundred black Haitians" on Amelia Island. The aforementioned witness to these activities, John Houston McIntosh, reported that if "Aury's blacks . . . are not expelled from that place [Fernandina Beach] some unhappy consequence might fall on our country. It is said that they have declared that if they are in danger they will call to their aid every negro within reach. Indeed I am told that the language of the slaves is already such as to be extremely alarming" (Landers, *Black Society* 246). As in the example from Whiteman's deposition, these black mariners were anonymous brigands, simply known as "Aury's blacks." Significantly, the speaker believed that local slaves were paying attention to these activities, and that, somewhat hyperbolically, Aury and his allies were capable of mobilizing "every

FIGURE 18. Portrait of Alexandre Sabés Pétion. Lithograph (ca. 1807–18). Courtesy of the John Carter Brown Library.

negro in reach" if they encountered trouble. These events were occurring at the same time that Aury was reputed to have used "African rowers" to sell over one thousand Africans, and it is clear that the volume and operating logistics of the trade made a strong impression upon all who witnessed them. The significant question worth asking is, did observers find the presence of black mercenaries in their environs more unnerving than their actual activities? After all, they were engaged in the otherwise unremarkable business of trading slaves in a slave-holding territory.

Events in postrevolutionary Haiti provide a different, yet related angle from which to evaluate the geographic range of these adventurers. The well-documented but surprisingly understudied collaboration between Simón Bolívar and Haitian president Alexandre Pétion (figure 18) provides a fascinating glimpse into an unexpected set of eventualities resulting from these regional privateering collaborations. The years

1815–17 were pivotal in the independence struggles in Latin America, and the young Haitian republic offered support to the rebel Columbian, Venezuelan, and Mexican causes by providing a safe haven, as well as monetary and munitions aid. Famous leaders such as Bolívar, José Manuel de Herrera, and Francisco Javier Mina sojourned in the island. Paul Verna notes, "Haiti had been converted, during that terrible year of 1816, into the center of the American Revolution. Every week Port-au-Prince and Aux Cayes especially were filled with hundreds of expeditionaries and foreign sailors, preparing for the independence of Latin America under the protection of the Haitian government" ("Haití se había convertido, durante aquel terrible año 1816, en el centro de la Revolución americana. Puerto Príncipe y Los Cayos especialmente, se llenaban, cada semana, de centenares de expedicionarios, de marinos extranjeros, preparando bajo la protección del gobierno haitiano, la independencia de Hispanoamérica"; *Pétion y Bolívar* 280).[35] French commissioners visiting Haiti at the time commiserated with Spanish officials in Cuba, stating that they were "as distressed as you to see that Port-au-Prince has become the receptacle of all the adventurers who so actively menace the possessions of his Catholic Majesty" (281–82).

Savary and Aury were recruited into this milieu, running supplies back and forth between Louisiana, Haiti, Galveston, and other locations (Bell 62; Warren, "Documents," 1087, 1092; Verna, *Pétion y Bolívar* 279–80). While residing in the republic, these adventurers also recruited Haitian soldiers to man their expeditions. For example, Aury set himself up as military and civil governor of Texas under the auspices of the Mexican revolutionary government when establishing the privateer headquarters in Galveston that the Laffite association would eventually take control of after leaving Barataria. He worked closely with both Saint-Domingue exiles and resident Haitians. Fascinatingly, one such Haitian, a man named Jose Bellegarde, led a mutiny against Aury because of his "bad treatment" ("mal trato") of the sailors. Bellegarde went on to work for Bolívar and became an important figure in Venezuelan independence struggles (Olson 60–78; Verna, *Pétion y Bolívar* 292).[36]

Importantly, then, these collaborations provided a means for the Haitian Republic to influence inter-regional activities, an especially important possibility given that the new state was diplomatically isolated for most of the nineteenth century. From the time of Toussaint Louverture forward, foreign powers heavily policed Haiti's ability to develop a strong navy for fear of just this type of regional propagandizing.[37] These privateering slave traders thus became indirect players in the foreign policy of Petion's Haitian state and its desire to work its way out of debt and isolation by creating partnerships with neighboring territories in revolt. Much as Pétion made the best use of the labor available to him, fragile self-proclaimed Latin American republics issued letters of marque to harness the manpower they did not possess on their own. Revolutionaries such as Humbert and Herrera recruited soldiers with the resources available to them—mercenary privateers and filibusters who would fight for the cause of "liberty" when it promised personal gain. At a time when many of these black mariners and soldiers were impoverished, this world provided employment, even social mobility. This was evidently true for both Saint-Domingue exiles and those resident in the island a decade after the proclamation of Haitian independence.

To conclude this discussion of the itinerant population of free blacks from Saint-Domingue and postrevolutionary Haiti who worked in the privateer, slave-trading business, I return to the idea of black self-determination. Not only were people of African descent employed by this economy, they held influential positions and played a decisive role in the success of both business and military endeavors throughout the region. When few flags would welcome blacks as equals, it is not surprising that they fought for those who would pay. What then do we make of these masterless men who wanted to be free of both the state and slavery only to further their own success in life through slave trading?

From the perspective of abolitionists, these men were heinous traffickers in human flesh. Men such as the Laffites and Aury were predators who profited from the traffic in black bodies; as such, their accomplices did as well. That said, is it only historical distance that brings these paradoxes to light? Would contemporaries have seen them as such? The primacy of an economic system, in this case slave trading, does not mean that its contradictions are not evident to people. The paradoxical elements of these activities would have been abundantly clear to Savary. In the 1810s, once Haiti was established and Savary was working there, actively running money and leading expeditions using Haitian mariners, he would have been well versed in the official state policy of abolition. The revolutionary nature of the period, the omnipresence of discussions about the status of blacks, free and slave, would have been inescapable. As in Susan Buck-Morss's famous Hegelian example, it is only reasonable to conclude that Savary must have "known" about and been exposed to radical antislavery. I highlight intentionality to show that Savary was making a conscious choice. A politics that would have been consistent with his purported republicanism was sublimated. Thomas Jefferson's decision not to manumit his slaves, and Napoleon's perversion of the earlier antislavery edicts of the new French Republic demonstrate a similar choice. The lives of these free black pirate/privateers articulate the same problem that has spawned endless legal, literary, political and social commentary—the incompatibility of slavery with democratic ideals of revolution. The everyday repercussions of these contradictions were lived out in these Gulf of Mexico communities just as they were in the halls of Monticello or the French National Assembly. Whether Savary's politics evolved over time remains a mystery. What seems clear is that although he was free to travel to Haiti and able to collaborate with expeditionaries leaving from there, he did not fit into the post-revolutionary order. He was part of a diaspora that identified with Saint-Domingue, but his politics were not those of the abolitionist postrevolutionary state. He fomented and profited from transcolonial collusions, ones that at times were ostensibly liberty seeking and anticolonial, at times repressive and proslavery; much of the time they were simultaneously both.

THE CULTURAL AFTERLIVES OF IMPOSSIBLE PATRIOTS

I now return to Louisiana, just prior to the Battle of New Orleans. This moment presents a historical juncture when several of the key ideas discussed thus far intersect: the divide between slaves and free people of color, the ways in which nationalist lore occludes alternative community stories, and the lessons to be drawn from the aforementioned pairing of Jean Laffite and Joseph Savary. As we have seen, Savary fought alongside U.S. troops in the Battle of New Orleans, raising a battalion of free people of color from Saint-Domingue. Andrew Jackson was reportedly so impressed with their skills that he lauded him and his Second Battalion personally. At the close of the war, however, authorities ordered these same black troops out of the city, as many white Louisianans had always had doubts about their mobilization, vociferously denying that they should even be designated "americains."[38] For reasons that have invited no end of speculation, Laffite and his allies refused an alliance with the British and also opted to side with the Louisianans and Andrew Jackson.[39] Largely working as accomplished cannoneers in the army's Third Battalion, they were praised for their bravery and credited with saving the newly formed United States from defeat at the hands of their former colonial masters.

Two cultural artifacts capture this moment from a personal perspective. The first is a poem, "La Campagne de 1814–15." It forms part of a tradition, both artistic and scholarly, that has reevaluated black involvement in North American revolutionary struggles, particularly the War of 1812.[40] Attributed to Hippolyte Castra, pen name for a free man of color, it was published in Rodolph Desdunes's influential anthology outlining the accomplishments of Afro-creole men of note, *Nos hommes et notre histoire* (1911). The poem laments:

Je me souviens qu'un jour, dans mon enfance,	I remember that, one day, during my childhood,
Un beau matin, ma mère, en soupirant,	"One beautiful morning, my mother, while sighing
Me dit: "Enfant, emblème d'innocence,	Said to me, "Child, emblem of innocence,
"Tu ne sais pas l'avenir qui t'attend.	"You do not know the future that awaits you.
"Sous ce beau ciel tu crois voir ta patrie:	"You believe that you see your country under this beautiful sky
"De ton erreur, reviens, mon tendre fils,	"Renounce your error, my tender child,
"Et crois surtout en ta mère chérie . . .	"And believe above all your beloved mother . . .
"Ici, tu n'es qu'un objet de mépris."	"Here, you are but an object of scorn."
Dix ans après, sur nos vastes frontiers	Ten years later, upon our vast frontiers,
On entendit le canon des Anglais,	One heard the English cannon,
"Nous sommes tous nés du sang Louisianais."	"We were all born of Louisiana blood."
A ces doux mots, en embrassant ma mère,	At these sweet words, and embracing my mother,
Je vous suivis en répétant vos cris,	I followed you, repeating your cries,
Ne pensant pas, dans ma course guerrière,	Not thinking in my pursuit of battle,
Que je n'étais qu'un objet de mépris.	That I was but an object of scorn.
En arrivant sur le champ de bataille,	Arriving upon the field of battle,
Je combattis comme un brave guerrier:	I fought like a brave warrior;

Ni les boulets non plus que la mitraille,	Neither the bullets nor the shrapnel,
Jamais, jamais, ne purent m'effrayer.	Could ever fill me with fear,
Je me battis avec cette vaillance	I fought with great valor
Dans l'espoir seul de servir mon pays,	With the hope of serving my country,
Ne pensant pas que pour ma récompense,	Not thinking that for recompense
Je ne serais qu'un objet de mépris.	I would be the object of scorn
Après avoir remporté la victoire,	After having gained the victory
Dans ce terrible et glorieux combat,	In this terrible and glorious combat,
Vous m'avez tous, dans vos coups, fait boire,	All of you shared a drink with me
En m'appelant un valeureux soldat.	And called me a valiant soldier.
Moi, sans regret, avec un cœur sincère,	And I, without regret, and with a sincere heart,
Hélas! j'ai bu, vous croyant mes amis;	Helas! I drank, believing you to be my friends.
Ne pensant pas, dans ma joie éphémère,	Not thinking, in my fleeting joy,
Que je n'étais qu'un objet de mépris.	That I was but an object of scorn.
Mais aujourd'hui tristement je soupire,	But today I sigh sadly
Car j'aperçois en vous un changement;	Because I perceive the change in you:
Je ne vois plus ce gracieux sourire	I no longer see that gracious smile
Qui se montrait, autrefois, si souvent,	Which showed itself in other times, so often
Avec éclat sur vos mielleuses bouches.	Upon your honeyed lips.
Devenez-vous pour moi des ennemis? . . .	Have you become my enemies?
Ah! je le vois dans vos regards farouches:	Ah! I see it in your fierce looks,
Je ne suis plus qu'un objet de mépris.	I am but an object of your scorn.[41]

The narrator is cast as a valiant defender of his "country" ("pays"), loyal to the U.S. war effort and those who share his "Louisiana blood." Yet he ultimately remains subservient, scorned, and outcast, much as his mother predicted would be the case years earlier given that he belonged to a domestic "enemy" class. Often cited as evidence that African American dreams of racial equality were destined for failure, the poem is a requiem for the unrealized hope for black integration into the nation. Written almost one hundred years after the battle, the poem implies that these hopes remained unrealized.

Read alongside Castra's elegy, two anonymous verses preserved by George Washington Cable provide a useful point of comparison. Rather than identifying with the dominant class, the speaker here demonstrates a marked ambivalence toward their welfare. The singer states:

Fizi z'Anglé yé fé bim! Bim!	The English muskets went bim! Bim!
Carabin Kaintock yé fz zim! Zim!	Kentucky rifles went zim! Zim!
Mo di' moin, sauvé to la peau!	I said to myself, save your skin!
Mo zété corps au bord de l'eau;	I ran along the water's edge;
Quand mo rive li té fé clair.	When I arrived at home it was day.
Madam'li prend' ein coup d'colère;	Mistress flew into a rage;
Li fé donn' moin ein quat' piquié	She had me whipped at the fourstakes
Passeque mo pas sivi mouchie;	Because I didn't follow master;
Mais moin mo vo mie quat' piquié	But for me four stakes
Passé ein coup d'fizi z'Anglé!	Are better than a shot from an English musket![42]

The song's French Creole lyrics suggest that the speaker had French owners, probably natives of Louisiana or Saint-Domingue. For this man, loyalty to the Americans and their French creole compatriots was trumped by interest in his own safety. British or Kentucky rifles (a reference to Andrew Jackson's soldiers) and the interests they represented were of no interest to him; more specifically, perhaps he judged the two sides equally objectionable. Knowing that his mistress would be angered that he had abandoned his owner on the battlefield, this slave was nevertheless unwilling to risk his life alongside his master's in a battle he did not see as his own. A predictable whipping was preferable to dying senselessly. The verses are a cultural counternarrative of slave resistance that disputes North American readings of the 1815 victory as the triumph of upstart democratic ideals versus Old World despotism. Both pieces illustrate that blacks, free and slave, did not have a secure place in the new hemispheric American order that was emerging out of the throes of late mercantilism. Slaves as legal nonpersons perhaps realized this truth sooner than their free counterparts.

FIGURE 19. *The Battle of New Orleans.* Copy of engraving by H. B. Hall after W. Momberger (ca. 1861). Courtesy of the Picture Collection, The New York Public Library, Astor, Lenox and Tilden Foundations.

A print produced during the U.S. Civil War captures a third perspective on the battle (figure 19). Like the poem and the song, it illustrates the limits of black patriotism as an interpretive lens for understanding the transition from a masterless Caribbean to a coherent and contained North American polity. The image provides a more canonical reading of this event, with Andrew Jackson and the U.S. flag occupying a central, inspirational position. The army officers in uniform fight beside the irregulars. These men could perhaps represent the nonuniformed Baratarians who helped man the artillery during the conflict. In the lower center, a black man is hunched down and appears to be searching for something. His stillness and seeming irrelevance are remarkable in a scene replete with images of active combat: the loading of muskets, unsheathing of swords, and the concentrated perusal of a smoking battlefield. Only the two dead and dying victims beside him are more inert. I believe that this iconographic snapshot epitomizes how black actors are present, yet silent in this representation of creole patriotism; they work, yet are of negligible interest to those in charge. While placed in the center of the print, this man is still depicted at half the stature of his fellow combatants. The juxtaposition of these figures must be kept in mind when evaluating a larger context of black activity in the revolutionary Americas.

I conclude by returning to the place of privateers of all colors in collective memory. Savary and Laffite were two men from the Saint-Domingue diaspora, both privateers, both slaveholders, but only the latter has served as a palimpsest of public memory. I argue that the differential treatment of the two men and the many nameless associates who were loyal to both demonstrates how state authorities and cultural historians have marginalized the centrality of black actors to privateering activities and to North and South American political struggles. In Savary's case, his blackness and his proslavery activities make him particularly difficult to fold into either nationalist-oriented or abolitionist narratives. His activities serve as a reminder that there is nothing inherently emancipatory in the transcolonial.

As often noted by biographers, Jean Laffite "belongs to folklore rather than to history" (Schaadt 35). In later years, especially by the late nineteenth and early twentieth centuries, the memory of the Laffites' organization would be associated with a certain prestige and mystique. In the United States, once his organization was no longer a threat, Jean Laffite was an easy cultural hero to assimilate since his Baratarians "did the right thing" through their performance of militarized patriotism. His "cause," rather than a communalistic one with transcolonial dimensions, became U.S.-centric. Many studies of the Baratarians, books with titles such as *Gentlemen Rovers* (1913) and *Some Forgotten Heroes and Their Place in American History* (1922), both by Edward Alexander Powell, and Winston Groom's *Patriotic Fire: Jackson and Laffite* (2006), culminate with elegies praising the military service of these figures. What the North American state was not able to accomplish physically for many years by capturing Laffite, they accomplished ideologically by adopting a romanticized, "cleaned-up" version of his renegade activities. Like the frontier pioneers and the '49 gold miners, the privateers were figures that appealed to the legend of rugged individuals who tamed the wilderness through their own ingenuity. Their actions align with narratives of U.S. manifest destiny, as they can be read as a successful incorporation of Frenchness and the lawless Caribbean into the new state. Nationalization of Laffite thus allows for a certain homogenization; statehood becomes identified with racial hegemony and a linear coherence of capitalist, nationalist development. The iconography around Jean Laffite emphasizes that he cut a dashing figure: handsome, courteous, well dressed, romantically flawed, yet redeemable—an assimilable outlaw. This focus on Jean not only sidelines his brother Pierre's centrality to their enterprises but effectively downplays the roles of the nameless, stateless, desperate, and intelligent men (and women?) who worked alongside him.

Of greater interest is how folklore has treated the darker members of the Barataria establishment. Over time, as Louisiana itself became more (North) American and the U.S. South continued to evolve into a large-scale slave-holding society, black protagonists all but disappeared from accounts of the Gulf Coast privateers. The nature of the cultural production around Laffite and early Louisiana gradually reflected a different approach to black integration into the nation's foundational tales, both those of a patriotic vein and those that embodied a titillating counterculture of renegade piracy. Laffite is useful as a foil for showing the different treatment that white and black privateers have received over time, the latter appropriated, the former disregarded. Savary, for example, received a pension for his valor but was forgotten by the mainstream establishment. The events I have chronicled occurred at the moment when transcolonial piratical havens began their final collapse and nationalism in the extended Americas flourished. As their world was subsumed, white pirates had the choice of insinuating themselves into the nation by becoming national citizens, however "roguish" their pasts may have been. Consider the Baratarians pardoned by President Madison after the 1815 battle, or the incorporation of infamous men such as Renato Beluche, one of their associates, into Venezuelan nationalist lore. Savary and his fellow soldiers of color, on the other hand, would not have had the immediate option of citizenship in the United States or the other Latin American territories they worked for. Their stories indicate the fraught nature of black inclusion into the nation, even for those committed to the political economy of the day. Savary could not be converted into the symbol that Laffite would eventually become.

As was the case with Dominican historiography's treatment of General José Campos Taváres, Joseph Savary thus emerges as an impossible patriot. Armed black insurgents with vastly different politics, these two men created possibilities for themselves via transcolonial collaborations. They were collaborators in the secondary sense of the word as well in that they willingly worked with the "enemies" of their respective countries. Of course, if we recall the two dominant ideas of what the "country" of Saint-Domingue meant for the people depicted in the images from the preface, we can see that Savary collaborated with the ancien régime that provoked Romain's suicide, while Campos Taváres placed his faith in the new regime that was to replace it.

In the present moment, what one might call a generalized discomfort with the legacy of slavery in the United States also makes the centrality of slave trading to the Laffites' enterprise, or say, to the Bowie brothers of Alamo fame, a subject best left to specialists rather than to the commercial establishment. Black slave traders are also a curious anomaly. To invoke a blatantly contemporary example, it would be unpalatable if Johnny Depp's garrulous Captain Jack Sparrow, now arguably the most iconic pirate of the Caribbean, were seen trading, owning, and mistreating slaves. To continue the analogy, black protagonists have almost no speaking lines in the Disney franchise. As such, an audience could easily have the impression that the waters of the Caribbean were not regularly plied by and transporting into slavery the very populations who would eventually form the numeric majority in the islands. While the Disney-ization of Laffite is not surprising, the city of New Orleans itself perpetuates this violence and silencing as well. For example, it is immensely disturbing that one of the post-Katrina mixed-income housing redevelopment projects in New Orleans continues to proudly bear the Laffite name.[43]

This chapter demonstrates that attempts to use Savary's name in an effort to celebrate how early black residents of the city contributed to antislavery traditions would be equally misguided. When the issue of excision enters into how both popular and canonical histories are written, we must remember it is not simply a question of inclusion or reincorporation of people of African descent into these stories. What is important is the perspective that they add to any discussion, especially when class affiliations are taken into account. My goal is not to tie these stories up neatly, as their messiness has enormous value. They are evidence of paths that *were* taken, however much later historiography has tried to clean them up or excise them. Wading through the contradictions reaffirms the centrality of African Americans to regional development and points to the viability of alternative imaginings of collectivity, however short-lived the moment proved to be. In Hispaniola and along the Gulf coast, the transitory flourishes of community that accompanied the move across former colonial boundaries provided a limited, yet critical space for autonomy and self-fashioning. Among the enslaved, still other articulations of unity and discord could be seen in the circulation of emergent musical patterns and dance repertoires throughout the region.

CHAPTER 4

French Set Girls and Transcolonial Performance

The drumming on the abominably monotonous tum-tum,
the singing in chorus, accompanied by the simultaneous
clapping of the hands, are very well for once; but, the novelty
over, they become extremely disagreeable. . . . As a race of
utterly mindless people, the negroes are fond of noise, and in
a very short time, the barbarism of such sounds thoroughly
overpowers all other feelings.

—Charles William Day, Trinidad, 1852

One culture's knowledge is another's noise.

—Carolyn Cooper, 1995

Performative culture provides an excellent medium to study the dialogues that took place between members of mobile black communities.
The interconnectedness of the colonial landscape was evident in the
signifying practices of an intellectual citizenry of musicians and their
dancing adepts. I examine how people employed fashion, movement,
and sound to define themselves and community in the rigidly hierarchical context of plantation slavery. The constantly evolving practices
I discuss provide an example of how forced migrations resulted in a
deliberate use of transcolonial experiences to create new knowledge
bases of both a conceptual and a material nature.

I frame the discussion that follows by using a remarkable Jamaican painting from the 1830s. A close reading of the image leads to
other images, sounds, and eyewitness testimonies that reveal a story
of cooperation, competition, and ingenuity across colonial frontiers.
In a multilingual era when reading and writing were proscribed for
the enslaved, any investigation of circum-Caribbean contact and collaboration must take into account interactions that did not exclusively

use written or spoken language as the dominant criteria of meaning and belonging. I am interested in how nontextual, embodied practices highlight the importance of intellectual publics. In the field of Caribbean intellectual history, an enormous amount of attention has been devoted to the figure of the public intellectual, most often the man-of-words who has successfully melded artistic production with a political career. This chapter reverses such a model, placing a spotlight back on largely anonymous female creative artists.

The percussive-based idioms that I explore occurred in the context of festive plantation traditions oriented toward both survival and play. Performance was uniquely qualified to play this role, especially in the context of profound systemic oppression. As people moved in transcolonial circuits, most often against their will, it provided a mechanism of communication that counteracted linguistic isolation. Migrants thrown into contact with those whose language they could not understand could communicate through gesture, dance, and musical rhythms. As mnemonic devices, dance and music (both instrumental and lyrical) also created, stored, and disseminated memories of former homes with responses to new ones. This process occurred on a collective level, and performance was thus a mode for fostering participatory interactions and forging a sense of community. In addition, while many traditions evolved into secular ones, performance itself provided a kinesthetic, physic connection to spiritual forces. Such an outlet for the emotions could provide comfort in times of despair, stimulate opposition to abuse, or help process rage so that it was not directed against the self. What follows eschews facile equations of black performance with resistance, while probing what were indeed deliberate choices made by the slaves about how to spend time and develop practices of their own making within an intensely violent world.[1]

I begin by discussing the specificity of Afro-Frenchness as it came into contact with colonial British, Spanish, French, and African identities. The performances of communities styled as *negros franceses*, *nègres français*, or French negroes demonstrate how memories of Saint-Domingue and its revolution were staged in cultural interactions between slaves, masters, and freedmen and women. I then trace seven characteristics of an interisland performance aesthetic, one grounded in African-derived practices and European set dances. My focus is on Saint-Domingue as one center of cultural diffusion of traditions that can be found in Jamaica, Cuba, Puerto Rico, Trinidad, and Martinique. I believe that the contact occasioned by interisland migrations was a critical element in the development and dispersal of these performance traditions. This moment of collaboration is often downplayed in debates regarding cultural origins and in studies of individual (often nationalist) island histories.

As in previous chapters, I use *transcoloniality* to denote both a set of strategic practices in the late eighteenth and early nineteenth centuries and a methodological approach in the present to reconstruct how people understood and experienced their worlds. I complicate the structural dualities often used to categorize conflicts of the time—imperial loyalties versus creole nationalism, "educated" versus popular, master versus slave—as they cannot fully explain the nuances of the practices under consideration. This approach allows me to focus on questions pertinent to this historical moment that continued to be asked in different ways at later times. For instance, how has migration shaped cultural forms? How did African and new world identities coexist? Considering the tremendous ethnic and racial diversity in the region, how have these identities been mobilized in different ways for artistic or political reasons?

Given the importance of sound and movement to what follows, it bears noting that extant late eighteenth- and early nineteenth-century examples of what the music sounded like or how people danced to it are scarce. Practitioners handed down these traditions primarily via the body. And knowledge stored and disseminated through the body was necessarily precarious in an era when those same bodies had, to cite Chief Justice Roger Taney in the landmark 1857 *Dred Scott* decision, "no rights which the white man was bound to respect." Most slaves were tortured, pushed to the physical limit on a daily basis, and legally alienated from self-ownership or kinship claims. Yet these practices remained vibrant and well respected among their practitioners, both then and now. Fortunately, cultural patrimony groups and musical families have kept many of these traditions alive. As a result, for "enacted" examples my evidence relies on twentieth-century audio recordings, filmed examples, and personal eyewitness observations.

My methodology also involves speculation, a process contingent upon close reading of textual descriptions, visual prompts, and sonic sources.[2] These sources, though mediated through the voices of predominantly white observers, attest to the intellectual labor of populations that were rarely associated with intellectualism. Rather than expect to find "answers" to what the black actors here may have been thinking, we can view this evidence as running commentary on how the marginalized populations of free blacks and slaves made sense of new geographical and political contexts occasioned by what was for many another forced uprooting, this time from their bondage in Saint-Domingue.

THE FRENCH SET GIRLS

During the Christmas celebrations of 1836, the Jamaican artist Issac Mendes Belisario painted *French-Set Girls* as part of the series *Sketches of Character in Illustration of the Habits, Occupation, and Costume of the Negro Population in the Island of Jamaica*. His sketches depicted Jamaican cultural life in the early nineteenth century and were reproduced as color lithographs in 1837 (figure 20).[3] Who were these black "French Set girls," and how did they become part of the popular culture of the British colony of Jamaica? What is particularly French about them and their performance? The portrait documents circum-Caribbean migrations, specifically those occasioned by the Haitian Revolution.

Belisario's color portrait depicts seven black musicians and dancers performing in a festive, outdoor venue. The women are center stage, two of them dancing in the foreground alongside a male partner, while two dance behind a pair of drummers. All of the female figures are dressed in long white dresses with colorful ruffles along both the hem and the low-cut neckline. They are wearing white stockings and blue shoes, and their heads are wrapped in elaborately tied, multicolored headwraps. Beaded necklaces and large gold earrings adorn them. The male dancing partner is wearing long striped trousers, shoes, a shirt, suspenders, an intricately tied neck cravat, and a red-striped, long-sleeved jacket. He also holds a handkerchief, another critical accessory in the choreographic traditions under examination. In the right foreground, two male percussionists provide the musical accompaniment. They are sitting astride their drums and are more casually attired in loose-fitting red shirts, long trousers, and broad-brimmed hats.

The elaborateness of the performers' attire is striking. This is obviously a formal occasion. One imagines that the fullness of the skirts would have facilitated movement of the lower body and that the skirts, much like the handkerchiefs, could be used to communicate through gesture. The headwraps, ornate jewelry, and fancy clothing find their echoes in contemporary descriptions of the finery worn by French creoles, especially *gens de couleur*. Afro-creole women in particular were often remarked upon for their sense of style and flair. Classic works, such as Moreau de Saint-Méry's *Description . . . de la partie française de l'isle de Saint-Domingue,* note:

> As to the kerchief around the head, fashion has never had anything which lends itself better to every caprice, to everything whether gracious or bizarre. Sometimes it is very simple and has no other value than in its contours. If

FIGURE 20. Issac Mendes Belisario, *French Set Girls*. Sketch reproduced as lithograph. *Sketches of Character in Illustration of the Habits, Occupation, and Costume of the Negro Population in the Island of Jamaica* (Kingston: n.p., 1837). Courtesy of the Yale Center for British Art, Paul Mellon Collection.

the shape of a woman's headdress demands that ten or a dozen be put on, one over the other, to form a huge bonnet, then that is done. . . . Fine gold earrings of all shapes, necklaces of gold beads mingled with garnets, or even garnets alone, add to her ornamentation, as do gold rings. (Spencer, *Civilization That Perished* 62)

Et ce mouchoir qui ceint le chef, la mode-a-t-elle jamais rien trouvé qui se prêtât mieux à tous ses caprices, à tout ce qu'elle a de gracieux ou de bisarre. Tantôt il est simple, et n'a d'autre valeur que dans ses contours; tantôt la forme de la coiffure exige que dix ou douze mouchoirs soient successivement placés les uns par-dessus les autres, pour former un énorme bonnet. . . . De beaux pendants d'oreille d'or dont la forme varie, des colliers à grains d'or mêlés de grenats, ou bien de grenats seulement, ajoutent à l'ornement, ainsi que des bagues d'or. (*Description topographique* [2004] 1: 76)

This kerchief around the head indicated social status in a variety of ways. The quality of the cloth—perhaps the coveted *madras* cotton from India, or imported silk—often indicated the attachment of a wealthy lover. The mode of tying the cloth itself, the "contours" that Moreau refers to, was also critical. For example, in some parts of the

French West Indies, one pointed knot meant that one was single and available, three knots that one was romantically attached.[4] The volume *Recueil de vues des lieux principaux de la colonie françoise de Saint-Domingue* includes a series of plates (figures 21 and 22) that provide a vivid depiction of the sartorial splendor of men and women of color. These romanticized images circulated widely, presenting as quotidian what was in fact an extreme level of luxury consumption unavailable to the large majority of the black population. However, they demonstrate how ornamentation was used as a mode of self-expression within the very narrow confines allowed by the realities of financial hardship and the rigorous sumptuary laws established in many colonial spheres to regulate black expression. Fashion became a battleground, what the Haitian historian Jean Fouchard calls a "war of lace . . . that involved the entire colony in an all-out competition" (*Haitian Maroons* 43). Each time laws were enacted to mark distinctions between social classes, distinctions understood in terms of racial classification, an ingenious manner of working around those regulations emerged. For example, prohibiting women of color from wearing hats only made the art of adorning oneself with *mouchoirs* more sophisticated. Given the importance accorded to these cultural practices, it is understandable why French republican propaganda would incorporate one of these headwraps iconographically into an image of the new black *citoyenne* as shown in chapter 2 (figure 12). I return to the importance of fashion and its manipulation as a community marker below.

In commenting upon Frenchness, Belisario's image demonstrates how Jamaica became one of the primary sites of Saint-Domingue refugee resettlement. The British occupied Saint-Domingue from 1793 to 1798, returning to blockade the island after 1803 following the renewal of war with France.[5] Consequently, British naval vessels were anchored off the coasts of the island, and thousands of white and black colonists, many with those they claimed as their slaves, escaped via these vessels to the closest British colony. French prisoners of all colors were confined on the island, and the Jamaican Assembly felt compelled to pass legislation in order to "prevent any intercourse or communication, between slaves of this Island and foreign slaves of a certain description." Deemed a dangerous and unsettling influence on the local population, the legislation also required that whites with republican sympathies "embark themselves and their slaves upon certain vessels provided by the Government of this Island to transport and convey them, free of expense, to New Orleans" (P. Wright xxi). As

FIGURE 21. *Costumes des affranchies et des esclaves [Costumes of free women of color and slaves].* Engravings by Nicolas Ponce and Antoine Phelipeau based on a painting by Agostino Brunias. *Recueil de vues des lieux principaux de la colonie françoise de Saint-Domingue* (Paris: Chez Moreau de Saint-Méry, ca. 1791). Courtesy of the John Carter Brown Library at Brown University.

we have seen, circuits of travel occasioned by the Haitian Revolution connected several islands, in addition to the North American mainland. As was the case in most host territories, newcomers from Saint-Domingue were regarded with suspicion and hostility, though they were often made the beneficiaries of charity balls and other efforts designed to provide emergency relief.

A prominent eyewitness documents the influx of these refugees during the early 1800s. Lady Maria Nugent, wife of the Governor General George Nugent, captured the anxiety occasioned by the momentous events on the neighboring island. Excerpts from her journal detail the following apprehensions:

December 13, 1803
Many unpleasant and alarming reports, respecting the French prisoners on parole and the negroes in this town. . . . The rumours all day, of an understanding between the French prisoners and the free blacks, and

FIGURE 22. *Affranchis des colonies [Free people of color in the colonies].* Engravings by Nicolas Ponce and Antoine Phelipeau based on a painting by Agostino Brunias. *Recueil de vues des lieux principaux de la colonie françoise de Saint-Domingue* (Paris: Chez Moreau de Saint-Méry, ca. 1791). Courtesy of the John Carter Brown Library at Brown University.

their tampering with the negro slaves, was indeed most frightful. . . . I cannot describe the anxiety I suffered, nor the thousand horrid ideas that pressed upon my mind; and, especially, as there has appeared of late a general apprehension throughout the country . . . of the alarming state of the negro population, &c. Before we went to bed, Gen. N secured his own arms . . . and as the nursery door did not lock well, I begged to have it nailed up for the night. (187)

March 4, 1804
People here so very imprudent in their conversation. The splendour of the black chiefs of St. Domingo, their superior strength, their firmness of character, and their living so much longer in these climates, and enjoying so much better health, are the common topics at dinner; and the blackies in attendance seem so much interested, that they hardly change a plate, or do anything but listen. How very imprudent and what *must* it all lead to! (198)

As these entries indicate, residents from every class background paid close attention to Saint-Domingue refugees. Slaveholders feared retribution if their own slaves were moved to revolt, a palpable anxiety captured clearly in a mother's decision to nail up the nursery door. In a climate of revolutionary activity and ongoing war between the British and French, it is easy to imagine why an understanding between Saint-Domingue blacks, radical French republicans, and Jamaican blacks was dreaded. The avid "interest" of the local Jamaican free black and slave population likewise confirms that there was commentary in these communities about the revolution in Saint-Domingue and its potential ramifications at home. David Geggus reports that "in 1800, the year Toussaint Louverture became governor of Saint-Domingue, slaves sang in the streets of Kingston, 'Black, white, brown. All de same'" ("Slavery, War" 14). What little evidence survives suggests that musical commentary was a potent vehicle for expressing how slaves interpreted their role in local politics. And local politics had transcolonial dimensions that were all the more tangible as people moved between these colonies, bringing rumors and news with them.

In a brief, yet wonderfully detailed description accompanying the image, Belisario confirms that these "French Set girls" and their fellow male dancers and musicians were refugees from Saint-Domingue. He notes that they arrived in Jamaica in 1794 with their owners, "faithful slaves to the number of fifteen hundred or two thousand, amongst whom were Africans, as well as Creoles, who to their credit, have, with few exceptions, strictly abided by the compact they entered into, viz that of fidelity to their Owners, and a rigid observance of the Laws of the land so affording them protection" (Ranston 254). The patriarchal language of slave obedience and goodwill echoes idyllic descriptions we have already seen of the faithful bondsperson willing to adopt his or her master's fate as his own. As was the case with Romain's example cited in the preface, however, these "slaves" would have been recently declared free by the general abolition decree issued by French commissioner Léger-Félicité Sonthonax in August 1793, a decree ratified by the French National Convention in February 1794. This is a critical fact, as we must speculate as to whether these men and women were forced to accompany their former masters, effectively ensuring their continued bondage.

Regardless of the circumstances surrounding their departure, the French Set girls were part of a self-identifying Saint-Domingue diaspora inasmuch as they cultivated traditions associated with their homes in the French colony. More than forty years after their initial arrival, they seem to have actively socialized with others of like origins/interests and to have engaged in artistic practices that they identified as specifically theirs. As they adapted to local societal customs and began to celebrate the holidays Jamaican style, these performers did so in such a way that marked them as different. Hence they were captured in this painting performing an art form that Belisario considered a local subculture of foreign origin. Yet he still considered them "Jamaican" enough to be included in his series of paintings that included *jonkonnu*, "actor boy," and other archetypes of Jamaican folklore.

A well-documented Jamaican tradition was thus a product of contact between British West Indian residents and interisland migrants from the French Caribbean. The local element of the tradition is captured by the designation *set girls* itself. The term refers to the name given to groups of women who paraded together during Christmas celebrations in nineteenth-century Jamaica. They generally had a queen and were joined by a small band of musicians. These musicians accompanied them as they danced and sang in the streets and in the homes of prominent residents. In exchange, observers offered them sustenance and monetary tips. The formality of the performers' attire is hence explained, as the three days allotted to festive play were ones in which slaves and free people of color donned their best finery, clothing made or borrowed for the occasion.

Of note, while male slaves were active revelers during Christmas celebrations, women played a very prominent role. The sets were among the most visible of the performers, and their groupings could be quite large. They draw our attention to the primacy of female dancers to Caribbean cultural traditions. Copious descriptions from both European travelers and local inhabitants document the existence of these set girls, most notably the rivalries between the Red Sets and the Blue Sets, so named because of their costumes. Monk Lewis, who wrote one of the most well-known descriptions of plantation life on the island, notes how he had "been struck by the precision of their march, the ease and grace of their action, the elasticity of their step, and the lofty way in which they carried their heads" (qtd. in Abrahams and Szwed 244). Michael Scott, author of the novel *Tom Cringle's Log* (1834), confirms these descriptions, stating, "The beautiful part of the exhibition was the Set Girls. They danced along the streets, in bands of from fifteen to thirty. Each was dressed pin for pin alike. . . . They sang, as they swam along the streets, in the most luxurious attitudes" (243).[6] Hence there were sets of many different groupings, some identified by their choice of dress, others by their occupations. Interestingly, the French Set girls were specifically referred to according to their national (colonial) origin in a manner that presumed corresponding cultural ties.[7]

RECONSIDERING THE MIGRATION OF "FRENCH" CULTURAL CAPITAL

This question of cultural ties to Saint-Domingue speaks directly to transcolonial community identification in formation. Through performance, we get a glimpse of how people engaged with and commented upon their environments. The evidentiary record points to a deterritorializing of Saint-Domingue-ness. That is, Saint-Domingue was following people into exile and being re-created, however imaginatively. Refugees developed practices that served as a rallying point for members of the Saint-Domingue community. However, the associations called forth about lives on the island were vastly different depending on one's place in the racial hierarchies both at home and in exile. Likewise, the artistic modality of expressing these diasporic sentiments was varied.

As they migrated, French refugees of all colors were seen as carriers of cultural capital. Contemporary accounts written by and about them point to their association with the fine arts, especially music, dance, theater, and fashion. For example, they established the first theaters in Cuba and New Orleans.[8] In 1803, Lemmonier-Delafosse, one such refugee, confirms this French creole propensity to transport pleasure in the wake of misfortune. He wrote, "In Santiago, where the misery was killing us, or so we thought, we built a Tivoli. We made a ballroom and a delightful garden which soon attracted the admiration of the Spaniards. Building a temple of pleasure upon a land of exile watered by our tears . . . What greater proof of national frivolity is it possible to give?" (Debien, "Saint-Domingue Refugees," 53–54). In the early North American republic, another creole from Saint-Domingue presented his compatriots as masters of refined pleasures, especially music. He jokingly remarked that "in America, a pianoforte is as indispensable as a china cupboard. They owe this fad in part to the wives of the French emigrants, who, to aid in combating their poverty, offered their services as music teachers. Unfortunately, the passion for harmony in this country only extends, as yet, to six to eight months of lessons" (De Puech Parham 203). Corroborating these remarks, figure 23 shows a classified advertisement placed by a refugee in Louisiana offering his skills as a music instructor. Finally, in Jamaica, a May 1800

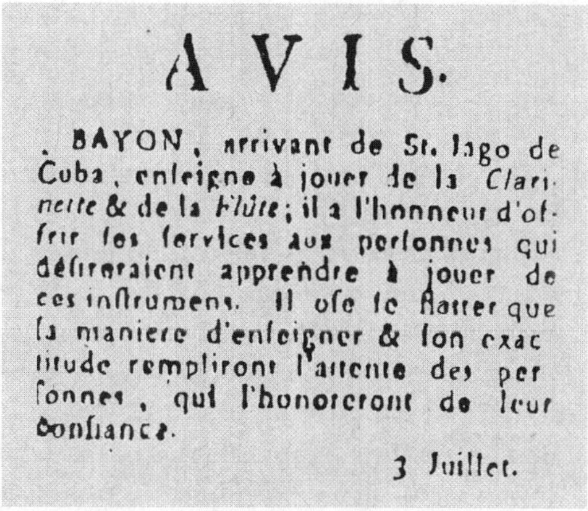

AVIS.

BAYON, arrivant de St. Iago de Cuba, enseigne à jouer de la *Clarinette* & de la *Flûte*; il a l'honneur d'offrir ses services aux personnes qui désireraient apprendre à jouer de ces instrumens. Il ose se flatter que sa maniere d'enseigner & son exactitude rempliront l'attente des personnes, qui l'honoreront de leur confiance.

3 Juillet.

FIGURE 23. Advertisement placed by M. Bayon, a Saint-Domingue migrant recently arrived in New Orleans from Santiago de Cuba, offering his services as a musical instructor of the clarinet and flute. "Bayon, arrivant de St. Iago de Cuba, enseigne à jouer de la Clarinette & de la Flûte; il a l'honneur d'offrir ses services aux personnes qui désireraient apprendre à jouer de ces instrumens. Il ose se flatter que la manière d'enseigner & son exactitude rempliront l'attente des personnes, qui l'honoreront de leur confiance." *Moniteur de la Louisiane,* July 1809.

announcement in the *Columbian Magazine, or Monthly Miscellany* reports that "from the sterility of public amusement in this town the community must necessarily confess itself highly obliged by the present Manager of the theatre for his endeavours to supply the deficiency, by satisfying at least one of the senses, namely the eye. It is not to be presumed that a truly British house . . . can be entirely gratified . . . by the hasty contemplation of French taste and the ear-lulling unintelligibility of French sounds" (R. Wright 302).[9]

These comments are rife with the usual colonial biases that the British, Spanish, and French held toward each other. Interestingly, however, a consistent association is made between French creoles and cultural savvy. They are sophisticated carriers of *la dernière mode.* Of course, the metropolitan French were likewise arbiters of good taste throughout Europe and the Americas; their fashions, dance styles, and language were just a few of the trappings of good breeding. Oscillation between Francophilia, most often associated with culture, and

Francophobia, associated with the taint of violent revolution, was arguably a worldwide phenomenon.

In Jamaica, the black French Set girls also seem to have stood out for what Belisario refers to as their "taste and decorum."[10] With regard to the former, he notes "the tasteful style in which the French Girls tie their kerchiefs on their heads, has ever been the envy of the Creole negroes of Jamaica, who make ineffectual efforts to imitate it." With regard to decorum, unlike other sets, this one didn't dance in the streets, "considering it derogatory to dance elsewhere than in dwelling-houses within walled premises; on no occasion are they found exhibiting on the light fantastic toe in the streets" (Ranston 261). Given that Jamaican Christmas celebrations were largely associated with movement through public spaces—down thoroughfares, from one Great House to another—this refusal to join other revelers in outdoor public spaces is noteworthy. It suggests a deliberately drawn status distinction between themselves and other local slaves, a manner of distancing themselves via cultural practices.

To make the case of self-distinction and hierarchies even more interesting, Belisario informs his subscribers that the French Set girls, "on becoming fixed residents [of Jamaica,] ... formed themselves into three bands or Sets at Christmas, denominated 'Royalists,' 'Mabiales,' and 'Americans.' The former was composed wholly of Creoles of St. Domingo, who considered themselves on that account of the highest grade—the 2nd, of Africans from Congo, and the latter of a portion of both. The two first names have ever been jealous of each other, and to such an extent have they carried their animosity at times, that many valuable domestics have fallen victims to the violence of blows received in their conflicts" (254). This information is provocative for several reasons. While the analyses of the French Set girls cited here are gleaned from white observers, the performances themselves corroborate black participants' own choices and practices. Not only were there divisions between the French sets and other sets in Jamaica, but internal divisions within the black French/Saint-Domingue diaspora community existed as well. It is clear that the creole-born versus African-born division that existed in many slave societies persisted among French-owned slaves after migration into Jamaica. At the time of the revolution in Saint-Domingue, the majority of the slave population was composed of native Africans.[11] Hence it is not surprising that among the French Set girls the "Mabiales" called upon their African, Congolese ethnicity as a communal marker. This retention of African ethnic affiliation was common in contemporary Jamaica, and some observers noted that many slaves celebrated Christmas with others of their own nations. For example, in an account published by James Kelly in 1838, "The Mangolas [sic], the Mandingoes, the Eboes, The Congoes, &c. &c formed into exclusive groups, and each strove to be the loudest in the music and songs, or rather yells, peculiar to their country; and their dance, if dance I must call it, was a display of unseemly gestures; the Creoles occupied the centre . . . and evidently considered themselves entitled to the best places" (Abrahams and Szwed 258). At the level of festive traditions, slaves therefore chose to convene in ways that fomented rivalries both between African ethnicities and between African-born and creole groupings. That some of these performers actually came to blows shows just how intense such rivalries and animosity could be.

This communication of ethnic pride, which might be interpreted as a politicization of ethnic identity, moved simultaneously backwards (toward roots and origins) and forwards (toward New World conflicts). I am interested in the performers' ability to articulate their subjectivity through both connection and difference. Hence the fact that some French Set women also chose to celebrate together under the banner of "Americans" is thought-provoking. A literal process of accretion, or the layering of multiple identities, is evident. That is, these revelers may have been African born, or creole Jamaican, and, in the case of the French set, self-consciously identifying as Saint-Domingue people as well. They were simultaneously many of these things, and each marker could be a cause of conflict, competition, or collectivity depending on the circumstances.

Many of the conventional conceptual categories for evaluating American plantation societies cannot adequately explain this fluidity. For example, the existence of individuals performing as French- Congolese-Jamaicans in the 1830s certainly complicates identity models that highlight the juxtaposition of (white) creole nationalism with loyalty to a colonial European metropole. Likewise, the uber-conflict that defined slave societies was between masters and slaves, most often lived in white-versus-black terms. This dynamic was in evidence here, yet the French Set girls demonstrate the shifting class and ethnic fault lines internal to the black Jamaican populations. As we have seen, these interblack tensions were ubiquitous, played out in a variety of circumstances that pitted people against one another.

For example, fault lines between black "French" communities and non-French slaves are evident in other colonial contexts. In Cuba, the largest site of Saint-Domingue refugee resettlement outside Louisiana, observers noted the distinct culture of the Saint-Domingue immigrants. Emilio Bacardí, whose maternal relatives were planters from Saint-Domingue, wrote a cultural history about the eastern areas around Santiago de Cuba that documents the activities of these migrants. He noted that the slaves working on the coffee estates in the region had "a special language: slang, French Creole, patois, a mixture of the French language with distinct dialects of African tribes. They communicated with their masters using it, amongst themselves and its use even extended beyond their own community to other slaves. . . . Perhaps due to contact with the refined luxury, even the sybaritism of their masters, perhaps due to the immediate environment, a more developed intellectual culture was evident in these slaves than that which was found amongst other slaves who weren't French property" (Bacardí y Moreau, *Crónicas* 508).[12] Beyond observing that this "intellectual culture" was most evident in music, he does not state on what grounds he evaluates its supposed superiority.

A few details of this commentary are worth remarking. First, black populations in Cuba were identifying as part of a Saint-Domingue diaspora. In addition, these "French" slaves, along with their masters, were associated with importing fine arts to the Spanish colony. It is clear that culture had presumed consequences for where one could belong in the social hierarchy, as the people who labored for French owners were considered more intelligent. The labeling of some slaves as superior to others is not unheard of in other contexts. Take, for example, how Muslim slaves were marked as different throughout the Americas because of their literacy and religious practices (Gomez, *Black Crescent*). The internal differentiation of slave populations into classes fomented competing claims to authority. In the aforementioned examples, authority could manifest itself in the realm of culture and/or performance; hence the labeling of these performers as a creative vanguard in the new geographic contexts in which they found themselves. If we imagine them as entering a context where they were seen as carriers of political emancipation as well, then authority had other parameters. I explore this possibility in detail below. What bears noting is that "French" girls were not fighting over who could best embody the cultural practices of the Parisian ancien régime. Assuming that some slaves would have indeed internalized a sense of French superiority as part of the hegemonic project of colonial slavery, there would also have been room for Frenchness to mean something quite distinct. In the

Americas during the Age of Revolution, this distinction was unquestionably linked to blackness and revolution.

In sum, many contemporary observers noted the "intellectual" superiority of slaves owned by French colonists. These observations assume that some of the "civilized" manners and cultural éclat associated with the French somehow rubbed off on their slaves. Transmission of "good taste" was imagined as moving from whites to blacks. However, French taste as an exclusively "white" attribute was already a problematic assumption given that in prerevolutionary Saint-Domingue white inhabitants of the island were incorporating black cultural traditions into their own lives. Contemporary observers, both metropolitan and native, noted the constant intimacy and intermingling of black and white populations at all levels of society. As such, French colonial taste already reflected both African and European cultural forms. This assertion comes as no surprise in the present given the varied and extensive scholarship on the process of creolization in the Caribbean.

A brief digression into the prerevolutionary artistic life of the colony makes this clear. Known throughout the Americas and Europe for its active theater life, Saint-Domingue supported theaters in seven cities, at least one of them opened and directed by a mulatto woman and her business partner (Fouchard, *Le Theatre* 11–102; Cornevin, qtd. in Fischer 208). In his exhaustive work on the colonial theater, Fouchard lists many of the spectacles publicly announced during the last decades of colonial rule. Alongside pieces written in Europe and performed by Europeans, local talent staged "comédies," "danses," and "pièces locales." Titles such as *Danses et pas de nègre* (1777), a piece billed as *Calenda, danse nègre* (1784), and *Les Amours de Mirebalais, parodie nègre* (1786), performed by a famous woman of color known as Lise, suggest that on the public stage performance was already heavily immersed in local realities (Fouchard, *Artistes et repertoires* 111, 145, 160). And these realities were necessarily inflected with slavery and attempts to define a creole identity vis-à-vis the constant influx of people and ideas from Europe and Africa. Nothing makes this ongoing process of cultural interaction and adaptation more clear than the fact that these pieces often incorporated Haitian Creole.[13] This language, one that Moreau claims that "creoles of all colors love to converse in" ("les Créols [sic] de toutes les couleurs aiment à s'entretenir") was a product of the local environment, a native vehicle of expression for those born on the island and the lingua franca for those coming from elsewhere (*Description topographique* [2004] 1: 82). When these characteristics of local performance are considered together, it is evident that the "Frenchness" that Saint-Domingue migrants exported to other parts of the Americas was heavily influenced by black cultural traditions.[14]

Speculation about just what practices and ideas were being circulated is critical. The politics of continuing to assert a Saint-Domingue connection for the enslaved would have been different from that of the former white colonists. How free people of color would have allied themselves is even more open to conjecture, given that some, such as Joseph Savary from the previous chapter, had been slaveholders themselves. All groups used the mnemonic properties of music, theater, and dance to link memories of home with responses to the new communities encountered during the course of migration. For the white exiles, however, there is ample evidence of an articulated nostalgia for an idyllic past, one predicated on a vicious regime of slave labor. This nostalgia is most evident in the many planter memoirs that circulated in France and the Americas in the decades after the revolution.[15]

Counterposed to this nostalgia for the "good old days," what many of these black performers were marking as Saint-Domingueness/Frenchness among both themselves and for outsiders was their own association with revolutionary struggle.[16] In the context of new encounters fraught with friction, competition for resources, and a desire for community approbation, these migrants would have needed to assert themselves. In the Jamaican Christmas parades, for example, "talking smack" was a key element of dominating members of opposing sets.[17] And what better way to stake a claim of superiority to other blacks than by embodying the specter of violence that whites most feared?

Using culture to perform Saint-Domingueness could become a way of asserting belonging to a place where the master class had been soundly defeated. Given the scarcity of sources written by former slaves, these performances are especially important, since they can be interpreted as meditations about the upheavals of the era. Accordingly, in addition to indicating a fashion or social statement about the wearers' identity, a certain way of tying a headwrap, for example, also indicated belonging to a place where racial hierarchies had been turned on their heads. The cachet that would have been tied to such boasting was enough to motivate otherwise jealous rivals (for instance, creoles versus Africans) to all voluntarily play the role of "French Set girls." While linguistically and culturally marked as "French," these performances were probably a coded way of making observers of all colors acknowledge the immediate presence within their own spheres of those who might have witnessed the revolution firsthand and perhaps brought some of that revolutionary spirit with them. As much as the state and local colonists tried to stifle any news of events on the neighboring island and to prohibit immigration of French slaves and freepersons when possible, these performances brought such ideas into the open. The "fear of French negroes" was ritualized in performance.

EMBODIED WISDOM AND ATTUNEMENT

Performance is one of the most recognizable intellectual traditions of the African diaspora. Beginning in the seventeenth and eighteenth centuries, observers such as Père Labat, J. G. Stedman, and Moreau de Saint-Méry wrote about the percussive, movement, and lyrical recreation activities of peoples of African descent transplanted in the Americas.[18] When practiced in groups, especially within what was observed to be a religious or festive carnival context, these activities were often feared to be a breeding ground for slave rebellion. More contemporary critics such as Fernando Ortiz, Samuel Floyd Jr., Guthrie Ramsey, Paul Gilroy, and John Storm Roberts have all identified music as a potential building block for racial collectivity and community formation. Ramsey calls it "a dynamic social text, a meaningful cultural practice . . . and a politically charged, gendered, signifying discourse" (18). Gilroy alerts readers to the epistemic and tutelar possibilities offered by musical production in the Black Atlantic, possibilities that are not always present in other forms of expression. He writes of a "distinct, often priestly caste of organic intellectuals . . . temporary custodians of a distinct and embattled cultural sensibility which has also operated as a political and philosophical resource." He recognizes their mode of cultural production as a bulwark of community identity and endurance, especially in a context of "complete exclusion from modern political society" (76).

Significantly, the musical repertoires under study were dance musics. In her work on Yoruba-derived sacred traditions in Haiti, Cuba, and Brazil, Yvonne Daniel discusses the "embodied wisdom" of participants and how "ritual dance performance was a repository of remembered movements and musical components but also a repository of complementary legends, beliefs, and attitudes, with contrasting and alternative resolutions for temporal problems." She asserts that "the dance and music forms 'housed' not only physical information about the human body in dance mode but also theoretical, emotional, aesthetic, and spiritual information. These data became blueprints with choices for possible action" (64). Like Gilroy, Daniel emphasizes the importance, even necessity, of performance as an integral element of a holistic worldview. These resources/blueprints had correlations to action, whether on an individual or a collective level. Action also implies a certain political valence. That is, any given problem might be addressed and worked upon through performance traditions that carried physical and philosophical information.

For the French Set girls, one could conceive of several temporal problems that could be confronted through these practices. For example: How might a new refugee best direct invective against a master? How might she decide how to celebrate her few days of freedom from forced labor? What would be the best way of teaching her children or neighbors about the world? How might she form allegiances in a new environment, allegiances that could afford protection or perhaps a monetary reward? In a context where politics for the enslaved and free blacks had no proper locus, these performative groupings took on an added importance (Hartman, *Scenes of Subjection* 61–65).[19] Since the state and its institutions (courts, schools, governance bodies) worked against their interests, alternative structures provided a mechanism for communal activity, decision making, and the institutionalization of knowledge.

Interpreting the meaning of these late eighteenth- and early nineteenth-century rituals requires imagination, especially as the sound and movement elements involved were rarely transcribed. However, observers did note some of the accompanying lyrics, and these provide a window into a politicized aesthetic consciousness on the part of the enslaved. For example, Belisario noted the words to a song of the Red Set girls, the most notable line being "Now pray my noble King, if you really love me well, Disband us from slavery, and set us at large" (Ranston 244). Belisario sketched his subjects during the apprenticeship period in the Anglophone Caribbean, a four-year stretch that provided for the gradual emancipation of slaves. Rather than feeling humbly grateful for such a "favor," the singers provocatively ask for immediate freedom. Emilio Bacardí's novel *Via Crucis* (14) incorporates the French Creole lyrics of one transcribed song, "Blan la yo qui sotí nan Frans," into the description of the *tumba francesa*, a Cuban performance tradition I discuss in detail below. As they drummed and danced, the slaves sang:

> Blan lá yó qui sotíi en Frans, oh, jelé!
> Yó prán madam yó servi sorellé
> Pú yó caresé negués

He provides a "literal translation" as "Blancos esos que salen de Francia, oh gridadlo, / Toman a sus senoras para que sirvan de almohadas para acariciar a las negras" (56) ("Those white men from France, oh shout it, they use their (white) wives as a pillow for caressing black women"). This latter song corresponds closely in content to the aforementioned Michael Scott's remembrance of a *jonkonnu* masquerader's verses in Jamaica. These male revelers were a fixture of Christmas celebrations, and Scott encountered one in the street who sang:

> But Massa Buccra have white love,
> Soft and silken like one dove,
> To brown girl—him barely shivel—
> To black girl—oh Lord, de Devil
> But when him once two tree year here,
> Him tink white lady wery great boder;
> De coloured peoples, never fear,
> Ah, him lob him de morest nor any oder . . .
> So always come-in two tree year,
> And so wid you, massa—never fear
> Brown girl for cook—for wife—for nurse;
> Buccra lady-poo-no wort a curse.
> (Abrahams and Szwed 238)

All three excerpts reference power emanating from a European metropole (kings, wives, newly arrived masters). For men, acclimation to the local environment correlates directly to the use of black women as sexual objects. White women are likewise pawns in this scenario, as their lovers abandon them in favor of darker-skinned (more vulnerable) partners. Sung in "playful" contexts, the songs nevertheless are barbed observations about racial and sexual hierarchies and the violence that became a matter of course under such regimes. Like the "Black, white, brown, All de same" song, this lyrical evidence provides clues as to how music was employed as social commentary, this time with reference to gendered inequalities.

However, attention to embodied wisdom is important precisely because it allows for a secondary, deeper level of intentionality to be seen. I propose the idea of attunement as a way of understanding the processes attendant to this intentionality. In its literal sense, the concept denotes an ability to bring disparate elements into alignment and unison. I am particularly concerned with how performers and their publics demonstrated a cultural sensitivity to stimuli—adapting the immediate environment into something usable as they collaborated with people from different backgrounds. The act of producing musical dance repertoires while living under slavery—constructing instruments, training performers, sewing costumes—is in itself an example of self-determination and choice. These artists learned how to reconcile their individual experiences into coordinated, collective new ones. In any situation, deliberate decisions made about how to best interact with one's surroundings are a precondition for conscious political engagement. It is thus crucial to examine a larger performative *context* as much as individual examples of performative acts. Specifically, context in these cases included an ensemble of fashion, lyrics, music, and dance choices. As such, lyrics are simply a more immediately discernible element of a larger framework of black self-fashioning.

Take, for example, the production of sound. It is critical to remember that slaves "lived in a world of sound; a world in which the spoken, chanted, sung, or shouted word was the primary form of communication" (L. Levine 157). As noted in the epigraph that opened this chapter, "one culture's knowledge" can indeed be "another's noise." An ability to distinguish between the two extremes is predicated on membership in a given community. While it is common to recall that white observers usually saw what they wanted to see (most often mindless beings that fit anywhere along a spectrum ranging from happy docile servants to barbarous hordes), it is also true that they heard what they wanted to hear. Put another way, they did not hear what they were not trained to understand. Hence, although many chroniclers noted the musical prowess of black musicians, just as frequently they complained of "backward," out-of-tune, or monotonous noise.

Again, Belisario's painting has much to teach us. He professed a desire to "furnish but sketches of character, steering clear of caricature, nature in her ordinary form alone having been the source" (Ranston 238). Attention to the detail of his subjects as they appeared "in nature" is significant because the painting not only provides a visual record of regional interchanges but also allows for a discussion of sound and movement. The instrumentation of the performance depicted is the first tradition worthy of note. As mentioned above, the percussionists are sitting astride their drums. They are also the only performers not wearing shoes. These details are critical, since sitting on top of a horizontally placed drum and using the heel to play is a Central African drumming technique found in certain Caribbean countries.[20] The heel is used to change the sound of the drum, and the cords crossing the center of both drums also produce a particular vibration. There are two drummers, and the drum on the right is slightly smaller than the one to the left. When this is the case, one drummer is usually playing the underlying, repeating rhythm while the other is improvising. The result is a syncopated, polyrhythmic sound. Finally, the female dancer in the foreground holding a rattle in her upwardly extended arm indicates further similarities between British, Spanish, and French Caribbean instrumentation. Typically made of a gourd or a piece of metal, then filled with seeds, this instrument is called *shaki-shaki* or *shaka* in Jamaica, a *chacha* in Cuba, and *chacha, syac,* or *chak-chak* in the French islands (Alleyne 110; Ranston 254).

French-Set Girls documents many of the elements of the interisland, transcolonial performance aesthetic proposed here: costume, sitting astride a horizontally placed drum, use of the heel to change the drum's pitch, and the presence of transverse cords on the drumhead. In addition, this aesthetic includes incorporation of a rhythmic signature called the *cinquillo*, use of an open-ended percussive instrument beaten with two sticks (the *catá, cuá,* or *tibwa*) that customarily plays the *cinquillo* rhythm, and the use of French Creole song lyrics and nomenclature for the instruments and dances themselves.

The rhythms, instrumentation, costume, and dancing styles depicted in the painting bear a striking resemblance to those found in other Caribbean performance traditions. The existence of the Jamaican French Set girls hence suggests that artistic traditions born out of interisland exchanges became incorporated into diverse local island cultures. The next section moves between different colonial territories to explore the intellectual knowledge contained in three: the Cuban musical dance repertoire known as the *tumba francesa,* the Puerto Rican *bomba,* and the Martinican/Trinidadian percussive tradition known as the *bèlè*/belair. The first two performance genres were associated with the French- and French Creole–speaking slaves who arrived in the eastern part of Cuba and the coastal regions of Puerto Rico in the extended aftermath of the Haitian Revolution. *Bèlè* is a tradition associated primarily with the French Caribbean islands. In the case of Trinidad, French settlers were recruited to the island during the last decades of the eighteenth century, and one can conjecture that the *bèlè* might have evolved from these interactions between the host society and new immigrants fleeing revolution in the Lesser Antilles.[21]

Thus, despite the history of imperial compartmentalization that divided the region into distinct linguistic, cultural, and political communities, these combined seven characteristics point to overlapping aesthetics. Undoubtedly, these similarities are attributable to shared African roots. Given that enslaved African men and women were brought into all these territories, one can surmise that the common denominator in these musics was the presence of African-derived practices that became incorporated in varying ways throughout the Americas.[22] In the context of classic historical and anthropological debates about African retentions, these examples point to the clear continued importance of African forms to the creative process. These performance traditions likewise show the process of creolization at work; African forms came into contact with and were influenced by European ones. For instance, both the *tumba francesa* and the *bèlè* were adaptations of European set dances.

My concern is with what meaning can be extracted from the existence of common practices across geographic locales. Instead of searching for roots, or filiation, to cite the Glissantian critique of the word, I am interested in what we can learn about how black populations dealt with the upheavals of the revolutionary colonial landscape when we examine a common point of contact.[23] Discussions that define eighteenth- and nineteenth-century Caribbean musics as examples of African retentions or as a complex mixture of African and European elements are enriched when we consider the importance of another level of fusion: the interaction of interisland migrants. Much like jazz or salsa music of a later period, these musics were built upon the migratory labor of black artists and their publics. Saint-Domingue, and the French Caribbean more generally, became one center of diffusion for elements of these collaborative traditions throughout the region.[24]

CIRCUM-CARIBBEAN REPERCUSSIONS OF SAINT-DOMINGUE

I trace the connections between Saint-Domingue and other Caribbean performative genres via rhythm, instrumentation, and to a lesser extent movement, specifically as the latter can be speculated about through costume props. In this context, rhythm was most commonly associated with the polyrhythmic sound produced by some combination of

FIGURE 24. *Cinquillo* rhythm.
Reproduced in Alejo Carpentier, *La música en Cuba* (México: Fondo de Cultura Económica, 1972).

multiple drums, idiophones, clapping, and singing. I document one rhythmic signature in particular, the *cinquillo*, as well as the use of a single-headed drum and an instrument called the *catá*. The *cinquillo* is a five-note pattern (ta-pi-ta-pi-ta) with the accent falling most heavily on the first beat (figure 24). The rhythm has been the subject of excellent scholarship, most notably Samuel Floyd Jr.'s work on the "cinquillo-tresillo matrix," which "stands as a symbol of circum-Caribbean unity" (29).[25] Paul Austerlitz, in discussing the *cinquillo* and its relation to Dominican *merengue*, states that it is a "syncopated duple rhythm (consisting of two pulses with off-beat accents) rather than a true quintuplet (of five equal durations)" (16). Like Floyd, he refers to the *cinquillo* as the "Caribbean *cinquillo*" with much the same sense of the rhythm's transcolonial dimensions that I explore in this argument.

The rhythm eventually found its way into music throughout Latin America and the Caribbean. I propose that one way it began to do so was as a result of the transcolonial Saint-Domingue diaspora. A cornerstone of Haitian music, the originality of this five-note pattern is mentioned as early as 1888. Occilius Jeanty, a Haitian musician and director of the Ecole Centrale de la Musique in Port-au-Prince, published a "petite grammaire musicale" that included a discussion about the *quintelet* (the *cinquillo*) and its importance as a core musical base of Haitian music (quoted in Dumervé 141). Later regional circulations of other musical forms, such as the *contradanza*, kept it in continuous evolution.

Given its importance to Haitian music, it is not surprising that the *cinquillo* resurfaced in communities where Saint-Domingue migrants resettled. Cuba provides a case in point. As in Jamaica, Saint-Domingue refugees flooded Cuba in the mid-1790s and again between 1801 and 1803. Largely dedicating themselves to the cultivation of coffee in the environs of Santiago de Cuba and Guantánamo, many of these refugees became very wealthy, initiating an economic and cultural renaissance in Oriente province. As noted by Bacardí above, the planters,

FIGURE 25. *Tumba francesa* society in Guantánamo, Cuba.
Photograph courtesy of Kay R. Torres (July 1997).

free people of color, and slaves living on these plantations developed distinctive traditions, including the continued use of French and French Creole. These traditions also included the *contradanza,* which eventually developed into the *danzón* (Gruson 5–7), various *comparsas*, and the *tumba francesa*.[26]

Alejo Carpentier wrote one of the most cited studies of Afro-French influences on Cuban music.[27] Fernando Ortiz likewise wrote an important study on the instruments of the *tumba francesa*. Commonly considered to have been a creative adaptation of a French minuet, the form contains three movements: the *masón*, the *yubá,* and the *frente.* Two of these movements feature women partnered by men. The tradition was eventually practiced mostly by *cabildo*-like societies in Oriente, the mutual aid organizations organized by African *naciones* during slavery. It is notable for the elaborate attire of its performers, its call-and-response dynamic, and the artistic use of handkerchiefs that are integral to the choreography (figures 25 and 26).[28] For example, these latter accessories are used to form a tunnel-like structure beneath which couples dance and are tied around a male dancer's body during his solo performances. This innovation is especially interesting given how meaningful head and shoulder scarves were in colonial Saint-Domingue and the fact that Belisario features one of his dancers with a kerchief in his hand.

It is in the *masón* that the *cinquillo* predominates. Choreographically the most "European" of the three styles in that it was danced in lines, the dancers use very erect posture and employ mannerisms of

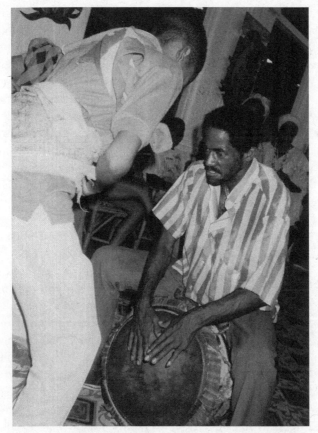

FIGURE 26. *Tumba francesa* society in Guantánamo, Cuba. A male dancer, with multiple scarves wrapped around his body, is in dialogue with a drummer who is sitting astride his instrument. Photograph courtesy of Kay R. Torres (July 1997).

courtly behavior such as bowing and curtsying. In the subsequent two movements this gives way to a more African-based dance aesthetic that is inclined toward the earth.

The *cinquillo* rhythm is played on an instrument called the *catá*. Not common to other Cuban musical traditions, the *catá* is a hollow piece of wood, usually cut from one tree trunk. It is an idiophone, having no membranes/skins covering either end. Perched horizontally on a wooden platform, the instrument is played by two sticks called *baquetas* or *buá-catá* and is the first instrument to start any of the three *tumba* dances. Fernando Ortiz's multivolume masterpiece documenting the instruments of Afro-Cuban music includes a photograph of both the *catá* and a percussionist using the heeled-drumming technique. He described the latter as follows: "Sometimes certain percussionists who play their instruments mounted astride them use their feet, or at least one of their heels, applying it briefly, like a pedal, on the vibrating membrane in order to cover or stop the sound, or to strike it with a muted sound; or also to make the heel-bone slide on the membrane and produce a certain smack. This is what we see in the rhythms of the *tumba francesa* and in *yuka* drumming" ("A veces ciertos tamboreros que tañen su gran instrumento montados a horcajadas en él, utilizan sus pies, al menos uno de sus talones, aplicándolo momentáneamente, a modo de pedal, sobre la membrana vibrante, para 'tapar' o parar su sonido, o para percutirla con son apagado, o también para hacer resbalar en ella el calcañar y producir cierto zurrido. Así hemos visto en toques de tumbas francesas y en tambores de yuka"; Ortiz, *Instrumentos* 2: 294).

The *cinquillo* also resurfaces in the Puerto Rican tradition of *bomba*. Commonly described as the "most African" in the spectrum of Puerto Rican musical traditions, *bomba* is a predominantly percussive music and dance genre. Although we have little information about *bomba* in its formative stages, there are clues that it was influenced by inter-Caribbean migratory contact.[29] Historically, performers used long, flowing dresses and formal suits similar to those depicted in Belisario's painting and the ones worn by the few remaining *tumba francesa* performers in Cuba. As the form is practiced today, these skirts allow for ease of movement. Like the kerchiefs, they also serve as a critical choreographic accessory. Skirts are gathered in women's arms and regularly flicked to the beat of the drums. They are prime gesturing mechanisms between dancers and percussionists, "talking" instruments used to create meaning. As such, the dance depends on manipulation of these costumes; they are not just ornamental.

With regard to instrumentation, Puerto Rican musicologist Jorge Pérez-Rolón states, "Two or three drums of different sizes and pitches make up the foundation of the ensemble, which is rounded out by the *cuá* (wooden sticks that are struck on the side of the drum by another player) and maracas (gourd rattles)" (9). The *cuá* also refers to a narrow, hollowed-out piece of wood that is supported by a platform and played with two sticks. Both the name and design are notably similar to the *catá*, and the instrument frequently plays the *cinquillo* rhythm.

Evidence suggests that *bomba* was heavily influenced in its formative stages by French immigrants who settled in the plantation zones along the coast. Jorge Duany suggests that "the bomba probably originated with the migration of French planters and slaves from St. Domingue, Louisiana and other Caribbean territories after 1815, when a decree by the Spanish Crown facilitated their entry into Cuba and Puerto Rico. . . . Both the salon dances of the elite and the folk music of the masses were marked by this influence" (75). Of course, the French planters and slaves from Louisiana and the Lesser Antilles could have been Saint-Domingue refugees as well, given the circuitous routes that many traveled once leaving Saint-Domingue. Thousands of these refugees were expelled from Kingston and Santiago de Cuba, many eventually resettling in New Orleans, Martinique, and Guadeloupe, the latter two islands still under French control. Duany goes on to provide important semantic evidence of his theory, stating, "The French/Haitian origin of some *bomba* dances is clear in the names of six sub-types known as *bambulé, calinde, cuaya, grasima, léro* and *sica*." He cites the work of linguist Manuel Alvarez Nazario, who believed that "some *bomba* songs have Haitian lyrics, and that the *bomba* dances around the Loíza Aldea areas resemble French Antillean types" (76).

Bèlè, from the French *bel air,* is a percussive music that is likewise considered the traditional, most "authentically" African music of Martinique. Some variation of *bèlè* is found in Martinique, St. Lucia, Trinidad, Grenada, and Carriacou, and accounts of the tradition date back to the eighteenth century. An 1844 witness in St. Lucia noted that "the most important personage next to the sovereign is the *chanterelle,* or female singer, upon whom devolves the task of composing their belairs, and of reciting them at their public dances" and that "some, indeed, are of a higher order than one would be entitled to look for from untutored Negroes: and it is but natural to suppose that they are assisted in these by their friends among the educated classes" (Abrahams and Szwed 264, 265).[30] In this testimony, white skepticism about the intellectual powers of black artists vies with a startled recognition of talent and virtuosity. The only way the observer can explain this incongruity is that the "untutored" performers must have had aid from "educated" friends. But literacy in this context was defined, not by European book learning, but by alternative knowledge bases that were indeed the domain of "untutored negroes."

I cite this account because I wish to foreground women's primary role as inventors and carriers of this and the other traditions we have seen. Doing so is especially important given how marginalized they remain in studies of Caribbean intellectual history. This includes studies of Caribbean music that tend to focus on musicians, often male percussionists and singers, at the expense of female artists, who are often relegated to the background as "just" dancers.[31] Male writers-turned politician-pedagogues were prominent at the expense of their female counterparts in the nineteenth century (think Eugenio Maria de Hostos, the Marcelin brothers, and José Martí) and remained so in the twentieth (Aimé Césaire and Eric Williams are prime examples). However, contemporary reports are replete with details about women's dynamism as leaders, their ferocious competitive edge, and their artistic acumen. They were equally represented, if not more common, as inter-island migrants in the wake of the Haitian Revolution, and any complete picture of the time period must incorporate their contributions.

One further example, this time drawn from Trinidad, confirms women's roles as creators and custodians of performative knowledge. Charles William Day, the caustic observer from the chapter's opening epigraph, attended what we can surmise was a *bèlè* celebration. I include his lengthy description because it provides a vivid summary, however racistly conceived, of the performance aesthetic we have seen thus far. He wrote:

> One night, hearing a horrible drumming on the tum-tums, I followed the sounds, and in the suburbs of the town came to a very characteristic scene—a negro *ladies'* ball. . . . At the head of this dingy *salon de danse* were five huge negroes, thumping might and main on casks, the tops of which were covered with parchment. Ranged on one side were twenty negresses roaring a chorus, each being in motion, turning half round alternately without moving from the spot. . . . In front of the choristers were about a dozen other ladies, having their woolly hair enclosed by a Madras handkerchief. . . . Enormous bunches of ear-rings hung from their ears, and their necks were adorned with a perfect gorget of gold chains and beads. The waists of the Trinidad negresses are absurdly short, so that a skirt, or *jupe,* always of a different colour, bags out, when the wearer is at rest. . . . Each of the ladies was performing a set of ludicrous evolutions, turning quite independently of her neighbour; and such jerkings, and courtesies, such genuflections and whirls as I beheld, baffle description! All danced with bare feet [and] men rarely join the festive throng, [having] to pay a small sum for the pleasure. (294–96)[32]

The bodily fashion and movement aesthetic is strikingly similar to ones we have seen in Saint-Domingue, Jamaica, Cuba, and Puerto Rico. Groups of women led the festivities, singing and dancing to the music produced by male percussionists. The account suggests that they were the arbiters of style, not simply its passive receptacles.

To return to the formal musical characteristics of the *bèlè*, the tradition is divided into eight separate figures including work songs, fighting songs, and so forth (Berrian 212).[33] The *cinquillo* rhythm is extremely prominent and is commonly played on the *tibwa*. Like the *catá* and the *cuá*, it is a cylindrical, open-ended instrument played with two sticks. Traditionally, an additional drummer crouched behind the primary percussionist, who was sitting astride the instrument, and played syncopated rhythms such as the *cinquillo* near the back of a horizontally positioned drum.[34] Hence, even when a separate instrument is not incorporated, the technique still involves beating two sticks against one of the main drums. In both the *bèlè* and the *tumba francesa*, the *tibwa* and *catá* are usually the first percussive instruments to begin. They establish the rhythm of the other instruments.

In an intriguing commentary on the origins of the *tanbou bèlè* in Martinique, also known as a *djouba* drum, the Martinican musician and musicologist Sully Cally suggests that this drum may have originated in Haiti. He states:

> In Martinique, no element allows us to identify the ethnic African origin of this drum. But if we go to Haiti . . . we will find in Haitian Vodou a ceremony dedicated to the *lwa* of the peasants named Zaca, where the musical element accompanying this ritual is called Djouba. In certain regions of Haiti, this same drum is called the Martinique drum. *Djouba* represents the name of the drum as well as the musical form it interprets and the accompanying dance. . . . One plays the instrument exactly as it is played in Martinique, the musician is seated astride it and the rear part of the instrument is tapped by another musician with the aid of two "ti-bwa." The drummer uses his heel on the membrane to change the timbre. . . . All of these details make me suppose that the authenticity of the Martinican drum, called the *bèlè,* can be found in its purest form in Haiti.

> En Martinique aucun élément ne nous permet antérieurement d'identifier l'origine ethno-africaine de ce tambour. Mais rendons nous en Haïti, ancienne colonie française sous le nom de Saint-Domingue . . . et nous retrouverons dans le vaudou haïtien une cérémonie vouée au culte du dieu paysan Zaca ou l'élément musical accompagnant ce rituel est nommé Djouba. Dans certaines régions d'Haïti ce même tambour est appelé Tanbou matinik. . . . Djouba représente aussi bien le nom de l'instrument que la forme musicale interprétée par celui-ci, ainsi que la danse qu'il accompagne; le Djouba dansé. . . . On l'utilise [l'instrument] exactement comme à la Martinique, le musicien est assis à califourchon sur l'instrument qui est frappé sur sa partie arrière par un autre musicien à l'aide de deux "ti-bwa." Le tambouyé utilise son talon sur la membrane pour changer le timbre de celui-ci. . . . Tous ces éléments me font supposer que l'authenticité du tambour martiniquais dit bèlè dans sa forme la plus pure pourrait se retrouver en Haiti. (18–19)

Hence according to Cally the "purest" form of the *bèlè/djouba* drum can be found in Haiti, and it is played using virtually identical techniques. The fact that this same drum is called the *tanbou matinik* in Haiti is a semantic circle that certainly complicates the question of origins while emphasizing the constant interisland movements, both before and after the Haitian Revolution, that made such commonalities possible.

I close with a useful visual artifact provided by the intrepid traveler Lafcadio Hearn. It documents the techniques involved in the sound production of the *bèlè* and, by extension, the *tumba francesa*, the *bomba*, and Belisario's performance of "frenchness." In a series of descriptions chronicling his 1888 visit to Martinique, Hearn included a photograph and a description of the music he had heard while on a plantation in Grande Anse. The image, entitled *Manner of Playing the Ka*, depicts "the best drummer in the settlement" sitting astride his drum (figure 27). *Ka* is a generic term for drum, more specifically called the *tanbou bèlè*. A young boy is seated behind the percussionist to his left, who "keeps striking the drum at the uncovered end with a stick, so as to produce a dry clattering accompaniment." This accompaniment may well have been the rhythm of the *cinquillo*. As for the drums themselves, Hearn provides the following description:

> Both ends of the barrel having been removed, a wet hide, well wrapped about a couple of hoops, is driven on and in drying the stretched skin obtains still further tension. The other end of the ka is always left open. Across the face of the skin a string is tightly stretched, to which are attached, at intervals of about an inch apart, very short thin fragments of bamboo or cut feather stems. These lend a certain vibration to the tones. . . . . The skillful player straddles his ka stripped to the waist, and plays upon it with the finger-tips of both hands simultaneously—taking care that the vibrating string occupies a horizontal position. Occasionally the heel of the naked foot is pressed lightly or vigorously against the skin, so as to produce changes in tone. This is called "giving heel" to the drum—*baill y talon*. (143–47)

Hearn's detailed description, documented by a printed image, provides remarkable evidence of the musical corollaries between different islands: sitting astride the drum, using the heel, and incorporating the catta sticks.

These correspondences are further demonstrated in the aforementioned presence of the horizontal chords on the drumhead. Octavo Alén, a noted scholar of the *tumba francesa*, mentions that a string called a *ficelle* was often stretched across the membrane and that it

FIGURE 27. *Manner of Playing the Ka*. Photograph.
Reproduced in Lafcadio Hearn, *Two Years in the French
West Indies* (New York: Harper & Brothers Publishers,
1889). Courtesy of the Library Company of Philadelphia.

was "a band of twisted skin in the middle of which was a chicken
or buzzard feather" ("una cinta de piel torcida en cuyo centro había
una pluma de gallina o de aura"; Alén, *Musica de las sociedades* 49).
Fascinatingly, Belisario provides almost identical testimony to that
provided by Hearn and Alén in the short description that accompanied the *French-Set Girls*. The text of the Belisario sketch reads as
follows: "They have their Queen, and allow male companions to join
in their dances, during which, two drums or 'Tamboos' are played,
and an instrument is shaken, called a 'Shaka.' . . . They are formed of
barrels, having both ends taken out, and a parchment of goat's skin
strained over them. A fiddlestring, with several pins, and pieces of quill
stuck on it, is affixed across the drum; these produce a buzzing sound
on coming in contact with the parchment during the vibration of the
same. The player sits on the instrument" (Ranston 254). The parallels

of such minute instrumental details, such as the presence of a feather or quill attached to a horizontal cord, speak volumes for the dialogues between slaves from different islands who developed a common musical vocabulary. Belisario's reference to the queen is also critical, for *tumba francesa* societies, as well as traditional *bomba* and *bèlè*, were hierarchically organized along aristocratic lines.

These details highlight the self-reflexivity involved in the performance of all of these traditions. Complicating a notion common to early observers that black music was primarily improvisational, these artisans set standards of discipline and methodology. An adaptable, yet systematized worldview explains the parallel rhythms and instrumentation. An aesthetic sensitive to nuance explains the subtlety and complexity we have seen. The performance traditions that passed from one generation to the next represented a system of knowledge that musical intellectuals spread and developed as they migrated from one colonial sphere of influence to another. Technical skills were needed to make the drums—carving ability, knowledge of what trees and animals skins provided maximum sound quality, and the know-how to properly assemble, tune, and bless the instruments.[35] Training and practice were indispensable—knowing where to place the hands on the drumhead, implementing complex rhythms, mastering footwork and gestures. Add to these requirements an ability to sing cleverly about current affairs in a variety of languages learned by necessity, and one has a sense of how black artists and their publics expended their creative energy and developed pedagogical tools. Taken together, an extremely multifaceted, difficult-to-master set of practices emerges. They exemplify both the physical repositories of knowledge and the conceptual standards that undergird the work of these intellectual publics.

The implications for such behaviors are many. A common musical vocabulary illustrates how play idioms were assertions of small-scale, quotidian politics that were inimical to the logic of dehumanization that characterized chattel slavery.[36] When these convergences are seen at a regional level, they corroborate J. Lorand Matory's contention that "lifeways, traditions, and the social boundaries they substantiate endure not *despite* their involvement in translocal dialogues but *because* of it" (1). In the context of forced migration from Saint-Domingue to other locales in the circum-Caribbean, these knowledges remained relevant precisely because they transformed into something new, something equally vibrant. Hence adaptations to the tradition of set girl performance allowed people to still practice and disseminate this knowledge in Jamaica. In a colonial system that allowed slaves and free people to form *cabildos*, the creation of *tumba francesa* societies in Cuba permitted the traditions to flourish there.

The idea of repercussions is thus fitting. These performative discussions were always being restaged and renegotiated. They moved from island to island, connecting people, doubling back (to Saint-Domingue, to Africa), and reverberating in such a way that we can see the burgeoning cultural life that linked the enslaved across colonial frontiers. As these practices transformed themselves, a consistent core set of material rituals and conceptual framings remained. And therein we see what practices these mobile communities chose to maintain under extraordinary circumstances.

LEGACIES

As noted above, in Martinique and Puerto Rico the *bèlè* and *bomba* forms are commonly described as "the most African" musics in the spectrum of local traditions. In Cuba and Jamaica, very similar performance genres are marked as French, albeit Afro-French. Just as "one culture's music is another culture's noise," one could posit that one culture's Africa is another culture's France. It is no surprise that in Martinique and Puerto Rico, territories that struggle with what many consider twenty-first-century colonial relationships, a desire to emphasize what is most different from French or U.S. influence is strong. Reclaiming African heritage has been a vital strategy of cultural nationalism.[37] In all contexts, accounting for distinction reveals a set of conscious choices. This was likewise the case for the French Set girls, who alternatively emphasized their African ethnicities (Congolese, Dahomeyan), their creole pedigrees (Jamaican, Cuban, Haitian), or one of many colonial labels (British, Spanish, French) depending on the circumstances.

Different methodologies have taught us much about these traditions. Africa-centric models, creolization theories, and colonial/national historiography have all succeeded in rescuing what were once scorned as mindless slave traditions from neglect, even oblivion. I believe that a transcolonial focus is also of particular use in demonstrating the flourishing of a regional counterplantation aesthetic during the Age of Revolution, an era that necessitated the constant renegotiation and restructuring of black community life. Such attention to the interstices of cultural production across today's national frontiers continues to be fruitful. In the contemporary Caribbean, for example, particular music genres are generally associated with specific nations: calypso with Trinidad, *bomba* with Puerto Rico. A circum-Caribbean lens illustrates the critical role played by interisland migrants to the development of these and other local traditions. While the "nationalization" of performance has strategic use, it is often at the expense of acknowledging the artistic acumen of a migrating group of black artists who provided the building blocks for these same practices.

By way of conclusion, we have seen how performers and their audiences were forced to come to grips with the dynamic tension that produced both togetherness and apartness depending on the political and intellectual choices they made. The underlying aesthetic of these late eighteenth- and early nineteenth-century performance idioms still resonates with more contemporary debates. Both state-sponsored projects such as the 1960s West Indies Federation and popular mobilizations such as Rastafarianism have pursued iterations of black collectivity that move across borders and frontiers. In each of these cases, centripetal forces require(d) a politics of possibility, a faith that oppressed people across the region could form strategic alliances in the face of common challenges. This preoccupation is also evident in the chapter that follows, in which we see how free blacks developed the political and cultural project of transcolonial collaboration in a novel, printed form. By the 1830s, Saint-Domingue still served as a powerful regional symbol, although the arrival of migrant "French negroes" to neighboring parts of the Americas subsided as the Age of Revolution drew to a close.

CHAPTER 5

"Sentinels on the Watch-Tower of Freedom"

The Black Press of the 1830s and 1840s

It has long been our anxious wish to see, in this slave-holding, slave-trading, and negro-hating land, a printing-press and paper, permanently established, under the complete control and direction of the immediate victims of slavery and oppression.

—Frederick Douglass and Martin Delany, editors of the *North Star* (1847–51)

Between 1830 and 1845 the political economy of American slavery came under renewed attack. Slave revolts such as Samuel Sharpe's Baptist War (Jamaica, 1831–32), Nat Turner's rebellion (Virginia, 1831), the Muslim Revolt / *Revolta dos Malês* (Brazil, 1835), and the Second Seminole War (1835–42) signaled a continuation of the armed resistance against planter control that occurred at the turn of the century during the unfolding and immediate aftermath of the Haitian Revolution.[1] For example, Jose Chirino's rebellion (Venezuela, 1795), the Second Maroon War (Jamaica, 1795–96), the Boca Nigua revolt (Santo Domingo, 1796), Gabriel Prosser's revolt (Virginia, 1800), Charles Deslondes's rebellion (Louisiana, 1811), and the Aponte conspiracy (Cuba, 1812) were just a few of the well-documented uprisings that threatened slave-holding regimes in the circum-Caribbean. Metropolitan ideological shifts likewise occasioned dynamic transformations in the operation of plantation economies, from the birth of the French Republic to the British abandonment of mercantilism that resulted in the end of their participation in the transatlantic slave trade. During the later hemispheric moment examined in this final chapter, the British abolished slavery in their Caribbean colonies under an apprenticeship system of gradual emancipation between 1834 and 1838. In direct contrast to these antislavery agendas, however, neighboring territories still expanded slavery's domain. Cuba, Brazil, and the southern and western United States were the most notable cases. In a climate of intense debates about the future of the institution, everyone paid close attention to these events, since they had direct implications for the social and economic status quo.[2]

In this charged atmosphere of possibility and repression, a number of black newspapers emerged that knit the region together through an aggressive campaign designed to promote unity and "open a channel of communication for the interchange of thought" (Jacobs 229). Motivated by a desire to advance regional abolition, advocate cultural exchange, and actively lobby in the interests of both free blacks and the enslaved throughout the Americas, the work of black journalists played a fundamental role in elaborating a transcolonial American consciousness in the public sphere. For the first time, black communities had their own written media outlets, and the information they disseminated was unique because it evaluated events according to criteria that measured the welfare of people of African descent. The papers were the most vocal print manifestations of the politicized, aesthetic consciousness I have documented thus far, evidence that colonial frontiers did not impinge upon the formulation of various inter-American projects committed to defending the rights of the oppressed community of Afro-America. Their work is thus a published, meditative accounting of how generations of people negotiated the interconnectedness of the Americas, often as a result of free and forced migration. Unlike the figures from previous chapters, however, the men who directed these papers expected their voices to be recorded, going to great lengths to ensure that their news would be broadcast to as large a public as possible and that their work could serve as a resource for politicizing readers.

The internationalist black press of the 1830s and 1840s demonstrates that the viability of inter-American collaboration was informed by the realities of multilingualism, the existence of migrating labor forces in a regional economy, and competing claims of racial, national, and regional self-identification. Collaboration and, equally important, insight into the methodology most appropriate to achieving this collaboration qualify these newspapers as the arbiters of a tremendously important sensibility that makes them a precursor to the more well-known nineteenth-century inter-American imaginary associated with figures such as Ramón E. Betances, Eugenio Maria de Hostos, and José Martí from the 1860s to the 1890s. But newspapers, as distinct from the lives of these migratory radicals, deserve our attention precisely for the promise they offered of ongoing communication in the absence of direct physical contact. Relatively neglected by scholarship on the Caribbean, these texts demonstrate that black intellectuals of the francophone and anglophone Americas placed discussions of regional autonomy and development alongside the compelling necessity of black self-determination. That these polemical writings predate the more closely studied ones is only part of the story; they also demonstrate how the field of early nineteenth-century inter-American studies had some of its most developed articulations at the juncture of antislavery ideology. I use the word *field* deliberately because the papers I have chosen to examine were intentionally pedagogical; their business was providing nuanced, artfully framed knowledge to a readership they wished to educate and mobilize.

As was the case in previous chapters, attention to cultural forms also brings into focus the variation in black communities, variation that impinged upon the ability to make sustainable cross-cultural connections, however persistent the desire was to do so. I examine three issues that highlight both the expansive and restrictive nature of these collaborations. These periodicals imaginatively constructed a model of inclusionary participation while reinforcing class, religious, and regional hierarchies. The editors were the elite of their respective black communities: literate and educated in a time of great illiteracy, free in an era of slavery, and devout, "hard-working" Christians, characteristics that they believed gave them a certain superiority over those who engaged in "frivolous" or "pagan" pursuits. Their biases emerge frequently in their writings. The politics of the freemen explored here differed greatly from the ones on exhibit at an earlier moment in the Gulf South, however, and though the papers' contributors may have seen themselves as more sophisticated and worthy of respect than their slave counterparts, they were still resolutely abolitionist.

In addition, while there is a sense of hope and promise in these pages, there is also a latent frustration. The intellectuals I study constantly meditated upon the limits of their own circumscribed freedom. During their dispirited moments, the editors would no doubt have agreed with the assertion documented in chapter 3 that the very term *free person of color* was mockingly paradoxical given the enormous power of a hemispheric economic and social system designed to ensure their continued exploitation. Sharing that frustration with an extended public was a mechanism through which free people of color could combat their isolation and their stymied political and social aspirations.

I use three papers to explore the literary dimensions of inter-American interchanges: the *Colored American* (New York, 1837–41), the *Revue des Colonies* (Paris/Martinique, 1834–42), and *L'Union* (Haiti, 1837–39). *Transnational* is a more accurate description of their editors' perspectives than *transcolonial,* given that two of these papers were published in the first independent nations of the Western hemisphere. That said, much of their coverage concerned nearby colonies. By reconstructing published debates, I show that black intellectuals defined a regional Afro-American identity (racial, cultural, and political) that depended on black collusion at a time when writers and readers were living in extremely hostile environments.[3] The papers' coverage of issues affecting blacks in all corners of the Americas— from Martinique, to Brazil, to Jamaica—is evidence of communication networks that engaged both the papers' collaborators and their readerships. As primary-source material, their contents deserve to be juxtaposed in the present, as there is ample evidence that they were in dialogue with one another at the time of their publication.

I thus conclude this study of transcolonial/transnational collaboration with an examination of the printed word as an antislavery, community-mobilizing mechanism. I do this through an analysis of three issues of public debate that served as a means of making communities of color both legible and relevant to one another. First I discuss an international diasporic literacy campaign that was promulgated out of a political necessity to stay informed about the most up-to-date news affecting people of African descent. Second, I examine how these papers helped broker the relocation of North American black laborers to the Caribbean and South America during an era of state-sponsored emigration initiatives. Finally, I focus on how the papers aggressively lauded the accomplishments of the Haitian Revolution in an effort to promote the political aim of a Caribbean confederation.

Ultimately, despite a deliberate effort to highlight the interconnectedness of black people in the extended Americas, these papers prioritized the assimilation of their readerships into their respective national home societies. As one article declared, "With the character of the country we are identified, and with its character we intend to sink or swim."⁴ With the glaring exception of many islands in the Caribbean, most colonial states in the region had become national ones. The inter-American literacy project examined below, while politically oriented and historically grounded, was not conceived to explore the objective of a black separatist, institutionalized political unit beyond that which already existed in Haiti.

PERIODICAL CAMPAIGNS: PROMOTING AN AFRICAN DIASPORIC LITERACY PROJECT

The conscious positioning of local struggles in an international framework was accomplished through an aggressive use of the medium of print journalism.Newspapers were the most widely read popular literary genre during the early nineteenth century and were a primary source of public knowledge.⁵ The three papers under examination established themselves as *porte-paroles* of their respective communities, becoming self-appointed arbiters of political, social, and cultural affairs. As the editors of the *Colored American* asked their readers, "Who can tell the power of the press, and who can measure its influence? Ever since it came into use, it has been about the first means resorted to to bring about any great change in Church or State. . . . And so it is with reformers at the present day" (September 25, 1841). The periodical press was thus the genre of choice for the literate, reform-minded members of these African diasporic communities, a consciously selected tool for disseminating information geared toward improving the life possibilities of their readerships. More than simply being attentive to the news that their publics were interested in reading, the editors of all three papers deemed it their job to *tell* the public what they *should* be reading. This section explores how transcolonial consciousness was expressed via methodologies designed to actively obtain information, translate it when necessary, and provide a framework that made the contents relevant. A critical element of this framing entailed the promotion of what can be considered an African diasporic literary canon, the first of its kind in the Americas.

I begin with the *Colored American* (1837–41), the fourth African American newspaper founded in the United States. Published every Saturday in New York City, its editors and proprietors were Samuel Cornish, Philip A. Bell, and Charles Ray, a group of African American Protestant ministers with prior journalistic experience (figure 28).⁶ It was one of many short-lived black periodicals in publication during the antebellum period in the United States. The January 13, 1838, edition

FIGURE 28. Portrait of Philip A. Bell. Lithograph. Irvine Garland Penn, *The Afro-American Press and Its Editors* (Springfield: Willey & Co. Publishers, 1891). Courtesy of the Manuscripts, Archives and Rare Books Division, Schomburg Center for Research in Black Culture, The New York Public Library, Astor, Lenox and Tilden Foundations.

notes that the newspaper had 1,800 subscribers and "10,000 who read it." Constantly in danger of financial ruin, the editors repeatedly appealed to their readership for support, reminding them:

> It is your own paper, the only weekly paper that we have. . . . It visits thousands, and ought to ten thousands; and would were the people awake to their duty and interest. Take your paper along then, to your meetings, and read some extracts, and let your friends see what is happening—what can be done. Facts will interest, and cheer and encourage them. There is no paper in the world that contains so much that should interest us. There is none of which we have so much reason to be proud. A sentinel on the watch-tower of freedom, it pleads our rights. If it lives it will thunder the terrors of omnipotent truth in the ears of the oppressor and proclaim hope to the Oppressed. (April 22, 1837)[7]

The attempt to create a public forum for a discussion of current events and a platform for future mobilization was the cornerstone of the paper's philosophy. Convinced of the urgency of its message as part of a divine (Christian) plan for the redemption of the black race, the *Colored American* published a well-researched collection of information concerning blacks throughout the Americas.

The *Revue des Colonies* (1834–42) was the brainchild of Cyril Charles-Auguste Bissette, a free mulatto merchant from Martinique (figure 29). He was exiled from the French Caribbean colonies for his alleged role as a political agitator in the 1823 distribution of the polemical pamphlet *De la situation des gens de couleur libres (Of the Situation of Free People of Color)*. Branded on the shoulder, deprived

FIGURE 29. Portrait of Cyrille Charles Auguste Bissette. Lithograph by François Villain. In Joseph Elzéar Morénas, *Précis historique de la traite des noirs et de l'esclavage colonial, contenant: L'origine de la traite, ses progrès, son état actuel, et un exposé des horreurs produits par le despotisme des colons* (Paris: n.p., 1828). Courtesy of the Manuscripts, Archives and Rare Books Division, Schomburg Center for Research in Black Culture, The New York Public Library, Astor, Lenox and Tilden Foundations.

of his property, and imprisoned by the French authorities as subversive, he became a cause célèbre in Paris, where he founded the paper. As was the case with Joseph Savary from chapter 3, Bissette had also been a slaveholder at one time. His experiences radicalized him, however, and he eventually came to recognize that free people of color and slaves had common interests.[8] Bissette directed the *Revue*, a "receuil mensuel de la politique, de l'administration, de la justice, de l'instruction et des moeurs coloniales," with indefatigable energy and a penchant for making enemies of both the planter lobby in France and potential allies. Its objective was clearly stated in the first issue's prospectus as follows: "These reclamations, these grievances, in order to be successfully addressed, must receive the greatest publicity; that is the object of our Review. The weak will find within support and protection, the oppressor, punishment, the bureaucrat the justifiable blame for his illegal actions" ("Ces réclamations, ces griefs, pour avoir du succès, doivent recevoir la plus grande publicité: c'est l'objet de notre Revue.... Le faible y trouvera appui et protection, l'oppresseur, châtiment, le fonctionnaire, blâme mérité de ses actes illégaux"; July 1834). Just as the editors of the *Colored American* were earnest about the role that the paper played as a "sentinel on the watch-tower of freedom," the *Revue des Colonies* was equally dogged in its staunch defense of the rights of the weak. Remarkable for its acerbic, aggressively abolitionist, and uncompromising tone, the paper existed to inform and sway the court of public opinion by publicizing events that violated the principles of the 1789 Déclaration des Droits de l'Homme et du Citoyen (Declaration of the Rights of Man and the Citizen). Bissette acknowledged this document as the ideal foundation of all just and equitable societies. Thus his critiques, while strident, were tempered by his republican loyalty to the principles of the French Revolution. Like the editors of all three papers, he was a reformer interested in having his native country live up to the principles of its founding documents. While the *Colored American* numbered its subscriber base at between 1,800 and 2,000 people, the *Revue* had a more limited circulation of 250 subscribers according to Bissette's own estimate. Most if not all of them were outside his native French Caribbean, since there "authorities did everything possible to impede its circulation."[9]

As a monthly publication, the *Revue* was longer in format than the two weeklies.[10] Issues averaged about thirty-five pages, and some of the longer ones totaled close to seventy. The writers of *Revue* dismantled the arguments of their proslavery enemies point by point, affording their readers a detailed inventory of some of the most momentous public debates of the time. The paper primarily published updates on French Caribbean and African colonies, while a section devoted to "colonies etrangères" covered news concerning the British and Spanish Caribbean in great depth.

The third paper, *L'Union* (1837–39), was published in Port-au-Prince by E. Nau and A. Blackhurst. It was promoted as a "Receuil Commercial et Littéraire." Although little is known about Blackhurst, Emile Nau was a celebrated journalist and historian, an advocate of the development of a national Haitian literature, and the author of a study of the indigenous population of the island, *Histoire des caciques d'Haiti* (1855).[11] A weekly journal that averaged about four pages per issue, *L'Union* was characteristic of the aggressive campaign waged by Haitian intellectuals in the years after the Haitian Revolution to "vindicate the Black race" by refuting claims of African inferiority. The underlying political philosophy of the paper was its recognition that Haitian national sovereignty depended on developing commercial and diplomatic ties with its closest neighbors.

L'Union was used as a forum for the publication of information that focused on three major categories: news from abroad / *nouvelles etrangères,* commercial and economic tracts / *notices commerciales,* and essays on history and literature. Both domestic and international affairs received critical attention, and the paper vigorously advocated the integration of its readership into debates about the future of the new republic. This goal was especially important given that the population was increasingly unhappy with the presidency of Jean-Pierre Boyer and the Revolution of 1843 was on the horizon. This is the same President Boyer who integrated the western and eastern territories of Hispaniola for twenty-two years.

Given the content of all three papers, I argue that their editors developed a shared sensibility concerning the news worth reporting. Regional coverage typified the 1830s/1840s black press. For example, the print dimensions of transcolonial networks of communication are demonstrated in the impressive accumulation of facts concerning the emancipation process in countries all over the Americas. The June 1837 issue of the *Colored American* alone provides headlines concerning events in Saint-Domingue, Guadeloupe, Chile, Colombia, Mexico, the British West Indies, and even the state of affairs of the "Hottentots" in South Africa.[12] The editors examined here used journalism to promote what VèVè A. Clark has conceptualized as diaspora literacy, a term connoting a "reader's ability to comprehend the literatures of Africa, Afro-America, and the Caribbean from an informed, indigenous perspective."[13] The papers covered news with the assumption that this informed, historicized perspective would stimulate readers' consciousness and then mobilize them to lobby in the interests of their brethren at home and abroad. Literacy was viewed as a self-help mechanism, evidence of the relationship between text, self-empowerment, and social change that is well documented by scholars of the African diaspora.[14]

By definition, however, the readership of these papers was limited in societies where the majority of the population of color had been legally barred from learning to read. Even when free, people had inadequate opportunities to acquire such a skill. Unlike the music and dance repertoires examined in chapter 4—inclusive and participatory manifestations of a black public sphere that incorporated the enslaved and the free—these periodicals were run and presumably consumed by those with some access to formal education. For example, in the case of *L'Union*, published less than thirty years after Haitian independence, the paper was produced in an environment in which the majority of the population of former slaves did not speak, much less read, French. Despite such formidable challenges, these papers sought to cast as wide a net of publicity as possible. Papers were often read aloud in community gatherings to a larger audience, and exchange reading rooms were established that kept newspapers on hand for subscribers and nonsubscribers alike. The establishment of communal spaces for reading and discussion has much in common with the strategies used later by activists involved in turn-of-the-century Cuban nationalist parties or the modern North American labor movement. All used public readings as a forum for political instruction.[15] Hence, while Sophia A. McClennen argues that the academic pursuit of inter-American studies began in the 1930s, I believe that these papers were also quintessentially "academic," especially at a time when universities were not admitting people of African descent.[16] Their editors researched, analyzed, and disseminated data about the extended Americas with the explicit goal of educating their readers about locales and events that were propitious for the progress of the black race.

The educational project under way was extremely ambitious in that the papers were undertaking a de facto literacy campaign to inspire and mobilize their readerships around "momentous" events in the African diaspora. Coverage of Haiti was especially detailed in *Revue* and the *Colored American,* much as it was the focus of *L'Union.* Accounts of the Haitian Revolution and the life of Toussaint Louverture figured prominently among these celebratory panegyrics. Just as white Saint-Domingue refugees used the periodical press to vilify the sanguinary "rebels," now black authors and their readers had their own forums to publicly defend black self-determination. Even Macandal, the legendary slave who initiated a successful poisoning campaign throughout the island in the 1750s, was eulogized (*L'Union* August 9, 1838). However, the historical distance of these particular events in Saint-Domingue seems to have made them "safer" subjects of analysis. Significantly, the armed revolts chronicled in the opening of this chapter, many of them contemporaneous to the papers' publication, received almost no attention. Instead, as the manumission process unfolded in the British colonies, extensive coverage of industrious and peaceful ex-slaves was used to justify why emancipation should be effected immediately versus on a more gradual time line. Reports were full of information about how "well behaved" the newly freed were, and how little prone to agitation and destruction. This suggests that the editors ultimately endorsed reform and nonviolent struggle as models of protest.

One notable exception to this pattern was coverage of the second Seminole War (1835–42). Attention to this struggle occurred within a larger context whereby the *Colored American* made an argument for why black Americans ought to take an interest in Native American affairs. In a forceful analysis of common interest, the editors suggested that the U.S. government had repeatedly betrayed the two communities. For example, they expressly employed the term *native* to describe both black North Americans and the "Indians." These groups were juxtaposed to recent European immigrants who, unlike them, were afforded the possibility of integration and social acceptance. During the years of the paper's publication, both the Seminole conflict and the Cherokee removal, also known as the Trail of Tears (1838), were under way as a result of the 1830 Indian Removal Act. One issue published a poem demanding that Americans "Prove that ye are not Slavery's slaves! At Slavery's beck, the very hands Ye lift to heaven, to swear ye're free, Will break a truce, to seize the lands of Seminole or Cherokee!" (June 23, 1838). The newspaper paid especially close attention to the Seminole War, given that many Seminoles were of African descent and that the conflict had implications for the extension of U.S. slavery. Chapter 1 examined how similar transcolonial warfare strategies were used to subdue both black and indigenous insurgents during these battles, and the aforementioned speeches of Congressman Joshua Giddings were reprinted in full over several 1841 issues. On a side note that further demonstrates African American interest in Native American affairs, an announcement from the April 22, 1837, edition stated that "an Indian will lecture on Monday evening in the first African Methodist Episcopal Church [on] the manners and customs of his people." The notice then added, "He will appear in the full dress of an Indian Chief" and suggested that people arrive early, as the event promised to be crowded.

I now turn to an analysis of methodology as it speaks to the issue of editorial intent.[17] I have found two strategies to be of particular importance to the black press. First, to keep abreast of events throughout the Americas, fluency in the languages of the region was a methodological necessity. It is clear that all three newspapers employed polyglots comfortable in a number of languages simultaneously, and the editors presented news to their readers as if it had always been in their native French or English. That is, the actual act of translation was silent and often unacknowledged, but it was an inevitable step in the process of regional integration. Coverage of events gleaned from original sources in French, French Creole, English, Spanish, and Portuguese was commonplace and demonstrated an ability to negotiate the multilingual realities of the greater American polity. Intellectual paradigms that balkanize the region according to linguistic variance do not acknowledge the importance of efforts made to promote the common interests of the region's populations despite this variance. The 1830s black press provides eloquent evidence of the commitment to overcoming the potential divisiveness of linguistic difference.

Second, information gathering relied on the availability of sources, and the types of sources used by these authors are evidence of the particular objectives they held and the challenges they faced when reporting. The editorial staffs made it their mission to locate and print any document that might shed light on both past and current affairs of relevance to people of African descent. The September 1840 issue of *Revue des Colonies* provides one example of the work that went into obtaining primary sources of interest. Bissette told his readers, "Mais voilà qu'en feuilletant des archives nous trouvons sous la main une série de pièces officielles dans le genre." "Leafing through the archives" of a wide range of sources, including primary documents housed by the French colonial minister of the marine, was an analytic strategy.

As far as was practicable, investigative journalism was also employed, and the papers used agents to provide firsthand reports about events. This was the case with the emigration ventures examined below. Given the dangers inherent in inter-American travel for free blacks in the slave-holding societies of the Caribbean Basin, however, employing agents to investigate information was risky. Olaudah Equiano's memorable distress at seeing many of these free men forcibly kidnapped and enslaved is instructive. Disgusted with customs in the West Indies, where "might too often overcomes right," he wrote, "hitherto I had thought only slavery dreadful, but the state of a free negro appeared to me now equally so at least, and in some respects worse, for they live in constant alarm for their liberty, which is but nominal, for they are universally insulted and plundered" (107).[18] All three papers were often forced to rely heavily on information disseminated in other periodicals of the time, making accounts second- or thirdhand. This practice of recycling news from other papers was common in the nineteenth century. However, these editors recognized that depending on printed sources for accurate, up-to-date details about the welfare of black people was also a problem given that information was intentionally withheld.

The issues of censorship and access to information should not be underestimated. For example, the *Colored American* reprinted an article from the Afro-American periodical *Emancipator*, edited by the well-known activist David Ruggles. The paper complained, "So stupid or so willful are the conductors of the American newspapers, that we have to depend on English newspapers for our information of what is passing at our doors. Not one American newspaper that we have seen has given publicity to the following official document [announcing that all classes of apprentices in Montserrat and Barbados are free]" (June 9, 1838). When news was available, several publications were repeatedly cited as sources, including the *Emancipator* and the *Morning Journal of Jamaica*. Significantly, the three papers studied here also cited each other. For instance, the November 1, 1838, issue of *L'Union* mentions an article in the *Colored American* outlining recent developments in the effort to procure formal U.S. recognition of Haitian independence. Likewise, a September 15, 1838, issue of the *Colored American* mentions that via the *Jamaica Dispatch* they received a copy of *L'Union*. With some difficulty, they maintained a dialogue with one another and with the international abolitionist press.

It is worth highlighting that in the case of *L'Union*, this was an especially precarious practice given attempts to isolate Haiti in the region. The governing polemic was the incongruity of a self-governing independent nation (in the age of colonialism), self-defined as a black republic (in the age of slavery), in the geographic center of Europe's prized colonial possessions and the neighboring U.S. South. The editors' anxiety and resentment at being kept out of the loop is palpable. As one editor notes, "It seems extraordinary that, while in Haiti we are so well and regularly informed about news in Europe and of the littlest events that happen two thousand leagues from us, we are completely ignorant, or are only informed very late, of events that took place in our immediate vicinity, given that the deplorable colonial system that rules the majority of the neighboring islands and territories forbids us from having any direct relations with them" ("Il paraîtrait extraordinaire que, tandis que nous sommes en Haïti si bien et si régulièrement informés des nouvelles d'Europe et des plus petits événmens [sic] qui y arrivent quoiqu'à 2,000 lieues de nous, nous ignorions tout à fait ou ne connaissions que fort tard les faits qui ont lieu dans notre voisinage immédiat. Bien que le déplorable système colonial que régit la plupart des îles et terres circonvoisines nous interdise toute relation directe avec elles").[19] Any perusal of documents from the postrevolutionary period demonstrates the frustration experienced by the Haitian government as it fought to combat this isolation. As one author once wrote when Haitian citizens were publicly assaulted while in the United States, "The day may yet come when it will be in our power to cause the name of Haytiens to be respected abroad, and particularly so by our arrogant neighbors" (September 13, 1838).

The editors of these papers thus circulated news from each other's publications and shared a journalistic aesthetic that prioritized similar content, multilingual sources, and publicity as an activist tool. Did their transnational focus extend to their audiences such that their reading publics also crossed colonial/national boundaries? These newspapers point to a process through which an imaginative, cognitive map of community was being drawn that was very different from the nation-grounded models of newspaper consumption suggested by scholars of creole nationalism such as Benedict Anderson.[20] There is ample evidence not only that all three newspapers were in (remote) dialogue with one another but also that each attracted readers throughout the Caribbean Basin. Consider the question of subscribers. The *Revue* published a letter to the editor from A. Broard, a "subscriber from Santo Domingo," stating: "I wanted to tell you how much we applaud your efforts, or better said, your success. Athletes emerging victorious from the ring, we don't forget that your cause and ours is the same. And if we are not allowed to enter the ring with you, we are at least permitted to encourage you with our acclamations" ("j'ai voulu vous dire combien nous applaudissons à vos efforts, ou pour mieux dire à vos succès. Athlètes, sortis victorieux de l'arène, nous n'oublions pas cependant que votre cause et la nôtre sont les mêmes; et s'il ne nous est pas permis d'y descendre avec vous, il nous est du moins permis de vous encourager par nos acclamations"; May 6, 1835). The subscriber thus acknowledged a sense of common cause between Haitians and other black Americans. Aware that Haiti could not fight directly alongside its neighbors, he felt that its citizens could at least support such a struggle.

This sense of having common interests that superseded nationality was echoed in an August 1, 1840, letter to the editors of the *Colored American* entitled "Cheering from Jamaica." A subscriber by the name of John Berger appended a list of nineteen new subscribers that he had recruited in Jamaica and donations from twenty-three Jamaican supporters. He stated that he was "agreeably surprised to receive the *Colored American* again, for my friends as well as myself. Your long silence caused us to think the worthy publication was numbered among the dead. But thrice happy am I, in unison with my friends, to find that it has appeared again in all its splendor with renewed zeal and vigor in the cause of truth and justice to the men of color all over the habitable globe." The information published in all three newspapers thus attracted readers throughout the Caribbean Basin. Subscribers in the United States evinced an interest in learning about their brethren abroad, and residents in the Caribbean were likewise interested in events in the United States and neighboring islands. This interest corroborates the evidence that we have seen throughout the book: racial solidarity was not confined to those living within the same national and/or colonial borders.

I close this discussion of periodical campaigns to promote an African diasporic literacy project by considering in detail the theorization of diaspora and a corresponding African diasporic literary canon. The word *diaspora* is not used in any of these papers; however, the concept of a shared cultural, historical, and, by extension, political set of beliefs is fundamental to the tenor and social projects of each. More concretely, regional slavery and the universal scorn heaped upon both the enslaved and free blacks resulted in a perceived need to unify the oppressed in a common struggle. Hence terminology such as "our brethren," "our oppressed humanity in other countries," or "men of color all over the habitable globe" stands in for a racialized collectivity. A communal resistance to oppression seems to have mobilized these communities more than any articulation of shared values due to dispersion from a common African homeland. This is not surprising given that the black elite in a variety of contexts often shared a colonialist European view of the backwardness of the African continent. Undoubtedly, however, all of these editors espoused an aggressively racialized point of view in a time period when both the local and metropolitan elite took pains to prevent collaboration among the region's disenfranchised and enslaved majority.

How did this perspective manifest itself? The *Revue*, for example, categorized its published literary canon using terms such as "Littérature des noirs," "Célébrités africaines," and "Nègres remarquables." This canon defined what was perceived to be as useful knowledge. Featured authors were grouped according to subtitles that encouraged the self-conscious creation of a black tradition that was largely literary in nature. The *Revue* was in fact the most traditionally "literary" newspaper of the three, publishing poems and short stories alongside expository essays and biographical author sketches.[21] Fiction was given prominence in the battle to educate the public mind and advance the cause of racial equality.[22] The paper was replete with information about late eighteenth- and early nineteenth-century literary figures that are now considered the founders of African diasporic discourse. Hence, much as Clark suggests that the central component of twentieth-century diaspora literacy implies that "names such as *Popul Vuh*, Legba, Bélain d'Esnambuc, Nanny, José Martí, Bigger Thomas, and Marie Chauvet represent mnemonic devices whose recall releases a learned tradition" ("Developing Diaspora Literacy" 42), in the 1830s the names that would trigger similar familiar reactions include those promoted in the *Revue des Colonies*—Olaudah Equiano, Phillis Wheatley, the Haitian journalist and poet Ignace Nau, the Jamaican poet Francis Williams, the Louisianan playwright Victor Séjour, and the Afro-British author Ignatius Sancho. As demonstrated by the list above, *Revue* presented information about the best-selling black authors of its time, forming a veritable "Who's Who" of the early Black Atlantic.[23]

In addition to providing biographical sketches, the paper served to anthologize authors' works. The texts of the pioneers of Afro-American letters were published in its pages, many presented and translated for the first time for a foreign audience. Just as the newspaper's coverage was interdisciplinary as a whole, its literary coverage was similarly multigeneric, as demonstrated by the inclusion of slave narratives, short stories, poetry, *pièces de théâtre*, and theoretical treatises. For example, the newspaper published French translations of three of Phillis Wheatley's poems, originally published in English in 1773. These were accompanied by a reproduction of her portrait and a sketch of the circumstances of her extraordinary life.[24] Likewise, Francis Williams, the earliest known Jamaican poet, who, like Wheatley, was educated as part of an experiment to ascertain the potential of the black race, was included as a "remarkable black." Williams's only surviving poem, a 1759 ode written in Latin to the then governor of Jamaica, George Haldane, was translated into French and published in its entirety. Had it not been for the original publication of Williams's work in Edward Long's canonical *History of Jamaica* (1774), the poet's one extant poem might have been lost. By reprinting and translating it in *Revue*, however, Bissette challenged Long's racist assessment of Williams's work, making both the poet and the poem part of a larger African diasporic tradition that coexisted alongside the virulently racist body of work about the Caribbean written from the perspective of the planter elite.[25]

Thus these papers proactively fought to keep their inter-American (and French) publics informed. They did so despite great obstacles, including financial distress and difficulties obtaining up-to-date and accurate information. Conflict with mainstream white abolitionists also seems to have been a problem. In the case of the *Revue*, Lawrence Jennings notes that "Bissette operated outside the mainstream of emancipationism, and was largely discredited by a series of bitter disputes that alienated him from other prominent French abolitionists. [He] stood out for the radicalism of his approach" ("Cyrille Bissette" 56). One can suppose that his call for immediate emancipation, a radical one in French abolitionist circles of the time, led to his marginalization and an increasingly desperate financial situation. In the case of the *Colored American*, a letter to the editors during one of the paper's many financial crises also suggests how black newspaper publics had differences of opinion with white abolitionists. The editors describe how "men of high distinction in the abolitionist ranks have said that it must no longer be supported. Men for whose names we have ever had the highest veneration, have said, 'No more money for the Colored American.' But what am I to say to those colored men who are weakly and blindly aiding and abetting in this unprovoked, unjustifiable homicide! Are they aware that if this paper is now silenced, in a short time there will not be another paper in the United States in which we can express our opinions free and untrammeled?" (November 16, 1839). As noted in the opening epigraph, an independent black printing press and paper were perceived to be absolutely necessary if black public intellectuals were to express their opinions without censorship and to decide for themselves the most pressing issues facing their communities.[26] Participation in white abolitionist circles was not sufficient and sometimes proved alienating and counterproductive. This tension between black intellectuals and white abolitionist circles certainly plagued both Frederick Douglass and Martin Delany. The search for the means by which people of African descent would be autonomous, both their bodies and ideas untrammeled, is one I examine in more detail below.

CLASS, MIGRATION, AND TRANSCOLONIAL LABOR RELATIONS

Black newspapers played a vital role in another of the key political projects of the mid–nineteenth century. Given this book's concern with the importance of black mobility, in this section I examine the migration of approximately thirteen thousand North American blacks to Haiti (including the integrated Spanish-speaking part of the island), Trinidad, Jamaica, and British Guyana.[27] Inasmuch as one can call the decision to relocate "voluntary" given the obstacles these free black migrants encountered in their home communities, these stories highlight a sustained interest in how life outside the place of one's birth could potentially be advantageous. These migrants were recruited in the pages of the *Colored American* and *L'Union* to emigrate to territories promoted as more solicitous of their welfare and open to their advancement. Below I focus on the recruitment process itself as a method of examining the complicated relationship between the regional literacy espoused in these papers and the physical movements of black migrants from one locale to another. I am interested in the material realities embodied in inter-American collaborations. The motivation behind such movement centered on a fundamental concern: Where was it possible for people of African descent to live in a society that would ensure their protection and their ability to live with honor and legitimation?

Before continuing, I want to reassert the primacy of class to my discussion of the black press. A heterogeneous group of people with different life experiences due to factors such as economic status and racial heritage, free blacks had even more differences in life possibilities when compared to their enslaved counterparts. Yet the former often found that the whole edifice of stability and respectability they had carefully constructed around themselves could be leveled instantaneously, perhaps even permanently, when they were confronted by white violence on an individual or state-sponsored level. There is a material/bodily vulnerability in evidence in these stories, from the scars left on Bissette from being branded, to the difficulties faced by traveling black agents, to Haiti's inability to protect its citizens abroad. The frustration that I alluded to earlier about the limits of freedom is one that saturates these pages. Even in less perilous circumstances, the psychological burden of having "prejudice [following a free person of color] wherever he goes, pointing at him the finger of scorn and contempt," was enormous.[28] For example, one article indignantly asked, "Do not our white brethren know, that at least some of us, have as keen sensibilities, as refined tastes, and as good an education as they have? That some of us were bred and born as respectably as they? That we have used the same industry and enterprise, and accumulated as much wealth as most of our fellow-citizens?" (*Colored American* September 30, 1837). This example is not simply indicative of a craving for "white" approval. Rather, these editors and their publics were acting as insurgents in a way that corresponded to their beliefs. While not clamoring for armed struggle, they verbally assaulted the institution of chattel slavery and the corresponding degradation of all people of African descent. This strategy entailed seeking out international support to counterbalance the fact that their respective nations did not respect them, however respectable they aspired to be.

Likewise, the Haitian elite who wrote and read *L'Union* frequently differentiated themselves from the uneducated masses. One issue commends the merits of a condescending speech made to slave apprentices in Jamaica, noting that "our readers will admire with us the simplicity of language that the author used when addressing this class of listeners, still so little advanced in their civilization" ("Nos lecteurs admireront avec nous la simplicité du langage, dont l'auteur s'est servi . . . en s'adressant à cette classe d'auditeurs encore si peu avancée dans la civilisation)" (April 5, 1838; reprinted from a story published in a black Jamaican newspaper called the *West Indian*). Despite their genuine concern for people of African descent in every guise, it would be a mistake to consider any of these papers as consistent, representative advocates of the black underclass, slave or free. This limited perspective would color how migrants interacted with each other when coming into personal contact in the context of resettlement.

Returning to the question of emigration to the Caribbean, all three papers covered news of the West Indies with great frequency. The *Colored American* alone contained over 175 references to the Caribbean region between 1837 and 1841.[29] The paper's connection with Haiti was especially strong, as the editors believed that "they [the Haitians] have not only many moral and political institutions for the benefit of their own citizens, but they have a respectable society, organized for the express purpose of promoting the cause of humanity throughout the world, and especially for the amelioration of their oppressed brethren in this country" (March 11, 1837). Of note, the paper pointed out the educational institutions open to Haitian citizens, declaring that "there are not less than fifteen male and female schools," an indication that opportunities were available to both men and women. After Haiti, the countries that received the most attention in the *Colored American* were Trinidad, British Guyana, and Jamaica. This focus was justified by the fact that all three countries were seen as potential sites for the resettlement of North American blacks in the antebellum U.S., post–British abolition era.

Debates about the future of blacks within the body politics of the United States, the Caribbean colonies, and even Haiti, which was undergoing a moment of severe constitutional instability, reverberated around the question of belonging. While some used international struggles for racial equality as a platform to lobby for changes at home, others entertained the notion of moving abroad. This was particularly the case in pre–Civil War North America when emigration movements were regaining popularity. As we have seen, acute racial prejudice strictly limited the opportunities available to free blacks, not to mention slaves, and many activists investigated alternative solutions to the "race" question. For those who believed that integration and assimilation into U.S. mainstream society would never be possible, emigration was a potential solution, and emigration and colonization societies were established in all of the major cities along the Northeast corridor. Although many black Americans bitterly resented plans to send them to the African colonization sites of Liberia and Sierra Leone, places they considered heathenish and superstitious, where "they [wear] a small cloth around the loins and are ornamented with rings and gregres," the Caribbean seemed a more reasonable solution (October 9, 1841). Haiti in particular seemed a promising alternative because of its proximity and status as an independent black nation.[30]

With regard to the viability of emigration movements to Haiti, Trinidad, Jamaica, and British Guyana, the reports published about these efforts were extremely detailed and the pages of the papers were used as a forum for information sharing. They all involved positioning the *Colored American* and *L'Union* as "middlemen" in U.S.-Caribbean relations. In addition to the aforementioned historical coverage of the Haitian Revolution, official correspondence from the representatives of Haitian, Trinidadian, and to a lesser extent, Guyanese emigration societies was directly addressed to the black population of the United States. This included correspondence from President Boyer and his secretary of state Joseph Inginac (dubbed the black Talleyrand), as well as letters from British colonial planters. These documents all provided contractual information about employment and living conditions, such as the series "Letters on Haiti" that appeared in March of 1838.[31] Paid advertisements from emigration agents were also published, including specific departure information. For example, one recurring advertisement stated "FOR TRINIDAD—Free industrious persons of color, of good character, desirous of becoming independent, wishing to emigrate to the British Island of Trinidad, can secure their passage in the first class American brig George Washington. . . . Agriculturists and laborers, with their families, will be taken out and found with ample provision, free of any expense or claim on their services after arrival. . . . Men of character with families, recommended for honesty, industry and sobriety, will be entitled to free passage, and that in every instance the proportion of female to males must be as 4 to 5."[32] There were also travelogue accounts that documented the climate, the state of the land, and "what to take."[33] The journal thus served as a guidebook of sorts for potential migrants seeking information as they decided whether to relocate.

Despite staunch advocacy of the liberation struggles occurring throughout the Caribbean, the aforementioned prejudices of both papers are evident. For example, the *Colored American* often evinced a marked cultural imperialism. Its coverage rearticulated social hierarchies between classes, religions, and ultimately regions, as the United States assumed a morally superior role of advancing "progress" among black people in other parts of the globe. The Presbyterian publishers were not tolerant of other religions, and the paper had a strong anti-Catholic and anti-"pagan" sentiment, coupled with a general Northeast American elitism vis-à-vis southern, including Caribbean, cultures. For instance, on November 4, 1837, the paper published an excerpt from Joseph Kimball's *Ruin of the West Indies*, a refutation of rumors circulated by proslavery apologists about the decline of the British West Indies after emancipation. The editors endorsed the work, asserting, "It will have weight with all who are willing to know the truth." The excerpt, originally published in the New Hampshire Anti-Slavery Society's *Herald of Freedom,* noted:

> There is a dark side too. Our travelers would meet much to grieve them and make their hearts sigh for the domestic joys and free institutions of their own land. They would not see the noble farms of the free North. . . . They would not behold the towns built up by the yeomanry of America. . . . They would not find the intelligence, nor the moral feeling, nor the religious principle of puritan New England. . . . The records of the system of depopulation and ruin, which destroys alike the spirit of intrepid enterprise, of letters, and of true religion, which suffocates genius and virtue, and all spirituality in the stews of a most horrible and bestial sensualism . . . are written in, too deeply and durably on the whole fabric of West Indian society, to be yet erased.

The article is tinged with an exclusivism that equates Protestant New England society with the epitome of "civilized" culture, rejecting the "bestial sensualism" of Caribbean societies. Such elitist ethnocentrism no doubt prejudiced the paper's readership, many of whom may have had no other exposure to the West Indies.

Black North Americans were not the only ones guilty of superior attitudes toward their hosts, however. The Haitians themselves also showed a limited willingness to make the physical embodiments of diasporic literacy work. During the time period under consideration, Haiti was suffering under the weight of the colossal indemnity she was forced to pay France in order to gain that country's recognition, while simultaneously engaged in the aforementioned unification project incorporating the former Spanish colony of Santo Domingo. The newly freed preferred to engage in subsistence farming on small plots rather than return to large plantations. Much as the U.S. South passed antivagrancy laws after the Civil War to ensure a steady labor force, Haiti, the denizen of black freedom, implemented the infamous 1826 Rural Code to force laborers back to the land in an effort to reinstate the large-scale production of export crops that had characterized colonial economic policy. Ironically, Haitian "yeomen" were engaged in exactly the kind of small-scale, privately owned, and community organized farm work extolled above, while the state wished to reinstate a model that was not in the best interests of either native or migrant laborers.

President Boyer and his successors were chiefly interested in contracting North American black immigrants who were either skilled artisans or agricultural laborers. Strict regulations stated that immigrants should remain in the rural areas and should not come to settle to a life of "indolence" in the urban centers. There is evidence that Haitians considered themselves superior to their North American brethren, as the latter had not succeeded in breaking the chains of slavery in the violent and conclusive manner that characterized Haitian independence. While Boyer's administration may have been partially motivated by fraternal solidarity, its attempts to find an alternative source of cheap labor echoed attempts to import Chinese and East Indian labor into other Caribbean nations after emancipation.[34] Disgruntled migrants reported that few could afford to buy the land promised in recruitment advertisements and that they could barely make ends meet. They were decimated by disease and forced to subsist on an "almost unvarying" diet of "yams, plantain and saltfish" (July 18, 1840). Eventually, when it became obvious that American recognition would not be forthcoming despite Haiti's attempts to help the United States by "solving" the problem of what to do with its free population of color, Boyer dropped the scheme.

This disaffection proved equally strong with emigration to Trinidad and, by extension, the other British colonies of British Guyana and Jamaica. In an April 1840 issue, the *Colored American* announced that the British Anti-Slavery Society had declared that emigration to Trinidad and other British colonies was not a good idea for black Americans. This report, coupled with the *Colored American*'s own investigations, led the editors to condemn the scheme. On April 11, 1840, an article entitled "News from Trinidad" chronicled the investigative journalism of one Mr. Walker, a "friend" of the paper who had gone to Trinidad for six weeks to "reconnoiter" and "investigate matters." Detailing the lack of opportunities for women, and the "great hostility" between the "native laborers" and the Americans, he concluded that emigration was not a good idea and that the natives were "too low in moral degradation to associate with." Again, class and cultural biases impeded the successful integration of black North American immigrants. Elsewhere the paper did acknowledge, however, that tension between the native Trinidadians and North American immigrants was a result of competition and that the planters in fact wanted to "displace the present [laborers] and thus gratify the grudge they owe them for being free . . ." (November 7, 1840).

By publishing firsthand accounts by correspondents, initially in an effort to abet the recruitment process and later with a mind to publicize the perils of emigration, the journalists of the *Colored American* vacillated between their ties to an unfriendly native country and the possibilities of exploring their opportunities elsewhere in the Americas. Eventually, "sensible that we occupy a position, between our people and this matter, in which we can exert an influence, for or against," the paper ceased to support emigration, taking their position as the political and moral vanguard of its subscriber community very seriously.[35] They proudly proclaimed that if "the planters of those Islands expect from the present free colored population of this country, a class of men to emigrate there, to be long the cultivators of their fields, they miss the figure—they have reckoned wrong upon the character of the 'colored Americans'" (November 7, 1840).

Thus the inter-American partnerships espoused by early nineteenth-century black intellectuals in the United States and the Caribbean met with limited success. Activist journalists and their readers who were imaginative enough to initiate contact with one another encountered pitfalls even as they acknowledged their common interests. A large body of correspondence has survived documenting these efforts to collaborate across colonial frontiers at the level of both theory and praxis. One need only understand the aforementioned period of coercive Haitian labor relations, the civilizationist discourse of the most redoubtable of early Pan-Africanists, or the contemporary resonance of debates over everything from language to fashion among black North Americans to recall what thinkers as diverse as Michael Gomez, C. L. R. James, and

Katherine Dunham have detailed—the crucial place of the class question within systems of racial domination. Here, then, is a connection that binds seemingly divergent figures such as the furiously antislavery Philip A. Bell to slaveholder Joseph Savary; that connects the hopeful affirmation of emigrationism to the hard reality of saltfish and yams; and that highlights the delicate balance between regional revolt and the restoration of servitude by a new name. A hemispheric black press allowed a crucial class of relatively enfranchised free blacks to break free from their local isolation. Yet within its pages those who sought to write their own stories like the ones that unfolded in Southampton or Salvador de Bahia could rarely find either the sympathy, or, more importantly, a strategy, that could re-create the sorts of temporary fusions across cleavages of language, degree of intermixture, place of birth, or status under white law that might reproduce the events of Saint-Domingue from which so many drew inspiration.

CARIBBEAN FEDERATION: ADVANCING NATIONAL INTERESTS THROUGH A REGIONALIST LENS

I close this chapter by looking at how the experiments examined here—both literacy projects and migratory labor arrangements—were accompanied by articulations of a regional confederation project that would first and foremost protect the interests of its black citizens. By *confederation* I am referring to political projects that called for either a centralized government that would unite different territories under one aegis or a more loosely organized, decentralized structure that would have different member states voluntarily collaborating on agendas of mutual interest. It is logical that the earliest public records theorizing a Caribbean confederation located Haiti as the center of this political entity. Given that Haiti had already achieved national independence and had a state infrastructure, the young nation stood alone in the region and was predictably in search of allies. Acknowledging that similar histories of colonization and slave labor marked all of the island societies of the region, Haitian intellectuals reached out to their closest neighbors, and these same neighbors responded with varying degrees of enthusiasm. It is crucial to remember, of course, that with the exception of Haiti and the Dominican Republic, islands in the Spanish, French, British, and Dutch Caribbean were still colonies until at least the late nineteenth century. Hence any agenda of Caribbean federation necessitated political independence from a European metropole.

Below I cite two articles at length from *L'Union* and the *Revue des Colonies*. Both are remarkable because they establish that conceptualizations of formalized inter-American union, ones that privileged the participation of the Caribbean, were being published in international forums by the 1830s. I maintain that this articulation is significant for several reasons. First, although this project has demonstrated the importance of interactions that crossed colonial boundaries between 1790 and 1840, published, outright proclamations of an ideology of inter-Americanism, either from an abolitionist or a proslavery stance, are rare. This is partly the case because these projects were often illegal and hence surreptitious. Second, the inclusion of the Caribbean, much less a Haiti-centered, black-run Caribbean, in a project of this nature is a distinct rupture from Bolivarian agendas. Commonly credited as one of the earliest and most dedicated promulgators of Latin American confederation, Bolívar very consciously excluded Haiti from his plans and made no gestures toward including islands beyond Puerto Rico and Cuba.[36]

Third, in the field of Caribbean studies, and to a lesser extent in Latin American and hemispheric American studies, there has long been interest in *la confederación antillana* and the idea of pan-Caribbean consciousness. Most discussions have focused on intellectuals of the Spanish Caribbean and Latin America such as the aforementioned Simon Bolívar, Ramón Emeterio Betances, Eugenio María de Hostos, Gregorio Luperón, Antonio Maceo, and José Martí. Scholars locate the 1860s as the watershed decade for integrationist movements, culminating in the 1880s and 1890s Caribbean confederation initiatives in the Greater Antilles.[37] These articles, and by extension the papers that printed them, demonstrate not only that the latter moments had a historical, if unacknowledged precedent but that this precedent was set by Afro-Americans in the francophone and anglophone territories. The papers' comprehensive coverage of the Americas, polyglot nature, and insistence that regional strength depended on the equality of the black race illustrate how the transcolonial collaborations imagined and practiced by those of African descent were just as developed as those that emerged among creole populations of the extended Americas during both the early and later eras.

Returning to the articles at hand, in the first, entitled "Hayti et les Etats-Unis," the anonymous author proposed the political integration of islands from different linguistic (i.e., colonial) backgrounds in a united front (*L'Union* September 27, 1837). He concretely espoused the political and commercial project of confederation, although he gave no systematic explanation of what he meant by the term or how to implement the logistics. The text claims:

> In the past, our relations with the other transatlantic peoples were purely commercial. All of this archipelago in the middle of which is our island, should, by its importance, its position, and its extent, form the center of a powerful confederation; this archipelago is closed to us in all directions, so much do they fear the contagion of liberty. So much do they fear, and perhaps rightfully so, that we could be propagandists! . . . Now that our political existence is solemnly recognized by France, the other European powers . . . will no longer delay, without doubt, in engaging with us in friendly relations. Likewise, the English colonies in our hemisphere, where the emancipation of slaves is consummated, will enter into direct relations with us, and they have already solicited this [interaction] from their metropole. The French islands will open to us, because there also, despite the indecision and slowness of the mother-country, emancipation is imminent. What can then stop the Spanish islands and the most important South American republics?

> Autrement, nos relations avec les autres peuples transatlantiques n'ont été que purement commerciales. Tout cet archipel au milieu duquel notre île eut semblé, par son importance, sa position et son étendue, doit être le centre d'une puissante confédération, cet archipel nous est fermé de toutes parts, tant on craint la contagion de la liberté! Tant on a redouté, et peut-être avec raison, que nous puissions faire de la propagande! . . . Maintenant que notre existence politique est solennellement reconnue par la France, les autres puissances européennes . . . ne tarderont pas, sans doute, à venir traiter d'amitié avec nous. D'un autre côté, les colonies anglaises de notre hémisphère ou l'émancipation des esclaves est consommée, entreront en communication avec nous, et déjà même, elles le sollicitent de leur métropole. Les îles françaises elles mêmes nous seront ouvertes, car là aussi, en dépit de l'indécision et des lenteurs de leur mère-patrie, l'émancipation est imminente. Qui retiendrait des lors les îles espagnoles et les plus importantes des républiques de l'Amérique du Sud?

The future communion of "American island nations" is a striking phrase, given their colonial status at the time. Such a communion was first and foremost predicated on emancipation. With this goal accomplished, Haiti, as the geographic center of the Greater Antilles, was posited as a logical choice for the center of a unified confederation. The scorn evinced for metropolitan authority, which was characterized as indecisive and out of step with local interests, is explicit, and the author implied that once the metropolitan powers were dispensed with, the local populations would recognize the benefits of an "opening out" within the archipelago. "Transatlantic peoples of the Americas" would then be free to act upon their common interests—interests that were more than just commercial ones. The terminology is striking on all levels, as it combines nationalist rhetoric with a theorization of a distinct regional consciousness based on common geographic and social histories. Just as Haiti had thrust its own existence as an autonomous state onto the colonial world stage, the writer took the next step of offering its closest neighbors a chance to be equally independent/ interdependent in the American arena.

A second source that further elucidates how black intellectuals in the 1830s imagined the future configuration of the region appeared as the front-page article in the August 1836 issue of the *Revue*. Entitled "L'Espagne, sa Révolution: Son influence sur l'abolition de l'esclavage colonial," the article pondered how metropolitan politics in Spain, especially the gaining ascendancy of the Liberal movement, might affect its Caribbean colonies. Bissette outlined the possibilities for Cuba and Puerto Rico in the event that they wished to secede from Spain. These possibilities included outright independence or membership in a union of federated Caribbean states. He wrote:

> Havana and Puerto Rico one to the west, the other to the east of Saint-Domingue, find themselves exposed naturally and topographically to frequent relations with this republic of blacks. Sooner or later Haiti cannot fail to exercise a sovereign power over the whole Antillean archipelago that her politics will tend to unite in a single confederation of insular states, of which Saint-Domingue will be the center. Alas, no more masters and no more slaves. This will be the day of the radical cessation of the rule of the strongest, and [mark] the complete regeneration of the African race. Before that comes to pass, England, already mistress of the biggest part of the archipelago, will perhaps try, through her vice-royalty in Jamaica, to effect this federation under its patronage and protection . . . to cut out Haiti. . . . We repeat it, there is only one clever and just politics on the part of the Spanish government that can protect it from the loss of the islands of Cuba and Puerto Rico. . . . It must follow the example of England and proclaim the abolition of slavery. . . . This grand act of justice is necessary to reattach this mass of islands that do not cease to have their eyes turned toward Jamaica and toward Haiti from which they await their deliverance. Their gratitude and the products of liberty will more than compensate you for the complaints of a few planters.

> La Havane et Porto-Rico, l'une à l'ouest, l'autre à l'est de Saint-Domingue, se trouvent exposés naturellement et topographiquement à de fréquentes relations avec cette république de nègres. Haïti, ne peut manquer d'exercer tôt ou tard un pouvoir souverain sur tout l'archipel des Antilles que sa politique tendra à réunir en une seule fédération d'états insulaires dont Saint-Domingue sera le centre. Alors, plus de maîtres et plus d'esclaves. Ce sera le jour de l'abolition radicale du droit du plus fort, et de la régénération

complète de la race africaine. Avant cette époque, l'Angleterre, déjà maî-
tresse de la plus grande partie de cet Archipel, essaiera peut-être, par sa
vice-royauté de la Jamaïque, d'effectuer cette fédération sous son patronage
et son protectorat . . . pour devancer Haiti. . . . Nous le répétons, il n'y a
qu'une politique habile et juste de la part du gouvernement espagnol qui
peut préserver la perte des îles de Cuba et Porto-Rico. . . . Il faut suivre
l'exemple de l'Angleterre et proclamer comme elle le principe de l'abolition
de l'esclavage. . . . Il faut par ce grand acte de justice rattacher par la reconnaissance à la métropole cette masse d'îlotes qui ne cessaient d'avoir
les yeux tournés vers la Jamaïque et vers Haïti d'où ils attendaient leur
délivrance. Leur reconnaissance et les productions de la liberté vous récom-
penseront largement des imprécations de quelques planteurs.

Bissette thus predicted that Haiti had the potential to serve as the
center of a federation of insular states, an event that would mark the
definitive end of societies composed of slaves and their masters. He
gauged Haiti's influence on the region as considerable, strong enough
that England might seek to counteract its pull by initiating a Caribbean federation of its own with Jamaica as the administrative center.
His assertion that "cette masse d'îlotes" was waiting for either of these
fellow island neighbors for deliverance is curious and certainly exag-
gerated. However, it provides some sense of the possibilities that black
intellectuals of the time imagined as alternative models of future Caribbean political development. The model of federation was based not
solely on racial alliances but on a "natural" partnership resulting from
geographic proximity and common commercial interests. Interestingly,
Bissette did not specifically name his native Martinique as a potential
member of this union. The fact that Bissette "advised" Spain on how
to maintain the allegiance of its Caribbean colonies demonstrates his
unique perspective. He was staunchly abolitionist, yet not anticolonial.
Despite France's continued abuse of the *gens de couleur* and slaves in
its colonies, Bissette was interested in reforming, not ending, colonial
rule in the French territories.

Nationalist ties complicated this consciousness of the social, political, and commercial potential involved in promoting an interest in and
loyalty to a larger confederated (and African diasporic) community. This
was at least the case for the editors, if not their reading publics. Consequently, *L'Union* was first and foremost a Haitian paper interested in
its Haitian readers. By positing Haitian struggles within a global perspective, however, the editors hoped to challenge Haiti's isolation in the
region and facilitate new alliances that had the potential to radically
change the Caribbean landscape. Likewise, the *Colored American* was

firmly aligned with the country of its birth. In the words of the editorial staff, "Our people will settle down, each to his own calling, until he can find a more lucrative and better one here, in our country, where we ought to be and where we are undoubtedly better off as a whole, or in any mass, than we can be in any other country" (April 4, 1840). While the *Revue*'s editor was committed to his native Martinican community, he was thoroughly French, lauding the higher moral standard of the "mère patrie" while demanding equal treatment for the residents of its Caribbean colonies. Believing that "the principle of all sovereignty essentially resides with the nation" ("le principe de toute souveraineté réside essentiellement dans la nation"), Bissette was loyal to France, however much he acknowledged the potential of a Caribbean federation.

All did recognize, however, that nationalist allegiances did not preclude strategic alignment with other oppressed populations of the black diaspora. Essentially, these periodical pages demonstrate that a shift took place from the earlier moments documented in this project: nationalist ties had become the principal assumed identity for many black intellectuals, and transcolonial or African ties had become secondary. This shift cannot be interpreted as a generalized statement concerning black subjectivity in the mid–nineteenth century, as there were many Afro-American intellectuals who ceaselessly critiqued the nation and investigated the possibility of abandoning their countries of birth and living elsewhere. Martin Delany, Frederick Douglass, and, at a much later moment, W. E. B. DuBois are some of the most prominent examples. But with the exception of DuBois, who ended his days in Ghana, even these vociferous detractors of the United States ended up serving the nation: Delany as a major in the Union Army and Douglass as the U.S. ambassador to Haiti.

Yet a transcolonial, inter-American imagination would return as a significant framework for Caribbean literature, politics, and thought. Specifically, the aforementioned work of activists of the 1860s is one example, as are projects from the 1890s. Newspapers were a tool in these later movements as well, as demonstrated by the importance of publications such as *Patria* to Martí's Partido Revolucionario Cubano. A crucial difference between the two moments is that the latter were characterized by efforts to promote a color-blind society as a prerequisite of both national and regional integration rather than by a focus on the primacy of race as an organizing factor. This is partly attributable to the fact that by the turn of the century abolition was accomplished, even if the objective of racial equality certainly was not.

In addition to the important role played by the periodical press, there are other remarkable parallels between these historical moments. The anonymous Haitian writer quoted at length above concerning his promotion of a Caribbean confederation addressed one such similarity. He stridently warned readers of the threat that the United States posed to any communion of the "people of the Americas," stating, "We are not unaware that their government feels disdain for ours and we are taking note of the outrages that on certain occasions our citizens have had to endure" ("Nous ne nous dissimulons pas que leur gouvernement affecte le dédain contre le nôtre et nous prenons note des outrages qu'en certaines occasions nos concitoyens . . . ont eu à subir"; *L'Union* September 27, 1838). He continued: "In this proximate communion of the peoples of the Americas with us, only the United States will be held at a distance. As long as slavery exists there, there cannot be a sincere rapprochement between us. And if one reflects on the future of the American nations, it seems, on the contrary, that a serious collision will occur sooner or later between Haiti and the United States" ("Dans cette communion prochaine des peuples de l'Amérique avec nous, les Etats-Unis seuls se tiendront à l'écart! . . . Or, tant que l'esclavage existera dans les Etats de l'Union, il n'y aura pas de rapprochement sincère possible entre eux et nous; et si l'on réfléchit sur l'avenir des nations de l'Amérique, il semble au contraire qu'une collision sérieuse tôt ou tard souviendra entre Haïti et les Etats-Unis"). The author's certainty of an eventual collision with the United States was prophetic, given the eventual U.S. invasion and nineteen-year occupation of the island, in addition to the U.S. invasions of many of its neighboring republics such as the Dominican Republic, Puerto Rico, and Cuba. His foresight concerning the need to formally unite the Caribbean in order to resist U.S. hegemony in the region was likewise ahead of its time.[38]

Writing more than fifty years later, Jose Martí made a strikingly similar statement, noting that North Americans "study and chronicle us with merely a hasty glance and with obvious ill-humor, like an impoverished nobleman in the predicament of asking a noted favor of someone he does not regard as his equal" ("nos estudian e historian a meras ojeadas, y con mal humor visible, como noble apurado que se ve en el aprieto de pedir un favor a quien no mira como igual suyo").[39] The perspective offered in the 1830s black press and the visions later proffered by Martí and Hostos all recognized that one of the most effective means of making this disdain irrelevant was the creation of a united front of Caribbean societies dedicated to protecting local interests.

Promoting a sense of regional consciousness was a prerequisite to any formal inter-American alliance, and the 1830s press laid the groundwork for future endeavors.

Just as the turn of the twentieth century in the Spanish Caribbean marked a renewed interest in inter-American ideals, this moment marked the beginning of another avant-garde movement in the United States that was also interested in prioritizing a regionalist view of the Americas, in this case, one with a particular interest in the welfare of those of African descent. Alain Locke's classic text of the Harlem Renaissance, *The New Negro* (1925), introduced the movement as follows:

> Fortunately there are constructive channels opening out into which the balked social feelings of the American Negro can flow freely. . . . A Negro newspaper carrying news material in English, French and Spanish, gathered from all quarters of America, the West Indies and Africa has maintained itself in Harlem for over five years . . . In terms of the race question as a world problem, the Negro mind has leapt, so to speak, upon the parapets of prejudice and extended its cramped horizons. In doing so it has linked up with the growing group consciousness of the dark-peoples and is gradually learning their common interests. . . . Persecution is making the Negro international. (13–15)

If "group consciousness" of the common interests of the "dark-peoples" was a characteristic of the modernist advance guard, then the "new Negro" of the 1920s was not nearly as new as Locke believed.[40] Over a century earlier the *Colored American*, a black periodical also published in New York City, not to mention the other Caribbean papers studied here, displayed a remarkable sense of the persecuted Negro's internationalness. That Locke may have been unaware of the work of his editorial predecessors indicates how knowledge documenting the racialized, transcolonial/transnational consciousness exemplified by early black periodicals has been lost. The gap between Locke's moment and the previous century illustrates the difficulty in creating continuities capable of linking diasporic moments of movement and possibility. In the absence of such knowledge, it has been all too easy to conclude that things were as they were without the participation—oppositional or otherwise—of the millions of black people, free and slave, African and creole, men and women, for whom the circum-Caribbean was to be both a connected and a circumscribed world.

Epilogue

Decades after the Haitian Revolution, stories of willing and forced migration across colonial frontier were still news. The May 1841 edition of the *Revue des Colonies* opened with a five-page article recounting the vicissitudes of a family of manumitted slave women entitled "Un épisode de l'histoire de l'esclavage à la Martinique." Although the title of the piece situates the tale in Martinique, it is a transcolonial American narrative about bondage, relocation, and the struggle for liberty and self-determination. According to the details presented, three domestic female slaves of "le Sieur C****" left Saint-Domingue with their owners at the onset of the revolution. After resettling in Philadelphia, Pennsylvania, then Charles Town, South Carolina, the women were manumitted upon their owner's death. In 1795, the three servants and one of their daughters, born a free black in the United States, accompanied their former masters to the French colony of Martinique, living together until 1821. Their employers eventually re-enslaved them, however, violating the integrity of a decades-long relationship. Only by escaping to Dominica (a British island) and St. Thomas (a Danish island) did the four women regain their freedom.

For people of African descent, networks of transcolonial migration and information sharing thus served as both an avenue to freedom and a means of imposing their continued servitude in slave-holding territories. As was the case with these four women, being forced to leave one place for another or the decision to stay or go could determine the fate of the family line for generations, especially as slavery followed the status of the mother. For every slave or free person of color who may have improved his or her life circumstances by moving across colonial frontiers, there are countless examples of transcolonial collaborations that contributed to a thriving inter-regional slave trade and buttressed the system in moments of crisis.

Returning to the conceptual framing provided by the "fear of French negroes, " the stories I assemble should trigger a response that moves beyond a consideration of the well-documented anxiety that insurgent blacks occasioned in slave-holding systems; they should refocus our attention on the wide variety of emotional and strategic responses that people of African descent had to the collapse and reconsolidation of the colonial world. This book has examined a particular moment in time, an era of revolutionary struggle when much of the conventional wisdom of the day was upended, even as reactionary forces violently tried to repress meaningful transformation. The experiential constant for the subjects of this study was adaptation to changing circumstances: from rich to poor, from slavery to freedom and back again, from "Spanish" to "French" to "Haitian." What were the choices individuals could make under such circumstances? What compels my interest is how black people formed a range of intentional, thoughtful, if often short-lived alliances. Expressive culture provides a transcript of politics that are often hidden from view. Because these decisions were not solely, even predominantly, guided by imperial loyalties, a methodology guided by nation-based considerations inevitably provides an incomplete picture. After all, the Haitian leader Toussaint Louverture strategically fought alongside both the Spanish and the French as he rose to power, much as slaves in what is now the United States fought for both British forces under Lord Dunmore and the American patriot cause. Allegiance to the metropole in control was one of many considerations people took into account when determining their best interests.

Ultimately these stories teach us about the persistence of a transcolonial framework as an active, viable tool of organization and self-expression for a diverse group of black figures eager to form alliances with those whom they imagined common cause. For example, it afforded a means for both José Campos Taváres and Joseph Savary, one a slave, one a slaveholder, to find room for personal advancement. Collaborating across colonial frontiers afforded sanctuary and helped meet the pressing need for shelter, food, and employment. It also stimulated the resilience of something less tangible: hope. This hope was inevitably connected to the desire for freedom. Freedom, of course, meant vastly different things to different people. Freedom from brutal field labor and freedom from domestic chores in the service of others; freedom from sexual predators and freedom to parent children for their natural lives; freedom to profit from the dominant economic system of the time by owning one's own slaves, and freedom to associate with the people of one's choice; freedom to move around and, all too often, simply freedom to sit still. Even the latter eventually became well nigh impossible in post-Emancipation societies throughout the Americas that quickly criminalized autonomy as vagrancy, shiftlessness, and rebellion.

The evidence I have collected here suggests that by the mid–nineteenth century a more consistently developed inter-regionalism, a more sophisticated attempt not only to maintain but to actively ruminate about the *importance* of maintaining dialogue between distinct American geographies, was present among the diverse classes of black Americans under study than among the region's white inhabitants. It should not astonish us that in a social and political world structured around racial hierarchies, those relegated to occupy society's most precarious positions were more anxious, and hence more creatively committed, to change their life possibilities by challenging state policies designed to minimize unsanctioned intercolonial interactions. For the wealthy planter classes in the hemisphere, life was largely agreeable before the advent of revolutionary activity. Thus the appeal of collective action between those of similar station in other territories was more functionalist in nature, born out of force of circumstance: when their cities were set on fire, they needed dogs for protection, or there was tremendous profit to be made.

I also hope to have added to the body of scholarship documenting the nuances of interblack conflict. When evaluating historical events through the lens of the "oppressed" versus the dominant, it is critical to remember that black actors have always been implicated in the persecution of people of like hue. This is true in the more obvious cases of those who owned slaves or worked as overseers in charge of discipline, or for those who served as policing agents and informers. It is also true in the more subtle, yet ubiquitous examples of those who contributed in myriad ways to the psychological oppression and self-hate inherent to a system predicated upon extreme violence. The idea of black collectivity examined here is framed as a struggle for unity amid the realities of division. Hence this book does not wish to invoke a triumphalist narrative about black resistance. Rather, it is about survival, about how people tried to exercise the limited choices they had so that life might improve for them and the subsequent generations.

Fascinatingly, much as the term *French negroes* evoked an immediate reaction for audiences in the past, the name Haiti has itself become a descriptor that provokes cognitive associations tending toward images of racialized extremes. For example, in the dominant imagination of the contemporary moment, the stock epithet "the poorest country in the Western Hemisphere" has replaced the colonial era's modifier "pearl of the Antilles." In virtually all coverage of the January 2010 earthquake, for example, the opening lines of any story in the mass media began with this epithet, as if such a description replaced any need to contextualize the situation. I believe that these two epithets are related. In a historically conditioned act of association, the often unspoken, yet unerringly present event that supposedly accounts for this transition from an alleged state of Edenic existence to a subsequent state of abjection becomes the Haitian Revolution itself. This assumption is evident not only in the predictably outrageous comments of someone like Pat Robertson, who explained the earthquake's devastation as a result of revolting slaves' centuries-old "pact [with] the devil," but even in purportedly sympathetic assumptions concerning the origins of present-day challenges. For example, many years ago at an excellent series of panels on the Haitian Revolution organized for the American Historical Association's annual meeting in Washington, D.C., a member of the audience earnestly asked if the revolution had been "worth it." I believe that such a question subconsciously presupposes the idea that such a violent expression of black self-determination could only have led to disaster—that if abolition had happened under different, more "reasonable" circumstances, then somehow Haiti would not be in a dire situation now. Those who challenged the system then come under critique, rather than the violence of the system itself that demanded such concentrated efforts to defeat. Despite this tendency to discuss either the revolutionary era or the present moment in ways that employ race, specifically blackness, as a bogeyman that elides systemic analyses of the relevant conflicts, there is no doubt that the revolution has had tremendous inspirational value across the centuries. For contemporaries such as the martyred Cuban free black José Antonio Aponte, late nineteenth-century scholars such as W. E. B. DuBois, writers of the Harlem Renaissance, and anticolonization crusaders such as Aimé Césaire, the boldness and success of Haitian revolutionaries keep them at the forefront of any discussion of the "black international." This legacy of Haiti-inspired artistic, activist, and scholarly work has made it possible for "Haiti" writ large to now function as its own "keyword" for specialists in hemispheric American studies.

The polemics examined in this book thus find echoes in contemporary times. Indeed, for each chapter here I could point to iterations of disturbing temporal continuities. Consider the use of dogs trained at the U.S. base in Guantánamo, Cuba, to torture prisoners in Iraq's Abu Ghraib prison. Or consider the effective use of Dominican campaign materials employing racist visual iconography to compare the 1994 presidential candidate José Francisco Peña Gómez, a politician of Haitian descent, to Jean-Jacques Dessalines and Henry Christophe, two Haitian generals portrayed as murderous fiends, in an effort to foment racial and national antagonisms. While today's events are in no way simple repetitions of the past, they are not historically isolated. Paradigms of what people "matter" and the hierarchies of power that determine or are determined by such assessments have been remarkably consistent from the nineteenth century into the present.

At a moment of diminishing access to social equality worldwide, the politics motivating both regional collaboration and migration continue to garner attention. First, competing inter-American frameworks, what today would be transnational rather than transcolonial conceptualizations, are especially evident when we consider the latest calls for a regional organization that would serve as a counterweight to the U.S.-backed Free Trade Agreement of the Americas (FTAA). One such alternative is the aforementioned ALBA, an umbrella organization that supports economic and social integration of Latin America and the Caribbean. The association explicitly critiques neoliberal policies of the World Bank and the International Monetary Fund that have led to massive debt, privatization of state resources, and incentives that privilege transnational capital at the expense of local economies. In a related vein, at a time of current unrest in the United States concerning "illegal" immigration from Mexico and countries from the "other" America, and Mexican discomfort with increasing immigration from neighboring central American countries, it is worth remembering that migrants have always been demonized through complex allusions to their difference as a systematic means of creating popular distrust of their presence. As is the case in the present, questions of "safety," "national security," and "loyalty" emerged again and again during the early nineteenth century, as continual wars between European powers and the threat of slave rebellion made the security of extended

American societies a daily concern. Consequently French- and French Creole–speaking migrants from Saint-Domingue living in Spanish colonies were feared for their purported republican (i.e., potentially antimonarchical, anti-Catholic, and racially egalitarian) ideals, just as their presence in Louisiana threatened to undermine loyalty to the United States. If history has taught us anything, it is that in times of extreme economic and political unrest, people move, sometimes voluntarily, at other times against their will. They rarely stay put. When physical borders intervene, whether these are colonial or national, creative ways of circumventing them abound. Then as now, innovative alliances serve as a coping strategy for migrants and are a key element in their capacity to generate communal action.

Notes

PREFACE

1. "Humanitas" asserts that slavery in the West Indies was crueler than that which was practiced in the United States. Prior to the tragedy, Romain's owner, Anthony Salaignac, had solicited the courts of New Jersey to determine if he was free to return to his native land with his slaves. Granted the court's consent after two previous refusals, the party was en route to Newcastle, from which the slaves would sail. It was thus a U.S. court ruling that recognized Salaignac's claim to Romain as a question of property rights, allowing the former to export said property abroad.

2. Immediately preceding his departure from Trenton, Romain had been "confined in gaol," an indication that he had a previous history of resistance toward his master (Humanitas 12). In addition to the aforementioned accounts documenting the suicide and inquest, a classified advertisement provides more information. Immediately after the trial, Anthony Salaignac published a runaway announcement outlining his situation. Arriving in the United States seven years earlier for what he and many other Saint-Domingue refugees had hoped would be a temporary period of exile, by 1802 he had decided that "the present state of affairs in St. Domingo, making him hope for a sufficient tranquility," made it possible to return. Planning to take his slaves with him, he was foiled when his "property" refused to cooperate. In addition to the suicide of Romain, and the "absconding of the said negro wench Marie Noel and her son Garcin," we learn that Romain and Marie Noel's other daughter Ann was "seized." His slave Clementine and her mulatto child Charlotte, age three, "did likewise abscond." Salaignac was thus deprived of six slaves. He openly threatened to sue those who "bribed, protected, or harboured" them, and his rage and refusal to recognize that nothing short of outside "councils of

insubordination" could have caused them to flee is palpable. See *Philadelphia Gazette and Daily Advertiser,* November 15, 1802.

How do we interpret the fact that all these slaves fled their master and refused to continue in his employ, either in Saint-Domingue or in New Jersey? Surely Romain and his associates cannot be construed as contented house-hold slaves whose earnest devotion caused them to emigrate with their masters to the United States in order to stay happily united as extended members of the Salaignac family. Rather, Romain's actions, as well as those of his fellow slaves, serve as strong evidence of their opposition to involuntary servitude, evidence that is corroborated in the many runaway ads that offered rewards for escaped "French negroes" in the United States, Cuba, and Jamaica, all sites of Saint-Domingue refugee resettlement during the unfolding of the Haitian Revolution. For once wealthy planters turned indigent refugees, the disappear-ances of these slaves, who had often been the sole support of their owners, were especially "inconvenient," as they needed them to sell, rent out, and take care of them in some semblance of the style they had grown accustomed to back in Saint-Domingue. For instance, readers of the April 22, 1809, *Mercantile Advertiser* were asked to feel special sympathy for the refugee Madame Montamard, as her fifteen-year-old slave Rozette, of a "melancholy cast," had run away and left her mistress and four children "without any means of sup-port." The supposed object of pity is thus the impoverished white family, not the young slave girl, who by her owner's own admission was disposed toward sadness. For an overview of how free blacks from Saint-Domingue integrated into the population of free blacks in New York City, see Shane White. He cites newspaper accounts suggesting that Saint-Domingue migrants were "involved in most of the black unrest in the city in the following decade [post 1793]" (450–51).

3. The promise of abolition granted by a legislative decree from abroad versus freedom attained by localized combat is exemplified linguistically in Daniel Maximin's statement, "Equality speaks French, but freedom speaks Creole." *L'isolé soleil* 252, quoted in Kadish xiv.

4. Although migrants left in gradual waves from 1791 to 1804, several cri-ses occasioned hurried, mass mobilizations. These include the 1793 conflagra-tion of Cap Français and the final defeat of the French army in 1803.

5. Louise Augustin Fortier, a descendent of Saint-Domingue refugees who resettled in Louisiana, wrote one such narrative. In her short story "Le bon vieux temps" ("The Good Ole Days"), the young male and female French pro-tagonists are hidden from a raucous mob of slaves by their "bon vieux nègre Pierre" (53) who carries them to safety in his "bons bras fidèles" (59). When this slave realizes that the same rebels have decapitated the elder master of the house, he throws himself on his master's dead body with a "convulsive trem-bling," and seconds later his "faithful heart had ceased to beat" ("coeur fidèle avait cessé de battre"; 61). His grief at his master's death was too much to bear. Another such story is A. Fresneau's *Theresa at San Domingo: A Tale of the Negro Insurrection of 1791* (1889). The plot centers on a white creole family in Saint-Domingue. Because they have always treated their slaves kindly, the "faith-ful" negroes sweep them away to safety during the revolts. Not only do these

slaves save their lives, they actually have someone locate the children who are later living in poverty in France in order to return their inheritance to them, an inheritance that was buried by the "revolting insurgents." The historical record confirms that some slaves, probably including Toussaint Louverture, saved their masters during the course of the revolution. However, these particular accounts attribute such acts of mercy to slave contentment and absolute devotion to the master class. Personal affection, a discomfort with violence, and fear of possible retribution could also have motivated these life-saving gestures. All translations contained herein are mine unless otherwise noted.

6. There is an extensive body of work documenting the experience of white Saint-Domingue refugees, much of it written by themselves and their descendants. See Debien's research for a sampling of some of their letters. For other well-known memoirs, see McIntosh and Weber; de Puech Parham; Aquin; Arredondo; and Palaiseau. Another genre that captured white creole exile experience was the periodical press. Proslavery in nature, several newspapers were founded and patronized by Saint-Domingue exiles. These papers maintained a public sphere of discussion among fellow exiles in dispersal. For example, see *Journal des Revolutions*, a paper that was published briefly in Philadelphia. Popkin, *Facing Racial Revolution*, also contains first-person accounts, all but one of the nineteen written by white witnesses. Despite his gesture toward the importance of presenting a more representative perspective, the result is a necessarily skewed evaluation of the Haitian Revolution, iconographically epitomized by the cover art of two captive white women surrounded by black men holding muskets.

7. This project is greatly indebted to seminal historical scholarship that has explored the flow of revolutionary ideas throughout the Caribbean Basin during the last decades of the eighteenth century and the first decades of the nineteenth. The Haitian Revolution's impact abroad has been the subject of a wide variety of scholarly research. See especially the work of C. L. R. James, David Patrick Geggus, Carolyn Fick, Michel-Rolph Trouillot, Laurent Dubois, Joan Dayan, Alfred Hunt, Deborah Jenson, Franklin Knight, Robin Blackburn, Sibylle Fischer, and Anthony Maingot. Historical studies that have documented local Saint-Domingue refugee communities abroad, such as Alain Yacou's and Gabriel Debien's work on Cuba, Emilio Cordero Michel's, Jean Price-Mars's, and Franklyn Franco's work on the Dominican Republic, and Rebecca Scott's, Thomas Fiehrer's, Gabriel Debien's, and Paul Lachance's work on Louisiana, have provided invaluable analyses of primary-source documents. These sources include census figures; notarial records; ecclesiastical records of births, marriages, and deaths; personal papers in private collections; and diplomatic correspondence in both local archives and the major European repositories of colonial history, including the Archives Nationales of France, the British Colonial Archives, and the Archivo General de las Indias. Garraway, *Tree of Liberty*, contains a series of articles on the cultural ramifications of the revolution in the Caribbean and France, as does Munro and Walcott-Hackshaw.

INTRODUCTION

1. There is an extensive bibliography on secondary economies, black markets, and what Dawdy calls "rogue colonialism." For example, see the discussion of the early seventeenth-century "devastaciones" in northern Hispaniola in Benítez-Rojo, *Isla que se repite*. Also, see the essays in Knight and Liss; Dawdy; and Obadele-Starks. Dorsey carefully documents the interisland slave trade. While beyond the scope of this book, the Dutch Caribbean is a logical focus for the study of intercolonial black markets as well.

2. Matory succinctly reminds us that "territorial jurisdictions might command great loyalty from their citizens and subjects, and they might impose significant restraints on their conduct; however, territorial jurisdictions have never monopolized the loyalty of the citizens and subjects they claim, and they are never the sole founts of authority or agents of constraint in such people's lives. Such is true of the nation-state now, as it was and is of kingdoms, acephalous republics, and fiefdoms" (2). Generations of Caribbeanists have documented the importance of migration in the region, and my work is built upon their insights.

3. The most commonly used text providing an overview of the Age of Revolution is Hobsbawm. For more nuanced attention to the revolutionary age in the Americas with a particular focus on people of African descent, see the work of scholars such as Sylvia Frey, Gary Nash, Ada Ferrer, C. L. R. James, Laurent Dubois, Peter Blanchard, and Douglas R. Egerton.

4. For examples of this scholarship, see J. Scott; Linebaugh and Rediker; Gilroy; Glissant; Matory; Nwankwo; Stephens; the volume edited by West, Martin, and Wilkins; and the special issue of *Radical History Review* edited by Brock, Kelley, and Sotiropoulos. Julius Scott's groundbreaking work was especially influential in conceptualizing this project. Centered on the viability of a "common wind" in Afro-America that functioned as a substantial channel of shared information, his research cites exhaustive archival evidence provided by British, Spanish, and French diplomatic correspondence to document the "networks of news and rumor" established in the late eighteenth century that enabled blacks to remain highly informed about events happening throughout the region and how they might best manipulate struggles between European metropoli to their own advantage. These networks were composed of those he calls "mobile fugitives"—the runaway slaves, military deserters, and deep-sea sailors that regularly crisscrossed the region. See J. Scott, "Common Wind." More recently, Nwankwo's work on "black cosmopolitanism" in the nineteenth century suggests that "race, nation and humanity were three major referents through which individuals defined themselves and others in the . . . Atlantic world, but only one of these three referents was allowed people of African descent—race" (10). In the tradition of scholars such as Anthony Maingot who have argued that the Haitian Revolution resulted in a "terrified consciousness" for white inhabitants in the region, Nwankwo argues that "Whites' fear of the revolution and its presumably contagious nature forced people of African descent throughout the Americas, particularly those in the public or published eye, to name a relationship to the Haitian Revolution, in

particular, and to a transnational idea of Black community, in general. The revolution made a fear of uprising and, by extension, of transnationally oriented notions of Black community, into a continent-wide obsession" (7–8). Her examples are culled from a later time (mostly 1830–80s), but the principal ideas are still relevant.

5. Another fascinating critique of the American Revolution is echoed in an anonymous article in the September 27, 1838, issue of the Haitian newspaper *L'Union*. The author wrote, "Notre caste aux Etats-Unis a tout perdu à l'indépendance des colons et malheureusement pour elle, cet événement est survenu au moment ou le mouvement philanthropique en sa faveur prenait naissance, précisément en Angleterre. Dès lors l'influence de la métropole lui a manquée et sa condition a de plus en plus empirée." The British metropole was thus seen to promote the interest of slaves, whereas the new American Republic was seen as denying them their liberty. These comments are much milder in tone than Frederick Douglass's famous Fourth of July oration in 1852, which asserted: "Your high independence only reveals the immeasurable distance between us. The blessings in which you, this day, rejoice are not enjoyed in common. The rich inheritance of justice, liberty, prosperity, and independence bequeathed by your fathers is shared by you, not by me. . . . To drag a man in fetters into the grand illuminated temple of liberty, and call upon him to join you in joyous anthems, were inhuman mockery and sacrilegious irony. Do you mean, citizens, to mock me by asking me to speak today? What, to the American slave, is your Fourth of July? I answer: a day that reveals to him, more than all other days in the year, the gross injustice and cruelty to which he is the constant victim. To him, your celebration is a sham; your boasted liberty, an unholy license; your national greatness, swelling vanity; your sounds of rejoicing are empty and heartless; your denunciation of tyrants, brass-fronted impudence; your shouts of liberty and equality, hollow mockery; your prayers and hymns, your sermons and thanksgivings, with all your religious parade and solemnity, are, to Him, mere bombast, fraud, deception, impiety, and hypocrisy."

6. Many twentieth-century fictional texts capture the interrelatedness of the Caribbean Basin and the particular importance of the Haitian Revolution to regional development. These include the most well-known ones, such as Carpentier's *El siglo de las luces [Explosion in the Cathedral]* and *El reino de este mundo [The Kingdom of This World]*, Maximin's *L'isolé soleil [Lone Sun]*, and the voluminous theatrical works by authors such as Aimé Césaire, Derek Walcott, Jeanne Brierre, and Edouard Glissant. Very recent works such as Marlon James's *The Book of Night Women* and Isabel Allende's *La isla bajo el mar [Island beneath the Sea]* continue to explore this legacy. Fischer provides an excellent account of the ramifications of the Haitian Revolution for the Caribbean, particularly Caribbean literary traditions.

7. Wood and Kriz are historically grounded studies that provide nuanced analyses of the role of visual culture in debates about slavery and race in the Americas and Europe.

8. Reference to her young mulatto daughter, also up for sale, suggests the possibility of sexual violence occurring in the household.

9. There is an extensive bibliography about Protestantism in black communities. For example, see Frey, *Come Shouting to Zion*. Evangelicals such as George Liehle worked in Jamaica, and a host of people from North America traveled to Africa for missionary purposes. A September 7, 1839, notice in the *Colored American* entitled "West Indian Mission" notes that "a Society has been established in the city of Troy, by the colored people of that place, to promote the spread of the gospel among the freed men of the British West Indian Islands. Thus, while some of our brethren have been contemplating the establishment of a commercial company, to fill their coffers with the silver and gold of those Islands, these Christian philanthropists of Troy have been considering the duty of scattering among the inhabitants of those Islands, 'the unsearchable riches of Christ.' Citizens of Troy, well done! Well done!" I discuss the issue of religious ethnocentrism in chapter 5.

10. See above, Preface, note 7, for an overview of work in Haitian revolutionary studies. The work of scholars such as Edouard Glissant, Vera Kutzinski, Eric Sundquist, Antonio Benitez-Rojo, and Stuart Hall laid the foundations for what became inter-American studies. In the past few years, the following special issues have continued this research: Levander and Levine; R. Saldívar and Moya; Shukla and Tinsman; and Fox. Attempting to put the hemispheric context back into the term *American,* these and other studies range widely in terms of their focus. Much pioneering work has been done examining North American imperialism, the social and economic forces behind migrations between the United States and its neighbors, and excellent work on the "transamerican" nature of both Latino writing and the (North) American Renaissance. For example, see Rowe, *Literary Culture;* Gruesz, *Ambassadors of Culture;* Brickhouse, *Transamerican Literary Relations;* Smith and Cohn, *Look Away!;* and Levander and Levine's edited volume, which assembles the work of many of these scholars.

11. On the relation between slavery and inter-American studies, see Blanchard, "Pan Americanism." In his analysis of the 1826 Congress of Panama, he concludes that "prospects thus seemed favorable for Spanish America's black populations; delegates approved Article 26 of the Treaty of Union, League, and Perpetual Confederation that called for cooperation in ending the African slave trade and declaring as pirates those involved with the trade. . . . However . . . Article 26 amounted to very little. Pan Americanism failed to secure abolition, citizenship rights for blacks, and racial equality because of various factors. . . . The failure of abolition as a Pan American mandate reflected the self-interest of the independent nations' new rulers, which also helped to undermine Pan Americanism more generally in the decades after independence" (14–15).

12. For example, slave traders transported men and women between ports such as Kingston and Havana. They may have used ships built in Baltimore for the purpose. In addition, merchants supplied the provisions needed to feed them—salt fish from New England and rice from the Carolinas were shipped to Caribbean planters. Runaways desperately sought to escape enslavement by fleeing across colonial frontiers—they left Saint-Domingue for Spanish Santo Domingo or fled Georgia for Spanish Florida. Planters moved throughout the

region to establish their enterprises, from Barbados to South Carolina, for example, and later to circumvent abolition or flee revolution.

13. For more on the concept of staggered development, see E. Williams, *From Columbus to Castro*. Much like Antonio Benítez-Rojo's paradigm of the repeating island in *La isla que se repite,* staggered development is a particularly useful tool for comparative work on Caribbean societies.

14. Hulme writes, "It should be made clear that by 'the Caribbean' is meant not the somewhat vague politico-geographic region now referred to by that term, but rather what Immanuel Wallerstein calls 'the extended Caribbean,' a coastal and insular region that stretched from what is now southern Virginia in the USA to the most eastern part of Brazil. . . . It emphasizes those features, environmental and ideological, that lay beyond national differences. The Caribbean is then the tropical belt defined ecologically or meteorologically . . . as the most suitable area for growing the tropical crops of cotton, tobacco and sugar. . . . Equally important, this was the area where, broadly speaking, the native populations were replaced by slaves brought from Africa" (*Colonial Encounters* 3–5).

15. Resurrecting circum-Caribbean history through the lives of individual men and women has produced fascinating recent scholarship. The work of Rebecca J. Scott provides an especially compelling narrative on the peregrinations of individual Saint-Domingue migrants throughout the Americas. See "Public Rights" and "Atlantic World." Also Jane Landers's use of Spanish colonial archival sources to narrate the stories of black Atlantic revolutionary figures such as Georges Biassou, Juan Bautista Whitten, and Francisco Menéndez in their own words is exemplary. See *Atlantic Creoles.*

CHAPTER 1

The epigraphs to this chapter are from Médéric Louis Élie Moreau de Saint-Méry, "Discours de Moreau de Saint-Méry, sur les affranchis des colonies, prononcé par lui dans l'assemblée publique du Musée de Paris," ms., April 7, 1785, Collection Moreau de St-Méry, F3, 156, Archives Nationales d'Outre Mer, and from Vastey, *Notes à M. le Baron* 11–12. An abridged translation of the French is quoted in Heinl, Heinl and Heinl, 26–27. For more on Vastey, see Nicholls, "Pompée Valentin Vastey." When Dessalines declared independence, he invoked this history of torture, asking, "Citizens, look about you for your wives, husbands, brothers, sisters. Look for your children, your nursing babes. Where have they gone? They have fallen prey to these vultures. . . . Whenever they near our shores may the French tremble, if not from the guilt of past atrocities then from our resolve to slaughter any person born French whose footprint henceforth contaminates our land of liberty!" (125). By appealing to the bonds of family and friendship between his audience and their dead, he affirmed their humanity, no small task in the immediate aftermath of a system that attempted to natally alienate bonds of kinship among those considered "property." In one of his most famous speeches, he asserted that he had "rendered to these true cannibals, war for war, crime for crime, outrage for outrage; yes, I have saved my country; I have avenged America" (qtd. in Rainsford 448).

1. One of the founders of comparative, inter-American historiography, Moreau is best known for his *Description topographique, physique, civile, politique et historique de la partie française de l'île de Saint-Domingue,* a detailed account of life in colonial Saint-Domingue. Born in Martinique, he resettled in Saint-Domingue after completing a law degree in Paris. Marrying into the local elite, he became involved with the Cercle de Philadelphes, a group interested in a variety of scholarly pursuits. He was appointed to the Conseil Superior and returned to the metropole in 1783 in order to use government archives for job-related research. With the eventual threat of execution during the Terror, however, he fled France with the intention of returning to Saint-Domingue, only to be foiled by the outbreak of the Haitian Revolution. Instead he settled in Philadelphia from 1794 to 1798 where he published *Description topographique* and other volumes. The sheer number of his texts on themes as disparate as colonial laws throughout the French Caribbean, Vodou, the correct way to grow sugarcane, and the nature of quadrupeds in Paraguay is some indication that he was passionately interested in classifying the world around him in the hope that his qualitative analyses would advance the interests of the ruling elite in colonial America. Throughout this book, French page citations to *Descriptions topographique* are taken from the 2004 reprint.

2. An extended critique in the introduction to the study, an appendix entitled "Some Account of the Nature and History of the Blood-Hounds used in the American Colonies," and two engravings commented upon this subject.

3. Marcus Rainsford seems to have been acquainted with Quarrell, one of the main protagonists of Robert C. Dallas's *The History of the Maroons* (1803). A note in Rainsford's text cites Dallas's work, so it is strange that he never mentions the use of dogs in the British context. Quarrell's personal escapades while on this mission, including tales of great fortitude in the midst of illness, privateering battles, run-ins with the local Spanish authorities and so forth, make an interesting companion narrative to Rainsford's own tales of imprisonment, meetings with Haitian revolutionary leaders, and other exploits in Saint-Domingue. Both of their narratives were popular adventure stories about white self-preservation amid the threat of black hostilities.

4. Madiou includes another exchange between a soldier and Rochambeau on the island of La Tortue. When he was asked whether to feed the dogs meat or bread, Rochambeau replied, "Donnez-leur de la chair de nègre et mulâtre; n'en existe-t-il pas à la Tortue?" (2: 507).

5. Of Noailles's mission, Ardouin writes, "Le fils d'un maréchal de France conçut l'idée de se mettre en rapport avec des éleveurs de chiens. . . . Il consentit à aller débattre avec de tels êtres le prix de ces animaux qu'il accompagna lui-même à Saint-Domingue, pour traquer des hommes qui défendaient leur liberté naturelle! Quelle dégradation! Quelle ignominie!" (5: 74).

6. In the background of the image, men in uniform are attacking several figures. One victim is in a posture of supplication and appears to be praying toward the sky. Interestingly, a large serpent is in the tree immediately above him, and I wonder if Rainsford was depicting a slave praying to the serpent itself. Accounts of popular religiosity, or Vodou, were published in Moreau's

aforementioned 1797–98 *Description topographique,* which includes a sensationalist account of how black slaves worshipped serpents. Rainsford's introduction makes it clear that he read most eighteenth-century sources about Saint-Domingue, so he may have been familiar with this text.

7. For the classic account of cruelty toward slaves in colonial Saint-Domingue, see C. L. R. James, the chapters "The Owners" and "The Property."

8. For a history of the Jamaican maroons, see Campbell; ch. 7 deals specifically with the 1795 war between Trelawny Town and the British government. See Price, *Maroon Societies,* for an overview of marronage in the Caribbean. For a discussion of the potential impact of the Haitian Revolution in Jamaica, see Geggus, "Enigma of Jamaica."

9. Far from being traditional allies, the Jamaican maroons and slave populations had long been enemies. As part of their accord with the British government, the maroons agreed not to harbor any new fugitives and to return escapees seeking asylum. Tensions between the slaves and maroon communities were high, and during the 1795–96 conflict slaves were not roused to join forces with Trelawney Town; even residents of Accompong, a neighboring maroon town, helped fight against them. Another interesting inter-American story could be written about the maroons' subsequent forced migration to Canada.

10. Dallas asserts that Quarrell's trip was inspired by a conversation the latter had with a "Spaniard," a man later revealed to be a native of Cuba. This man informed him that when the Spanish had faced opposition from the Miskito Coast Indians, they had imported "thirty six dogs and twelve chasseurs" from Cuba to wage war against them, and he asserted that "these auxiliaries were more formidable than the finest regiment of the most warlike nation," allowing the Spaniards to "drive the Mosquitos from the coast" (5). This commentary probably refers to conflicts between the Spanish and the Miskitos during the 1790s. The Miskitos had formerly been allies of the British.

11. Franklin Knight (*Caribbean,* esp. 90–106) describes two types of societies in the seventeenth- and eighteenth-century Caribbean. The first was the "organized and formal colony" composed of "struggling settlers, prosperous planters, exasperated officials, machinating merchants, suffering slaves and ambivalent free persons of color." The second was a "variegated group of individuals, commonly considered transfrontiersmen—people who chose to operate outside the conventional confines of the colonies." These ranged from "highly organized communities of Maroons" to the "defiant, stateless, peripatetic collectivity of buccaneers or freebooters" (90).

12. Other evidence about the breeding of these Cuban dogs is found in the diary of J. B. Dunlop, a Scotsman who spent two years traveling in Cuba. He wrote, "I also visited on this occasion, one of the neighboring Estates in which Blood hounds are kept and trained to prevent the Negroes from running away, or the too near approach of the maroons. These Dogs are a species of hound and *remarkable for the suspicious hue of the eye, in which no confidence can be placed even by their master. They are kept constantly confined in Iron Cages and are taught to have a fierce antipathy to the Negroes, whom they*

attack whenever they get loose. The owner had the complaisance to shew us how they were trained. He ordered one of his Negroes to go into the Woods and after he had been gone some time one of the Dogs was let loose after being first muzzled. The animal seemed to know his Duty well, for sniffing about the yard for a few minutes he got the scent of the Negroes foot and darted with the force of lightning with his Nose upon the track into the Woods. Shortly after a tremendous howling was heard in the woods and then 2 large Dogs were let loose, who in a few minutes brought back the Negroe. *But either owing to the looseness of muzzle or the force [of] the Dogs jaws the poor Negroe was nipped rather severely.*" Italics mine; qtd. in A. Mohl 244. This "demonstration" of the dog's ability to hunt human beings illustrates how such an activity had an element of sport to it, not unlike the Spaniards' engagement in the *montería infernal* during the Conquest, a sportive event during which dogs were used to hunt and kill indigenous peoples.

13. Dallas continues, "The muzzled dogs with the heavy rattling chains ferociously making at every object, and forcibly dragging on the chasseurs, who could hardly restrain them, presented a scene of tremendous nature, well calculated to give a most awful colouring to the report which would be conveyed to the Maroons" (120). Campbell writes, "There was an old black woman cooking in the open, and one of the dogs attempted to seize a piece of her meat, whereupon she struck it and was instantly killed by the bloodhound; on another occasion a soldier of the 83rd regiment, having seized one, was severely torn in the arm and only with great difficulty saved; again, two of the dogs went into fighting, and the keeper was forced to kill one of them, since they never let go of their hold" (229).

14. For the use of dogs during the Seminole War, see Covington. Given that the dogs did not prove as "successful" in Florida combat as they had elsewhere in the Americas, Covington astoundingly surmises that "it is possible that these dogs also failed because they had been trained to pick up a scent left by the Negroes of Cuba who had a different racial odor than the Seminoles of Florida" (118–19). For a nineteenth-century source that outlines the debates about use of the Cuban dogs, see former congressman Joshua Giddings's narrative of the Seminole Wars in *Exiles of Florida* 264–73.

15. An excellent multimedia site chronicling the history of the Black Seminoles is provided by Bird. Five images of the bloodhounds, dating between 1840 and 1848, are included. One contemporary print (ca. 1840) shows three bloodhounds being presented with awards from the Van Buren administration for their aid in the war. The caption reads: "Fellow citizens & soldiers! In presenting this standard to the 1st Regiment of Bloodhounds, I congratulate you on your promotion, from the base & inglorious pursuit of animals, in an uncivilized region like Cuba, to the noble task of hunting 'men' in our Christian country! our administration has been reproached for the expense of the Florida war, so we have determined now to prosecute it, in a way that's 'dog cheap!'" Finally, another pro-Democratic party caricature shows Taylor climbing a pole to flee some hounds hot in pursuit. He says, "When Cuba is Annexed I hope these Foreigners will no longer be imported to annoy the 'Natives' in this way."

16. For an overview of the use of dogs in warfare, from ancient Greece,

to Napoleon's use of them in the Egyptian campaigns, up to the twentieth century, see Sloane.

17. The French may have heard of the dogs' successful sojourn in Jamaica during the 1795–96 conflict. Rochambeau was temporarily stationed in Saint-Domingue in 1795, a time when the British occupied the western part of the colony. It is possible that he became aware of the dogs then.

18. Much scholarship points to the escalation of Cuban sugar production and its corresponding dependence on slavery as a consequence of the island's deliberate attempt to fill the vacancy left on the global sugar market by the collapse of Saint-Domingue. Planter Francisco Arango y Parreño's much-discussed 1792 *Discurso sobre la agricultura de la Habana y medios de fomentarla* often serves as evidence of the enthusiasm for a renewed interest in large-scale plantation production. For example, see Benítez-Rojo's interesting "Power/Sugar/Literature."

19. Dubois, *Avengers,* cites Ardouin's *Études* and Dayan's *Haiti, History* (155) for this example.

20. Both Antonio de Herrera y Tordesillas and Bartomolé de Las Casas include accounts of how the Spanish conquistadores (Christopher Columbus, Juan Ponce de Leon, Vasco Nuñez de Balboa, and so forth) used dogs to subdue the indigenous populations of the Caribbean and Latin America. This particularly horrified Las Casas, and later editions of his work included an engraving depicting human meat markets where body parts were sold. Varner and Varner, authors of a monograph on the use of dogs during the Conquest, write, "The dogs of the conquerors and early settlers were, in the main, war dogs and were trained purposely to relish Indian flesh. Thus, in combat or after a struggle was over, they gorged on the bodies of the victims. Not only was this destruction permitted, it was encouraged, both as an effective maneuver in the cruel process of subjugation and . . . as an easy means of providing them food" (13). These stories fed what would become the black legend / *la leyenda negra* about the Spanish Conquest. For an examination of their use from the Conquest to Abu Ghraib, see S. Johnson, "You Should Give Them Blacks to Eat."

21. The review of Dallas's work is quite extensive, totaling twenty-three pages (31–41, 246–59). The editors go on to explain that "enough, however, was explained at that period to divert the censure of the House, and the subject was not afterwards renewed" (247).

22. The quote from George III is in Campbell, letter from Portland to Balcarres, March 3, 1796.

23. To attest to Quarrell's character, Dallas writes, "The commissioner's humanity and kindness to his own black people are well known in Jamaica; I myself bear witness to it, having had an opportunity, by residing at his house for a considerable time, to be well acquainted with his disposition; and I believe that his slaves enjoyed a far greater portion of happiness than the generality of the poor in any country upon the face of the earth. But had it been otherwise, had the suggestion proceeded from a despotic and ferocious spirit, bent on the extermination of some of the human species by a barbarous expedient, it is not likely that a mild, humane, and beneficent mind, like that of Lord Balcarres,

or that the majority of any assembly of educated men, would have concurred in the experiment. It appeared to them at that time, as it must appear now to every rational man, a choice of two evils; and the one wisely chosen was trivial in comparison with the magnitude of the other" (2: 18).

24. See the commentary in Bird, under "Trail Narrative," "Exile," "Shifting Alliances," "National Debate," accessed December 18, 2007, <http://www.johnhorse.com/trail/03/a/08.htm>.

25. Qtd. in *Colored American* April 10, 1841. More on this African American newspaper follows in chapter 5.

26. This is not to say that life in late eighteenth-century Europe was devoid of torture outside the plantation zone. Jay Winik writes, "On European soil, it was also an age of horrid cruelty. As the historian J. H. Plumb once wrote: 'life was cheap.' Torture was universally employed for all manner of crimes, from speaking ill of the king to stealing a tradesman's wages or even loaves of bread. Rarely was there mercy. To be sure, one might be hanged, drawn and quartered — that was simple. But ordinary criminals and political dissidents alike were routinely beheaded, burned, or broken alive on the wheel. Or slowly crushed by the infamous peine forte et dure. Or they were subjected to the rack and the rope. Or the knout. Treason, but not only treason, often yielded more creative methods. Rapists, for one, were castrated. Counterfeiters were punished by pouring molten metal down their throats. Curiously, those speaking ill of the sovereign were, to a point, more fortunate: They simply had their tongues ripped out" (3). The ubiquity of torture during the time period makes it all the more remarkable that some contemporaries took such an intense dislike to the project of using dogs against slave and maroon insurgents.

27. There is a rich visual record of engravings depicting slaves being hunted and mauled by dogs, especially in antislavery literature from the United States in the immediate antebellum period. The trope of the runaway slave, often in the company of his family, being mercilessly chased by bloodhounds is evident in countless novels and prints. For an example of how ubiquitous slave-hunting dogs were in the North American imagination, consider Abel C. Thomas's primer *Gospel of Slavery*. The letter "B" included the following entry alongside of an engraving of a slave being attacked by three hounds:

B stands for bloodhounds. On merciless fangs
The Slaveholder feels his "property" hangs,
And the dog and the master are hot on the track,
To torture or bring the black fugitive back.
The weak has but fled from the hand of the strong,
Asserting the right and resisting the wrong,
While he who exults in a skin that is white,
A Bloodhound employs in asserting his might
-Oh chivalry-laymen and dogmatist-priest,
Say, which is the monster, the man or the beast?

28. Carpentier famously declared in the prologue to his novel that "the story about to be read is based on extremely rigorous documentation. A documentation that not only respects the truth of events, the names of characters—including the minor ones—of places and streets, but also conceals, beneath

its apparent atemporality, a minute correspondence of dates and chronology" (qtd. in Paravisini-Gebert 116). In the chapter "Saint Calamity" he has an almost verbatim summary of the above-mentioned incident as recorded by Madiou and Ardouin when the anonymous slave, a servant of French General Boyer, is eaten alive on stage.

29. Dogs have evoked memories of racial hatred in a global context well into the twentieth century. A few examples suffice. The film *When We Were Kings* (1996) showcases the famous 1974 "Rumble in the Jungle" between Muhammad Ali and George Foreman. In a scene when Foreman arrives in Kinshasa, he emerges from the plane with a large shepherd. According to the film, he lost many local fans who associated him with the Belgians, the former colonizers who had terrorized the native population with their attack dogs. Likewise, images of police dogs attacking peaceful civil rights protestors in 1963 Alabama are a stark reminder that dogs have been regularly used to police populations deemed a threat to the status quo. The final riot scene in the 1973 cult classic film *The Spy Who Sat by the Door* includes a scene when dogs are introduced to control angry citizens and it only whips them to further fury. As one black character says, "The dogs, why did they have to go and bring in the dogs?" To this day, African American popular culture is replete with jokes about dogs being racist.

CHAPTER 2

1. Very little information is available about Domingo Echavarría. According to one study, he was born in Ozama in 1805 and died in 1849. In addition to being an engraver, he was also a painter. See de los Santos, *Memoria* 143–45.

2. In 1697, the Spanish monarchy officially ceded the western third of Hispaniola to the French under the Treaty of Ryswick. Although the island was subsequently divided into French and Spanish colonies, the border separating the two was highly permeable. Populations regularly crossed from one side to the next, and it was not until the 1777 Treaty of Aranjuez that legal disputes regarding an official border were temporarily settled. To the present day, however, the border between Haiti and the Dominican Republic remains permeable, and estimates vary widely about the number of Haitians and people of immediate Haitian descent living in the Dominican Republic. This has especially been the case after the January 2010 earthquake. Whether in search of work or networking with family, the people who travel from one side to the other and often back again have negotiated their own criteria about the relationship between the two countries. See Lundahl for an excellent overview of the relationship between the two countries from the seventeenth to twentieth centuries. There is a large body of scholarship concerning Haitian-Dominican relations, both social and cultural, including work by Franklyn Franco, Emilio Cordero Michel, André Corten and Isis Duarte, Marcio Veloz Maggiolo, Maurice Lemoine, Pedro Mir, Jean Price-Mars, Edwidge Danticat, René Philoctète, Sibylle Fischer, David Howard, Ernesto Sagás, and Eugenio Matibag. Inoa provides a detailed accounting of the resources available for a

variety of themes related to interisland relations in the nineteenth and twentieth centuries. Mariñez is another resource.

3. The first half of the nineteenth century was marked by a series of Haitian attempts to integrate the eastern part of the island, specifically in 1801, 1805, 1822, 1849, and the late 1850s. See San Miguel's overview of Dominican historiography dealing with these events, especially ch. 2, "Racial Discourse and National Identity, Haiti in the Dominican Imaginary."

4. For a discussion of the anti-Haitian sentiment commonly found in Rodríguez Demorizi's work, see Scheker Mendoza. Writings of Joaquín Balaguer, former president of the Dominican Republic, are also well known for their virulent anti-Haitianism: see, for example, *Isla al revés* or *Centinela de la frontera*. Haitian historiography, as a whole, has had kinder judgments about this period. For example, see Jean Price-Mars's very detailed *République d'Haïti*. However, the aforementioned Thomas Madiou, one of a handful of canonical nineteenth-century Haitian historians, relied heavily on Dominican chronicles, and as such his assessments often repeat the biases found in accounts from elite easterners that argued against integration.

5. The insight offered by this cultural analysis is of contemporary significance given the worldwide attention that has focused on relations between the Dominican Republic and Haiti in recent years. Several documentaries and international campaigns launched by the Anti-Slavery Society have brought major human rights abuses committed against migrant Haitian sugarcane workers / *braceros* to light, often comparing contemporary working and living conditions to those under slavery. Studied in conjunction with the dictator Rafael Trujillo's 1937 massacre of upwards of fifteen thousand Haitian workers, scholarship on Dominican-Haitian affairs has largely been dominated by an interest in these events and their place within twentieth-century border and migration studies. The present-day animosity between the two nations also manifests itself in electoral politics. Elsewhere I have examined racialized caricatures from the hotly contested presidential campaign of 1994, when Jose Francisco Peña Gómez ran as the candidate of the Partido Dominicano Revolucionario (PRD). Of Haitian descent, Peña Gómez was ruthlessly attacked for his purported sympathy toward his western neighbors. These images speak to the continued manipulation of anti-Haitian feeling in the Dominican Republic and the role that visual culture plays in perpetrating these sentiments. See my discussion in an earlier version of this chapter: S. Johnson, "Integration of Hispaniola." Many thanks to Elka Sheker for sharing these images. For an overview of the overt racism involved in the 1994 campaign, see Howard's chapter "Race and Nation in Dominican Politics."

6. Disturbingly little historical information is available about Campos Taváres. His absence from Dominican historiography is especially interesting in light of other "Haitian" generals who have claimed critical attention. For example, Antonio Duvergé Duval (1807–55) was the son of Haitian parents (from Mirebalais and Croix des Bouquets). Born in Mayagüez, Puerto Rico, to a mixed-race refugee family from Saint-Domingue, he resettled in the Dominican Republic in 1808 and became a hero for his role as leader in the Azua battle against the Haitians in 1844 during the separatist movement. Celebrated as

the "sentinel" of the *frontera*, he has been the subject of several studies, including Balaguer's aforementioned *Centinela de la frontera*. Duvergé was killed by firing squad under the orders of Pedro Santana in 1855. Another interesting figure is Placide Lebrun, Haitian governor of Las Vegas, who seems to have been well liked by some of his Dominican colleagues.

7. Arredondo fled Santo Domingo in April 1805 and resettled in Puerto Príncipe, Cuba. In 1905 the writer's nephew sent the manuscript from Cuba to the Dominican historian José Gabriel García.

8. See above, Preface, note 6, for an overview of some of these narratives. When examining genealogies of knowledge from the era, one can see how important inter-American migrations were to early Caribbean letters. For example, although many families fled Hispaniola (both the Spanish and French territories) and became involved in affairs in other countries such as Cuba, Venezuela, or the United States, they still wished to document their "glorious pasts" in Santo Domingo and in Saint-Domingue. The trope of reversal of fortune is ubiquitous in exile cultural production. As the elite moved, they became nostalgic, and their attachment to their former homes led to the creation of a diasporic literature from Hispaniola. Culturally, then, they expressed a creole consciousness that at times had elements of burgeoning nationalism. This creole consciousness was sometimes even hemispheric in nature, as they read one another's work (this was the case with Leonardo del Monte and Moreau de Saint-Méry, for example) and identified with their fellow citizens in their adoptive homelands. These texts demonstrate how the Haitian Revolution was critical to the content and material conditions surrounding the production of much of this early Caribbean literature.

9. Many passages describe the magnificence of the Haitian palaces, and it is clear that these delegates had a personal tête-à-tête with Dessalines, who regaled them with stories of French perfidy and Haitian military prowess.

10. For an interesting essay on the naming of Haiti, particularly the use of indigenous symbolism, see Geggus, *Haitian Revolutionary Studies,* the chapter "The Naming of Haiti," 207–20.

11. Madiou records Dessalines's speech in his *Histoire d'Haiti.* Marcus Rainsford documents a similar speech in a May 8, 1804, proclamation by Dessalines in Appendix 16 of his *Historical Account,* 453–56.

12. The idea of Hispaniola as "one and indivisible" confronted the reality of a territory where constantly shifting alliances and priorities between and among metropolitan governments and local actors defied linear progress from colony to nation, from Spanish to French to Haitian, from enslavement to freedom. That is, the history of Santo Domingo during the first half of the nineteenth century was enormously complex. It is poetically epitomized in the oft-cited verses, "Yesterday I was born a Spaniard, in the afternoon I was French, by the evening I was Ethiopian [black], and today they say I am English, I don't know what will become of me!" ("Ayer español nací, a la tarde fui francés, a la noche etíope fui, hoy dicen que soy ingles, no sé que sera de mi"; Torres-Saillant 50–51; Fischer 131). In addition to noting shifting imperial/political ties, the poem could just as easily have commented on how one experienced the anguish of being a slave during childhood, freedom for

a few years during adolescence, re-enslavement for another fifteen years or so, and a permanent freedom at the onset of middle age. Few laws, including those mandating abolition, were stable and enduring. Sibylle Fischer's nuanced analysis of repetition and nonlinearity as a mode of understanding Dominican history allows her to conclude that "Spanish Hispaniola seemed to be set on a course of eccentric loops, punctuated by violent disruptions and reversals that reproduced dependency instead of ushering in a new golden era of the modern nation state, and left traces of traumatic memories that reasserted the power of the past at every turn" (132).

13. See Deive, *Emigraciones dominicanas* and *Refugiados franceses*.

14. Toussaint Louverture seems to have abolished slavery in the eastern territory, as his 1801 Constitution included Samaná and presumably the entire expanse of Hispaniola. Article 3 stated that "There cannot be slaves on this territory, servitude is there forever abolished. All men are born, live, and die free and French." What the postslave subject was allowed to do was another matter entirely. The newly titled *cultivateurs* throughout the island were subject to many restrictions regarding work and mobility. Arredondo cites the vigilance of Haitian forces regarding attempts to leave the island with slaves or free people of color, stating that one could suffer the death penalty for this offense, even if one wished to emigrate with those who, he suggests "didn't wish to separate from those with whom they had passed their youth receiving blessings." He notes that Haitian troops went so far as to search houses "while former masters were still in bed, looking for hidden negroes" (134).

15. Excellent scholarship examines women's participation in the French Revolution and the use of women as republican symbol. See, for example, the figure of Marianne. For women's role in the revolution, see Melzer and Rabine, particularly Landes's essay, which provides useful context for the Bonneville image.

16. In Saint-Domingue, most of the well-known leaders of the revolution, such as Louverture, Dessalines, Christophe, and Boyer, engaged in continued conflict with popular leaders such as Jean- Baptiste Sans Souci, Goman (Jean-Baptiste Perrier), and Jean-Jacques Accau.

17. A host of official documents are cited in R. González 184–224. Most are located in the Archivo General de Indias and in Incháustegui's *Documentos para estudio*.

18. Antivagrancy laws were ubiquitous in the Americas, especially in the aftermath of slave abolition. Implemented as a form of maintaining control over the workforce, they made a host of activities illegal and many punishable by forced labor. R. González (205) quotes Pedro Catani's *Informe sobre la isla Española, por Pedro Catani, oidor de la Audiencia de Santo Domingo* as evidence of how the Crown wished to exert control over free blacks. Catani suggested that "deberia formarse un padrón de todos ellos y del lugar de su residencia, no permitiéndoles ubicarse en lo más interior de los montes, sino en parages circunvecinos a los caminos reales y principales veredas, y obligarles a trabaxar [sic] lo proporcionado a sus fuerzas."

19. Catani's mention of runaway slaves / *cimarrones* is a reminder that

maroon communities crossed the frontiers established by European treaties for decades before the Haitian Revolution. For instance, Maniel, one of the most famous *palenques*, was situated along the border, "stretching from the western limits of Jacmel, in the (French) South, and extending well into the Spanish part of the island" (Fick 51–52). The existence of populations that did not recognize either French or Spanish control is important as it demonstrates alternative community loyalties of both African-born and creole blacks. Like the "transfrontiersmen" and privateers operating in the region, maroons existed outside at the periphery of state control. Catani's original language stated that he would "limpiar esta tierra de osjosos, vagamundos, ebrios y ladrones. . . . Esta clase de hombres no tienen conucos, ni labranzas, ni otro oficio honesto con que mantenerse. . . . Estos, como interesados a ocultar sus vicios, los atribuyen a simarrones [sic] y si algunos de estos hay, los favorecen y abrigan, como a sus compañeros. . . . Aquellos son los destructores de las haciendas, los que matan reses, cavallos [sic] y otros animales causando grandes perjuicios a los hasendados. . . . Lo que esto es, nadie lo puede creer sin verlo: es todo una rochela de pícaros, sin ley, ni religión, viven como árabes. . . . Y dígame vuestra merced ahora, de qué sirve estas gentes en una republica?" (qtd. in R. González 198–200).

20. As the town assessor, Arredondo was given the role of apprehending those guilty of writing and disseminating the pamphlets. Unfortunately, his text does not specify who the accused parties were, and I have not located any of these popular verses.

21. Outrage at being "traded" by the Spanish, especially to the French, was profound. One anonymous verse captures Heredia's sentiments perfectly. "Oh! Qué terrible maldad!, Que mi noble jerarquía, Vuelve el francés a porfía, a una infame igualdad!" (Rodríguez Demorizi, *Poesia popular dominicana* 22). Heredia's bitter disappointment that being the "cradle" of Spanish civilization in the Americas did not save Santo Domingo from being "forsaken," is indicative of a long history of Dominican pride in all things identified with Columbus. Joaquín Balaguer's enormously expensive Faro a Colon / Columbus's Lighthouse is the most recent iteration of this sentiment. The 1844 manifesto published by some leaders of the separatist movement invoked the Conquest as a justification for why Santo Domingo should no longer be integrated into Haiti. They wrote that "más derecho tenemos los de Oriente a dominar a los de Occidente que al contrario, si remontamos a los primeros años del descubrimiento del inmortal Colón." See *Documentos para la historia* 13.

22. Another commentary published in the periodical *El Dominicano* regarding the 1801 arrival of the Haitian army is relevant because it differs in content and tone from those cited above. Dr. Alejandro Llenas documents the welcome extended to the Haitians by some segments of the population. He documents that with "Toussaint's entrance to the city, Joaquín Garcia presented him the keys to the city on a table. 'Mr. President," said the Haitian, 'please be kind enough to put them in my hands. If not, it will look as if I have taken them.' After regularizing the administration and taking care of the country's necessities . . . the new governor retired from Azua and San Juan, showered with the blessings of the Dominicans" (Rodríguez Demorizi,

Invasiones haitianas 187–88). Llenas implies that these blessings were generalized, not solely forthcoming from the black population. Louverture is portrayed as gracious and eloquent, capable of "regularizing" administrative necessities that affected the quality of life of the whole population. This benign portrait of Louverture greatly differs from the anti-Haitian invective often found in narratives produced by slave holders and Trujillo bureaucrats. Azua and San Juan were provinces closer to the border, where much of the economy, both under French colonial rule and with the newly independent Haitian government, was closely tied to business with inhabitants to the west. Saint-Domingue served for a century as the principal market for cattle and wood exports coming from the east. Thus people involved with these industries had reason to promote amicable relations. See "Apuntes históricos sobre Santo Domingo, Ocupación de Santo Domingo por Toussaint Louverture," *El Dominicano*, Santiago, no. 17 (May 1874), qtd. in Rodríguez Demorizi's *Invasiones haitianas*, 185–88.

23. In 2005, a new edition of Arredondo's "Memoria de mi salida" was published on the occasion of the "Bicentennial of the Throat-Slitting" *(Bicentenario del Degüello)*. The cover reads, "Jean-Jacques Dessalines' Haitian army massacred thousands of Dominicans in the Cibao region. This is the terrifying story of the genocides in Moca and Santiago, written by a survivor" ("El ejercito haitiano de Juan Jacabo Dessalines llevó a cabo una matanza de miles de Dominicanos en la region del Cibao. Este es el espeluznante relato del genocidio en Moca y en Santiago, escrito por un sobreviviente"). Hence the reprint encourages anti-Haitian sentiment, referring to the 1805 conflict as a genocide related in all of its particulars by an eyewitness.

24. Ferrand's complete decree of January 6, 1805, is available in Rodríguez Demorizi, *Invasiones haitianas* 101–04. It also demanded that "male children from ten to fourteen years old and black and mulatto girls from twelve to fourteen years old will be deliberately sold and exported" ("los niños varones de diez a catorce años y las negras, mulatas, etc. de doce a catorce años, serán expresamente vendidas para ser exportadas"; 102). Louisiana's French-language newspaper *Moniteur de la Louisiane* published reports on how Ferrand's army was faring. Planter exiles were clearly interested in the latest developments and saw this army as continuing to fight in their interests. On the western side of the island, the French had also reinstituted both slavery and the slave trade upon the arrival of Leclerc. For example, Madiou states that "la presqu'île du Sud faisait avec Cuba un trafic très actif d'esclaves. Le bâtiment de l'Etat l'Intrépide . . . transportait à St-Yague ces infortunés qui étaient vendus à l'encan" (2: 503).

25. A perusal of many blogs mentions the 1805 events as if they happened yesterday.

26. See Martinez-Fernández, who uses correspondence of Dominican church officials to gauge their role in Dominican nationalist and annexationist struggles. He cites the Haitian state's abolition of church fees, its appropriation of some of their land, and its cessation of the Spanish practice of paying priests' salaries as reasons behind the church's significant resistance toward Haitian integration.

27. For details about the 1821 declaration of independence from Spain, in which José Núñez de Cáceres attempted to place Spanish Haiti under the jurisdiction of La Gran Colombia, see Moya Pons, *Dominican Republic* 119–24. Information about these events is elusive, yet they are another iteration of projected inter-American alliances that did not come to fruition.

28. Elizabeth Freeman was permanently disfigured when her mistress hit her with a hot shovel.

29. Rodríguez Demorizi, *Poesía popular dominicana* 52–53. Rodríguez Demorizi notes that the verses were recited by two Dominicans, Mercedita Del Monte and Arturo Alardo. They resonate with the African American slave song from whence Ira Berlin draws the title of his influential study *Many Thousands Gone*. After announcing the end of the days of the auction block, the driver's lash, and the peck o'corn (slave rations), the song announces, "No more mistress call for me, no more, no more, No more mistress call for me, Many thousands gone, Many thousands gone" (xii). The song and poem are a reminder of the role that women played as abusive owners in slave systems throughout the extended Americas.

30. As early as 1791, Olympe de Gouges issued her biting *Déclaration des droits de la femme et de la citoyenne,* which pointed out the limits of republican ideology and demanded equality for women.

31. There is a large body of scholarship dealing with the limits of emancipation in various American contexts. For example, see F. Cooper, Holt, and R. Scott; Sheller, *Democracy after Slavery.* For consideration of how slavery and emancipation affected women in particular, see Moitt; Gaspar and Hine; Scully and Paton; Stevenson.

32. The June 14, 1838, edition of *L'Union* included an excerpt from the diary of a soldier who had participated in the 1822 campaign in the Dominican Republic entitled "Notes extraites du carnet d'un soldat." Along with Campos Taváres's testimony, it provides a rare firsthand account of the military intervention from the point of view of a black soldier. He wrote, "The name of the place, Puerto Rico, occasioned a play of words amongst the soldiers of the division that said, since they were in Puerto Rico (an allusion to the island of that name), the army could easily make a promenade through the islands of this archipelago to bring liberty to the unhappy slaves. This wish could truly have existed in their hearts" ("Le nom du lieu, Puerto-Rico, fut l'occasion d'un jeu de mots des militaires de la division . . . qui [lui] disaient que puisqu'on était à Puerto-Rico (allusion à l'île de ce nom) l'armée pouvait bien faire une promenade dans les îles de cet archipel, pour y donner la liberté aux malheureux esclaves. Ce voeu pouvait bien exister réellement au fond de leur cœurs"). The Haitian army on a "promenade" through the archipelago, conferring freedom to unhappy slaves, is a forceful image. The author obviously recognized Haiti's position as the vanguard of populist rebellion in the region, a position that he and his fellow soldiers were proud to support.

33. Franklyn Franco's *Los Negros* includes references to primary sources from the 1820s, when residents of the east had to decide between continued Spanish rule, an alliance with La Gran Colombia, or integration into the Haitian state. The latter option seems to have been most popular with "las masas"

(132). For example, he cites a letter written to Haitian general Magny informing him that the residents of (San Fernando de) Monte Cristi had decided to
"hoist the Haitian flag" ("enarbolar la bandera haitiana") with hopes that the
Haitian government would "protect this city, and that from this day forward
it would form part of the Haitian Republic" (131–32). Cordero's study cited
above is another example of this revisionist perspective. These works represent
the most detailed scholarship supporting the possibility that Haitian integration accorded with many Dominicans' desires. By the end of Boyer's reign,
however, there was widespread dissatisfaction throughout the island. His government implemented the infamous Rural Code, a form of forced labor, and he
was responsible for negotiating the unpopular, extremely expensive indemnity
payment reimbursing former slave owners in exchange for official recognition
from France. By 1843 there was a revolution in Haiti, and he was forced into
exile.

34. During the first three decades of the twentieth century, iconographic
representations of Haitians in uniform were used to objectify and stereotype
them on the basis of deep-seated social fears often revolving around religion,
poverty, and disease. Following a wave of Haitian immigration to the eastern
part of Cuba, for example, many newspapers published caricatures of Haitians depicting them in military uniforms. Aline Helg's study of the Cuban
Partido Independiente de Color includes several caricatures from the period
of the 1912 Race War. One in particular, *El hombre de la bulla*, satirizes a
leader of the party, Pedro Ivonnet, who was of Haitian descent. He is decked
out in full military regalia, and the caption reads, "The Noisemaker: Here is
Ivonete, a light mulatto Cubo-French and rebel chief who is the one putting
Cuba under pressure. He shows off the Haitian uniform of his rank and hierarchy and believes he will become Afro-Cuban marshal any day." See Helg,
Our Rightful Share 229.

35. Rodríguez Demorizi's commentary on the Echavarría image has influenced all subsequent, if scant, commentary, down to other sources citing the
general as being "recargando de galones en contraste con sus rústicas sanda-
lias." For example, see Yépez 14. In a footnote, Rodríguez Demorizi states that
the work is "a caricature worthy of Cham, in vogue in France at that time, who
victimized Soulouque and other Haitians with his pen. From Cham we still
have some funny caricatures, offensive to the Haitians, the object of his jokes"
("una caricatura digna de Cham, tan de moda en Francia en aquella epoca,
quien hizo victima de su lapiz a Soulouque y a otros haitianos. . . . De Cham
conservamos algunas comicas caricaturas por demas ofensivas a los haitianos,
objeto de sus burlas"; 7–8). Cham, the pseudonym for the extremely popular nineteenth-century French cartoonist Amédée de Noé, is lauded for his
admittedly offensive caricatures of Haitians, especially the Haitian Emperor
Soulouque. However, *General haitiano en marcha* does not share the unam-
biguous, unflattering depictions characteristic of Cham's work.

36. I have chosen to use the commonly accepted orthography *Vodou* and
lwa, although these terms are often spelled as *Voudoun/Vaudou* and *loa*.
Likewise, Ogou, Ogun, and Ogoun are used interchangeably according to the
usage in cited sources. This *lwa* has many manifestations that are indicative

of particular personalities, or paths, including Ogun Ferray, Ogun Badagri, and so forth.

37. Patrick Polk documents how flags and other military regalia were highly valued in French colonial society as well as after the Haitian Revolution. He writes, "With the coming of Independence, military reviews were quickly and firmly established as part of the official ritual of the national armed forces. Well aware of the fact that the military was the primary source of their sovereignty, Haitian leaders devoted much energy to the continued readiness of their troops" (341). Hence the Haitian appropriation of military uniforms cut in what often appears to be a "European/French" style should not primarily be understood as an imitation of fashion modes characteristic of European regiments stationed in the former Saint-Domingue. Rather, they have their own, historically and spiritually loaded meanings.

38. A large body of scholarship explores Ogou's importance in Haiti and his association with masculinity and militarism. See Sheller, "Sword-Bearing Citizens." Also see the work of Leslie Desmangles, Richard Burton, Maya Deren, and Karen McCarthy Brown, whose "Systematic Remembering" provides a good introduction. In classical texts of Haitian literature, Ogou is often the *mèt tèt* of protagonists, as in Marie Chauvet's *Fond des negres* and Jacques Roumain's *Gouverneurs de la rosée.* See Dayan, *Haiti, History,* for an excellent analysis of the aforementioned texts. I find her contention that "vodou practices must be viewed as ritual reenactments of Haiti's colonial past, even more than as retentions from Africa" (xvii), especially provocative and compelling. In the Dominican Republic, Ogou manifests himself as Ogún Balindyó. "Vodou practitioners see him as a distinguished military man, valiant, mounted on a white horse, and protected by his shield. He habitually falls in love, smokes and drinks rum. His color is red and he specializes in diplomatic, social and family affairs. He loves tobacco and rum." See J. James, Millet, and Alarcón 166.

39. Donald Cosentino's helpful article "It's All for You, Sen Jak," 243–63, provides a detailed description of the various manifestations of Sen Jak/Ogou in Vodou iconography. He writes, "Through fantastic processes of appropriation, major events in Haitian history have thus been refigured through the lineaments of a Spanish warrior saint. . . . St. Jacques Majeur (St. James/Santiago/Ogou), patron-saint of Spain and dominating figure of the Conquest, has become an outstanding figure in the Vodou pantheon . . . at the core of Vodou sacred art" (246). In addition, figure 9.18 of Cosentino, *Sacred Arts* 251, shows a worshipper ridden by Ogou, who wears one version of the military uniform under discussion.

40. Alix's poem "Diálogo cantado entre un guajiro dominicano y un Papá bocor haitiano en un fandango en Dajabón" (1874), in his *Décimas* 199–212, is a thirteen-page masterpiece that chronicles the encounter of a Dominican peasant and a spiritual leader of Haitian Vodou in the border town of Dajabón. Although Dominican literary historians characterize the poem as anti-Haitian, I would not dismiss it as such. A remarkable bilingual document written half in Spanish and half in Haitian Creole, it evinces a marked familiarity with the customs of populations who constantly interacted with one another on

both sides of the border. The *décima* serves as a reminder that national ties did
not preclude interchanges that undercut linguistic and national balkanization.

41. Toussaint's 1801 Constitution recognized only Catholicism, and it is
rumored that Dessalines targeted Vodou practitioners as objects of his wrath.
In the 1940s, a massive "campagne anti-superstitieuse" was launched to perse-
cute Vodou practitioners. See Nicholls, *From Dessalines* 181–83.

42. Nineteenth-century poetry is rife with these sentiments. Felix Maria
del Monte's famous "Cantos dominicanos" from 1875 (in Rodríguez Demorizi, *Poesia popular dominicana* 246–48) contains the following verses. Note
that the priest in particular uses his authority to threaten excommunication
for "quien tiene lazo de unión." The need for this threat, along with the idea of
some Dominicans sharing a meal with Haitians, implies that there were indeed
Dominicans who lived and worshipped alongside them.

> Canuto: sé buen cristiano
> dale al caido la mano
> y tu pan al indigente,
> sé humilde, fiel, obediente,
> buen vecino; buen amigo;
> pero una cosa te digo,
> que esta doctrina que vés
> la practiques al revés,
> con el mañé tu enemigo'
> Con ese no hay compasión
> ni se debe transigir
> bajo pena de infringir,
> nuestra Santa Religión,
> Quien tiene lazo de unión
> con esos diablos sañudos
> que beben sangre y desnudos
> en pacto con Belzebú,
> bailan su horrible bodú
> y comen muchachos crudos?
> El Cura me ha asegurado,
> que el que con ellos trafica
> al punto se dañifica
> porque queda excomulgado . . .
> Y aseguro (acá entre nos)
> que el propio dominicano,
> que mire con el haitiano,
> comiendo en el mismo plato,
> fresco y a tiempo lo mato;
> porque ese es mal ciudadano!

43. See in particular Fischer's discussion of the murder of "Las Virgenes
de Galindo," 174–79.

44. Pierre, like other Vodou practitioners, "sees no contradiction between
painting and his priesthood. On the contrary, since every piece is devoted to
the spirits' glory, he understands his art as a principal means of demonstrating his reverence" (Stebich 167). In several of his oils on masonite from the

1960s, for example, most of the male *lwa*, including Agoué and Dambala, are depicted in uniforms complete with epaulettes, hanging swords, buttoned-up shirts decorated with elaborate embroidery-like designs, waist sashes, and knee britches. For example, see *Le labyrinthe du panthéon vaudou*, *Agoué, Loa of the Sea, Saluting His Ship* (ca. 1962), *Immamou* (ca. 1966), and *Damballa* (ca. 1963).

45. Many view this figure as an example of Dominican folklore and legend, rather than a story based in fact. Howevêr, Raymundo González's documentation makes it clear that the Spanish Crown and colonial representatives were greatly alarmed about a series of brutal homicides in the 1790s and that they initiated several investigations. It has never been proven whether or not the *comegente* was in fact one person or many. The 1792 version appears in Rodríguez Demorizi, *Tradiciones* 269–75, while Moya's story appears in the same volume, 175–95.

46. For an overview of the pervasiveness of racial prejudice in the Dominican Republic, including during the colonial period and the nineteenth century, see Deive, "Prejuicio racial." He cites the work of Malagón to show that the author of the 1784 *Codigo Negro Carolino* believed that "Africans are very superstitious and fanatical, prone to seduction and vengeance, naturally inclined towards the poisonous arts" ("los africanos son supersticiosos y fanáticos, muchos fáciles a seducción y a la venganza e inclinados naturalmente a las artes venenosas"). As a means of controlling them, he cites the existence of the above-referenced *cedula*. That said, a characteristically gruesome *comegente* murder was that of an Apolonaria Ramos, who was "abierta desde la hoya hasta el pubis, le saco el Corazon que se llevo juntamente con la mano derecha y le clavo un palo por sus pudendas, tambien le corto una porcion de la empella, y con ella le cubrio la cara" (274). This violence is striking in any context.

47. The proslavery lobby always asserted that "philosophers" from abroad, abolitionist agitators, or "friends of the blacks," were giving bad ideas to their "good negroes."

48. *Bokò* is a term for a Vodou spiritual leader, and it is distinguished from *oungan*. The former is often associated with dark powers, vengeance, and "working with the left hand."

CHAPTER 3

1. A long history of pirating in the Caribbean, often sanctioned as privateering under monarchs such as Elizabeth I, has been well documented. In the more immediate past, during the late eighteenth century several communities were associated with these activities and were precursors of the Laffite commune. Originally operating out of Northern American seaports in the New England and mid-Atlantic regions, privateers began to come under increased scrutiny from the U.S. government as part of the 1794 Neutrality Act. They reestablished themselves in Charleston, a little further south, and had a stronghold there from 1793 to 1795. This was in great part facilitated by the French consul of the city, Edmund Genêt. When Victor Hughes arrived

in Guadeloupe, a new era began between 1794 and 1796. These years marked the height of French efforts to work with blacks to foment republicanism, what Robin Blackburn has called the "revolutionary emancipationist offensive" of the time, or the "*Corsairs de la liberté*" (17). The time marked a strong challenge to the British in the Caribbean, as privateers waged an aggressive campaign against British shipping. Of course, the British, France's sworn enemy, called this time period the "Brigands' War," which demonstrates that the difference between privateering and piracy was a matter of perspective. Privateering required not only ships and letters of marque but prize courts to which these ships could go to have their claims officially sanctioned. Point-à-Pitre was one such prize court. Once this court was closed, many of these privateers relocated to the eastern ports of Cuba and the Barataria region of Louisiana.

2. For French creoles living in the United States, Laffite and the Baratarians served the function of proving their community's patriotism while also highlighting the supposed differences between themselves, the "natives" of the region, and the expansionist, unlettered *americains*. Such a reading further propagates the romantic, cultured, and masculinist myths of the heroic "Louisiana creoles." This desire to integrate Laffite into U.S. history while simultaneously connecting him to a French creole imaginary is apparent in the proliferation of work about him in the 1880s post-Reconstruction moment when French creoles were positioning themselves as the true guardians of local customs. See Tregle's excellent discussion of this period. In the so-called Gilded Age, once the frontier was a thing of the past and reactionary nationalism was at its height, mythmaking around figures such as these abounded throughout the United States, as is evident in dime novels about Buffalo Bill and the Laffites themselves. For example, both Charles Gayarré and George Washington Cable, well known for their works of Louisiana cultural history, wrote about Laffite and the Baratarians in the 1870s and 1880s. Today, the old pirate stomping ground can still be experienced at the Laffite house in the French Quarter, now a candle-lit bar where the decor is in keeping with a tradition that honors Laffite as both a rogue and a patriot.

3. This revisionist tendency includes the work of historians such as Thomas Madiou, Paul Verna, Caryn Cossé Bell, and Roland McConnell.

4. While it is unclear whether people associated with Barataria and Galveston ever hoisted the Jolly Roger, they alternately assumed the flags of France, Cartagena, or Mexico when convenient and were certainly armed predators of merchant ships, whatever paperwork they may or may not have been carrying. Their ships were manned by the aforementioned "motley" crews of the working poor of different nations. For an excellent study of the role of pirates in both formation of and resistance to the European maritime state in the seventeenth and early eighteenth centuries, see the "Hydrarchy" chapter in Linebaugh and Rediker 143–73. The authors write, "Atlantic piracy had long served the needs of the maritime state and the merchant community in England. But there was a long-term tendency for the control of piracy to devolve from the top of society to the bottom, from the highest functionaries of the state (in the late sixteenth century), to big merchants (in the early to middle seventeenth century), to smaller, usually colonial merchants (in the late

seventeenth century), and finally to the common men of the deep (in the early eighteenth century). When this devolution reached bottom, when seamen—as pirates—organized a social world apart from the dictates of mercantile and imperial authority and used it to attack merchants' property . . . then those who controlled the maritime state resorted to massive violence, both military (the navy) and penal (the gallows), to eradicate piracy. A campaign of terror would be employed to destroy hydrarchy, which was thus forced below decks and into an existence that would prove both fugitive and durable" (156). Elsewhere, Rediker contends that "pirates constructed a culture of masterless men. They were as far removed from traditional authority as any men could be in the early eighteenth century. Beyond the church, beyond the family, beyond disciplinary labor, and using the sea to distance themselves from the powers of the state, they carried out a strange experiment. The social constellation of piracy, in particular the complex consciousness and egalitarian impulses that developed . . . provides valuable clarification of the more general social and cultural patterns among seamen in particular and the laboring poor in general" (286). Although focusing on early eighteenth-century piracy, his remarks are helpful in the context of the later period.

5. There are other examples of "revolutionary " blacks selling fellow blacks into slavery. Ada Ferrer's forthcoming work provides excellent documentation.

6. Perhaps the two were born in the Bordeaux region of France in the 1780s, but their origins cannot be confirmed. The lack of definitive historical data accords well with what seems to have been a penchant on the brothers' part to deliberately obscure their past. Throughout the chapter I opt to spell the Laffite name as it appears in the few extant signatures of the brothers, with two "f"s and one "t."

7. See Arthur's influential *Jean Laffite, Gentleman Rover* (1952). The working-class background outlined in Laffite's journal and in the historical record makes it all the more interesting that novels about Laffite and Laffite's biographers insist on his "gentlemanly ways." Allusions to a certain presumed genteel education and code of comportment have succeeded in sanitizing his image and making his lifestyle more palatable. With regard to his gentlemanly comportment, nineteenth-century fiction is full of melodramatic plot twists linking some imagined tragic occurrence with his decision to renounce his middle-class or even noble status for a life at sea. A brief survey of the titles of Laffite biographies supplies some flavor of the romantic side: Mitchell Charnley's *The Buccaneer: The Story of Jean Lafitte, Gentleman Smuggler* (1934); Theresa Hunter's *The Saga of Jean Lafitte: Word Portraits of a Picturesque Southern Pirate: History and Romance of the Texas Coast* (1940); and Jack Ramsay's *Jean Lafitte: Prince of Pirates* (1996).

8. See Cecil DeMille's *The Buccaneer,* originally made in 1938 and remade in 1958, with Yul Brynner playing the role of Jean Laffite and Charleston Heston playing the role of Andrew Jackson. In the 1950s, there was a television series, *Cavalcade of America,* about the Laffites, and Jean Laffite and some of his circle, usually his brother Pierre or his infamous colleagues Renato Beluche and Dominique You, show up in series as diverse as *Bonanza, The Adventures of Jim Bowie,* and special Hallmark Hall of Fame episodes. There is also a

proliferation of young adult literature on Laffite, from authors as well-versed in Louisiana lore as Robert Tallant (*The Pirate Lafitte and the Battle of New Orleans*, 1951) and Lyle Saxon (*Lafitte, the Pirate*, ca. 1930) to more contemporary pieces such as Aileen Weintraub's *Jean Lafitte: Pirate-Hero of the War of 1812* (2002). In addition to his image being used as a marketing tool in New Orleans, "Lafitte's Landing" is a popular Disneyland attraction located directly across from the Pirates of the Caribbean ride; one can take a replica Mississippi River Steamboat across the water to the pirate haunt.

9. See, for example, the business ventures of Saint-Domingue refugee Honoré St. Gême. The St. Gême Family Papers in the Historic New Orleans Collection cover material relating to his privateering operations out of Santiago de Cuba and New Orleans.

10. Obadele-Starks briefly discusses how people of African descent fit into this smuggling world, and his assessment of Laffite's crew is not at all romanticized. For example, he attributes Laffite's decision to fight with Jackson and the United States against the British to the fact that the British had abolished the slave trade and that if they had won the war Laffite's business would have suffered serious losses. Also see Kendall, who asserts that the prime activity of the Laffite smuggling ring was slave trading.

11. Crew list for the ship *La Diligente*, Manuscript MSS 56, Williams Research Center, Historic New Orleans Collection.

12. Deposition of José Rodriguez, Ernest Sabourin Papers, Tulane University Library Special Collections, New Orleans.

13. For example, when the aforementioned Governor Claiborne first arrived in New Orleans to claim the territory for the United States, he was so worried about the divisive factions threatening to impede U.S. control that he wrote the following to Secretary of State James Monroe: "England has her partisans; Ferdinand the Seventh, some faithful subjects; Bonaparte, his admirers, and there is a fourth description of men, commonly called *Burrites*, who would join any standard which would promise rapine and plunder." See Cable, *Creoles of Louisiana* 158–59. For a thought-provoking series of essays about colonial New Orleans and the impact of the American purchase, see Hirsch and Logsdon. A large amount of material was generated in recognition of the bicentennial of the Purchase Treaty, including a major exhibit at the Louisiana Cabildo in New Orleans. The classic text on Saint-Domingue immigration into Louisiana remains Brasseaux and Conrad's collection, which includes essays by Thomas Fiehrer, Gabriel Debien, Rene Le Gardeur, and Paul Lachance.

14. See Lachance's "1809 Immigration" 278. By 1803, estimates put the total population of the city at 8,050 residents, 1,335 of whom were free blacks and 2,775 of whom were slaves. In the 1809 exodus of Saint-Domingue refugees from Cuba, the official report of the mayor's office cites the arrival of 2,731 whites, 3,102 free people of color, and 3,226 slaves, a total of 9,059 persons (figures cited in Lachance, "1809 Immigration" 247). Much has been written about the impact of these refugees on the local community, as they effectively doubled the size of the population and reinforced Gallic sentiments at a time when Claiborne and the U.S. government were aggressively trying to

Americanize the territory. A recent exhibit at the Historic New Orleans Collection in 2006 did a comprehensive job exploring the connections between these two former colonies; see Lemmon et al.

As an example of how ingrained some of these figures became in U.S. history, Homer Plessy of the "separate but equal" legal decision in *Plessy versus Ferguson* was Homère Plessy, a descendant of Saint-Domingue immigrants. Laguerre has a helpful chapter on nineteenth-century Haitian migrations into the United States.

15. In the late 1930s and 1940s, the *Louisiana Quarterly* devoted many articles to the question of relations between the southern United States (Louisiana, Florida, and Texas) and revolutionary struggles in Latin America. See, for example, Lagarde; Wellborn; Wilgus, "Spanish American Patriot Activity" and "Some Activities." Especially noteworthy is the detailed work of Stanley Faye, who provides some of the most exhaustive research on the Baratarians. See "Privateers of Guadeloupe," "Great Stroke," and "Commodore Aury." All of these pieces historicize the inter-American nature of the Baratarians' activities. A few historians mention black participation in this world, although none of them discuss it in any detail.

16. George Washington Cable's work, arguably the most popular source documenting the foundational myths of Louisiana creole society, paints the scene. Consider his short story "Café des Exilés," published as part of the collection *Old Creole Days*. Although set in the New Orleans of the 1830s, at least fifteen years after the events in this chapter, this particular story establishes the ambience of the time and complements Cable's *Creoles of Louisiana*, which suggests that during the 1810s the cafes were "full of filibusters" (218). The title of the piece refers to the cafe established by M. D'Hemecourt, a refugee from Saint-Domingue, where "the exiles came like bees, pushing into the tiny room to sip its rich variety of tropical syrups, its lemonades, its orangeades, its orgeats, its barley waters, and its outlandish wines, while they talked of dear home—that is to say, of Barbadoes, of Martinique, of San Domingo and of Cuba" (87). While not one of Cable's better-developed stories, the main action revolves around the filibustering plans that take shape among this community of exiles. All are anxious to regain their former fortunes, and by tale's end it becomes clear that the protagonists are running guns and ammunition. Destitute as refugees, exiles were often employed as mercenaries and found filibustering an appealing occupation. There was a historical Café des Refugiés on rue St. Philippe, whose host, Jean Baptiste Thiot, was a Saint-Domingue refugee famous for serving tropical refreshments (Arthur 19). Also see Verna's *Pétion y Bolívar*, cited in detail below.

17. Jean-Joseph Humbert is best known for his unsuccessful 1798 invasion of Ireland at the head of French troops, an invasion designed to aid the republican cause there. After a stint in Saint-Domingue during the revolution, he seems to have fallen out of favor with the French government and moved to the United States, from whence he participated in various Latin American filibustering campaigns. Louis Aury is likewise an interesting figure. From a poor French family, he initially came to the Americas in the French navy and then joined the Latin American independence struggle, working both as a privateer

and in the service of Bolívar and others. Like Laffite, he has his partisans, and a trilingual Internet blog provides an idea of his legacy's continued appeal. Its stated goal is "De faire mieux connaître ce corsaire hors norme . . . injustement passé sous silence à travers les siècles. Este blog tiene por objectivo de defender la memoria y luchar por la reablitation [sic] de este corsario fuera de lo común. This blog pretends to defend the memory, reputation and honor of this unbelievable privateer." See <http://louisaury.blogspot.com/>. The French republican cause in Saint-Domingue is associated with Léger-Félicité Sonthonax and Etienne Polverel, two civil commissioners of the French Republic that were originally sent to Saint-Domingue to restore order. In August 1793, in the face of planter hostility, they issued a general abolition proclamation, which was later ratified by the French National Convention in February 1794. André Rigaud and others worked closely with them as generals of the French army. Many free men of color returned with the French army and navy during the 1802 Leclerc expedition and were deceived by Napoleon's covert plans to restore slavery and subjugate free men of color.

18. In the U.S.-acquired Orleans territory, the Baratarian swamps remained beyond the easy arm of the law. Just west of the Sabine River, Galveston was a contested territory that Spain, the Mexican revolutionaries, and the U.S. all sought to control. Like Barataria, it was too isolated for any of these state authorities to effectively govern.

19. Debates about the journal's authenticity started in the 1940s when a supposed descendant of Jean Laffite, John A. Lafitte, announced that he had inherited the journal along with other family memorabilia. See Marshall for an edition and translation of the journal and Schaadt for an introduction to it that provides an excellent overview of the controversy. Members of the Laffite Society in Texas, especially historian Robert C. Vogel, tend to agree that the journal is a forgery, although handwriting experts have not confirmed this. Whether we take the journal as historical truth or as the cultural imagining of a forger, its importance remains in its details of transcolonial life, details that relegate Laffite's famous service on the battleground of Chalmette to a few brief pages in a much longer narrative about his adventures throughout the extended Americas. If Laffite was indeed the author, he located himself within a tradition of outlaw pioneers with idealistic leanings, consciously adopting the language of collective entrepreneurship. With regard to the terminology he uses to describe his enclaves, one example concerns his fears for their survival. He writes, "My future hopes concerning the unity of America were weakened after the victory at New Orleans. . . . If I continued to fulfill my privateering mission and if I helped the revolutionaries of the province of Texas and Mexico against Spain, in the future I would have to contend with armed bands led by so-called generals, who would put my communes in danger . . ." (Marshall 108).

The biography sketched in the journal documents birth in Saint-Domingue and an early life that included travel throughout the Caribbean Basin, including Louisiana, Cuba, and the Lesser Antilles. Its anti-Spanish invective explains his lifelong choice of allies and victims during his years at sea, as his implacable hatred toward these "despots" made Spanish merchantmen his chosen enemies. However, extensive documentation confirms that the Laffites were also in the employ of the Spanish government. See Faye, "Great Stroke." The British are castigated in similar terms partially because they, like the Spanish, "instigated" slaves in Saint-Domingue to rebel, resulting in the death of many of his "countrymen." While identifying strongly with his Saint-Domingue countrymen, and with French creoles in general, Laffite's restraint when writing of the Haitian Revolution is noteworthy. In a tone very different from that found in most white exile accounts, he suggests a sense of the inevitability of events. There is no mention of lost property, or invective about a past idyllic lifestyle destroyed at the hands of a ferocious black mob. Not only does he refrain from lamenting the past, he also seems to have no qualms about establishing trade relations with the new rulers of the country after independence. He does note, however, that he "encountered a certain resistance in Haiti among the lethargic black officials working in Port-au-Prince" (129). The diary is full of the victorious news of successful slave raids against "prizes in Negroes coming from Cuba and the high sea" and the profitable reselling of these slaves in Mobile, Charleston, and Savannah (126). Fascinatingly, the last section of this journal outlines Laffite's connections with European radical traditions. In it he claims that he financially supported Marx and Engels.

20. Upon the final dissolution of his Galveston community in 1821, a place he and his followers had named Campeche, Laffite writes, "Everyone regretted the disappearance of this egalitarian empire to whose formation I had dedicated four years" (Marshall 151). "Egalitarian" is a strong conceptual way of organizing community, and unfortunately little eyewitness testimony has survived to verify or refute these claims. This lack of information pertains to how black participants were treated as well. Antiauthoritarian, perhaps even utopian, the crew engaged in regional anticolonial struggles when it appeared that these associations would work to their advantage.

21. The history of territorial Louisiana provides an excellent example of how formal and informal sectors relied on intra- and transcolonial relationships. The massive territory included in the Louisiana Purchase had been controlled by the French (1699–1769), the Spanish (1769–1803), the French again (1803), and finally the United States upon conclusion of the Purchase Treaty. This historical periodizing does not reference the various Native American groups who inhabited the territory and had a long history of struggle with conquering forces. The relationship that existed between each European master of Louisiana and neighboring colonies points to a long history of regional competition and cooperation. For example, as Thomas Fiehrer states, "It is important to remember that Saint-Domingue was the parent colony of Louisiana, she gave birth to her and sustained her to maturation" ("Saint Domingue/Haiti" 7). Ties between Saint-Domingue and Louisiana predated the migrant flows occasioned by the Haitian Revolution. Likewise, during the Spanish period when Louisiana was under the jurisdiction of the governor-general of Cuba, all money for the colony and decisions about its welfare came from that island. It is no surprise, then, that the population had conflicting loyalties; not only was it accustomed to a string of various imperial authorities, it was also used to interacting with neighboring colonies that

housed business associates, family, and friends. Transcolonial interactions were the norm rather than the exception. As Dawdy has shown in her work on Louisiana during the French period, "Intercolonial commerce fostered a far-reaching social and cultural network and carved out a niche of relative independence from the greater Atlantic" (226).

22. For my purposes, letters of marque are cultural artifacts that speak directly to the nationalisms at play in the extended Americas during the period under study. This letter, a license issued by a state government, gave authority to a private party to equip an armed ship, and during times of war to use it to attack and plunder the ships of enemy combatants. The Laffites and their crews purportedly sailed under letters of marque issued by both the French government and the newly declared Republic of Cartagena. By the time they moved to Galveston, they were hoping to have letters of marque from the Mexican Revolutionary Junta. In all cases, the relationship was mutually beneficial; the sponsoring states saw Spanish Royalist or British forces attacked, and the privateers were legalized to take any and all booty. Declaring themselves in possession of letters of marque allowed Laffite associates to escape the gallows if captured and accused of pirating but doesn't seem to have limited them in many other ways. Profit sharing with national governments and use of official prize courts were the privateering niceties that they did not always observe. Some contemporaries doubted whether the Laffite brothers were ever in possession of valid letters of marque at all. For example, one official noted that they had "neither knowledge nor belief in the existence of a Mexican Republic, and the sole object and view of the persons comprising the establishment of Galveston, were to capture Spanish property, under what they called the Mexican flag, but without an idea of aiding the revolution of Mexico" (qtd. in Bollaert 441). The presumption of the legality, if not the morality, of their raids against enemy shipping, however, essentially afforded them the possibility of being in control of their own community of men for roughly a decade before the United States shut the business down for good when they closed the Galveston operation in 1821. For a fictional rendition of the fluidity of pirate loyalties, see Maxwell Philip's *Emmanuel Appadocca; or Blighted Life. A Tale of the Boucaneers* (1854), considered the first anglophone Caribbean novel.

23. There is a vast body of scholarship on black seafaring, some of the best work done by Julius S. Scott, "Common Wind" and "Crisscrossing Empires," and W. Jeffrey Bolster. As Bolster notes, "Seamen wrote the first six autobiographies of blacks published in English before 1800. Finding their voices in the swirling currents of international maritime labor, seafaring men fired the opening salvo of the black abolitionist attack and fostered the creation of a corporate identity. . . . That culture created an ambiguous world in which black men simultaneously could assert themselves within their occupation and find with white sailors common ground transcending race, while also being subject to vicious racist attacks" (4–5). For more on the use of black troops throughout the Americas, see Ben Vinson II's work on colonial Mexico, *Bearing Arms,* and the collection by C. Brown and Morgan. Dubois, "Citizen Soldiers," provides an overview of how republican France used troops of color.

Peter Blanchard's "Slave Soldiers" explains how slaves often fought for the royalists against creole "patriots." Again, this choice highlights how many people of African descent associated creole patriotism in the Americas with slaveholders.

24. Deposition of Andrew Whiteman, July 18, 1813, Ernest Sabourin Papers, Tulane University Library Special Collections, New Orleans.

25. Foley to Williams, Collector of the Port, New Orleans, May 1, 1813, National Archives, Southwest Region, Fort Worth, Texas, Record Group 21, Records of District Courts of the United States.

26. This critic is cited in Orians 353. It is not surprising that during the onset of Jacksonian America tales of unlettered but bold, antiauthoritarian, enterprising (white) men had a ready audience, especially tales of men who had once been close allies of "Old Hickory."

27. Little is known about Joseph Savary. Bell's chapter "The Republican Cause and the Afro-Creole Militia" in *Revolution, Romanticism,* remains the most thorough account of his life in Louisiana. However, her work consistently uses terminology such as "French Jacobins of the most radical stamp" to refer to Aury (47) and makes comments such as "The free black veterans of the Haitian Revolution preserved their republican idealism" (42). Of course, *republican* is a term that is hard to nail down since it meant something radically different in 1794 than in 1803. However, her account presents a triumphal, idealistic narrative that curiously elides the politics indicated in the historical record. Rothman (153) asserts that Joseph Savary's father was a Charles Savary, perhaps the same Charles Savary who was a leader in Saint Marc, Haiti during the British occupation of the island.

28. See William C. Davis's popular history, which makes use of extensive historical documentation and is one of the most detailed biographies of the brothers' professional lives.

29. See Geggus's overview of the *gens de couleur libres* in chapter 1 of *Haitian Revolutionary Studies.* Commenting on this population's unusual size and wealth, he concludes that they "covered an extremely broad social range, from recently freed African slaves to rich landowners and tradesmen who were almost indistinguishable in appearance and culture from their white counterparts. They constituted merely a legal category (those who were neither slave nor white) rather than a class" (6). Also, see Garrigus and S. King's work on free people of color in colonial Saint-Domingue. There is a large body of scholarship on the unique situation of free people of color in many American contexts, including Berlin, *Slaves,* and the edited collection by Cohen and Greene, *Neither Slave nor Free.*

30. There is a vast scholarship on struggles between black and mixed-race people in Haiti. For a good overview, see Nicholls, *From Dessalines to Duvalier.*

31. For example, in Cuba, free blacks had created a niche for themselves by the early nineteenth century, most famously as skilled artisans and musicians. The severe Spanish reprisals following the alleged 1842 La Escalera conspiracy would result in the execution of many of this community's most prominent members.

32. The author continues, "Free indeed! when almost every honourable incentive to the pursuit of happiness, so largely and so freely held out to his fairer brother, is withheld from him. A freeman! when prejudice binds the most galling chains around him! drives him from every mechanical employment, and situations of trust, or emolument; frowns him from the door of our Institutions of learning; forbids him to enter every public place of amusement, and follows him, wherever he goes, pointing at him the finger of scorn and contempt." *Weekly Advocate* January 14, 1837, qtd. in McHenry 107.

33. Going back a few years to the initial arrival of many of these Saint-Domingue blacks from Cuba, the mayor of New Orleans placed an advertisement in *Le Moniteur* asking resident people of color, "wherever they were born" ("quel que soit le lieu de leur naissance"), to support those of their class by starting a public subscription on behalf of "the many women of color recently arrived and caring for young children" ("plusieurs femmes de couleur récemment arrivées . . . surchargées d'enfans en ba-âge [sic]") given "the distress" ("la détresse") in which they found themselves. The ad notes that two men of color had collected funds and rented a house for them on Bourbon Street (June 28, 1809). Free people of color from a variety of colonial backgrounds thus mobilized to support each other in a time of crisis.

34. In *A General History of the Pyrates* (1724), Daniel Defoe, using the pseudonym "Captain Charles Johnson," wrote, "It is no Wonder that, when an honest Livelihood is not easily had, they run into one so like their own; so that it may be said, that Privateers in Time of War are a Nursery for Pyrates against a Peace" (4).

35. A fascinating manuscript written by an anonymous French soldier who participated in these expeditions is available in Moreau de St.-Méry's papers at the Archives Nationales d'Outre Mer. He claims Bolívar was a weak leader who was totally unprepared for battle, letting himself be led by adventurers who did not have the proper military experience. Foreigners, such as himself, even when better equipped to make strategic decisions, were reportedly treated as second-class members of the expedition. See "Quelques détails sur la dernière expédition de Bolivar à Venezuela depuis son départ des Cayes . . . ," Collection Moreau de St-Méry, F3, 155.

36. Verna writes, "Las patriotas mexicanos Toledo y Herrara, refugiados en Nueva Orleans, entablaron negociones con Pedro Gual, con el propósito de lograr la ayuda haitiana, la cual permitiría realizar un ataque en el Golfo de México, contra Tampico o Veracruz. A tal efecto, enviaron dos agentes a Haití, Pierre Girard y José Savary, encargados de preparar el reclutamiento de voluntarios haitianos. Pétion les abrió los puertos de la República y les permitió contratar a marinos haitianos, comprar armas y preparar la expedición en suelo haitiano" (*Pétion y Bolívar* 278–79). Referencing the Aury expedition into Galveston, he states that Bellegarde and fellow "haitianos, furiosos por el mal trato recibido de parte de Aury, se sublevaron el 6 de septiembre de 1816, con Bellegarde a su cabeza. . . . Aquel dia el corsario frances salvó milagrosamente la vida pues recibió de uno de los Haitianos un balazo que le perforó la mano derecha y parte de las costillas" (279–80). After shooting Aury and leaving him for dead, apparently "200 of them took $60,000 in goods and three

ships and sailed for their native Saint-Domingue" (Olson 62). Renato Beluche, another Baratarian, was also very involved with the Venezuelan struggle and went on to become a famous general. Verna concludes by stating, "Se puede imaginar lo que debía ser la capital haitiana para aquella época, con tantos expedicionarios de la 'libertad.' Por una parte, Bolívar con sus seguidores, luego los 250 hombres de Mina, los marinos de los corsarios que habían hecho de Puerto Príncipe una de sus bases, y por otra parte, los numerosos emigrados de Nueva Granada . . ." (281–82). See 312-317 for a discussion of Petion's policies concerning slave-trading privateers. See also Verna, *Bolívar y los emigrados* (Caracas: Graficas la Bodoniana, 1983).

37. There were in fact two Haitian states at the time, Pétion's republic in the south, and Henri Christophe's kingdom in the north. For Haiti's isolation in the nineteenth century, see Stinchombe. See Girard for an overview of Toussaint Louverture's foreign policy at an earlier moment.

38. See McConnell's aforementioned discussion. Negative reaction to Andrew Jackson's recruitment of people of color is captured in Gayarré's summary of events. In his discussion of the "American Domination" period he writes, "This proclamation was looked upon by many as exceedingly objectionable, on the ground of its putting the colored men too much on a footing of equality with the whites. It was denied that the native mulattoes of Louisiana were entitled to the appellation of 'sons of freedom,' and that the colored refugees from St. Domingo had any claim to being called the 'adopted children' of the State. It was still more strenuously denied that they could, whether 'natives' or 'adopted children,' be properly designated as 'Americans,'—a question which was judicially raised years afterward, and which was decided in the negative by the Supreme Court of the United States. Even those who were the best disposed toward that peculiar class of the population objected to their being raised to the dignity of being denominated as the 'fellow-citizens' and the 'countrymen' of the white race" (356). He goes on to add that "it was deemed bad policy by many to address them in terms which were not in accordance with the inferiority of their social position, and which might tend to raise hopes that could never be gratified. There were some who predicted that it was a precedent of a dangerous nature. These apprehensions, in the course of time, have been strangely realized; for these two addresses of General Jackson to the men of color, and the use which he made of their services, were afterward seized upon by a far more barbarous foe than the English, as a pretext for putting in Louisiana the Blacks on a footing of equality with the Whites" (409).

39. Approached by the British to serve as their allies during the waning days of the War of 1812, the Baratarians' participation was solicited largely because of their intricate knowledge of the low waters downstream of the city. This back-channel access to New Orleans was crucial in the war, as the British stood to gain control over the city and hence the lower Mississippi River. Popular convention holds that they could have effectively gained control over the central corridor of the continent, owning a swath of land from Canada all the way to the Gulf; the original U.S. states would have been cut off from expanding into any territory further west.

40. Scholars such as Benjamin Quarles, Philip Foner, Sylvia Frey, and Gary

Nash have evaluated the involvement of U.S. blacks in North American revolutionary struggles. For a comparative British perspective on black involvement in the War of 1812, see Bolster's excellent chapter "The Boundaries of Race in Maritime Culture" in *Black Jacks*.

41. Castra's poem is often cited in studies of free blacks in Louisiana. For example, see Hanger, *Bounded Lives* 219–20 nn.; McConnell 107–08; Bell; and Bruce and Gipson. The work of these poets is likewise cited as exemplars of non-English American literature.

42. See Courlander, *Treasury* 557. Courlander cites Cable as the source for the verses, and this printing employs a very French/etymological orthography.

43. The former Lafitte Projects in the Sixth Ward, severely damaged during Hurricane Katrina and later demolished, were reopened early in 2011 as the Faubourg Lafitte.

CHAPTER 4

1. In my discussion on performance, I take seriously the warning posited by scholars that slave play traditions cannot be viewed uncritically as evidence of resistance, agency, or autonomy. Saidiya Hartman, for example, cites Frederick Douglass's comment that plantation festivities were "safety-valves to carry off the explosive elements inseparable from the human mind when reduced to the condition of slavery." She warns that "the promotion of innocent amusements and harmless pleasures was a central strategy in the slave owner's effort to cultivate contented subjection." See *Scenes of Subjection* 47, 49. Richard Burton, in his wonderful work on play traditions in Jamaica and Haiti, concludes that though they "challenge the status quo and in so doing provide those who engage in them surrogate satisfactions for the deeper dissatisfactions of their lives, they also, by their very richness, reconcile the disempowered to the political, social and economic inequalities. . . . There is scarcely one cultural form discussed in this book that is not at the same time a revolt against things as they are and a form of adjustment to them" (263–64). Work on carnival traditions has been especially attentive to this dynamic. I do, however, strongly believe that evaluating play traditions as panaceas and "safety valves" is as limiting as viewing them as unmitigated sites of resistance. With regard to dance specifically, see the work of Bill Maurer, who critiques the tendency of some scholarship to "view Caribbean dance in terms of political resistance to, coercion by, or complicity with some dominant force or hegemonic narrative." He argues that "the resistance/complicity and coercion/consent dichotomies are inadequate for the analysis of dance in the Caribbean because of their predication upon western bourgeois liberal constructions of an individuated subject—constructions which may not obtain in the Caribbean and which certainly remain to be demonstrated before they are assumed in any particular case." Although Maurer doesn't explicitly state that they may not pertain in the Caribbean specifically because of the legacy of slavery, this is one implied interpretation of such a critique. See "Caribbean Dance."

2. This chapter is predicated on close listening, and it is imperative to hear the sounds under study in order to understand the correlation between these

musical genres. A CD with interviews and commercial recordings of *bomba, bèlè,* and *tumba francesa* accompanied my dissertation upon which this chapter is based.

3. Many thanks to Judith Bettelheim for introducing me to this image. See her chapter on the *tumba francesa* and the *tajona* in *Cuban Festivals.* For a study of Belisario's world alongside a beautiful color reproduction of his entire 1838 series, see Ranston, from which all of Belisario's quotations in this chapter are taken. Belisario told subscribers that his work was to "nothing extenuate nor set down in malice . . . drawn after nature and in lithography . . . [purposing] to furnish but Sketches of Character, steering clear of Caricature: nature in her ordinary form alone, having been the source from whence all the original drawings were derived." The artist thus expressed his desire to capture his immediate environment in a realistic way that did not employ stereotypes of his black subjects but rather documented their cultural traditions with respect. For Belisario's preface, see Ranston 238; the French Set images and commentary appear in Ranston 254–56. The image continued to inspire twentieth-century artists. The National Dance Theatre of Jamaica used it as a basis for the costume designs for the piece *Dance Time in Cascade* (1964). See Nettleford 110.

4. Headwraps were used throughout Africa and the Americas. For example, the original Brunias image was drawn after a "French" woman of color in Saint Vincent. For more on the use of dress as a field of contestation in slave societies, see the chapter on clothing in Fouchard, *Haitian Maroons* 41–49. Also, see Buckridge.

5. See Geggus, *Slavery, War,* for an account of this period.

6. Interestingly, Moreau includes a note about how women of color in Saint-Domingue also promenaded together, "dressed pin for pin alike" on special occasions. Called "l'assortiment," this happened when "elles s'habillent plusieurs d'une manière absolument uniforme, pour aller se promener ou danser" (*Description topographique* 2004] 1: 77).

7. There is little evidence of whether "French Set girl" traditions in Jamaica, specifically the musical ones, have survived. Musicologists Kenneth Bilby, John Storm Roberts, and Mervyne Alleyne mention Jamaican percussive traditions that use the transverse heeling technique as well as a variation of the *catá,* techniques I discuss below. Referring to the technique as documented in Martinique, Bilby states that it is "virtually identical to the method used to change pitch in . . . Jamaican *tambo*" (Bilby and Marks 12). Alleyne (110) cites Roberts's observations of a *tambo* drummer in Wakefield, Trelawny parish "who muted his drum with his heel [as] this drummer's son used a pair of catta sticks to beat out a second rhythm on the side of the tambo." Hence the Jamaican musical tradition most reminiscent of Belisario's early nineteenth-century musical image seems to be *tambo.* Olive Lewin, a specialist in Jamaican music, mentions the possible French Caribbean / Haitian connections of this tradition, stating that "its songs and dances were accompanied by a large single-headed drum played by a man who straddled it, using his heel to change the pitch, and a percussionist who stood behind the drummer using two wooden sticks to beat an intermittent pattern on its sides. . . . The style

of drumming was quite new to me. At the start there was often no discernible beat being produced except by the catta 'ticks" (171–77).

8. For example, see Kmen. Leonora Sansay commented about the establishment of theaters in Cuba by Saint-Domingue immigrants in her *Secret History*. She wrote, "A company of French comedians had built a theatre here, and obtained permission from the governor to perform. They played with éclat, and always to crowded houses. The Spaniards were delighted. . . . But the charm was suddenly dissolved by an order from the bishop to close the theatre, saying that it tended to corrupt the morals of the inhabitants. But it is supposed the order was issued to vex the governor, with whom the bishop is at variance. . . . It is impossible for him to know that even the vices of the French lose much of their deformity by the refinement that accompanies them, whilst those of his countrymen are gross, disgusting and monstrously flagrant" (156–57).

9. R. Wright notes that "the last year of the century is fairly deluged with refugee concerts." He confirms that people of color were attending the theater by citing a February 1802 announcement that the "French theatre, managed by Augustus Tessier, has erected a vast and most commodious amphitheatre for the accommodation of the people of colour, to which he has added a row of the second boxes adjoining the circus, by which means the people of colour will have a very spacious, airy and distinct place to which they can ascend by a separate passage" (305–06).

10. Belisario also observed that "this set as much distinguished for the neatness of style in their dress, as their general deportment, differing in these respects greatly from all others, as may be perceived in the subjects of the same class already represented, where every description of finery is employed, without the slightest regard being had to the selection of colours, or the mode in which the garments are worn" (Ranston 254).

11. For a discussion of the African workforce in Saint-Domingue, see ch. 2 of Dubois, *Avengers*. For work on creole-versus-African-born slave divisions, see Smallwood. Scholarship continues to reinforce the importance of African ethnicity in the extended Americas. See, for example, Gomez, *Exchanging Our Country Marks;* G. Hall, *Slavery and African Ethnicities;* and Thornton. For an overview of the polemics between "Africa-centric" models and creolization ones, see Price, "On the Miracle."

12. The original text reads "Dejar de mencionar el 'francés criollo' . . . sería dejar de pasar por alto algo muy típico de nuestra comarca. . . . Con la venida a esta ciudad de familias de nacionalidad francesa, huyendo de la rebelión de la colonia haitiana, se importó al mismo tiempo que idioma, costumbres, industria y cultura, un gran número de negros esclavos, con los cuales se emprendió el fomento de los primeros magníficos cafetales. Los esclavos de franceses tenían una habla especial: 'la jerigonza, francés criollo, patuá,' mezcla de la lengua francesa y de distintos dialectos de tribus africanas. Con ella se entendían con sus dueños, con ella entre si, e hiciéronla extensiva también, no sólo a sus convecinos de la misma condición de raza y suerte, sino aun a los demás esclavos a quienes la maldad humana continuó introduciendo procedentes de las costas de Guinea. Quizás por el refinado lujo, y hasta el sibaritismo

de los amos se determinó en el esclavo ya por contacto, ya por el medio ambiente, una cultura intelectual mayor que la que poseía el otro esclavo, que no era propiedad francesa; y cultura debemos llamar a la expansión del sentimiento de la raza oprimida, que al exteriorizarlos había de hacerlos brotar, como en todo tiempo han brotado al igual en los pueblos que sufren, valiéndose de dos artes al servicio siempre de los oprimidos: la poesía y la música. Parecerá esto una paradoja, pero es así" (Bacardí y Moreau, *Crónicas* 508).

13. Hazaël-Massieux examines one such Creole-language production.

14. See ch. 9 of Fischer. There is a growing body of literature on how whiteness as a social and cultural category was understood through blackness. The works of Toni Morrison, Saidya Hartman, Werner Sollors, Theodore Allen, Joan Dayan, and Doris Garraway are a few examples. Garraway writes, "Slaves were essential to white Creoles' conceptions of themselves, not merely as a negative self-definition but more importantly as the mirror in which they recognized their own cultural specificity and affirmed their difference from the French" (*Libertine Colony* 246).

15. See above, Preface, note 6, for examples.

16. The fact that creole French Set performers called themselves "Royalists" is fascinating. Jamaican authorities probably would not have allowed residents of the island to openly identify as "republicans" during the 1790s, even had they wanted to outwardly identify with the French Republic. Scholarship has shown that professed monarchical "loyalties" among slaves were common, probably because many believed that the "king" had their best interests in mind but local planters were refusing to obey laws sent out from the metropole. Of course, exile planters were often monarchists, associating the upheavals in Saint-Domingue with the excesses of the French Revolution. Even if slaves assumed the mantle of royalism, they could still support the revolutionary movement in Saint-Domingue.

17. Belisario goes on to state that "the degree of jealousy heretofore existing between the Rival Sets, can scarcely be conceived. The writer has been credibly informed, their animosity some twenty years back, was of so inveterate a nature, that their meetings in public, seldom passed without violent affrays: proving fatal in most instances, to their articles of dress, if not also to their persons, in the struggle for pre-eminence. Such *unladylike conduct* in the present day, being regarded as highly indecorous, this description of warfare is rarely witnessed—the parties contenting themselves with the expression of epithets only without resorting to more *striking* proofs of their hatred" (Ranston 242).

18. There is a long history of scholarship on black performance in the Americas. In the seventeenth and eighteenth centuries, for example, canonical figures such as Labat and Moreau documented the use of two different-sized drums, the smaller often called the *bamboula*, which were played in a horizontal position and produced polyrhythmic sounds. Twentieth-century scholarship by researchers including Fernando Ortiz, Lawrence W. Levine, Harold Courlander, Lydia Cabrera, and Errol Hill has exhaustively documented the richness and complexity of black expressive culture in music, dance, and oral literature. My work is made possible by the research of these predecessors

who forthrightly argued for the "*espíiritu intellectual*" that animated these traditions.

19. Hartman goes on to eloquently note that her approach "emphasizes both the preponderance of resistance and the absence of a proper locus that would grant autonomy to these practices. These practices are significant in that they are local assaults and pedestrian challenges to slavery, the slave owners, the law and the state and, at the same time, they are provisional and short-lived and exploit the cleavages of the social order. However the focus on the contingent and transient character of these practices is not an attempt to underestimate the magnitude of these acts, for they are fraught with utopian and transformative impulses that are unrealizable within the terms of the current order precisely because of the scope of these implicit, understated, and allegorical claims for emancipation, redress, and restitution" (*Scenes of Subjection* 62–63).

20. See the liner notes by Bilby and Marks in the Alan Lomax collection of *Caribbean Voyage: The 1962 Field Recordings* (Rounder Records, 1999). They refer to this technique as Central African in origin but provide no further details. Thus far, it seems that what the musicologist Julian Gerstin refers to as "transverse heeled drumming" is found in Puerto Rico, Cuba, Martinique, and Dominica. See Gerstin, "Traditional Music" 110. Also, Martha Ellen Davis documents the use of similar techniques in the Dominican Republic in "Bi-Musicality."

21. For more on the legacy of the Haitian Revolution in Trinidad, see Brereton's excellent article. Scholarship has also shown that Saint-Domingue refugees and their descendents had a tremendous influence on music in Louisiana, especially New Orleans. Jelly Roll Morton may perhaps be one of the most famous of these musicians. The music of Louis Moreau Gottschalk also capitalized on Caribbean themes, as did early jazz. See Starr's *Bamboula!*, which includes a recounting of how Gottschalk performed with *tumba francesa* drummers on a Havana stage. Also, see Fiehrer, "From Quadrille to Stomp." Washburne studies the *cinquillo*, *tresillo* and *clave* rhythms as fundamental elements in the development of early jazz.

22. John Storm Roberts details elements of the proposed aesthetic in discussions of "neo-African" and "Afro-American" musics throughout the Americas. See *Black Music* 1–36.

23. For a nuanced discussion of the dangers of filiation, see Glissant, *Poétique de la relation*.

24. Evidence suggesting that these elements were incorporated into traditions in Spanish and British colonies through contact between local residents and Saint-Domingue refugees is compelling. This assertion acknowledges the tremendous influence that Central African traditions originally had on musical traditions in French colonial territories. It is crucial to remember that inter-island, transcolonial migrations, especially between many of the islands of the Lesser Antilles ruled by the French and the British, occurred both before and after the Haitian Revolution. Migrants carried their traditions with them, and it is hence impossible (and I'd argue unnecessary) to say with absolute certainty that the traditions under examination here originated in one place or

traveled as a result of only one trajectory of historical events. Rather, it is more productive to speculate that years of interisland migration, specifically from French territories into neighboring ones, resulted in the creation of genres that were constantly evolving with the participation of myriad performers. Post 1791, knowledge of and perhaps firsthand experience of the Haitian Revolution and revolutionary activity in neighboring Martinique and Guadeloupe would have inflected how "Frenchness" was interpreted in cultural forms.

25. Samuel Floyd suggests that "the cinquillo and tresillo have been in continual flux—existing as fugitive rhythms that, having escaped both the African time line and European-derived divisive meter, find themselves free to roam and manifest themselves, chameleon like, in ever-changing additive patterns of 3 +3+2, 2+3, 2+2+3, and other such formulations. The cinquillo-tresillo matrix, as the common denominator in Latin American and West Indian performance practices, stands as a symbol of circum-Caribbean unity." He notes that Haiti may have been a source of regional diffusion for this rhythmic cell in the early twentieth century ("Black Music" 28–29).

26. For various studies of the French communities in Cuba, see Lamore; Yacou, "Refugiados franceses," "Santiago de Cuba," and "Révolution française."

27. In *La música cubana*, Alejo Carpentier provides an excellent overview of how the French *contredanse* was transformed into the Cuban *contradanza*, discussing the role that black musicians played in this process. For a more recent overview of Cuban music, including information about Haiti's influence, see Sublette.

28. Alén's research on the *tumba francesa* documents the historic origins, instrumentation, song lyrics, and precise performance patterns of the style as studied in the cabildo Sociedad Pompadú de Guantánamo and the Sociedad Santa Catalina de Riccis, also in Guantánamo. He studied the *fiestas* held by these *sociedades,* especially as they have persisted after the 1959 Cuban Revolution. With regard to the clothing worn during celebrations, Alén describes how "women who attend the festivities [wear] pale, beltless, stiff, well-ironed dresses with broad collars, sleeves and ruffles, trimmed with lace and ribbons. The broad skirt hangs to her feet, with a short train behind. . . . Colored, artfully-knotted bandanas are worn on the head and large kerchiefs on the hand. The women also wear necklaces with the low-necked gowns, along with earrings, bracelets, and huge finger rings with fancy jewels. . . . The men wear predominantly white shirts and trousers. Traditionally they attended festivities wearing a suit, formal shirt, and necktie, with large kerchiefs around their necks when dancing" ("Tumba Francesa Societies" 80–81). See also Alén, *Música de las sociedades.*

29. See Morales Carrión for a description of the circumstances surrounding the arrival of refugees in Puerto Rico. Luque de Sánchez gives a more complete picture of the impact of these refugees on Puerto Rican society. She states that most refugees from Saint-Domingue initially resettled in the environs of Mayagüez. Members of the legendary Cepeda family in Puerto Rico, who continue to document and perform the *bomba,* confirm that *bomba* was born in Mayagüez. In an interview in the documentary film *Bomba: Dancing the*

Drum (2001), a granddaughter of Rafael Cepeda speculates about the psychic meaning of the dance. She says, "When those people gathered under the trees in the cane fields, what were those people trying to let go of? The exhaustion from their work, their sweat. The pain they carried inside from being slaves. And what did they express in their dance? All that pain and fury. Let's release all that. Let's liberate ourselves from all that. And let's enjoy ourselves. Why, because when I release all that, I will feel better."

30. The observer continues, "In order to gratify their propensity for dancing the Negroes have formed themselves into two divisions, or societies, under the somewhat fantastic style of Roses and Marguerites. . . . It appears that at one period they were invested with a political character; and their occasional allusions to English and French, Republicans and Bonapartists would seem to confirm this impression. Their connexion with politics must have ceased with the termination of the struggle between England and France, from which period their rivalry has been confined to dancing and other diversions . . ." (Abrahams and Szwed 263–64). Rose and Marguerite societies still exist in St. Lucia.

31. There are obvious exceptions to this tendency. Many studies of Caribbean religious traditions include women, as do studies of more contemporary genres such as zouk, dancehall, and so forth.

32. Day continues, "The place was surrounded by a crowd of dark men and women, quietly looking on, and smoking. The Terpsichoreans were chiefly servants and laundresses. I afterwards attended several of these balls, some of which were held in *demi toilette,* each of the characters holding in her hand a 'shock-shock,' a little calabash, filled with peas, by shaking which a rattling is produced in cadence with the *tambours,* which keep admirable time. So fond of dancing are negroes, of all ages, that I traced two tum-tums to a private yard, where the chorus was composed of young negro females, and the dancers of old women, while the ball was lighted by two tallow candles, held by boys" (295–96).

33. For an overview of *bèlè,* see Gerstin, "Traditional Music"; Cally; and Berrian.

34. As noted above, this is the same position observed by musicologist John Storm Roberts when studying the *tambo* tradition in Jamaica. It is found in *bomba* as well. Harold Courlander, the noted historian of Haitian culture, writes of the Haitian context that "the Juba, or Martinique drum, is similar to the Pétro or Congo but wider and squatter. It is laid on its side for playing, the drummer sitting astride and pressing his heel against the drumhead to mute it or change the pitch. For Juba, or related music, a second man, called the catalier (the one who catas), beats sticks against the body of the instrument behind the drummer" (*Drum and the Hoe* 195).

35. For an excellent description of the very detailed processes involved in making drums, see the discussion of *batá* drum creation in Vélez 119–27.

36. This vocabulary was not limited to corresponding techniques; it was evident in the actual nomenclature of the instruments as well. For example, in *tumba francesa* there were originally three drums used: the *premier,* the large drum used for improvisation, and the two smaller, equally sized drums used

to set the underlying rhythm, the *bulá* and the *segón*. In the Guadeloupan percussive tradition known as *gwoka*, there are two drums: the larger called the *markè* and the other called the *boula*. Like the *bulá* in *tumba francesa*, the *boula* also maintains the rhythm while the larger drum improvises. In all cases, the percussionists play part of the repertory while sitting astride and the drums are single-headed. Likewise, the three *arada* drums used in Haitian Vodou are called the *manman, moyen/seconde,* and the *bula/bébé* (Courlander, *Drum and Hoe* 190, 193). That a *djouba* drum and a *matinik* rhythm are found in Haitian Vodou, and that *boula/bulá* drums are used in Guadeloupe, Haiti, and Cuba, testifies to the inter-regional interchanges that make Caribbean music so rich.

37. There is an extensive literature on the intersections of dance, race, class, and nation. For example, see Quintero Rivera, "Somatology of Manners"; Chasteen; Roberts, *Latin Tinge;* Munro, *Different Drummers;* and Gerstin's "Allure of Origins."

CHAPTER 5

1. There is a wealth of literature on these uprisings. For example, see Craton; Paquette; Reis; Genovese; Aptheker; and Blackburn.

2. The French would not abolish slavery in their American colonies until 1848; final abolition in the Spanish islands occurred in 1873 (Puerto Rico) and 1886 (Cuba). Brazil was the last to abolish slavery via royal decree in 1888. For an examination of how U.S. slaveholders moved to Brazil and Cuba after the Civil War in an effort to maintain their wealth and privilege, see Guterl.

3. I use the term *Afro-American* to refer to blacks living throughout the Americas. When referring to blacks in the United States, I use the modifier *African American* or *North American.*

4. The writer emphatically states, "Some say, let the colored people leave the country! We reply, NO BRETHREN. We would rather die a thousand deaths in honestly and legally contending for our rights, in this our native country. . . . We will stay, and seek purification of the whole lump. . . . If the country sink in disgrace, we will perish amidst its ruins, yet seeking its regeneration and salvation" (*Colored American* September 30, 1837).

5. The use of print journalism during the 1830s corresponds to the enormous amount of pamphlet and tract literature published at the same time in the service of reform campaigns such as the temperance movement and benevolence societies. The editors of the *Colored American* were Protestants, and the paper is full of notices for various church and reform-minded activities. In one issue, for example, temperance and being a subscriber to the paper went hand in hand. One editor wrote, "Allow me, reader, to commune with you; to ask a few plain questions, and suggest a few practical thoughts. Do you belong to a temperance society founded upon the only right principle, *total abstinence?* Are you a worthy, consistent, and a faithful member? Are you a subscriber to *The Colored American?* Do you faithfully read its invaluable columns from week to week? Do you appreciate your privilege? As a friend of your down-trodden fellow-men—as one who feels deeply for the interest and

prosperity of your 'countrymen in chains'—as having a heart imbued with the divine and glorious principle of benevolence—a soul glowing with lofty aspirations, 'panting to realize fame' in another and a better world—do you take *The Colored American*, the *only* paper in this country, that from week to week, *from colored men*—speaks to colored men" (October 17, 1840). For a sense of the comparative circulation of these Afro-American papers, the United States had upwards of 512 newspapers in 1820. The 1830s saw the emergence of the penny press, especially in cities such as New York and Philadelphia. As a result, new publications such as the *New York Herald* had a circulation of seventy-seven thousand by the Civil War. This puts the *Colored American*'s circulation of approximately two thousand in perspective. See Tebbel. In early North America newspapers were considered to be "literary," in contrast to fiction, which had no useful purpose. See Michael Warner's work about newspapers as a means of promoting citizenship in the early American republic.

6. The three periodicals under examination have survived in almost complete run with isolated missing issues. Housed in archives and studied in conjunction with the national journalistic histories of which they were part, the papers have yet to be looked at comparatively. The first three North American black newspapers were *Freedom's Journal* (1827–29), *Rights of All* (1829), and the *Weekly Advocate* (1837). Samuel Cornish was a principal editor of all three before starting the *Colored American*. Philip A. Bell had a long and distinguished career in journalism and has been referred to as "the Napoleon of the early Negro Press." See Hutton 19. I used the University of California, Berkeley, collection of the *Colored American*. I consulted the issues of *L'Union* preserved in the newspaper collection of the University of Florida's Latin American collection. For *Revue des Colonies*, I consulted Stanford's collection for the years 1834–35 and 1842 as well as the University of California, Santa Barbara, collection for the years 1836–41.

7. The *Colored American* was frequently in financial distress. See a June 12, 1841, letter to the readers that stated, "It has been some time since we made a direct appeal to you in behalf of our paper. We had hoped not again to have to have been under the necessity. . . . First, we ask of those subscribers who are in arrears, to come up without delay and remit what they owe. You know the amount—the bill has more than once been sent to you. . . . We have served you with the paper—will you now serve us with the money?" In a more direct, rather over-the-top appeal, the editors state, "We strike off weekly 2,250 copies—2000 of which go to subscribers, and the remainder we use in exchange with other journals. One half of these subscribers live in the city [New York] and its immediate vicinity. . . . But if our people be taken as a body and their patriotism judged of by their support of the ONLY PAPER conducted by themselves and consecrated to their interests, every intelligent mind would say, they mostly deserve to be slaves. . . . *Colored American* will be published as long as water runs and grass grows. If we cannot get the means to publish it weekly, we will publish it *monthly*, and if not monthly, *quarterly*, and if not quarterly, yearly. Its publication shall be sustained" (April 12, 1838; italics and capitalization in original). With regard to the *Revue*, Bissette's

financial dealings earned him a bad reputation, and Lawrence Jennings notes that "it mattered little that Bissette was experiencing personal hardship and apparently devoting every franc he could garner to financing his campaign for the black cause. . . . At a time when overwhelming debt and outright bankruptcy were not only a serious social stigma but a crime, Bissette's financial dealings had made him a pariah in the eyes of respectable philanthropists." See Jennings, "Cyrille Bissette" 56.

8. Bissette was a complicated man. He was the son of a free couple of color, and his mother was the black (illegitimate) daughter of the Tacherie family, making Bissette an unacknowledged cousin of Empress Josephine Bonaparte. He worked as a merchant in Fort Royal. After his arrest, he lost his property and was initially sentenced to death. After 1835, he was in favor of immediate abolition (Jennings, "Cyrille Bissette" 58–59). See Bongie's brilliant and entertaining discussion of Bissette in *Islands and Exiles* 262–347; Kennedy, "Bissette Affair"; and Cook. For a glimpse of how Bissette is still evoked in contemporary local politics in Martinique, see Baber. More recently, the third chapter of Brickhouse, *Transamerican Literary Relations,* contains an excellent discussion on the importance of *Revue* to the field of comparative American studies.

9. See Bissette's letters to John Scoble, April 28 and September 14, 1840, cited in Jennings, "Cyrille Bissette," 54 and n. 18. For a comparative perspective on French colonial journalism in France, see Jennings, "Slavery."

10. Not only the *Revue*'s content but also its format was unique. Bissette evidently saw his paper as a future resource for those interested in a study of the Caribbean colonies and the particular situation of black men and women in the region. I argue that the paper formed a self-conscious cornerstone of the literary canon he endorsed. Bissette's conviction concerning the paper's worth was evident in his methodology. For example, each issue included a table of contents beneath the front-page heading, and an exhaustive alphabetical index of every subject covered was published at the end of each year. These organizational tools are rare in early nineteenth-century periodicals. The following countries received regular, detailed coverage in the paper: Martinique, Guadeloupe, French Guiana, Algeria, Sénégal, l'Ile Bourbon, Haiti, St. Thomas, Saint Lucie, Cuba, Jamaica, Grenada, Dominica, St. Vincent, Trinidad, Antigua, Barbados, and the Bahamas.

11. The byline on the title page of the paper lists "E. Nau" as the publisher and distributor. Emile Nau had an equally famous brother, Ignace Nau (1808–45), who was a journalist, poet, and short story writer. He is credited for promoting the earliest national school of Haitian literature. He was a frequent contributor to both *L'Union* and the *Revue des Colonies.* Some confusion is evident, as several sources cite Ignace Nau as the managing editor of *L'Union.* See, for example, Herdeck 464.

12. As a further example, in the March 15, 1838, edition of *L'Union,* the editors provided news of various Latin American independence movements. With reference to Brazil, they described a revolt in the regions of Rio-Grande, Para, and Bahia, stating that the local Brazilian press "scorn the insurgents because they are principally composed of trash, mixed-race people of color

and blacks" ("méprise les insurgés parce qu'ils sont composés principale-ment de *canaille, gens de couleurs et noirs*"; italics in original). In an explicit self-acknowledgment of Haiti's power in the regional imagination, the paper continued: "We are far from suggesting a war of extinction, the shedding of blood, or as they say, a repetition of the 'catastrophes of Saint-Domingue' between the two classes in Brazil. But if this *trash* that makes up the vast majority of its population could show itself this firm and decisive throughout the empire, without however exceeding the bonds of humanity, the infamous slave trade would be forever extinct" ("Nous sommes bien loin de souhaiter une guerre à outrance, l'effusion de sang, ou, comme l'on dit, la répétition 'des catastrophes de St. Domingue,' entre les deux classes au Brésil. Mais si cette canaille, qui fit la grande majorité de sa population, pouvait se montrer dans tout l'empire aussi ferme et décidée, sans toutefois dépasser les bornes de l'humanité, l'infâme traite des noirs se trouverait à jamais éteint"). This ironic stance regarding a "repetition of the catastrophe of St. Domingue" confirms that Haitian intellectuals were well aware of how the revolution was being maligned in the larger world, while acknowledging that Haiti's path was a desirable one for the majority of the region's black populations. By appropriat-ing the oft-cited phrase for themselves, the authors of the article demonstrated that the perspective of the *canaille*, a class composed of Afro-Brazilians, would designate catastrophe as triumph. Moreover, the fact that Haitian intellectuals perused Brazilian papers to keep abreast of events further demonstrates the information channels open to those dedicated to lobbying on behalf of the region's black majority. This revolt, while it remains unnamed, was likely a reference to the Sabinada revolt of 1837–38 in Bahia, Brazil, and more cover-age is provided in the April 12, 1838, edition. Many thanks to João Reis for discussing this matter (pers. comm. July 2004).

13. See Clark, "Developing Diaspora Literacy" 42.

14. Just as many authors described the attainment of literacy as a turning point in their personal quests for freedom, the existence of an international reading audience equipped with knowledge about blacks living throughout the "habitable globe" indicates how much this same knowledge was valued for its potential to affect the lives of diasporic communities. See McHenry's discus-sion of the development of literary character.

15. I'm thinking here of the work of labor organizers such as Samuel Gom-pers and José Martí, the latter's mobilization of exiled Cuban tobacco work-ers via public readings by the factories' *lectores* being a case in point. At the time period under discussion, this practice of reading aloud shows how impor-tant oral transmission continued to be in societies that prohibited slaves from learning to read and write. Caribbean papers seemed to have been very popu-lar in these North American reading rooms. For instance, one 1838 issue (no date available) states, "Files of *The Barbadian* to the 9th of September, have been received at the Exchange reading room." The article then goes on to note the *Barbadian*'s coverage of events in the *St. Vincent Chronicle*, the *Trinidad Standard*, and the *St. Vincent Gazette*.

16. See McClennen's influential article.

17. Edwards discusses the way that diasporic black intellectuals in the

francophone and anglophone world attempted to frame and translate their experiences to one another in the interwar period. His discussion of anthologizing and translating practices is relevant to this much earlier period.

18. In Edward P. Jones's Pulitzer Prize–winning *The Known World*, one of the main characters, a free black man named Augustus Townsend, is kidnapped, and the law provides neither him nor his family any protection. In one of the novel's most moving and memorable scenes, a poor white slave catcher literally eats Townsend's free papers, and in one act permanently deprives him of his liberty. Jones writes, "Travis began to eat the rest of the papers, making a loud show of it, and when he was done eating, he licked his fingers. . . . 'Now wait a minute,' Augustus said. 'You stop right now . . .' 'Harvey, for god's sakes, them papers belong to him,' Barnum said. 'What he gon do? . . . That ain't right, Harvey. That just ain't right.' Travis wiped his mouth with the back of his hand. 'Right ain't got nothing to do with it'" (212).

19. According to the editor, the only method of circumventing this information blockade was to capitalize on the interisland commercial steam boats, often mail boats, that provided a timely means of contact between Haiti and other colonial ports. In the April 5, 1838, edition, for example, the editors reminded their readers that "l'inappréciable établissement des bateaux à vapeur qui distribuent dans tout cet archipel la malle anglaise qu'apportent régulièrement à chaque quinzaine les paquets, pourrait bien être aussi le moyen de lier des rapports avec ces différentes contrées, de manière à être au courant, dans un temps très rapproché, non seulement de ce qui se passe chez elles, mais même dans ces autres contrées intérrantes de la Côte Ferme qui touchent presque à quelques unes de ces îles." Likewise, a June 21, 1838, article further comments on the difficulties experienced in obtaining recent information from nearby nations. It informs its readers, "Si nos communications avec les Etats-Unis étaient régulières, comme par le passé, ces nouvelles auraient eu toujours l'avantage de la nouveauté. Nous avons déjà exprimé dans un de nos numéros précédens [sic], nos regrets sur l'inconvénient de les recevoir par une voie si longue et si détournée."

20. These papers were nationalistic as well. Their rich content makes simultaneous agendas visible: some locally bound, others transnational/colonial. All were concerned primarily with black advancement. See Anderson, especially the chapter "Creole Pioneers." Gruesz, *Ambassador of Culture*, and Lazo.

21. With regard to the work of his contemporaries, Bissette regularly published poetry by francophone authors, most often Haitian poets such as Ignace Nau and Coriolan Ardouin. Common themes included exile and odes to local natural wonders, family, and close friends. In addition to poetry, the pages of the *Revue* regularly contained short stories, some published in their entirety during one issue, others appearing as serial installments. One of the first pieces of Haitian fiction, "Isalina, ou un scene créole," a short story written by Ignace Nau, was serialized between July and September 1837. Likewise, the short story "Le Mulâtre," by Victor Séjour, a New Orleans–born playwright from a Saint-Domingue refugee family, was published in the March 1837 issue and is now considered the first African American work of fiction. See Gates and McKay

286–99. Articles on literature were remarkable for the articulated desire to develop a local literature that wasn't imitative in either content or form. E. Nau expressed his conviction that "it is necessary to modify and adapt the French language to our needs and our localities, transplanted in a foreign climate; imitation of the style of European poets is more disagreeable and sterile here than elsewhere. We say to our poets and to those who wish to be poets, the source of your inspiration is within you and in your surroundings" ("il faudra la [la langue française] modifier et l'adapter à nos besoins et à nos localités, transplantée sous un climat étranger . . . l'imitation de la manière et du faire des poètes européens est plus ingrate et plus stérile ici qu'ailleurs . . . Nous dirons enfin à nos poètes ou à ceux qui aspirent à l'être: la source de l'inspiration pour vous est en vous et chez vous"; November 16, 1837).

22. Bongie writes that the *Revue* made "attempts at rendering visible an indigenous literature that, while bearing an undoubted resemblance to that of the metropolitan center, was nonetheless identifiably on its margins exploring a different geographical and psychological terrain" (271). The *Revue* did not restrict itself to commentary on texts by black authors, offering vociferous, often bitingly humorous critiques of works by European authors and white creole planters from the Caribbean. For example, the May 1835 issue favorably reviewed *Les Créoles, ou la vie aux Antilles* (1835), by M. Jules Levilloux, just as it mercilessly vilified and mimicked the novel *Outre-mer* (1835), by M. Louis de Maynard de Queilhe, a planter from Martinique. Bissette likewise published a scathing critique of the work of M. Poirié Saint Aurèle, a white Guadeloupan poet. Laden with adjectives such as *foolish* and *insipid*, his ironic descriptions of racist material are well documented in Chris Bongie's excellent chapter on the relationship between Maynard de Queilhe and Bissette, a relationship that pitted a "white creolist discourse" against one aligned with the *gens de couleur*.

23. See Equiano; Cugoano; and Sancho.

24. The paper culled these translations from an unspecified earlier translation by the Abbé Grégoire. For Wheatley, see *Poems*. There were more than eleven editions of the volume by the time *Revue* published her work.

25. See Van Wyk Smith. Four of the five authors designated there as key eighteenth-century black writers—Wheatley, Cugoano, Sancho, and Equiano—were included in Bissette's journal.

26. Physical violence was also a real danger, especially in border or southern states. For example, Elijah Lovejoy, editor of the *Alton Observer* in St. Louis, was murdered by a mob and his printing press destroyed because of his abolitionist activities.

27. See Bethel 828. Migrants settled in both Haiti and what is today the Dominican Republic, since the island was united under one rule at the time. The figure of thirteen thousand refers specifically to the number of migrants who settled in Haiti, as I do not have access to estimates of the numbers who may have settled in Trinidad, Jamaica, and British Guiana. Presently, in the Samaná peninsula of the Dominican Republic, there are Dominicans who are direct descendnts of these North American black settlers. English is still spoken by some. See Martha Davis for further descriptions of these communities in *Himnos y anthems*.

28. For the full quote, see above, chapter 3, note 32.

29. See Jacobs's excellent index.

30. For an overview of colonization efforts, see Forbes; Miller; Burin; and Alexander's "Black Republic." Colonization efforts met with mixed reactions among populations of African descent, and there was a general disapproval of the African Colonization Society's motivations. Founded in 1817, the society established a colony in West Africa in what would eventually become Liberia. Many African Americans felt that this was a ploy to get rid of them, and, as the passages below indicate, they were not far from the mark. In the *Colored American,* one text published in London and written by an unnamed traveler was highlighted as evidence of "A Colored Community, Taking care of themselves!" Speaking of Haiti in this case he wrote, "I have never seen a government really free before. Every colored person is a citizen from the moment of his arrival, and entitled, upon application to the commandant, to nine acres of good land for himself. . . . The population as yet hardly amounts to a million, but there is room for ten times that number, besides all the black and colored population of the Untied States; and being so near, *it would be well to get rid of them* in that way, seeing that they bid fair to becoming very peaceable neighbors" (July 1, 1837; italics mine). Another letter from a Florida planter stipulates that emigration plans were in the best commercial interests of the United States, writing, "Is it not our best policy . . . to encourage as far as possible the industrious and most respectable part of our free colored population, especially the agricultural part, to migrate to that country? The natural prejudices of those emigrant towards the country of their birth, would greatly tend to promote a reciprocal national attachment, and would produce harmony and good will by an assimilation *[sic]* of manners, customs, and language, tending to strengthen the chain of commercial relations much to our advantage" (*Colored American* August 11, 1838). Emigration movements would once again gain in popularity in the 1850s and 1860s. Men such as James Redpath sponsored emigration to Haiti with the belief that blacks would never be accepted into North American society. Some of these migrants became successful members of Haitian society. During the Civil War Abraham Lincoln was willing to sign a contract allowing blacks to be resettled in Haiti, as he could not imagine a peaceful coexistence of whites and blacks in the United States.

31. For example, they published official correspondence between Haitian and American officials such as Dewey and Boyer's volume. See immediately below for a recurring notice from an emigration official in Trinidad.

32. A similar advertisement read:

—FOR TRINIDAD—Free industrious persons of color, of good character, desirous of becoming independent, wishing to emigrate to the British Island of Trinidad, can secure their passage in the first class American brig George Washington, to sail from this port 20th of March. Agriculturists and laborers, with their families, will be taken out and found with ample provision, free of any expense or claim on their services after arrival. Laborers are in great demand, and can meet with permanent employment immediately on arrival, at high wages. —For freight or passage, apply to the Captain on board, foot of Brad Street, pier No, East River (March 7, 1840).

33. Emigrationists focused on sharing practical information. This was the case in the August 31, 1839, article "Description of the Island of Trinidad and of the Advantages to be derived from Emigration to that Colony." The anonymous author wrote of how "from its happy position, it cannot fail of becoming the great commercial emporium, the New York in fact of that part of the world. Placed at the mouth of the splendid river Orinoco, it commands the commerce of a country as fertile and extensive as the valley of the Mississippi. . . . On going aboard, [the immigrant] will require to take with him only the wearing apparel necessary for himself and family during the passage. Everything requisite for his and their comfortable maintenance while on board will be provided for at the expense of the colony of Trinidad." In later years, James Redpath's *Guide to Hayti* tells his readers, "For clothing, take as many summer suits as you can afford, light-colored linen or cotton clothing is the best, every family ought to have a saw, hammer and nails, and washing-machines, tubs and sewing machines would be invaluable for your women folk, for you can buy none of those useful allies of the housewife in Hayti" (169–70).

34. In the August 30, 1838, edition, a reader cited the success of measures initiated by British planters to import an East Indian workforce to Demerara, suggesting a similar policy in Haiti. He wrote, "La manque de bras se fait de plus en plus sentir . . . la conséquence nécessaire de la subdivision des propriétés; à mesure que le cultivateur acquiert une portion de terre, il 'y retire avec sa famille est ses proches. Ainsi, nos grandes habitations périclitent." The *Colored American* eventually voiced a steadfast opposition to emigration schemes and posted an article questioning whether immigrants induced to come from other countries, including India, were in fact prospering. It stated, "*Immigrants* not a few, Scotch, Irish, German, Portuguese, Maltese, and Indian, have already been introduced into the West Indies; and from none of them have we heard the tidings, 'We are happy.' None of them are multiplying like a flock, or sending letters of invitation to their relatives or friends to follow them. Many of them have gone into a premature grave, and the rest are for the most part, we may say almost without exception, pining away the remainder or a short life of hopeless and helpless sorrow" (May 2, 1840). For more on Chinese and Indian immigration to the Caribbean and the United States, see Kale and Jung.

35. "We learn by the *Sun*, of Thursday the 8th that a British vessel sailed from Baltimore on the 3rd, with two hundred and fifty migrants for Trinidad. We know not what were the condition of these men at home, but we may safely say, that *three fourths* them will be sadly disappointed and wish to return. *We have some sympathy for these brethren because they live beyond the reach of those influences which would counteract these operations—they live where it is dangerous to receive those papers which thunder out against this system. They therefore become the dupes of the Emigrationists, who have ceased operations here, and resorted there, where their false pretences of equality, which in contrast with the oppression to which the people in that city are exposed, becomes at once a great stimulant.*" Italics mine.

36. Historically, the political manifestation of pan-American ideals is credited to the "Libertador" of Latin America, Simon Bolívar. Bolívar understood the importance of uniting Latin America in an effort to counteract Spanish

and North American hegemony in the region as early as 1815. In his oft-cited "Carta de Jamaica" and in comments made during the 1825 Congreso de Panamá, he broached the idea of a Pan-American federation. A critical element of this political ideal involved providing military support in the armed liberation struggles of Cuba and Puerto Rico, islands that would then have the choice of becoming incorporated into this federation. While Bolívar initially succeeded in founding a unified Gran Colombia, and the five nations of Central America also remained unified for approximately twenty years under the Federación de los Estados de la América Central, the Caribbean was never integrated into these political projects. Although Bolívar did not succeed in uniting the Antilles under the auspices of his federations, his legacy had a tremendous impact on the region. As seen in chapter 3, he spent eighteen months in exile in Jamaica and Haiti when Alexandre Pétion provided political asylum to him upon his being expelled by the Spanish government from South America. When Bolívar was ready to resume the Wars of Independence, Pétion provided the Venezuelan leader with critically needed arms and soldiers. Bolívar subsequently excluded Haiti from the influential Congress of Panama in 1826. See Maingot for an analysis of Bolívar's motivations.

37. For an overview of Caribbean confederation movements, see Mathews.

38. U.S. involvement with Haiti, and the Caribbean in general, became increasingly more complex after the 1823 Monroe Doctrine, which declared the region a U.S. sphere of influence in an effort to counteract European hegemony.

39. Cited in Lewis, *Main Currents* 300. The original was published in the Argentinian newspaper *La Nación* as "La República Argentina en los Estados Unidos" (December 4, 1887) and was republished in Martí, 7: 329–35. The quote appears on 330.

40. In 1891, Irvine Garland Penn published a long, detailed study of the black press called *The Afro-American Press and Its Editors*. The 1920s and 1930s marked a renewed interest in the African diaspora, and editions of the NAACP's *The Crisis* magazine published during these decades were similar to projects undertaken in the 1830s black press. For example, one advertisement promoted a play, *The Abraham Lincoln of Haiti: A Super-photoplay entitled Toussaint L'ouverture,* by the Delsarte Film Corporation. Likewise, articles such as "The Negro in Cuba," by Margaret Ross Martin (January 1932), and "A Page of West Indian Poetry," by Nicolas Guillén (December 1931), had diasporic themes. A brief excerpt from Carleton Beals's story "Black Mexico" demonstrates an awareness of how promoting networks of communication between diasporic communities was deemed dangerous by some. He wrote, "Here is a charming description of a Negro-Mexican village. Most writers and travelers in Central and South America and the West Indies very carefully omit all mention of Negro blood. They seem desperately afraid that the Negroes of all the Americas should become acquainted with each other."

Works Consulted
and Discography

PERIODICALS

L'Abeille (New Orleans)

The American Star, or, Historical, Political, Critical and Moral Journal (Philadelphia)

The Anti-Jacobin Review and Magazine, Or, Monthly Political and Literary Censor (London)

City Gazette and Daily Advertiser (Charleston)

Commercial Advertiser (New York)

The Colored American (New York)

The Crisis (New York)

El Dominicano (Santiago, Dominican Republic)

Freedom's Journal (New York)

Journal des Révolutions de la Partie Française de Saint-Domingue (Philadelphia)

Littel's Living Age (Boston)

Le Manifeste (Port-au-Prince)

Mercantile Advertiser (New York)

Moniteur de la Louisiane (New Orleans)

Philadelphia Gazette and Daily Advertiser (Philadelphia)

Revue des Colonies (Paris)

L'Union (Port-au-Prince)

UNPUBLISHED MANUSCRIPTS

Althea de Puech Parham Working Papers, UC MSS 517, Monsieur P., "Mon Odyssée." Williams Research Center, Historic New Orleans Collection

Arsène Lacarrière Latour Archive, MSS 555.37–42, Williams Research Center, Historic New Orleans Collection

Assorted notarial acts of Narcisse Broutin, New Orleans Notarial Archives

Ernest Sabourin Papers, deposition of Andrew Whiteman. Tulane University Library Special Collections

Ernest Sabourin Papers, deposition of José Rodriguez. Tulane University Library Special Collections

Louisiana Papers, 1767–1816. Bancroft Library, University of California, Berkeley.

"Mémoire sur la police des gens de couleurs libres." Collection Moreau de St-Méry. F3, 91, Archives Nationales d'Outre Mer.

Moreau de Saint-Méry, Médéric Louis Élie. "Discours de Moreau de Saint-Méry, sur les affranchis des colonies, prononcé par lui dans l'assemblée publique du Musée de Paris." April 1785. Collection Moreau de St-Méry. F3, 156, Archives Nationales d'Outre Mer.

Moreau de Saint-Méry, Médéric Louis Élie. Various manuscripts in "Colonies anglaises, espagnoles, français, Etats Unis; refugiés de SD, correspondences des consuls francais aux EU 1792–1795." Collection Moreau de St-Méry. F3, 285, Archives Nationales d'Outre Mer

Pierre and Jean Laffite Collection, MSS 56. Williams Research Center, Historic New Orleans Collection

"Quelques détails sur la dernière expédition de Bolivar a Venezuela depuis son départ des Cayes . . . " Collection Moreau de St-Méry. F3, 155, Archives Nationales d'Outre Mer

Records of District Courts of the United States, Record Group 21. Foley to Williams, Collector of the Port, New Orleans, May 1, 1813, National Archives, Southwest Region, Ft. Worth Texas

St. Gême Family Papers, MSS 100. Williams Research Center, Historic New Orleans Collection

You Papers, MSS 55. Williams Research Center, Historic New Orleans Collection

PUBLISHED SOURCES

Abrahams, Roger D. *The Man-of-Words in the West Indies: Performance and the Emergence of Creole Culture*. Baltimore: Johns Hopkins University Press, 1983.

Abrahams, Roger D., and John F. Szwed, eds. *After Africa: Extracts from British Travel Accounts and Journals of the Seventeenth, Eighteenth, and Nineteenth Centuries Concerning the Slaves, Their Manners, and Customs in the British West Indies*. New Haven: Yale University Press, 1983.

Adresse à l'Assemblée nationale, pour l'abolition de la traite des noirs. Par la Société des amis des noirs de Paris. Paris: De l'Imp. de L. Potier de Lille, 1790.

Alén, Olavo. *La música de las sociedades de tumba francesa en Cuba*. Havana: Ediciones Casa de las Américas, 1986.

———. "The Tumba Francesa Societies and Their Music." *Essays on Cuban*

Music: North American and Cuban Perspectives. Ed. Peter Manuel. Lanham: University Press of America. 80–81.

Alexander, Leslie M. *African or American? Black Identity and Political Activism in New York City, 1784–1861.* Urbana: University of Illinois Press, 2008.

———. "The Black Republic: The Influence of the Haitian Revolution on Black Political Consciousness, 1817–1861." *African Americans and the Haitian Revolution: Selected Essays and Historical Documents.* Ed. Maurice Jackson and Jacqueline Bacon. New York: Routledge, 2010. 57–79.

Alix, Juan Antonio. *Décimas.* Ed. Joaquín Balaguer. Ciudad Trujillo: Librería Dominicana, 1961.

Allende, Isabel. *La isla bajo el mar.* New York: Vintage, 2009.

Alleyne, Mervyn. *Roots of Jamaican Culture.* London: Pluto Press, 1989.

Anderson, Benedict. *Imagined Communities: Reflections on the Origin and Spread of Nationalism.* New York: Verso, 1991.

Andrews, George Reid. *Afro-Latin America, 1800–2000.* London: Oxford University Press, 2004.

Anti-Jacobin Review and Magazine, or, Monthly Political and Literary Censor. Vol. 15. London: R. Bostock, 1803.

Aptheker, Herbert. *American Negro Slave Revolts.* 5th ed. New York: International Publishers, 1983.

Aquin, Hélène. *Souvenirs d'Amérique et de France, par une créole.* Paris: Imprimerie Marchessou Fils, 1883.

Ardouin, Beaubrun. *Études sur l'histoire d'Haïti suivies de la vie du Général J. M. Borgella.* 11 vols. 1853–60. Port au Prince: Chez L'editeur François Dalencour, 1958.

Armas Rigal, Nieves. *Los bailes de las sociedades de tumba francesa.* Havana: Editorial Pueblo y Educación, 1991.

Arredondo y Pichardo, Gaspar. "Memoria de mi salida de la Isla de Santo Domingo el 28 de abril de 1805." Rodríguez Demorizi, *Invasiones haitianas* 120–60.

Arthur, Stanley Clisby. *Jean Laffite, Gentleman Rover.* New Orleans: Harmanson, 1952.

Austerlitz, Paul. *Merengue: Dominican Music and Dominican Identity.* Philadelphia: Temple University Press, 1997.

Baber, Willie L. "Political Economy and Social Change: The Bissette Affair and Local-Level Politics in Morne-Vert." *American Ethnologist* 12.3 (1985): 489–504.

Bacardí y Moreau, Emilio. *Crónicas de Santiago de Cuba.* 1909. Madrid: Graf. Breogan, 1972.

———. *Via Crucis.* Barcelona: la Viuda de Luis Tasso, 1914.

Balaguer, Joaquín. *El centinela de la frontera: Vida y hazañas de Antonio Duvergé.* 1962. Santo Domingo: Editora Corripio, 1990.

———. *La isla al revés.* Santo Domingo: Librería Dominicana, 1983.

Barnes, Sandra, ed. *Africa's Ogun: Old World and New.* Bloomington: Indiana University Press, 1989.

Barton, Halbert E. "The Drum-Dance Challenge: An Anthropological Study of Gender, Race, and Class Marginalization of Bomba in Puerto Rico." Diss. Cornell University, 1995.

Basch, Linda, Nina Glick Schiller, and Cristina Szanton Blanc. *Nations Unbound: Transnational Projects, Postcolonial Predicaments, and Deterritorialized Nation States*. Langhorne: Gordon and Breach, 1994.

Bassett, John, ed. *Correspondence of Andrew Jackson*. Vol. 2. Washington, DC: Carnegie Institute of Washington, 1926.

Baud, Michiel. "Una frontera-refugio: Dominicanos y haitianos contra el estado (1870–1930)." *Estudios Sociales* 26.92 (1993): 5–28.

Baudry des Lozières, Louis Narcisse. *Second voyage à la Louisiane, faisant suite au premier de l'auteur de 1794 à 1798: contenant un mémoire sur la découverte du coton animal, un manuel botanique à l'usage des jeunes colons, un dictionnaire ou vocabulaire Congo, précédé d'une statistique des comptoirs de la côte d'Angole, le tout utile aux Américains cultivateurs qui n'entendent point les langues de l'Afrique, différens projets d'armemens, et tableaux de cargaisons pour l'avantage des jeunes colons, négocians, armateurs, capitaines de vaisseaux marchands ou de l'Etat, et même des administrateurs des ports, le coffre de chirurgie qui enseigne la nature des drogues et médicamens destinés au voyages de long cours, leur prix et leur usage, observations sur la botanique médicinale, d'une grande utilité pour la santé et l'instruction des planteurs américains, réflexions sur les chambres d'agriculture qui viennent d'être créées [sic] de nouveau pour les colonies, etc. etc. etc.* Paris: Chez Charles, 1803.

Baur, John. "International Repercussions of the Haitian Revolution." *Americas* 26.4 (1970): 394–418.

Béhague, Gerard, ed. *Music and Black Ethnicity: The Caribbean and South America*. Miami: North-South Center Press, 1994.

Belisario, Issac Mendes. *Sketches of Character in Illustration of the Habits, Occupation, and Costume of the Negro Population in the Island of Jamaica*. Kingston: n.p., 1837.

Bell, Caryn Cossé. *Revolution, Romanticism, and the Afro-Creole Protest Tradition in Louisiana, 1718–1868*. Baton Rouge: Louisiana State University Press, 1997.

Bellegarde-Smith, Patrick, and Claudine Michel, eds. *Haitian Vodou: Spirit, Myth and Reality*. Bloomington: Indiana University Press, 2006.

Benítez-Rojo, Antonio. *La isla que se repite*. Hanover: Ediciones del Norte, 1989.

———. "Power/Sugar/Literature: Toward a Reinterpretation of Cubanness." *Cuban Studies* 16 (1986): 9–32.

Bennett, Herman L. "The Subject in the Plot: National Boundaries and the 'History' of the Black Atlantic." *African Studies Review* 43.1 (2000): 101–24.

Berlin, Ira. *Many Thousands Gone: The First Two Centuries of Slavery in North America*. Cambridge, MA: Harvard University Press, 2000.

———. *Slaves without Masters: The Free Negro in the Antebellum South*. New York: New Press, 1974.

Berrian, Brenda. *Awakening Spaces: French Caribbean Popular Song, Music, and Culture*. Chicago: University of Chicago Press, 2000.

Bethel, Elizabeth Rauh. "Images of Hayti: The Construction of an Afro-American *Lieu de mémoire*." *Callaloo* 15.3 (1992): 827–41.

Bettelheim, Judith. *Caribbean Festival Arts*. Saint Louis: Saint Louis Art Museum; Seattle: University of Washington Press, 1988.

———. *Cuban Festivals: A Century of Afro-Cuban Culture*. Kingston: Ian Randle, 2001.

Bilby, Kenneth, and Morton Marks. Liner notes. *Caribbean Voyage: The 1962 Field Recordings*. Rounder, 1999.

Binder, Wolfgang, ed. *Creoles and Cajuns: French Louisiana—La Louisianne française*. Frankfurt: Peter Lang, 1998.

Bird, J. B. *Rebellion: John Horse and the Black Seminoles, the First Black Rebels to Beat American Slavery*. Southwest Alternate Media Project, June 2005. Web. 20 July 2008. <http://www.johnhorse.com/index.html>.

Blackburn, Robin. "Haiti, Slavery, and the Age of the Democratic Revolution." *William and Mary Quarterly* 63.4 (2006): 643–74.

———. *Overthrow of Colonial Slavery, 1776–1848*. London: Verso, 1988.

Blanchard, Peter. "Pan Americanism and Slavery in the Era of Latin American Independence." *Beyond the Ideal: Pan-Americanism in Inter-American Affairs*. Ed. David Sheinin. Westport, CT: Praeger, 2000. 9–18.

———. "The Slave Soldiers of Spanish South America: From Independence to Abolition." C. Brown and Morgan 255–73.

———. *Under the Flags of Freedom: Slave Soldiers and the Wars of Independence in Spanish South America*. Pittsburgh: University of Pittsburgh Press, 2008.

Bollaert, William. "Life of Jean Lafitte, The Pirate of the Mexican Gulf." *Littell's Living Age* 32 (March 1852): 433–46.

Bolster, Jeffrey. *Black Jacks: African American Seamen in the Age of Sail*. Cambridge, MA: Harvard University Press, 1997.

Bomba: Dancing the Drum. Dir. Ashley James. 2001. Film.

Bongie, Chris. *Islands and Exiles: The Creole Identities of Post/Colonial Literature*. Stanford: Stanford University Press, 1998.

Boxill, Ian. *Ideology and Caribbean Integration*. Kingston: Consortium Graduate School of Social Sciences, University of the West Indies, 1993.

Brana-Shute, Rosemary, and Rosemarijn Hoefte. *Bibliography of Caribbean Migration and Caribbean Immigrant Communities*. Gainesville: University of Florida Libraries, 1983.

Brasseaux, Carl A., and Glenn R. Conrad, eds. *The Road to Louisiana: The Saint-Domingue Refugees, 1792–1909*. Lafayette: Center of Louisiana Studies, 1992.

Brasseaux, Carl A., Keith P. Fontenot, and Claude F. Oubre, eds. *Creoles of Color in the Bayou Country*. Jackson: University Press of Mississippi, 1994.

Brereton, Bridget. "Hé St Domingo, songé St Domingo": Haiti and the Haitian Revolution in the Political Discourse of Nineteenth-Century Trinidad." Munro and Walcott-Hackshaw 123–49.

Brickhouse, Anna. "Hemispheric Jamestown." *Hemispheric American Studies*, Caroline F. Levander and Robert S. Levine, eds. New Brunswick: Rutgers University Press, 2008. 18–35.

———. "L'Ouragan de Flammes" ('The Hurricane of Flames'): New Orleans and Transamerican Catastrophe, 1866/2005." *American Quarterly* 59.4 (2007): 1097–127.

———. *Transamerican Literary Relations and the Nineteenth-Century Public Sphere.* Cambridge: Cambridge University Press, 2004.

Brierre, Jean F. *Petion y Bolívar: El adiós a la marsellesa.* Buenos Aires: Ediciones Troquel, 1955.

Brock, Lisa, Robin D. G. Kelley, and Karen Sotiropoulos, eds. *Transnational Black Studies.* Spec issue of *Radical History Review* 87 (2004).

Brown, Christopher L., and Philip Morgan, eds. *Arming Slaves: From Classical Times to the Modern Age.* New Haven: Yale University Press, 2006.

Brown, Karen McCarthy. "Systematic Remembering, Systematic Forgetting: Ogou in Haiti." *Africa's Ogun: Old World and New.* Ed. Sandra Barnes. Bloomington: Indiana University Press, 1989. 65–89.

Brown, William Wells. *The Black Man; His Antecedents, His Genius, and His Achievements.* Boston: J. Redpath, 1863.

———. *Clotel; or The President's Daughter.* 1853. New York: Penguin Books, 2004.

Browning, Barbara. *Infectious Rhythm: Metaphors of Contagion and the Spread of African Culture.* New York: Routledge, 1998.

Bruce, Clint, and Jennifer Gipson. "'Je n'étais qu'un objet de mépris': Degrés de résistance dans la littérature des Créoles de couleur en Louisiane au XIXe siecle." *Francophonies d'Amerique* 17 (2004): 5–15.

Buck-Morss, Susan. "Hegel and Haiti." *Critical Inquiry* 26.4 (2000): 821–65.

Buckridge, Steeve O. *The Language of Dress: Resistance and Accommodation in Jamaica, 1760–1890.* Kingston: University of West Indies Press, 2004.

Burin, Eric. *Slavery and the Peculiar Solution: A History of the American Colonization Society.* Gainesville: University Press of Florida, 2005.

Burton, Richard. *Afro-Creole: Power, Opposition and Play in the Caribbean.* Ithaca: Cornell University Press, 1997.

Cable, George Washington. *The Creoles of Louisiana.* 1884. Gretna, LA: Pelican, 2000.

———. *Old Creole Days.* 1879. Gretna, LA: Pelican, 2001.

Cabrera, Lydia. *El Monte.* Miami: Ediciones Universal, 2000.

Cally, Sully. *Musiques et danses afro-caraïbes: Martinique.* France: Madiana Editions, 1990.

Campbell, Mavis C. *The Maroons of Jamaica, 1655–1796.* Granby: Bergin and Garvey, 1988.

Canizares-Esguerra, Jorge. *How to Write the History of the New World: Histories, Epistemologies, and Identities in the Eighteenth-Century Atlantic World.* Stanford: Stanford University Press, 2001.

Carpentier, Alejo. *La música en Cuba.* Mexico: Fondo de Cultura Económica, 1972.

———. *El reino de este mundo.* 1949. Barcelona: Editorial Seix Barral, 1991. *The Kingdom of this World.* Trans. Harriet de Onís. New York: Farrar, Straus and Giroux, 1989.

———. *El siglo de las luces.* 1962. Havana: Letras Cubanas, 2009.

Casimir, Jean. *The Caribbean, One and Divisible.* Santiago: United Nations, Economic Commission for Latin America and the Caribbean, 1992.

Castor, Suzy. *Migración y relaciones internacionales (el caso haitiano-dominicano).* Santo Domingo: Universidad Autónoma de Santo Domingo, 1987.

Castronovo, Russ, and Susan K. Gillman, eds. *States of Emergency: The Object of American Studies.* Chapel Hill: University of North Carolina Press, 2009.

Chamberlain, Mary. *Caribbean Migrations: Globalised Identities.* London: Routledge, 1998.

Charnley, Mitchell. *The Buccaneer: The Story of Jean Lafitte, Gentleman Smuggler.* New York: Grosset and Dunlap, 1934.

Chasteen, John Charles. *National Rhythms, African Roots: The Deep History of Latin American Popular Dance.* Albuquerque: University of New Mexico Press, 2004.

Childs, Frances. *French Refugee Life in the United States, 1790–1800: An American Chapter of the French Revolution.* Baltimore: Johns Hopkins University Press, 1940.

Chinea, Jorge Luis. *Race and Labor in the Hispanic Caribbean: The West Indian Immigrant Worker Experience in Puerto Rico, 1800–1850.* Gainesville: University of Florida Press, 2005.

Clark, VèVè. "Developing Diaspora Literacy and *Marasa* Consciousness." *Comparative American Identities.* Ed. Hortense Spillers. New York: Routledge, 1990. 40–61.

———. "Haiti's Tragic Overture: (Mis)Representations of the Haitian Revolution in World Drama (1796–1975)." *Representing the French Revolution: Literature, Historiography and Art.* Ed. James A. W. Heffernan. Hanover: University Press of New England, 1992. 237–59.

Clark, VèVè, and Sara E. Johnson, eds. *Kaiso! Writings by and about Katherine Dunham.* Madison: University of Wisconsin Press, 2006.

Clerk, Astley. "The Music and Musical Instruments of Jamaica." *Jamaica Journal* 9.2 (1975): 59–76.

Cohen, David W., and Jack P. Greene, eds and introd. *Neither Slave nor Free: The Freedmen of African Descent in the Slave Societies of the New World.* Baltimore: Johns Hopkins University Press, 1972.

Cook, Mercer. *Five French Negro Authors.* Washington, DC: Associated Publishers, 1943.

Cooper, Carolyn. *Noises in the Blood: Orality, Gender and the Vulgar Body of Jamaican Popular Culture.* Durham: Duke University Press, 1995.

Cooper, Frederick, Thomas Holt, and Rebecca J. Scott. *Beyond Slavery: Explorations of Race, Labor, and Citizenship in Post-Emancipation Societies.* Durham: University of North Carolina Press, 2000.

Coopersmith, J. M. *Music and Musicians of the Dominican Republic.* Washington, DC: Pan-American Union, 1949.

Cordero Michel, Emilio. *La revolución haitiana y Santo Domingo.* Santo Domingo: Editora Nacional, 1968.

Córdova-Bello, Eleazar. *La independencia de Haití y su influencia en Hispano-américa*. Caracas: Instituto Panamericano de Geografía e Historia, 1967.

Corten, André, and Isis Duarte. "Five Hundred Thousand Haitians in the Dominican Republic." *Latin American Perspectives* 22.3 (1995): 94–110.

Cosentino, Donald. "It's All for You, Sen Jak!" Cosentino, *Sacred Arts* 243–65.

———. ed. *Sacred Arts of Haitian Vodou*. Los Angeles: UCLA Fowler Museum of Cultural History, 1995.

Courlander, Harold. *The Drum and the Hoe: Life and Lore of the Haitian People*. Berkeley: University of California Press, 1960.

———. *Haiti Singing*. Chapel Hill: University of North Carolina Press, 1939.

———. *A Treasury of Afro-American Folklore: The Oral Literature, Traditions, Recollections, Legends, Tales, Songs, Religious Beliefs, Customs, Sayings, and Humor of Peoples of African Descent in the Americas*. New York: Marlowe, 1996.

Covington, James W. "Cuban Bloodhounds and the Seminoles." *Florida Historical Quarterly* 33 (1954): 111–19.

Craton, Michael. *Testing the Chains: Resistance to Slavery in the British West Indies*. Ithaca: Cornell University Press, 1983.

Cugoano, Ottobah. *Thoughts and Sentiments on the Evil and Wicked Traffic of the Slavery and Commerce of the Human Species*. London: T. Becket, 1787.

Dain, Bruce R. *A Hideous Monster of the Mind: American Race Theory in the Early Republic*. Cambridge, MA: Harvard University Press, 2002.

Dallas, Robert Charles. *The History of the Maroons, from Their Origin to The Establishment of Their Chief Tribe at Sierra Leone: Including the Expedition to Cuba for the Purpose of Procuring Spanish Chasseurs; and the State of the Island of Jamaica for the Last Ten Years: With a Succinct History of the Island Previous to That Period*. London: Longman and Rees, 1803.

Daniel, Yvonne. *Dancing Wisdom: Embodied Knowledge in Haitian Vodou, Cuban Yoruba, and Bahian Candomblé*. Urbana: University of Illinois Press, 2005.

Danticat, Edwidge. *The Farming of Bones*. New York: Penguin Books, 1999.

Dash, J. Michael. *Haiti and the United States: National Stereotypes and the Literary Imagination*. Basingstoke: Macmillan, 1988.

———. "*Haïti Chimère*: Revolutionary Universalism and Its Caribbean Context." Munro and Walcott-Hackshaw 9–19.

———. *The Other America: Caribbean Literature in a New World Context*. Charlottesville: University Press of Virginia, 1998.

Davies, Carole Boyce. *Black Women, Writing and Identity: Migrations of the Subject*. New York: Routledge, 1994.

Davis, Martha Ellen. "Bi-Musicality in the Cultural Configurations of the Caribbean." *Black Music Research Journal* 14.2 (1994): 145–60.

———. *Himnos y anthems ("coros") de los "americanos" de Samaná: Contextos y estilos*. Santo Domingo: n.p., 1981.

Davis, William C. *The Privateers Laffite: The Treacherous World of the Corsairs of the Gulf*. Orlando, FL: Harcourt, 2005.

Dawdy, Shannon Lee. *Building the Devil's Empire: French Colonial New Orleans*. Chicago: University of Chicago Press, 2008.

Day, Charles William. *Five Years' Residence in the West Indies*. Vol. 1. London: Colburn, 1852.

Dayan, Joan. "Codes of Law and Bodies of Color." *New Literary History* 26.2 (1995): 283–308.

———. *Haiti, History, and the Gods*. Berkeley: University of California Press, 1995.

D'Costa, Jean, and Barbara Lalla, eds. *Voices in Exile: Jamaican Texts of the 18th and 19th Centuries*. Tuscaloosa: University of Alabama Press, 1989.

Debien, Gabriel. *Les esclaves aux Antilles françaises, XVIIE-XVIIIE siècles*. Basse-Terre: Société d'histoire de la Guadeloupe, 1974.

———. "The Saint-Domingue Refugees in Cuba, 1793–1815." Trans. David Cheramie. Brasseaux and Conrad 31–112.

Debien, Gabriel, and René Le Gardeur. "The Saint-Domingue Refugees in Louisiana, 1792–1804." Trans. David Chearamie. Brasseaux and Conrad 113–243.

Deive, Carlos Esteban. *Las emigraciones dominicanas a Cuba, 1795–1808*. Santo Domingo: Fundación Cultural Dominicana, 1989.

———. "El prejuicio racial en el folklore dominicano." *Boletín* 8 (1976): 75–96.

———. *Los refugiados franceses en Santo Domingo*. Santo Domingo: Universidad Nacional Pedro Henríquez Ureña, 1984.

———. *Vodú y magia en Santo Domingo*. 2nd ed. Santo Domingo: Taller, 1988.

Delany, Martin Robinson. *The Condition, Elevation, Emigration, and Destiny of the Colored People of the United States, Politically Considered*. 1852. New York: Arno Press, 1968.

De los Santos, Danilo. *Memoria de la pintura dominicana: Raíces e impulso nacional*. Vol. 1. Santo Domingo: Grupo León Jimenes, 2003.

De Puech Parham, Althea, ed. and trans. *My Odyssey: Experiences of a Young Refugee from Two Revolutions by a Creole of Saint-Domingue*. Baton Rouge: Louisiana State University Press, 1959.

Derby, Lauren. "Haitians, Magic, and Money: Raza and Society in the Haitian-Dominican Borderlands, 1900 to 1937." *Comparative Studies in Society and History* 36.3 (1994): 488–526.

———. "National Identity and the Idea of Value in the Dominican Republic." *Blacks, Coloureds and National Identity in Nineteenth-Century Latin America*. Ed. Nancy Naro. London: Institute of Latin American Studies, 2003. 5–37.

Deren, Maya. *Divine Horsemen: The Living Gods of Haiti*. London: Thames and Hudson, 1953.

Desdunes, Rodolph. *Nos hommes et notre histoire: Notices biographiques accompagnées de reflexions et de souvenirs personnels, hommage à la population créole, en souvenir des grands hommes qu'elle a produits et des bonnes choses qu'elle a accomplies*. Montreal: Arbour and Dupont, 1911.

Desmangles, Leslie. *The Faces of the Gods: Vodou and Roman Catholicism in Haiti.* Chapel Hill: University of North Carolina Press, 1992.

Dewey, Loring, and Jean-Pierre Boyer, eds. *Correspondence Relative to the Emigration to Hayti of Free People of Colour in the United States.* New York: M. Day, 1824.

Dixon, Chris. *African America and Haiti: Emigration and Black Nationalism in the Nineteenth Century.* Westport, CT: Greenwood Press, 2000.

Documentos para la historia de la República Dominicana. Vol. 1. Ciudad Trujillo: Editora Montalvo, 1944.

Dorsey, Joseph. *Slave Traffic in the Age of Abolition: Puerto Rico, West Africa, and the Non-Hispanic Caribbean, 1815–1859.* Gainesville: University Press of Florida, 2003.

Douglass, Frederick. "What to the Slave Is the Fourth of July?" July 5, 1852. http://teachingamericanhistory.org/library/index.asp?document=162.

Duany, Jorge. "Popular Music in Puerto Rico." *Salsiology: Afro-Cuban Music and the Evolution of Salsa in New York City.* Ed. Vernon Boggs. New York: Excelsior Music, 1992. 71–89.

Dubois, Laurent. *Avengers of the New World: The Story of the Haitian Revolution.* Cambridge, MA: Harvard University Press, 2004.

———. "Citizen Soldiers: Emancipation and Military Service in the Revolutionary French Caribbean." *Arming Slaves: From Classical Times to the Modern Age.* C. Brown and Morgan 233–54.

———. *A Colony of Citizens: Revolution and Slave Emancipation in the French Caribbean, 1787–1804.* Chapel Hill: University of North Carolina Press, 2004.

DuBois, W. E. B. *The Repression of the African Slave Trade to the United States of America, 1638–1870.* 1896. New York: Russell and Russell, 1965.

Dubroca, Louis. *Vida de J. J. Dessalines, gefe de los negros de Santo Domingo con notas muy circunstanciadas sobre el origen, caracter y atrocidades de los principales gefes de aquellos rebeldes desde el principio de la insurrección en 1791.* Mexico: Mariano de Zúñiga y Ontiveros, 1806.

Dumervé, Etienne Constantin. *Histoire de la musique en Haiti.* Port-au-Prince: Imprimerie des Antilles, 1968.

Edwards, Brent Hayes. *The Practice of Diaspora: Literature, Translation, and the Rise of Black Internationalism.* Cambridge, MA: Harvard University Press, 2003.

Egerton, Douglas R. *Death or Liberty: African Americans and Revolutionary America.* London: Oxford University Press, 2008.

———. *Rebels, Reformers, and Revolutionaries: Collected Essays and Second Thoughts.* New York: Routledge, 2002.

Elisabeth, Léo. "Gens de couleur et révolution dans les îles du Vent: 1789–janvier 1793." *Revue Française d'Histoire d'Outre-Mer* 76 (1989): 75–96.

Entiope, Gabriel. *Nègres, danse et résistance: La Caraibe du XVIIe au XIXe siècle.* Paris: L'Harmattan, 1996.

Equiano, Olaudah. *The Interesting Life of Olaudah Equiano, Written by Himself.* Ed. Robert Allison. Boston: Bedford Books, 1995.

Everett, Donald E. "Emigres and Militiamen: Free Persons of Color in New

Orleans, 1803–1815." *Journal of Negro History* 38 (October 1953): 377–402.

Faye, Stanley. "Commodore Aury." *Louisiana Historical Quarterly* 24.3 (1941): 612–97.

———. "The Great Stroke of Pierre Laffite." *Louisiana Historical Quarterly* 23.3 (1940): 733–826.

———. "Privateersmen of the Gulf and Their Prizes." *Louisiana Historical Quarterly* 22.4 (1939): 1012–94.

———. "Privateers of Guadeloupe and Their Establishment in Barataria." *Louisiana Historical Quarterly* 23.2 (1940): 428–44.

Fernández, Raúl. "Popular Music: Worksong of the Caribbean." Conf. "Caribbean Theories: Culture, Identity and Nation." Claremont Colleges, Claremont, CA. April 1999.

Ferrer, Ada. "The Archive and the Atlantic's Haitian Revolution." *Tree of Liberty: Cultural Legacies of the Haitian Revolution in the Atlantic World.* Ed. Doris Lorraine Garraway. Charlottesville: University of Virginia Press, 2008. 21–40.

———. *Insurgent Cuba: Race, Nation, and Revolution, 1868–1898.* Chapel Hill: University of North Carolina Press, 1999.

———. "Speaking of Haiti: Slavery and Freedom in Cuban Slave Testimony." *The World of the Haitian Revolution.* Ed. David Geggus and Norman Fiering. Bloomington: University of Indiana Press, 2009. 223–47.

Fick, Carolyn. *The Making of Haiti: The Saint Domingue Revolution from Below.* Knoxville: University of Tennessee Press, 1990.

Fiehrer, Thomas. "From Quadrille to Stomp: The Creole Origins of Early Jazz." *Popular Music* 10.1 (1991): 21–38.

———. "Saint-Domingue/Haiti: Louisiana's Caribbean Connection." *Louisiana History* 30.4 (1989): 419–37.

Fischer, Sibylle. *Modernity Disavowed: Haiti and the Cultures of Slavery in the Age of Revolution.* Durham: Duke University Press, 2004.

Flores, Juan. *From Bomba to Hip-Hop: Puerto Rican Culture and Latino Identity.* New York: Columbia University Press, 2000. Popular Cultures, Everyday Lives.

Floyd, Samuel A. "Black Music in the Circum-Caribbean." *American Music* 17.1 (1999): 1–38.

———. *The Power of Black Music: Interpreting Its History from Africa to the United States.* New York: Oxford University Press, 1995.

Forbes, Ella. "African American Resistance to Colonization." *Journal of Black Studies* 21.2 (1990): 210–23.

Fortier, Louise Augustin. "Le bon vieux temps." *Ecrits Louisianais du dix-neuvième siècle: Nouvelles, contes et fables.* Ed. Gérard Labarre St. Martin and Jacqueline K. Voorhies. Baton Rouge: Louisiana State University Press, 1979. 49–61.

Foster, Frances Smith. "How Do You Solve a Problem Like Theresa?" *African American Review* 40.4 (2006): 631–45.

Fouchard, Jean. *Artistes et repertoires des scenes de Saint-Domingue.* Port-au-Prince: Editions Henri Deschamps, 1955.

———. *The Haitian Maroons: Liberty or Death*. Trans. A. Faulkner Watts. New York: E. W. Blyden Press, 1981.

———. *Le théâtre à Saint-Domingue*. Port-au-Prince: Editions Henri Deschamps, 1988. Regards sur le temps passé.

Fox, Claire F., ed. *Critical Perspectives and Emerging Models of Inter-American Studies*. Spec. issue of *Comparative American Studies* 2.1 (2005).

Franco, Franklyn. *Cultura, política e ideologiá*. Santo Domingo: Editora Nacional, 1974.

———. *Los negros, los mulatos y la nación Dominicana*. Santo Domingo: Editora Nacional, 1969.

Franco, José Luciano, ed. *Ensayos históricos*. Havana: Editorial de Ciencias Sociales, 1974.

Fresneau, Armand. *Theresa at San Domingo: A Tale of the Negro Insurrection of 1791*. Trans. Emma Geiger Magrath. Chicago: A. C. McClurg, 1889.

Frey, Sylvia R. *Come Shouting to Zion: African American Protestantism in the American South and British Caribbean to 1830*. Durham: University of North Carolina Press, 1998.

———. *Water from the Rock: Black Resistance in a Revolutionary Age*. Princeton: Princeton University Press, 1991.

Garraway, Doris. *The Libertine Colony: Creolization in the Early French Caribbean*. Durham: Duke University Press, 2005.

———, ed. *Tree of Liberty: Cultural Legacies of the Haitian Revolution in the Atlantic World*. Charlottesville: University of Virginia Press, 2008.

Garrigus, John D. *Before Haiti: Race and Citizenship in French Saint-Domingue*. New York: Palgrave Macmillan, 2006. The Americas in the Early Modern Atlantic World.

Gaspar, David Barry, and Darlene Clark Hine, eds. *More Than Chattel: Black Women and Slavery in the Americas*. Bloomington: Indiana University Press, 1996.

Gates, Henry Louis, and Nellie McKay, eds. *The Norton Anthology of African American Literature*. New York: W. W. Norton, 1997.

Gayarré, Charles Etienne. *History of Louisiana*. 4 vols. 1866. Gretna, LA: Pelican, 1974.

Geggus, David Patrick. "The Enigma of Jamaica in the 1790s: New Light on the Cause of Slave Rebellions." *William and Mary Quarterly* 3rd ser. 44.2 (1987): 274–99.

———. "The French and Haitian Revolutions, and Resistance to Slavery in the Americas: An Overview." *Revue Française d'Histoire d'Outre-Mer* 76 (1989): 107–24.

———. *Haitian Revolutionary Studies*. Bloomington: Indiana University Press, 2002.

———, ed. *The Impact of the Haitian Revolution in the Atlantic World*. Columbia: University of South Carolina Press, 2001.

———. "Slavery, War, and Revolution in the Greater Caribbean." *A Turbulent Time: The French Revolution and the Greater Caribbean*. Bloomington: Indiana University Press, 1997. 1–50.

————. *Slavery, War, and Revolution: The British Occupation of Saint Domingue, 1793–1798*. New York: Clarendon Press, 1982.

————. "The Slaves and Free Coloreds of Martinique during the Age of the French and Haitian Revolutions: Three Moments of Resistance." *The Lesser Antilles in the Age of European Expansion*. Ed. Robert Paquette. Gainesville: University Press of Florida, 1996. 280–301.

Geggus, David Patrick, and Norman Fiering, eds. *The World of the Haitian Revolution*. Bloomington: Indiana University Press, 2009.

Geggus, David Patrick, and David Barry Gaspar, eds. *A Turbulent Time: The French Revolution and the Greater Caribbean*. Bloomington: Indiana University Press, 1997.

Genovese, Eugene D. *From Rebellion to Revolution: Afro-American Slave Revolts in the Making of the Modern World*. Baton Rouge: Louisiana State University Press, 1981.

————. *Roll, Jordon, Roll: The World the Slaves Made*. New York: Vintage, 1976.

Gerassi-Navarro, Nina. *Pirate Novels: Fictions of Nation-Building in Spanish America*. Durham: Duke University Press, 1999.

Gerstin, Julian. "The Allure of Origins: Neo-African Dances in the French Caribbean and the Southern United States." *Just below South: The United States and the Caribbean*. Ed. Jessica Devi. Charlottesville: University of Virginia Press, 2007. 123–45.

————. "Traditional Music in a New Social Movement: The Renewal of Bèlè in Martinique." Diss. U. of California, Berkeley, 1996.

Gibson, J. *A New and Correct Map of the West Indies, Drawn from the Best Authorities*. London: A. Millar, and J. & R. Tonson, 1762.

Giddings, Joshua R. *The Exiles of Florida: Or, the Crimes Committed by Our Government against the Maroons, Who Fled from South Carolina and Other Slave States, Seeking Protection under Spanish Laws*. 1858. Baltimore: Black Classic Press, 1997.

Gillman, Susan. *Blood Talk: American Race Melodrama and the Culture of the Occult*. Chicago: University of Chicago Press, 2003.

Gilroy, Paul. *The Black Atlantic: Modernity and Double Consciousness*. Cambridge, MA: Harvard University Press, 1993.

Girard, Phillippe R. "Black Talleyrand: Toussaint Louverture's Diplomacy, 1798–1802." *William and Mary Quarterly* 66.1 (2009): 87–124.

Giraud, Marcel. *Histoire de la Louisiane française*. Paris: Presses Universitaires de France, 1953.

Glissant, Edouard. *Le discours Antillais*. Paris: Seuil, 1981.

————. *Poétique de la relation*. Paris: Gallimard, 1990.

Gomez, Michael. *Black Crescent: The Experience and Legacy of African Muslims in the Americas*. Cambridge: Cambridge University Press, 2005.

————. *Exchanging Our Country Marks: The Transformation of African Identities in the Colonial and Antebellum South*. Chapel Hill: University of North Carolina Press, 1998.

González, José Emilio. "Hostos y la idea de la Confederación Antillana." *Vi-

vir a Hostos. San Juan: Comité pro Celebración Sesquicentenario del Natalicio de Eugenio María de Hostos, 1989.

González, Raymundo. "El Comegente, una rebelión campesina al final del período colonial." *Homenaje a Emilio Cordero Michel*. Santo Domingo: Academica Dominicana de la Historia, 2004. 175–224.

Goudie, Sean X. *Creole America: The West Indies and the Formation of Literature and Culture in the New Republic*. Philadelphia: University of Pennsylvania Press, 2006.

Gouges, Olympe de. *Déclaration des droits de la femme et de la citoyenne*. Ed. Emanuèle Gaulier. Paris: Mille et une nuits, 2003.

Grasset de Saint-Sauveur, Jacques. *Encyclopédie des voyages*. Paris: n.p., 1795–96.

Greene, Jack P., and Philip D. Morgan, eds. *Atlantic History: A Critical Appraisal*. New York: Oxford University Press, 2009.

Groom, Winston. *Patriotic Fire: Andrew Jackson and Jean Laffite at the Battle of New Orleans*. New York: Alfred Knopf, 2006.

Gruesz, Kirsten Silva. *Ambassadors of Culture: The Transamerican Origins of Latino Writing*. Princeton: Princeton University Press, 2001.

———. "The Gulf of Mexico System and the 'Latinness' of New Orleans." *American Literary History* 18.3 (2006): 468–95.

Gruson, Bart. Liner notes. *Cuba: Contradanzas y danzones*. Nimbus Records, 1996.

Guterl, Matthew Pratt. *American Mediterranean: Southern Slaveholders in the Age of Emancipation*. Cambridge, MA: Harvard University Press, 2008.

Hall, Gwendolyn Midlo. *Africans in Colonial Louisiana: The Development of Afro-Creole Culture in the Eighteenth Century*. Baton Rouge: Louisiana State University Press, 1992.

———. *Slavery and African Ethnicities in the Americas: Restoring the Links*. Chapel Hill: University of North Carolina Press, 2005.

Hall, Stuart. "Cultural Identity and Diaspora." *Identity, Community, Culture, Difference*. Ed. Jonathan Rutherford. London: Lawrence and Wishart, 1990.

Hamel, Reginald. *Louis-Moreau Gottschalk et son temps (1829–1869)*. Montreal: Guérin, 1996.

Hanger, Kimberly. *Bounded Lives, Bounded Places: Free Black Society in Colonial New Orleans, 1769–1803*. Durham: Duke University Press, 1997.

———. "Free Blacks in Spanish New Orleans." *Against the Odds: Free Blacks in the Slave Societies of the Americas*. Ed. Jane Landers. London: Frank Cass, 1996. 44–64.

Hartman, Saidya. *Lose Your Mother: A Journey along the Atlantic Slave Route*. New York: Farrar, Straus and Giroux, 2007.

———. *Scenes of Subjection: Terror, Slavery, and Self-Making in Nineteenth-Century America*. Oxford: Oxford University Press, 1997.

Hazaël-Massieux, Marie-Christine. "A propos de *Jeannot et Thérèse*: Une traduction du Devin du village en créole du XVIIIe siècle." *Creolica*, September 8, 2005. <http://www.creolica.net/A-propos-de-Jeannot-et-Therese-une>.

Hearn, Lafcadio. *Two Years in the French West Indies.* New York: Harper and Brothers, 1889.

Heinl, Nancy G., Michael Heinl, and Robert D. Heinl. *Written in Blood: The History of the Haitian People, 1492–1995.* 2nd ed. Lanham: University Press of America, 1996.

Helg, Aline. *Liberty and Equality in Caribbean Colombia, 1770–1835.* Chapel Hill: University of North Carolina Press, 2004.

———. *Our Rightful Share: The Afro-Cuban Struggle for Equality, 1896–1912.* Chapel Hill: University of North Carolina Press, 1995.

Heneken, T. S. (Britannicus). *The Dominican Republic and the Emperor Soulouque: Being Remarks and Strictures on the Misstatements and a Refutation of the Calumnies of M. D'Alaux in the article under the Above Title in the Revue des Deux Mondes.* Philadelphia: T. R. Collins, 1852.

Herdeck, Donald, ed. *Caribbean Writers: A Bio-Bibliographical-Critical Encyclopedia.* Washington, DC: Three Continents Press, 1979.

Heredia y Mieses, Jose Francisco de. "Informe presentado al muy ilustrísimo ayuntamiento de Santo Domingo, capital de la isla Española, en 1812." Rodríguez Demorizi, *Invasiones haitianas* 161–72.

Hill, Donald. "West African and Haitian Influences on the Ritual and Popular Music of Carriacou, Trinidad and Cuba." *Black Music Research Journal* 18.1/2 (1998): 183–201.

Hine, Darlene Clark, and Jacqueline McLeod, eds. *Crossing Boundaries: Comparative History of Black People in Diaspora.* Bloomington: Indiana University Press, 1999.

Hirsch, Arnold, and Joseph Logsdon, eds. *Creole New Orleans: Race and Americanization.* Baton Rouge: Louisiana State University Press, 1992.

Hobsbawm, Eric J. *The Age of Revolution: Europe, 1789–1848.* 1962. London: Abacus, 2008.

Holly, James Theodore, and J. Dennis Harris. *Black Separatism and the Caribbean, 1860.* Ed. Howard H. Bell. Ann Arbor: University of Michigan Press, 1970.

Holmes, Jack. "The Abortive Slave Revolt at Pointe Coupée, Louisiana, 1795." *Louisiana History* 11.4 (1970): 341–62.

Howard, David. *Coloring the Nation: Race and Ethnicity in the Dominican Republic.* Oxford: Signal Books, 2001.

Hulme, Peter. *Colonial Encounters.* London: Methuen, 1986.

———. "Postcolonial Theory and Early America: An Approach from the Caribbean." *Possible Pasts: Becoming Colonial in Early America.* Ed. Robert Blair St. George. Ithaca: Cornell University Press, 2000. 33–48.

Humanitas. *Reflections on Slavery; with Recent Evidence of Inhumanity, Occasioned by the Melancholy Death of Romain, a French Negro.* Philadelphia: R. Cochran, 1803.

Hunt, Alfred. *Haiti's Influence on Antebellum America: Slumbering Volcano in the Caribbean.* Baton Rouge: Louisiana State University Press, 1988.

Hunter, Theresa. *The Saga of Jean Lafitte: Word Portraits of a Picturesque Southern Pirate: History and Romance of the Texas Coast.* San Antonio, TX: Naylor, 1940.

Hutton, Frankie. *The Early Black Press in America, 1827 to 1860.* Westport, CT: Greenwood Press, 1993.

Idylles, ou, Essais de poësie créole par un colon de St. Domingue. New York: De l'imprimerie par Hopkins and Seymour, 1804.

Incháustegui, Joaquin Marino. *Documentos para estudio: Marco de la época y problemas del tratado de Basilea de 1795, en la parte española de Santo Domingo.* Buenos Aires: Academia Dominicana de la Historia, 1957.

Ingersoll, Thomas. "Free Blacks in a Slave Society: New Orleans, 1718–1812." *William and Mary Quarterly* 48.2 (1991): 173–200.

Ingraham, J. H. *Lafitte: The Pirate of the Gulf.* New York: Harper and Brothers, 1836.

In Motion: The African-American Migration Experience. Ed. Schomburg Center for Research in Black Culture. <http://www.inmotionaame.org/home.cfm>.

Inoa, Orlando. *Bibliografía haitiana en la República Dominicana.* Rio Piedras: Departamento de Historia, Universidad de Puerto Rico, 1994.

Jackson, Maurice, and Jacqueline Bacon, eds. *African Americans and the Haitian Revolution: Selected Essays and Historical Documents.* New York: Routledge, 2010.

Jacobs, Donald, ed. *Antebellum Black Newspapers.* Westport, CT: Greenwood Press, 1976.

James, C. L. R. *Black Jacobins: Toussaint L'Ouverture and the San Domingo Revolution.* 1939. 2nd ed. New York: Vintage Books, 1989.

James, Joel, José Millet, and Alexis Alarcón. *El vodú en Cuba.* Santo Domingo: CEDEE, 1992.

James, Marlon. *The Book of Night Women.* New York: Riverhead Books, 2009.

Jennings, Lawrence C. "Cyrille Bissette, Radical Black French Abolitionist." *French History* 9.1 (1995): 48–66.

———. "Slavery and the Venality of the July Monarchy Press." *French Historical Studies* 17.4 (1992): 957–78.

Jenson, Deborah. *Beyond the Slave Narrative: Politics, Sex and Manuscripts in the Haitian Revolution.* Liverpool: Liverpool University Press, 2011.

———. "Mimetic Mastery and Colonial Mimicry in the First Franco-Antillean Creole Anthology." *Yale Journal of Criticism* 17.1 (2004): 83–106.

Jiménez, Ramón Darío. *El Caballo de Troya: Gobernarán los haitianos a los dominicanos, otra vez?* San Juan: Impresos Félix, 1996.

Johnson, Charles [Daniel Defoe]. *A General History of the Pyrates.* 1724. Ed. Manuel Schonhorn. Columbia: University of South Carolina Press, 1972.

Johnson, Sara. "The Integration of Hispaniola: A Reappraisal of Haitian-Dominican Relations in the Nineteenth and Twentieth Centuries." *Journal of Haitian Studies* 8.2 (2002): 4–29.

———. "'You Should Give Them Blacks to Eat': Cuban Bloodhounds and the Waging of an Inter-American War of Torture and Terror." *American Quarterly* 61.1 (2009): 65–92.

Johnson, Walter. "On Agency." *Journal of Social History* 37.1 (2003): 113–24.

———. *Soul by Soul: Life inside the Antebellum Slave Market.* Cambridge, MA: Harvard University Press, 1999.

Jones, Edward P. *The Known World.* New York: Amistad, 2003.

Jung, Moon-Ho. *Coolies and Cane: Race, Labor, and Sugar in the Age of Emancipation.* Baltimore: Johns Hopkins University Press, 2006.

Kadish, Doris, ed. *Slavery in the Caribbean Francophone World: Distant Voices, Forgotten Acts, Forged Identities.* Athens: University of Georgia Press, 2000.

Kale, Madhavi. *Fragments of Empire: Capital, Slavery, and Indian Indentured Labor in the British Caribbean.* Philadelphia: University of Pennsylvania Press, 1998.

Kelley, Robin D. G. "'But a Local Phase of a World Problem': Black History's Global Vision, 1883–1950." *Journal of American History* 86 (December 1999): 1045–77.

Kendall, John. "The Huntsmen of Black Ivory." *Louisiana Historical Quarterly* 24.1 (1941): 341–68.

Kennedy, Melvin. "The Bissette Affair and the French Colonial Question." *Journal of Negro History* 45.1 (1960): 1–10.

King, Nicole. *C. L. R. James and Creolization: Circles of Influence.* Jackson: University Press of Mississippi, 2001.

King, Stewart R. *Blue Coat or Powdered Wig: Free People of Color in Pre-Revolutionary Saint Domingue.* Athens: University of Georgia Press, 2001.

Kmen, Henry. *Music in New Orleans: The Formative Years, 1791–1841.* Baton Rouge: Louisiana State University Press, 1966.

Knight, Franklin. *The Caribbean: The Genesis of a Fragmented Nationalism.* 2nd ed. New York: Oxford University Press, 1990.

———. "The Haitian Revolution." *American Historical Review* 105.1 (2000): 103–15.

———. "The Haitian Revolution and the Notion of Human Rights." *Journal of the Historical Society* 5.3 (2005): 391–416.

———. *Slave Society in Cuba during the Nineteenth Century.* Madison: University of Wisconsin Press, 1970.

Knight, Franklin W., and Peggy K. Liss, eds. *Atlantic Port Cities: Economy, Culture and Society in the Atlantic World, 1650–1850.* Knoxville: University of Tennessee Press, 1991.

Kriz, Kay Dian. *Slavery, Sugar, and the Culture of Refinement.* New Haven: Paul Mellon Centre for Studies in British Art, 2008.

Kutzinski, Vera. "American Literary History as Spatial Practice." *American Literary History* 4.3 (1992): 550–57.

———. "Borders and Bodies; The United States, America and the Caribbean." *New Centennial Review* 1.2 (2001): 53–86.

———. *Sugar's Secrets: Race and the Erotics of Cuban Nationalism.* Charlottesville: University Press of Virginia, 1993. New World Studies.

Labat, Jean Baptiste. *Nouvelle relation de l'Afrique occidentale contenant une description exacte du Senegal et des pais situés entre le Cap-Blanc et la rivière de Serrelionne . . . ; L'histoire naturelle de ces pais, les différentes nations qui y sont répandues, leurs religions et leurs moeurs avec l'état ancient et present des companies qui y font le commerce.* Paris: Chez G. Cavelier, 1728.

Lachance, Paul F. "The 1809 Immigration of Saint-Domingue Refugees to New Orleans: Reception, Integration and Impact." Brasseaux and Conrad 245–84.

———. "The Politics of Fear: French Louisianans and the Slave Trade, 1786–1809." *Plantation Society* 1 (June 1979): 162–97.

Laffite, or the Baratarian Chief: A Tale Founded in Facts. New York: n.p., 1828.

Lagarde, François, ed. *The French in Texas.* Austin: University of Texas Press, 2003.

Laguerre, Michel. *Diasporic Citizenship: Haitian Americans in Transnational America.* New York: St. Martin's Press, 1998.

Lamore, Jean, ed. *Les Français dans l'orient cubain, actes du colloque international de Santiago de Cuba, 16–18 Avril 1991.* Bordeaux: Maison des Pays Ibériques, 1993.

Landers, Jane. ed. *Against the Odds: Free Blacks in the Slave Societies of the Americas.* London: Frank Cass, 1996.

———. *Atlantic Creoles in the Age of Revolutions.* Cambridge, MA: Harvard University Press, 2010.

———. *Black Society in Spanish Florida.* Urbana: University of Illinois Press, 1999.

Landes, Joan B. "Representing the Body Politic: The Paradox of Gender in the Graphic Politics of the French Revolution." *Rebel Daughters: Women and the French Revolution.* Ed. Sara E. Melzer and Leslie W. Rabine. Oxford: Oxford University Press, 1992. 15–37.

Lanusse, Armand. *Les cenelles: Choix de poésies indigènes.* 1845. Nendeln: Kraus Reprint, 1971.

Largey, Michael. "Composing a Haitian Cultural Identity: Haitian Elites, African Ancestry, and Musical discourse." *Black Music Research Journal* 14.2 (1994): 99–117.

Laslett, Peter. *The World We Have Lost: England before the Industrial Age.* New York: Charles Scribner's Sons, 1965.

Latour, Arsène Lacarrière. *Historical Memoir of the War in West Florida and Louisiana in 1814–1815.* 1816. Gainesville: University of Florida Press, 1964.

Lazo, Rodrigo. *Writing to Cuba: Filibustering and Cuban Exiles in the United States.* Chapel Hill: University of North Carolina Press, 2005.

Le Gardeur, René. *The First New Orleans Theater, 1792–1803.* New Orleans: Leeward Books, 1963.

Lemmon, Alfred E., et al. *Common Routes: St. Domingue-Louisiana.* New Orleans: Historic New Orleans Collection, 2006.

Lemoine, Maurice. *Bitter Sugar.* London: Banner Press, 1985.

Lespinasse, Colette. "Prácticas culturales en la frontera." *Hacia una nueva visión de la frontera y de las relaciones fronterizas.* Ed. Rubén Silié and Carlos Segura. Santo Domingo: FLASCO, 2002. 269–75.

Levander, Caroline F., and Robert S. Levine, eds. *Hemispheric American Studies.* New Brunswick: Rutgers University Press, 2008.

Levine, Lawrence W. *Black Culture and Black Consciousness*. London: Oxford University Press, 1977.

Levine, Robert S. *Dislocating Race and Nation: Episodes in Nineteenth-Century American Literary Nationalism*. Chapel Hill: University of North Carolina Press, 2008.

Lewin, Olive. *Rock It Come Over: The Folk Music of Jamaica*. Kingston: University of the West Indies Press, 2000.

Lewis, Gordon. *Main Currents in Caribbean Thought: The Historical Evolution of Caribbean Society in Its Ideological Aspects, 1492–1900*. Baltimore: Johns Hopkins University Press, 1983.

———. "Migration and Caribbean Consciousness." *Migration and Caribbean Cultural Identity: Selected Papers from Conference Celebrating the 50th Anniversary of the Center*. Ed. Center for Latin American Studies. Gainesville: Center for Latin American Studies, University of Florida, 1981.

Lieth-Philipp, Margot. "Bamboula: Historical, Ethnological and Linguistic Evidence for a Forgotten Caribbean Music." *Ethnomusicology and the Historical Dimension*. Ludwigsburg: Philipp, 1989. 59–70.

Liljegren, Ernest. "Jacobinism in Spanish Louisiana, 1792–1797." *Louisiana History* 22 (1939): 47–97.

Linebaugh, Peter, and Marcus Rediker. *The Many-Headed Hydra: Sailors, Slaves, Commoners, and the Hidden History of the Revolutionary Atlantic*. Boston: Beacon Press, 2000.

Lionnet, Françoise. "Cultivating Mere Gardens? Comparative Francophonies, Postcolonial Studies, and Transnational Feminisms." *Comparative Literature in an Age of Globalization*. Ed. Haun Saussy. Baltimore: Johns Hopkins University Press, 2006. 100–13.

Locke, Alain, ed. *The New Negro*. 1925. New York: Atheneum, 1968.

Logan, Rayford W. *The Diplomatic Relations of the United States with Haiti, 1776–1891*. Chapel Hill: University of North Carolina Press, 1941.

Lowe, Lisa. "Autobiography Out of Empire." *Small Axe: A Caribbean Journal of Criticism* 28 (March 2009): 98–111.

Lukács, Georg. *The Historical Novel*. Lincoln: University of Nebraska Press, 1962.

Lundahl, Mats. "Haitian Migration to the Dominican Republic." *The Haitian Economy, Man, Land and Markets*. New York: St. Martin's Press, 1983.

Luque de Sanchez, María Dolores. "Colons français refugiés à Porto Rico au cours de la période révolutionnaire." *De la Révolution française aux révolutions créoles et nègres*. Ed. Michel L. Martin and Alain Yacou. Paris: Editions Caribéennes, 1989. 41–48.

Madiou, Thomas. *Histoire d'Haiti*. 1847–48. Port au Prince: Editions Henri Deschamps, 1989.

Maingot, Anthony P. "Haiti and the Terrified Consciousness of the Caribbean." *Oostindie* 53–80.

Maldonado-Denis. Manuel. *Eugenio María de Hostos y el pensamiento social iberoamericano*. México: Fondo de Cultura Económica, 1992.

Manzano, Juan Francisco. *Autobiografía de un esclavo*. 1937. Bilingual ed.

Trans. Evelyn Picon Garfield and Ivan Schulman. Introd. Ivan Schulman. Detroit: Wayne State University Press, 1996.

Mariñez, Pablo. *Relaciones dominico-haitianas y raices historico-culturales africanas en la República Dominicana: Bibliografía basica*. Santo Domingo: Editora Universitaria UASD, 1986.

Marshall, Gene, trans. The *Memoirs of Jean Laffite from Le Journal de Jean Laffite*. Philadelphia: Xlibris, 2000.

Martí, José. *Obras completas de José Martí*. Vol. 7. Havana: Centro de Estudios Martianos, 2001.

Martinez-Fernández, Luis. "The Sword and the Crucifix: Church-State Relations and Nationality in the Nineteenth-Century Dominican Republic." *Latin American Research Review* 30.1 (1995): 69–93.

Mathews, Thomas. "The Project for a Confederation of the Greater Antilles." *Caribbean Historical Review* 3/4 (1954): 70–107.

Matibag, Eugenio. *Haitian-Dominican Counterpoint: Nation, Race, and State on Hispaniola*. New York: Palgrave, 2003.

Matory, J. Lorand. *Black Atlantic Religion: Tradition, Transnationalism, and Matriarchy in the Afro-Brazilian Candomblé*. Princeton: Princeton University Press, 2005.

Maurer, Bill. "Caribbean Dance: Resistance, Colonial Discourse, and Subjugated Knowledges." *New West Indian Guide / Nieuwe West-Indische Gids* 65.1/2 (1991): 1–26.

———. "Movement, History and Theory: Contemporary Dance Scholarship in the Corpora of Power." *Plantation Society in the Americas* 5 (1997): 67–87.

Maximin, Daniel. *L'isolé soleil*. Paris: Editions du Seuil, 1981.

McClellan, James. *Colonialism and Science: Saint Domingue in the Old Regime*. Baltimore: Johns Hopkins University Press, 1992.

McClennen, Sophia A. "Inter-American Studies or Imperial American Studies." *Comparative American Studies* 3.4 (2005): 393–413.

McConnell, Roland. *Negro Troops of Antebellum Louisiana: A History of the Battalion of Free Men of Color*. Baton Rouge: Louisiana State University Press, 1968.

McHenry, Elizabeth. *Forgotten Readers: Recovering the Lost History of African American Literary Societies*. Durham: Duke University Press, 2002.

McIntosh, M. E., and B. C. Weber, eds. *Une correspondance familiale au temps des troubles de Saint-Domingue, Lettres du Marquis et de la Marquise de Rouvray à leur fille, Saint-Domingue-Etats Unis, 1791–1796*. Paris: Société de l'Histoire des Colonies Françaises et Librairie Larose, 1959.

Melzer, Sara E., and Leslie W. Rabine, eds. *Rebel Daughters: Women and the French Revolution*. Oxford: Oxford University Press, 1992.

Miller, Floyd J. *The Search for a Black Nationality: Black Emigration and Colonization, 1787–1863*. Urbana: University of Illinois Press, 1975.

Mintz, Sidney W., and Richard Price. *The Birth of African-American Culture: An Anthropological Perspective*. Boston: Beacon Press, 1992.

Mir, Pedro. "Acerca de las tentativas históricas de unificación de la isla de

Santo Domingo." *Problemas dominicos-haitianos y del Caribe*. Ed. Gerald Pierre-Charles. Mexico: Universidad Nacional Autónoma, 1973.

Mohammed, Patricia. "The Visual Grammars of Gender, Race and Class in the Caribbean in the Paintings of Brunias, Bellisario, Landaluze and Cazabon, Four Eighteenth- and Nineteenth-Century Painters." Proc. of Association of Historians Conference. Martinique: Université Antilles Guyane, Groupe de Recherche AIP-CARDH, 1997.

Mohl, Raymond A. "A Scotsman in Cuba, 1811–1812." *Americas* 29.2 (1972): 232–45.

Moitt, Bernard. *Women and Slavery in the French Antilles, 1635–1848*. Bloomington: Indiana University Press, 2001.

Moll, Herman. "A Map of the West Indies etc. or New Spain; Also ye trade winds, and ye several tracts made by ye galeons and flota from place to place." *Atlas Minor of a Set of Sixty Two New and Correct Maps of All Parts of the World*. London: Thomas and John Bowles, ca. 1730.

Monte y Tejada, Antonio del. *Historia de Santo Domingo*. Ciudad Trujillo: Biblioteca Dominicana, 1952–53.

Morales, Salvador. "Martí en la génesis de la solidaridad antillana." *Casa de las Américas* 90 (1975): 43–57.

Morales Carrion, Arturo. "El reflujo en Puerto Rico de la crisis dominico-haitiana, 1791–1805." *Eme Eme* 5.27 (1976): 19–39.

Moreau de Saint-Méry, Médéric Louis Elie. *A Civilization That Perished: The Last Years of White Colonial Rule in Haiti*. Trans., abr., and ed. Ivor D. Spencer. Trans. of *Description topographique, physique, civile, politique et historique de la partie francaise de l'ile de Saint-Domingue*. Lanham: University Press of America, 1985.

———. *Description topographique, physique, civile, politique et historique de la partie française de l'ile de Saint-Domingue*. Philadelphia: Chez Moreau, 1797–98.

———. *Description topographique, physique, civile, politique et historique de la partie française de l'ile de Saint-Domingue*. New ed. 3 vols. Introd. Marcel Dorigny. Philadelphia: Chez Moreau, 1796–97. Saint-Denis: Société française d'histoire d'outre mer, 2004.

———. *Moreau de St. Méry's American Journey, 1793–1798*. Trans. and ed. Kenneth and Anna M. Roberts. Garden City, NY: Doubleday, 1947.

———. *Topographical and Political Description of the Spanish Part of Santo Domingo*. Trans. William Cobbett. Philadelphia: Chez Moreau, 1796.

Morénas, Joseph Elzéar. *Précis historique de la traite des noirs et de l'esclavage colonial, contenant: l'origine de la traite, ses progrès, son état actuel, et un exposé des horreurs produits par le despotisme des colons*. Paris: n.p., 1828.

Morrison, Toni. *Playing in the Dark: Whiteness and the Literary Imagination*. New York: Vintage, 1993.

Moya, Casimiro N. de. "Historia del Comegente." Rodríguez Demorizi, *Tradiciones* 175–95.

Moya Pons, Frank. *La dominación haitiana, 1822–1844*. Santo Domingo: Universidad Católica Madre y Maestra, 1978.

———. *The Dominican Republic: A National History.* New Rochelle, NY: Hispaniola Books, 1995.

———. "The Land Question in Haiti and Santo Domingo: The Socio-Political Context of the Transition from Slavery to Free Labor, 1801–1843." *Between Slavery and Free Labor.* Ed. Manuel Moreno Fraginals, Frank Moya Pons, and Stanley Engerman. Baltimore: Johns Hopkins University Press, 1985. 181–214.

Munro, Martin. *Different Drummers: Rhythms and Race in the Americas.* Berkeley: University of California Press, 2010.

Munro, Martin, and Elizabeth Walcott-Hackshaw, eds. *Reinterpreting the Haitian Revolution and its Cultural Aftershocks.* Kingston: University of the West Indies Press, 2006.

Nadal, Marie-Josée, and Gérald Bloncourt. *La peinture haïtienne.* Paris: Editions Nathan, 1986.

Naro, Nancy, ed. *Blacks, Coloureds and National Identity in Nineteenth-Century Latin America.* London: Institute of Latin American Studies, University of London, 2003.

Nash, Gary B. *The Forgotten Fifth: African Americans in the Age of Revolution.* Cambridge, MA: Harvard University Press, 2006.

"El Negro Incognito o El Comegente." Rodríguez Demorizi, *Tradiciones* 269–75.

Nesbitt, Nick. *Universal Emancipation: The Haitian Revolution and the Radical Enlightenment.* Charlottesville: University of Virginia Press, 2008.

Nettleford, Rex. *Dance Jamaica: Cultural Definition and Artistic Discovery: The National Dance Theatre Company of Jamaica, 1962–1983.* New York: Grove Press, 1985.

Nicholls, David. *From Dessalines to Duvalier: Race, Colour and National Independence in Haiti.* 3rd ed. New Brunswick: Rutgers University Press, 1996.

———. "Pompée Valentin Vastey: Royalist and Revolutionary." *Revista de Historia de América* 109 (1990): 129–43.

———. "Work of Combat: Mulatto Historians and the Haitian Past, 1847–1867." *Journal of Interamerican Studies and World Affairs* 16.1 (1974): 15–38.

Nugent, Maria. *Lady Nugent's Journal of Her Residence in Jamaica from 1801 to 1805.* 4th ed. Kingston: Institute of Jamaica, 1966.

Nwankwo, Ifeoma Kiddoe. *Black Cosmopolitanism: Racial Consciousness and Transnational Identity in the Nineteenth-Century Americas.* Philadelphia: University of Pennsylvania Press, 2005.

Obadele-Starks, Ernest. *Freebooters and Smugglers: The Foreign Slave Trade in the United States after 1808.* Fayetteville: University of Arkansas Press, 2007.

Olson, R. Dale. "French Pirates and Privateers in Texas." *The French in Texas.* Ed. François Lagarde. Austin: University of Texas Press, 2003. 60–78.

Oostindie, Gert, ed. *Ethnicity in the Caribbean: Essays in Honor of Harry Hoetink.* London: Macmillan Education, 1996.

Orians, G. Harrison. "Lafitte: A Bibliographical Note." *American Literature* 9.3 (1937): 351–53.

Ortiz, Fernando. *Los bailes y el teatro de los negros en el folklore de Cuba.* 1951. Havana: Editorial Letras Cubanas, 1981.

———. *Los instrumentos de la música afrocubana.* 5 vols. Havana: Publicaciones del Ministerio de Educación, 1952.

Ott, Thomas. *The Haitian Revolution, 1789–1804.* Knoxville: University of Tennessee Press, 1973.

Palaiseau, Mlle de. *Histoire de mesdemoiselles de Saint-Janvier: Les deux seules blanches conservées à Saint-Domingue.* Paris: Chez J.-J. Blaise, 1812.

Palmié, Stephan. "Conventionalization, Distortion and Plagiarism in the Historiography of Afro Caribbean Religion in New Orleans." *Creoles and Cajuns.* Ed. W. Binder. Frankfurt: Peter Lang, 1998. 315–44.

Paquette, Robert L. *Sugar Is Made with Blood: The Conspiracy of La Escalera and the Conflict between Empires over Slavery in Cuba.* Middletown, CT: Wesleyan University Press, 1990.

Paravisini-Gebert, Lizabeth. "The Haitian Revolution in Interstices and Shadows: A Re-reading of Alejo Carpentier's *The Kingdom of This World.*" *Research in African Literatures* 35.2 (Summer 2004): 114-127.

Patterson, Orlando. "Migration in Caribbean Societies: Socioeconomic and Symbolic Resource." *Human Migration: Patterns and Policies.* Ed. William McNeill and Ruth Adams. Bloomington: Indiana University Press, 1978. 106–45.

———. *Slavery and Social Death: A Comparative Study.* Cambridge, MA: Harvard University Press, 1982.

Peabody, Sue, and Tyler Stovall, eds. *The Color of Liberty: Histories of Race in France.* Durham: Duke University Press, 2003.

Pedro, Alberto. "La semana santa haitiano-cubana." *Etnología y Folklore* 4 (1967): 49–79.

Penn, Irvine Garland. *The Afro-American Press and Its Editors.* Springfield, MA: Willey, 1891.

Pérez, Luis. "French Refugees in New Orleans in 1809." *Publications of the Southern Historical Association* 9 (1905): 293–310.

Pérez de la Riva, Juan. "La implantación francesa en la cunca superior del Cauto." *El barracón y otros ensayos.* Havana: Editorial de Ciencias Sociales, 1975. 361–433.

Pérez Firmat, Gustavo, ed. *Do the Americas Have a Common Literature?* Durham: Duke University Press, 1990.

Pérez-Rolón, Jorge. Liner notes. *Puerto Rico in Washington.* Smithsonian Folkways, 1996.

Pérotin-Dumon, Anne. "Révolutionnaires français et royalistes espagnols dans les Antilles." *Revue Française d'Histoire d'Outre-Mer* 56 (1989): 125–58.

Philip, Maxwell. *Emmanuel Appadocca; or Blighted Life. A Tale of the Boucaneers.* London: C. J. Skeet, 1854.

Philoctète, René. *Le peuple des terre mêlées.* Port au Prince: Editions Henri Deschamps, 1989.

Plummer, Brenda Gayle. "Firmin and Martí at the Intersection of Pan-Americanism and Pan-Africanism." *Jose Martí's Our America: From National to Hemispheric Cultural Studies*. Ed. Raul Fernández and Jeffrey Belnap. Durham: Duke University Press, 1998.

Polk, Patrick. "Sacred Banners and the Divine Cavalry Charge." Cosentino, *Sacred Arts* 325–47.

Ponce, Nicolas. *Recueil de vues des lieux principaux de la colonie françoise de Saint-Domingue*. Paris: Chez Moreau de Saint-Méry and M. Phelipeau, ca. 1791.

Popkin, Jeremy. "Facing Racial Revolution: Captivity Narratives of the Saint-Domingue Insurrection." *Eighteenth-Century Studies* 36.4 (2003): 511–33.

———. *Facing Racial Revolution: Eyewitness Accounts of the Haitian Insurrection*. Chicago: University of Chicago Press, 2007.

———. *Revolutionary News: The Press in France, 1789–1799*. Durham: Duke University Press, 1990.

Powell, Edward Alexander. *Gentlemen Rovers*. New York: C. Scribner's Sons, 1913.

———. *Some Forgotten Heroes and Their Place in American History*. New York: C. Scribner's Sons, 1922.

Powers, David M. "The French Musical Theater: Maintaining Control in Caribbean Colonies in the Eighteenth Century." *Black Music Research Journal* 18.1/2 (1998): 229–40.

Pratt, Mary Louise. *Imperial Eyes: Travel Writing and Transculturation*. London: Routledge, 1992.

Price, Richard. *Maroon Societies: Rebel Slave Communities in the Americas*. Baltimore: Johns Hopkins University Press, 1979.

———. "On the Miracle of Creolization." *Afro-Atlantic Dialogues: Anthropology in the Diaspora*. Ed. Kevin A. Yelvington. Santa Fe, NM: School of American Research Press, 2006. 113–45.

Price-Mars, Jean. *La République d'Haïti et la République Dominicaine*. 3 vols. Port-au-Prince, 1953.

Prince, Mary. *The History of Mary Prince: A West Indian Slave*. Ed. Moira Ferguson. 1831. Ann Arbor: University of Michigan Press, 1997.

Prudent, Lambert-Félix. *Des baragouins à la langue antillaise*. Paris: Editions Caribéennes, 1980.

Puig, Max. "La migración haitiana en la República Dominicana." *Anales del Caribe* 9 (1989): 253–60.

Putney Beers, Henry. *French and Spanish Records of Louisiana: A Bibliographic Guide to Archive and Manuscript Sources*. Baton Rouge: Louisiana State University Press, 1989.

Quilly, Geoff, and Kay Dian Kriz, eds. *An Economy of Colour: Visual Culture and the Atlantic World, 1660–1830*. Manchester: Manchester University Press, 2003.

Quintero Rivera, Angel. *Salsa, sabor y control: Sociología de la música tropical*. México: Siglo Veintiuno Editores, 1998.

———. "The Somatology of Manners in the Hispanic Caribbean." *Oostindie* 152–81.

Rainsford, Marcus. *An Historical Account of the Black Empire of Hayti, Comprehending a View of the Principal Transactions in the Revolution of Santo Domingo; With Its Antient and Modern State.* London: James Cundee, 1805.

Ramos Mattei, Andrés. *Betances en el ciclo revolucionario antillano: 1867–1875.* San Juan: Instituto de Cultura Puertorriqueña, 1987.

Ramsay, Jack. *Jean Laffite: Prince of Pirates.* Austin, TX: Eakin Press, 1996.

Ramsey, Guthrie. *Race Music: Black Cultures from Bebop to Hip-Hop.* Berkeley: University of California Press, 2003.

Ranston, Jackie. *Belisario: Sketches of Character. A Historical Biography of a Jamaican Artist.* Kingston: Mill Press, 2008.

Read, Martha. *Monima; or, The Beggar Girl. A Novel, Founded on Fact. Written by a Lady of Philadelphia.* Philadelphia: Eaken and Mecum, 1803.

Rediker, Marcus. *Between the Devil and the Deep Blue Sea: Merchant Seamen, Pirates, and the Anglo-American Maritime World, 1700–1750.* Cambridge: Cambridge University Press, 2006.

Redpath, James. *A Guide to Hayti.* Boston: Haytian Bureau of Emigration, 1860.

Reis, João. *Slave Rebellion in Brazil: The Muslim Uprising of 1835 in Bahia.* Baltimore: Johns Hopkins Press, 1995.

Rhys, Jean. *The Wide Sargasso Sea.* London: Deutsch, 1966.

Richardson, Bonham. "Caribbean Migrations, 1838–1985." *The Modern Caribbean.* Ed. Franklin Knight and Colin Palmer. Chapel Hill: University of North Carolina Press, 1989. 203–28.

Rigaud, Milo. *Vè-Vè: Diagrammes rituels du Voudou.* New York: French and European Publications, 1992.

Roach, Joseph. *Cities of the Dead: Circum-Atlantic Performance.* New York: Columbia University Press, 1996.

Roberts, John Storm. *Black Music of Two Worlds: African, Caribbean, Latin, and African-American Traditions.* 2nd ed. New York: Schirmer Books, 1998.

———. *The Latin Tinge: The Impact of Latin American Music on the United States.* New York: Oxford University Press, 1979.

Rodríguez Demorizi, Emilio, ed. *La caricatura y dibujo en Santo Domingo.* Santo Domingo: Editora Taller, 1977.

———, ed. *Invasiones haitianas de 1801, 1805 y 1822.* Ciudad Trujillo: Ed. del Caribe, 1955.

———. *Música y baile en Santo Domingo.* Santo Domingo: Librería Hispaniola, 1971.

———. *Pintura y escultura en Santo Domingo.* Santo Domingo: Librería Hispaniola, 1972.

———, ed. *Poesía popular dominicana.* Vol. 1. Ciudad Trujillo: Editorial La Nación, 1938.

———, ed. *Tradiciones y cuentos dominicanos.* Santo Domingo: Julio D. Postigo e hijos Editores, 1969.

Rosemain, Jacqueline. *La musique dans la société antillaise: 1635–1902, Martinique, Guadeloupe.* Paris: L'Harmattan, 1986. Collections Recherches et documents.

Rothman, Adam. *Slave Country: American Expansion and the Origins of the Deep South*. Cambridge, MA: Harvard University Press, 2005.

Rowe, John Carlos. *Literary Culture and U.S. Imperialism*. Oxford: Oxford University Press, 2000.

———. *The New American Studies*. Minneapolis: University of Minnesota Press, 2002. Critical American Studies Series.

Rowland, Dunbar, ed. *Official Letter Books of W. C. C. Claiborne, 1801–1816*. 6 vols. Jackson, MI: State Department of Archives and History, 1917.

Ryan, Marveta. "Border-Line Anxiety: Dominican National Identity in the 'Diálogo cantado." *Afro-Hispanic Review* 20.2 (2001): 23–33.

Ryman, Cheryl. "The Jamaican Heritage in Dance." *Jamaica Journal* 44 (1981): 3–14.

Sagás, Ernesto. *Race and Politics in the Dominican Republic*. Gainesville: University Press of Florida, 2000.

Saint-Domingue, ou Histoire des ses révolutions, contenant le récit effroyable des divisions, des troubles, des ravages, des meurtres, des incendies, des dévastations et des massacres qui eurent lieu dans cette île, depuis 1789 jusqu'à la perte de la colonie. Paris: Chez Tiger, Imprimeur-librairie, 1815.

Saldívar, José. *The Dialectics of Our America: Genealogy, Cultural Critique, and Literary History*. Durham: Duke University Press, 1991.

Saldívar, Ramon, and Paula Moya, eds. *Fictions of the Trans-American Imaginary*. Spec. issue of *Modern Fiction Studies* 49.1 (2003).

Sancho, Ignatius. *Letters of the Late Ignatius Sancho, an African*. 2 vols. London: J. Nichols, 1782.

San Miguel, Pedro L. *The Imagined Island: History, Identity, and Utopia in Hispaniola*. Chapel Hill: University of North Carolina Press, 2009.

Sansay, Leonora. *Secret History; or, the Horrors of St. Domingo, in a series of letters, written by a lady at Cape Francois, to Colonel Burr, late vice-president of the United States, principally during the command of General Rochambeau*. 1808. Freeport, NY: Books for Libraries Press, 1971.

———. *Zelica, the Creole: A Novel*. London: W. Fearman, 1820.

Saxon, Lyle. *Lafitte, the Pirate*. New York: Century, ca. 1930.

Schaadt, Robert A. Introduction. *The Memoirs of Jean Laffite from Le Journal de Jean Laffite*. Trans. Gene Marshall. Philadelphia: Xlibris, 2000.

Schaeffer, Wendell. "The Delayed Cession of Spanish Santo Domingo to France, 1705–1801." *Hispanic American Historical Review* 29.1 (1949): 46–68.

Scheker Mendoza, Elka. "Race, Nation, and Dominican National Discourse." *Desde la orilla: Hacia una nacionalidad sin desalojos*. Ed. Silvio Torres-Saillant, Ramona Hernandez, and Blas R. Jiménez. Santo Domingo: Ediciones Librería La Trinitaria, 2004. 389–400.

Schiller, Nina G, Linda G. Basch, and Blanc C. Szanton, eds. *Towards a Transnational Perspective on Migration: Race, Class, Ethnicity and Nationalism Reconsidered*. Proc. of a Workshop of the Same Name, May 1990, New York Academy of Sciences. New York: New York Academy of Sciences, 1992. Annals of the New York Academy of Sciences 645.

Schomburg, Arthur A. *Military Services Rendered by the Haitians in the*

North and South American Wars for Independence. Nashville, TN: A.M.E. Sunday School Union, 1921.

Scott, Julius. "The Common Wind: Currents of Afro-American Communication in the Era of the Haitian Revolution." Diss. Duke University, 1986.

———. "Crisscrossing Empires: Ships, Sailors, and Resistance in the Lesser Antilles in the Eighteenth Century." *The Lesser Antilles in the Age of European Expansion.* Ed. Robert Paquette. Gainesville: University Press of Florida, 1996.

Scott, Michael. *Tom Cringle's Log.* Edinburgh: Blackwood, 1834.

Scott, Rebecca. "The Atlantic World and the Road to *Plessy v. Ferguson.*" *Journal of American History* 94.3 (2007): 726–33.

———. *Degrees of Freedom.* Cambridge, MA: Harvard University Press, 2006.

———. "Public Rights and Private Commerce: A Nineteenth-Century Atlantic Creole Itinerary." *Current Anthropology* 48.2 (2007): 237–56

Scully, Pamela, and Diana Paton, eds. *Gender and Slave Emancipation in the Atlantic World.* Durham: Duke University Press, 2005.

Sevilla Soler, Rosario. "Las repercusiones de la Revolución Francesa en el Caribe español: Los casos de Santo Domingo y Trinidad." *Cuadernos Americanos* 3.5 (1989): 117–33.

Sheller, Mimi. *Democracy after Slavery: Black Publics and Peasant Radicalism in Haiti and Jamaica.* Gainesville: University Press of Florida, 2000.

———. "Sword-Bearing Citizens: Militarism and Manhood in Nineteenth Century Haiti." *Plantation Society in the Americas* 4.2/3 (1997): 233–78.

Shukla, Sandhya, and Heidi Tinsman, eds. *Our Americas: Political and Cultural Imaginings.* Spec. issue of *Radical History Review* 89 (June 2004).

Sloane, Charles F. "Dogs in War, Police Work and on Patrol." *Journal of Criminal Law, Criminology, and Police Science* 46.3 (1955): 385–95.

Smallwood, Stephanie. *Saltwater Slavery: A Middle Passage from Africa to American Diaspora.* Cambridge, MA: Harvard University Press, 2007.

Smith, Jon, and Deborah Cohn, eds. *Look Away! The U.S. South in New World Studies.* Durham: Duke University Press, 2004.

Starr, S. Frederick. *Bamboula! The Life and Times of Louis Moreau Gottschalk.* Oxford: Oxford University Press, 1995.

Stebich, Ute. *Haitian Art.* New York: Brooklyn Museum, 1978.

Stephens, Michelle Ann. *Black Empire: The Masculine Global Imaginary of Caribbean Intellectuals in the United States, 1914–1962.* Durham: Duke University Press, 2005.

Stevenson, Brenda. "The Question of the Female Slave Community and Culture in the American South: Methodological and Ideological Approaches." *Journal of African American History* 92.1 (Winter 2007): 74-95.

Stinchcombe, Arthur L. "Class Conflict and Diplomacy: Haitian Isolation in the 19th-Century World System." *Sociological Perspectives* 37.1 (1994): 1–23.

Suárez, Lucía M. *The Tears of Hispaniola: Haitian and Dominican Diaspora Memory.* Gainesville: University Press of Florida, 2006. New World Diaspora Series.

Sublette, Ned. *Cuba and Its Music: From the First Drums to the Mambo.* Chicago: Chicago Review Press, 2007.

Sundquist, Eric J. "Benito Cereno and New World Slavery." *Reconstructing American Literary History.* Ed. Sacvan Bercovitch. Cambridge, MA: Harvard University Press, 1986. 93–122.

———. *To Wake the Nations.* Cambridge, MA: Belknap Press, 1998.

Szwed, John F., and Morton Marks. "The Afro-American Transformation of European Set Dances and Dance Suites." *Dance Research Journal* 20.1 (1988): 29–36.

Tallant, Robert. *The Pirate Lafitte and the Battle of New Orleans.* New York: Random House, 1951.

Taylor, Diana. *The Archive and the Repertoire: Performing Cultural Memory in the Americas.* Durham: Duke University Press, 2003.

Tebbel, John. *The Compact History of the American Newspaper.* New York: Hawthorn, 1963.

"Theresa, A Haytien Tale." *Freedom's Journal* January 18, 1828; January 25, 1828; February 8, 1828; February 15, 1828.

Thomas, Abel C. *The Gospel of Slavery: A Primer of Freedom.* New York: T. W. Strong, 1864.

Thompson, Robert Farris. *Flash of the Spirit: African and Afro-American Art and Philosophy.* New York: Random House, 1983.

Thornton, John. "'I Am the Subject of the King of Congo': African Ideology in the Haitian Revolution." *Journal of World History* 4 (1993): 181–214.

Tinker, Edward Larocque. *Les écrits de langue française en Louisiana au XIXe siècle.* Nendeln: Kraus Reprint, 1970.

Torres-Saillant, Silvio. "Dominican Literature and Its Criticism: Anatomy of a Troubled Identity." *A History of Literature in the Caribbean.* Vol. 1. *Hispanic and Francophone Regions.* Ed. A. James Arnold, Julio Rodríguez-Luis, and J. Michael Dash. Amsterdam: John Benjamins, 1994. 49–64.

Touchstone, Blake. "Voodoo in New Orleans." *Louisiana History* 13.4 (1972): 371–86.

Tregle, Joseph G. "Creoles and Americans." *Creole New Orleans.* Ed. Arnold Hirsch and Joseph Logsdon. Baton Rouge: Louisiana State University Press, 1992. 131–85.

Trouillot, Michel-Rolph. *Silencing the Past: Power and the Production of History.* Boston: Beacon Press, 1995.

Van Wyk Smith, M. "Writing the African Diaspora in the Eighteenth Century." *Diaspora* 1.2 (1991): 127–42.

Varner, John Grier, and Jeanette Varner. *Dogs of the Conquest.* Tulsa: University of Oklahoma Press, 1983.

Vastey, Pompée V. *Notes à M. le Baron de V. P. Malouet, Ministre de la Marine et des Colonies, de sa Majesté Louis XVIII, et ancien Administrateur des Colonies et de la Marine, ex-Colon de Saint-Domingue, etc, en réfutation du 4eme volume de son ouvrage, intitulé, "Collection de mémoires sur les colonies et particulièrement sur Saint-Domingue," etc.* Cap-Henry: P. Roux, 1814.

Vélez, María Teresa. *Drumming for the Gods: The Life and Times of Felipe*

García Villamil, Santero, Palero, and Abakuá. Philadelphia: Temple University Press, 2000.

Veloz Maggiolo, Marcio. *Sobre cultura dominicana*. Santo Domingo: Editora Alpha y Omega, 1977.

Verna, Paul. *Bolívar y los emigrados patriotas en el Caribe*. Caracas: Ediciones de la Presidencia de la República, 1980.

———. *Petión y Bolívar: Una etapa decisiva en la emancipación de Hispanoamérica (1790–1830)*. 3rd ed. Caracas: Ediciones de la Presidencia de la República, 1980.

Viau, Alfred. *Negroes, mulatos, blancos; o, Sangre, nada más que sangre*. Ciudad Trujillo: Editora Montalvo, 1955.

Villaverde, Cirilo. *Cecilia Valdés; Novela de costumbres cubanas*. Mexico: Editorial Porrúa, 1986.

———. *Cecilia Valdés or El Angel Hill*. Trans. Helen Lane. Ed. Sibylle Fischer. Oxford: Oxford University Press, 2005. Library of Latin America.

Vincent, Charles, ed. *The African American Experience in Louisiana. Part A: From Africa to the Civil War*. Lafayette: Center for Louisiana Studies, University of Southwestern Louisiana, 1999. Louisiana Purchase Bicentennial Series in Louisiana History 11.

Vinson, Ben. *Bearing Arms for His Majesty: The Free-Colored Militia in Colonial Mexico*. Palo Alto: Stanford University Press, 2003.

Vitier, Cintio. "Visión martiana de Haití." *Casa de las Américas* 186 (1992): 10–18.

Warner, Michael. *The Letters of the Republic: Publication and the Public Sphere in Eighteenth-Century America*. Cambridge, MA: Harvard University Press, 1992.

Warren, Harris Gaylord, ed and trans. "Documents Relating to the Establishment of Privateers at Galveston/Campeachy, 1816–1817." *Louisiana Historical Quarterly* 21.4 (1938): 1086–1109.

———. "Pensacola and the Filibusters, 1816-1817." *Louisiana Historical Quarterly* 21.3 (1938): 806-22.

———. *The Sword Was Their Passport: A History of American Filibustering in the Mexican Revolution*. Baton Rouge: Louisiana State University Press, 1943.

Washburne, Chris. "The Clave of Jazz: A Caribbean Contribution to the Rhythmic Foundation of an African-American Music." *Black Music Research Journal* 17.1 (1997): 59–80.

Weintraub, Aileen. *Jean Lafitte: Pirate-Hero of the War of 1812*. New York: PowerKids Press, 2002.

Wellborn, Alfred Toledano. "Relations between New Orleans and Latin America, 1810–1824." *Louisiana Historical Quarterly* 22 (1939): 710–94.

West, Michael O., William G. Martin, and Fanon Che Wilkins, eds. *From Toussaint to Tupac: The Black International since the Age of Revolution*. Chapel Hill: University of North Carolina Press, 2009.

Wheatley, Phyllis. *Poems on Various Subjects, Religious and Moral*. London: n.p., 1773.

White, Ashli. *Encountering Revolution: Haiti and the Making of the Early Republic*. Baltimore: Johns Hopkins Press, 2010.

White, Shane. "'We Dwell in Safety and Pursue Our Honest Callings': Free Blacks in New York City, 1783–1810." *Journal of American History* 75.2 (1988): 445–70.

Wilgus, A. Curtis. "Some Activities of United States Citizens in the South American Wars of Independence, 1808–1824." *Louisiana Historical Quarterly* 14 (1931): 182–203.

———. "Spanish American Patriot Activity along the Gulf Coast of the United States, 1811–1822." *Louisiana Historical Quarterly* 8 (1925): 193–215.

Williams, Eric. *Capitalism and Slavery*. 1944. Chapel Hill: University of North Carolina Press, 1994.

———. *From Columbus to Castro: The History of the Caribbean, 1492–1969*. 1970. New York: Vintage Books, 1984.

Williams, Patrick G., S. Charles Bolton, and Jeannie M. Whayne, eds. *A Whole Country in Commotion: The Louisiana Purchase and the American Southwest*. Fayetteville: University of Arkansas Press, 2005.

Winik, Jay. *The Great Upheaval: America and the Birth of the Modern World, 1788–1800*. New York: Harper Collins, 2007.

Wolf, Donna Marie. "Double Diplomacy: Ulises Heureux and the Cuban Independence Movement." *Caribbean Studies* 14.1 (1974): 75–104.

Wood, Marcus. *Blind Memory: Visual Representations of Slavery in England and America, 1780–1865*. New York: Routledge, 2000.

Wright, Philip. Introduction. *Lady Nugent's Journal of Her Residence in Jamaica from 1801 to 1805*. By Maria Nugent. 4th ed. Kingston: Institute of Jamaica, 1966. xi–xxxiii.

Wright, Richardson. *Revels in Jamaica, 1682–1838*. 1937. New York: Benjamin Blom, 1969.

Yacou, Alain. "Los refugiados franceses de Saint-Domingue en la región occidental dela isla de Cuba." *Del Caribe* 23 (1994): 66–79.

———. "Révolution française dans l'île de Cuba et la contre-révolution." *De la Révolution française aux révolutions créoles et nègres*. Paris: Editions Caribéennes, 1989. 15–40.

———. "Santiago de Cuba a la hora de la revolución de Santo Domingo (1790–1804)." *Del Caribe* 26 (1997): 73–80.

Yépez, Arturo. *Humor a quien humor merece*. San Juan: La Editorial Universidad de Puerto Rico, 2005.

Yih, Yuen-ming David. "Music and Dance of Haitian Vodou: Diversity and Unity in Regional Repertoires." Diss. Wesleyan University, 1995.

DISCOGRAPHY

Antologia de la música afrocubana: Tumba Francesa. Vol 7. EGREM, LD-3606, 1981.

Augustin, Frisner. *The Drums of Vodou*. White Cliffs Media 9338, 1994.

Caribbean Island Music: Songs and Dances of Haiti the Dominican Republic, and Jamaica, Recorded in the Islands by John Storm Roberts. Nonesuch Explorer Series 72047-2, 1972.

Caribbean Revels: Haitian Rara and Dominican Gaga. Smithsonian Folkways SF 40402, 1991.

Caribbean Voyage, The 1962 Field Recordings. Rounder 11661-1721-2, 1999.

Cuba: Air Mail Music. Productions Sunset France SA 141024, 1998.

Cuba: Contradanzas y Danzones. Nimbus Records NI 5502, 1996.

Cutumba: Ballet folklórico Santiago de Cuba. Egrem CD 0256, 1997.

Folk Songs of Puerto Rico. Folkways Records FWO4412, 1971.

Grands Carnavals d'Amerique. Playasound PS 65008.

Grivalliers, Ti Raoul. *Mi Bèlè-A.* Auvidis B6828, 1996.

GrupoVocal Desandann. *Descendants.* Bembé Records 2022-2, 1999.

Katherine Dunham Presents the Singing Gods: Drum Rhythms of Haiti, Cuba and Brazil. Caney CCD 523, 2004.

Puerto Rico in Washington. Smithsonian Folkways SF 40460, 1996.

Voodoo Drums. Voyager CRG 140115, 202.

Index

Page numbers in italics indicate illustrations.

abolitionist movement: black newspapers
  and, 157–87; in British colonies, 158;
  colonialism and, 10, 183–84, 196n3,
  235n2; Haitian Revolution and, 41–42,
  59–62; in Santo Domingo, 70; slave
  autobiographies and, 10–11; white
  abolitionists' conflicts with black
  newspaper editors, 172–73
Abu Ghraib prison (Iraq), 193
Accau, Jean-Jacques, 210n16
African Colonization Society, 241n30
Alardo, Arturo, 213n29
Alén, Octavo, 152–53, 233n28
Alianza Bolivariana para los Pueblos de
  Nuestra América (ALBA), 6, 193
Alix, Juan Antonio, 78, 84, 215–16n40
Alleyne, Mervyne, 229n4
Alvarez Nazario, Manuel, 149
Amelia Island, Florida, 110
American Revolution: critique by *L'Union*
  newspaper, 199n5; slavery and, 10;
  slaves adopting loyalist cause, 71
Amézquita y de Lara, Pablo Francisco,
  83–86
Anderson, Benedict, 170
Anti-Jacobin Review, 39, 205n21
Anti-Slavery Society, 178, 208n5
Aponte, José Antonio, 86, 192
Aponte conspiracy (Cuba), 157
Aranjuez, Treaty of (1777), 207n2
Ardouin, Beaubrun, 26, 37–38, 41, 202n5

Ardouin, Coriolan, 239n21
Aristide, Jean-Bertrand, 76
Arredondo y Pichardo, Gaspar de: life
  and career, 53–54, 209n7, 211n20;
  "Memoria de mi salida," 53–56, 63–
  66, 68–69, 73, 210n14, 212n23
Atlantic crossing, 9
Aury, Louis-Michel: career, 221–22n17; in
  Florida, 92, 110; Savary and, 98, 102,
  112–13, 225n27, 226–27n36
Austerlitz, Paul, 145
Aux Cayes, Haiti, 91, 98, 110, 112

Bacardí, Emilio, 136, 145–46; *Via Crucis,*
  140–41
Balaguer, Joaquín, 208n4, 211n21;
  Centinela de la frontera, 209n6
Balcarres, Lord, 36, 39, 205–6n23
Baltimore, Haitian refugees relocated to,
  xix
bamboula drum, 231n18
baquetas (percussion sticks), 147
Barataria, Louisiana, 91, 92, 95–104, 110,
  119–21, 218nn1–2, 222n18
Barnes, Sandra, 76
Basle, Treaty of (1795), 57–58, 64–65
Battle of New Orleans (print), *118,*
  118–19
Beales, Carleton: "Black Mexico," 243n40
bèlè/belair percussive tradition, 143–44,
  149, 150–52, 154, 155

social stratification and class, 5; newspaper coverage and, 176–80; in Saint-Domingue diaspora, 92–93, 128–29, 136–37; slavery views and, 42
Sociedad Pompadú de Guantánamo, 233n28
Sociedad Santa Catalina de Riccis, 233n28
Société des Amis des noirs, 61
Sonthonax, Léger-Félicité, 130, 222n17
Spanish Chasseur of the Island of Cuba, A, 29, 30
Spy Who Sat by the Door, The (film), 207n29
staggered development, concept of, 16, 201n13
Stedman, J. G., 139

Tacherie family, 237n8
tambo drumming, 229–30n7, 234n34
Tampico, Mexico, 98
tanbou bèlè (drum), 151–52
Taney, Roger, 124
Taváres, Pedro, 52
Taylor, Zachary, 35–36, 40
Tessier, Augustus, 230n9
Thiot, Jean Baptiste, 221n16
Thomas, Abel C.: *Gospel of Slavery,* 206n27
tibwa (percussion instrument), 143, 151
trade, intercolonial: abundance of, 1–2; in bloodhounds, 21–48; British changes in, 157; nationalism and, 98–99; privateering and black marketing, 91–121; research on, 198n1; in slaves, 200–201n12
Trail of Tears (1838), 167
transcoloniality: Afro-French ethnic identity, 123–24, 134–35, 155–56, 160, 231nn16–17; appeal, 5; concept, 2–3, 124; evidentiary base for, 11, 48, 51–52, 141–42; fashion and, 125–27; inter-European exchanges of colonies, 57; labor relations, class, and migration, 173–80, 240n27, 241–42nn30–33; methodological considerations, 9–16; multilingual approach to, 12–14; of music and dance traditions, 139–55; new knowledge bases created by, 122, 154–55; newspapers' role in, 157–87; race and class axes, 6–8, 42, 52, 63–66, 68–70, 74, 87, 92–93, 136–37, 173–80, 191–92, 231n14; research on, 198n4; slaves' mobility, 9–10, 129–30, 178, 189–90; slave uprisings and, 157–58

"transfrontiersmen," 31, 203n11, 211n19
Trelawney Town Maroons, 29, 31–33, 203n8, 203n9
Trinidad: *bèlè*/belair in, 143–44, 149, 150–52; calypso in, 156; *Colored American*'s coverage of, 175; French settlers in, 143–44, 232n21; North American black emigrés to, 173–80, 241–42nn31–33; as resettlement site for Haitian refugees, xix, 123–24
Trinitario movement, 70
Trujillo, Rafael, 84, 208n5
tumba francesca Cuban musical dance repertoire, 140–41, 143, 144, 146–48, 151, 152–53, 229n3, 233n28, 234–35n36
tumba francesca societies, 146, 146–47, 147, 154, 155
Turner, Nat, 157

Underground Railroad network, 6
L'Union (Haitian newspaper), 18, 160; black emigration advocated by, 174, 175; coverage of Haitian news in, 166, 169; coverage of Latin American independence movements, 237–38n12; critique of American Revolution, 199n5; diary of soldier published by, 213n32; elite readership, 175; founding and editors, 164–65; Latin American confederation advocated by, 181–83; literacy campaign, 165; reprinting of stories from other papers, 169; role and purpose, 164–65, 184

Varner, Jeanette and John Grier, 205n20
Vastey, Pompée Valentin, 20, 21, 29, 201(headnote)
Venezuela: independence struggles, 112; Jose Chirino's rebellion in, 157; refugees from Hispaniola in, 59
Verna, Paul, 112
Vessey, Denmark, 86
Villard, Marie, 102, 105
Villaverde, Cirilo: *Cecilia Valdés,* 46
visual records of transcoloniality, 11
Vodou, 214–15n36, 215n38; *bokò* figure, 88–89, 217n48; drums used in, 151–52, 235n36; food used in, 76, 78; iconography, 74–83, 202–3n6; politicization of, 80; in Santo Domingo, 74–83, 88–90; signified in Echavarría Haitian general depiction, 50–51, 74–77

TEXT
10/13 Sabon Open Type

DISPLAY
Sabon Open Type

COMPOSITOR
Modern Language Initiative

TEXT PRINTER AND BINDER
IBT-Global